Defying victimhood

2 1 MAR 2024

WITHDRAWN

DCAF

a centre for security,
development and
the rule of law

The Geneva Centre for the Democratic Control of Armed Forces (DCAF) is an international foundation whose mission is to assist the international community in pursuing good governance and reform of the security sector. DCAF develops and promotes norms and standards, conducts tailored policy research, identifies good practices and recommendations to promote democratic security sector governance, and provides in-country advisory support and practical assistance programmes.

DCAF PO Box 1360 CH-1211 Geneva 1 Switzerland
www.dcaf.ch

Defying victimhood: Women and post-conflict peacebuilding

Edited by Albrecht Schnabel and Anara Tabyshalieva

**United Nations
University Press**

TOKYO · NEW YORK · PARIS

© United Nations University, 2012

The views expressed in this publication are those of the authors and do not necessarily reflect the views of the United Nations University.

United Nations University Press
United Nations University, 53-70, Jingumae 5-chome,
Shibuya-ku, Tokyo 150-8925, Japan
Tel: +81-3-5467-1212   Fax: +81-3-3406-7345
E-mail: sales@unu.edu   general enquiries: press@unu.edu
http://www.unu.edu

United Nations University Office at the United Nations, New York
2 United Nations Plaza, Room DC2-2062, New York, NY 10017, USA
Tel: +1-212-963-6387   Fax: +1-212-371-9454
E-mail: unuony@unu.edu

United Nations University Press is the publishing division of the United Nations
University.

Cover design by Andrew Corbett
Cover photograph by Tim McKulka/UN Photo

Printed in the United States of America for the Americas and Asia
Printed in the United Kingdom for Europe, Africa and the Middle East

ISBN 978-92-808-1201-5

Library of Congress Cataloging-in-Publication Data

Defying victimhood : women and post-conflict peacebuilding / edited by
Albrecht Schnabel and Anara Tabyshalieva.
    p. cm.
  Includes bibliographical references and index.
  ISBN 978-9280812015 (pbk.)
  1. Women in development—Developing countries. 2. Women—Developing
countries—Social conditions. 3. Women and war—Developing countries.
4. Postwar reconstruction—Developing countries. 5. Women—Political activity—
Developing countries. I. Schnabel, Albrecht. II. Tabyshalieva, Anara.
HQ1240.D44   2012
305.409172'4—dc23   2012014360

Contents

Figures and tables

Contributors

Ancil Adrian-Paul has been working on women's and children's issues for the past 20 years. She has a degree in education, a BEd (Hons) in sociology and an MSc in development practices and refugee studies from Oxford Brookes University and the Refugees Studies Centre, Oxford University. Born in Guyana, South America, Ancil Adrian-Paul lives in London, UK. She is an independent consultant focusing on human rights and democracy issues and has worked for the United Nations, civil society organizations, bilateral agencies and EU institutions. Most recently she has been involved in international long-term election observation for the European Union. She is currently employed as a consultant adviser on a DFID project supporting elections in Sierra Leone, and has worked on women's issues in Afghanistan, Liberia, Colombia, South Korea, Uganda, Kenya and Ethiopia, among many other countries. Much of her recent research, training and publications focused on the impact of UN Security Council Resolution 1325 on women and unpacking the resolution to enable women to use it effectively in their work on the ground.

Constantine P. Danopoulos is professor and chair of the political science department at San Jose State University. He has written or edited 11 books, numerous articles and book chapters, and dozens of conference papers. His publications deal with civil-military relations, national security, poverty, the bureaucracy and the environment. He served as election observer in Bosnia (1996) and editor of the *Journal of Political and Military Sociology*. He is the West Coast associate editor of *Mediterranean Quarterly* and serves on the editorial board of *Armed Forces and Society*,

Journal of Southern Europe and the Balkans and the *Annual Review of Political and Military Sociology*. From 1993 to 1999 he served as president/chair of the Research Committee on Armed Forces and Society of the International Political Science Association, and Fulbright Scholar to Greece (2008). Constantine P. Danopoulos is the recipient of the President's Scholar Award, the Warburton Award of Excellence in Research and Pi Sigma Alpha Professor of the Year.

Deborah Davis has a degree in political theory from the University of California, Berkeley. She has worked as a policy analyst and social development specialist at the World Bank for the past 20 years, with a focus on gender and local governance. Her fieldwork has included studies of democratization, gender empowerment and community justice in Indonesia, Rwanda and Afghanistan. She was the editor of three World Bank policy research reports on financial integration, community-driven development and engendering development. She was also a principle contributor to *Scaling Up Local & Community Driven Development: A Real World Guide to Its Theory and Practice*, which identified the elements of successful local-level political change. Before working in international development, Deborah Davis was an investigative reporter and author of a National Book Award-nominated biography of *Washington Post* publisher Katharine Graham, which analysed the power of the media in the United States during the Nixon era.

Hermine De Soto is a senior social scientist/anthropologist and works currently as independent consultant in international social development. Before retirement she worked as World Bank staff and consultant. At the World Bank she focused on social analyses, gender, minority studies/action plans, resettlement/ social policies and project management in the Europe, Russia and Central Asia region as well as in the Africa and East Asian/Pacific regions. She also served as country social scientist in Tajikistan and Albania, where she developed and implemented post-conflict social development programmes. Before joining the World Bank she held a research and teaching position at the University of Wisconsin-Madison. She is a widely published anthropologist, both within the Bank and in international academia. A recipient of various awards and recognitions, she is a fellow of the Woodrow Wilson International Center for Scholars and the Kennan Institute, both in Washington, DC. She holds a PhD in socio-cultural anthropology from the University of Wisconsin-Madison, USA.

Vanessa Farr is the social development and gender adviser at UNDP's Programme of Assistance to the Palestinian People, where she focuses on how gender impacts on individual experiences of the intra-Palestinian and Palestinian-Israeli conflicts. She is an expert on gendered experiences of armed conflict, including several aspects of security sector reform: the disarmament, demobilization and reintegration of women and men combatants after war; gender and policing; the impacts on men and women of prolific small arms and light weapons; and women's coalition-building in conflict-torn societies. For the past decade she has worked on gender mainstreaming in weapons collection programmes, written on gender in SSR and DDR processes, undertaken research on the gendered impact of small arms, published on Security Council Resolution 1325 (2000) and its operational implications and co-edited (with Henri Myrttinen and Albrecht Schnabel) *Sexed Pistols: The Gendered Impacts of Small Arms and Light Weapons* (UNU Press, 2009) and (with Albrecht Schnabel) *Back to the Roots: Security Sector Reform and Development* (LIT Verlag, 2012). She holds a PhD from York University, Canada.

Lyn S. Graybill is an independent scholar in Atlanta, Georgia. She has taught courses in African politics and international relations at various institutions since receiving her PhD from the University of Virginia in 1991. Her main research interests include religion and politics, gender and transitional justice. She is the author of *Truth and Reconciliation in South Africa: Miracle or Model?* (Lynne Rienner, 2002) and *Religion and Resistance Politics in South Africa* (Praeger, 1995). She co-edited (with Kenneth W. Thompson) *Africa's Second Wave of Freedom: Development, Democracy, and Rights* (University Press of America, 1998). Her articles have been published in diverse journals, including *Human Rights Review, Ethics & International*

Affairs, Conflict Trends, Current History, Africa Today, Women's Studies International Forum, Iris and *Third World Quarterly.*

Zlatko Isakovic, a native of Serbia, received his undergraduate education in the former Yugoslavia and earned his PhD in political science from the University of Belgrade. He has taught in a number of European and Canadian institutions of higher learning, including the Diplomatic Academy of the Serbian Ministry of Foreign Affairs and the Institute for European Studies in Belgrade. He served on the review board of *UPEACE Law Review* and has participated in many international conferences and seminars. He has published numerous books, articles and chapters (in Serbian and English) dealing with national security, civil-military relations, conflict and conflict resolution, and the Balkans.

Rose M. Kadende-Kaiser is a senior programme manager with the US Center for Disease Control in Kigali, Rwanda, coordinating the transition of HIV/AIDS clinical services from international partners to the Rwanda government's Ministry of Health. She previously worked as technical adviser for Kilimanjaro International, implementing the US African Development Foundation grants programme in Burundi. She also worked as regional manager for Southern Africa with Geneva Global, a Pennsylvania-based company that provides investment advice to donors interested in measuring the impact of their international giving. Prior to joining Geneva Global, she was an assistant professor of anthropology and director of the Women's Center at Mississippi State University. She moved to the University of Pennsylvania on a visiting scholarship through the Asch Center for Study of Ethno-Political Conflict and as research associate of the Women's Studies Program. Her research focuses on ethnicity, online identities and conflict management, and women and peacebuilding. She holds a BA in English language and literature from the University of Burundi and an MA and PhD in folklore and women's studies from Indiana University.

Kari H. Karamé has been a senior researcher at the Norwegian Institute of International Affairs since 1991. She has taught ethnology at the University of Oslo, the American University of Beirut and Saint Joseph University, also in Beirut. She has been a fellow of the Catherine T. and John D. MacArthur Foundation, Chicago. She has on several occasions served as a consultant for the Norwegian Ministry of Foreign Affairs on issues related to conflict, peace and gender. Her research has focused on gender perspectives of war and peacebuilding in multi-ethnic/multi-religious societies; the reintegration of combatants in the Middle East and – mainly – Lebanon; and women and peacebuilding in Africa.

Krishna Kumar is the senior evaluation adviser in the Office of the Director of Foreign Assistance at the US State Department. From 1996 to 2007 he was the sector team leader for democracy and humanitarian assistance in USAID's Center for Development Information and Evaluation, where he directed a series of multi-country studies and evaluations on elections, democracy promotion, international media assistance, women and women's organizations, and civil society and peacebuilding. Prior to joining USAID he worked at the World Bank and the East West Center. He has consulted with many international organizations, including the OPEC Fund for International Development, the UN Centre on Transnational Corporations, the World Food Programme and the Clingendael Institute. Krishna Kumar has written or edited 14 books, over 30 monographs, numerous articles in professional journals and chapters in edited books. His latest book, *Evaluating Democracy Assistance: Search for New Directions*, is forthcoming. He received his PhD from Michigan State University.

Sumie Nakaya is currently a political affairs officer in the UN Department of Peacekeeping Operations, covering Sudan/Darfur. Prior to joining the UN Secretariat, she worked with the Social Science Research Council and the UN Development Programme. Sumie Nakaya holds a PhD in political science from City University of New York and an MA in law and diplomacy from the Fletcher School. Her publications include book chapters and journal articles on gender and peacebuilding, aid effectiveness and post-conflict state-building.

Lisa Schirch is director of 3P Human Security: Partners for Peacebuilding Policy, a programme that connects civil society perspectives on conflict prevention and peacebuilding to US security policy-making. She is also a research professor at the Center for Justice and Peacebuilding, Eastern Mennonite University, and policy adviser for the Alliance for Peacebuilding. A former Fulbright fellow in East and West Africa, Lisa Schirch has worked in over 20 countries in conflict prevention and peacebuilding, most recently in Afghanistan, Pakistan, Iraq and Lebanon. She has written four books and numerous articles on conflict prevention and strategic peacebuilding. Her current research interests include the design and structure of a comprehensive peace process in Afghanistan, conflict assessment and programme design, civil-military relations and the role of the media in peacebuilding. She holds a BA in international relations from the University of Waterloo, Canada, and an MS and PhD in conflict analysis and resolution from George Mason University.

Albrecht Schnabel is a senior fellow in the Research Division of the Geneva Centre for the Democratic Control of Armed Forces. He studied political science and international relations in Germany, the United States and Canada (where he received his PhD in 1995 from Queen's University). He has held teaching and research appointments at Queen's University, the American University in Bulgaria, Central European University, the United Nations University, Aoyama Gakuin University, swisspeace and the University of Bern. His publications have focused on ethnic conflict, refugees, human security, armed non-state actors, security sector reform, conflict prevention and management, peacekeeping and post-conflict peacebuilding. His experiences beyond academia include military service in the German armed forces, participation in OSCE election monitoring missions, training and teaching for the UN System Staff College and a term as president of the International Association of Peacekeeping Training Centres. He currently works on the role and impact of security sector reform in the context of development and peace processes; the agency of women, youth and children in post-conflict peacebuilding; the operational utility of human security threat analysis and mitigation; the urban dimension of security sector governance and reform; and evolving non-traditional roles of armed forces.

Svetlana Sharipova is an international social development professional with over 15 years of experience in the World Bank and the IMF. In these two institutions she initially represented the government of Tajikistan at the corporate level. Later she was extensively engaged in projects and programmes implemented in countries of Eastern Europe and Central Asia, including Tajikistan. Her work mainly focuses on issues of post-conflict reconstruction and development, economies in transition, agriculture, education and gender. Her expertise on Tajikistan, her home country, covers the areas of education, scientific research and international relations. She has reviewed and edited a number of book manuscripts on socio-economic development issues, which were subsequently published in the United States. She holds a PhD in education and linguistics, and completed her postgraduate education at the St Petersburg Scientific Research Institute of Linguistics (Russia).

Konstantinos S. Skandalis received his PhD in management from the University of Peloponnese, Tripolis, Greece, and is currently a visiting scholar at the Claremont Graduate University, California. A native of Greece, he has published a number of articles dealing with entrepreneurship in Greece and other Balkan countries.

Anara Tabyshalieva is an assistant professor of history at Marshall University and a research fellow and former director of the Institute for Regional Studies in Bishkek, Kyrgyzstan. She has taught modern world history, Asian and Eurasian studies, Middle Eastern studies, sociology and political science at several universities in Kyrgyzstan and the United States. Her publications have focused on politics, history, development and gender issues. Among others, she co-edited (with Madhavan K. Palat) *Towards the Contemporary Period: From the Mid-nineteenth to the End of the Twentieth Century*, vol. VI of the UNESCO History of Civilizations of Central Asia project (UNESCO, 2005) and wrote the report "Promoting Human Security: Ethical, Normative and Educational Frameworks in Central Asia" (UNESCO, 2006). She has held visiting positions at the US Institute of Peace, Johns Hopkins University, the Centre for the Study of Islam and Christian-Muslim Relations, University of Birmingham, and the United Nations University. Her areas of expertise include modern history, international relations, human security, social development, and women and children in post-conflict societies. She holds a Master of International Public Policy from SAIS/Johns Hopkins University and MA and PhD degrees in history from the Kyrgyz National University.

Kristin Valasek has been active in research and training on gender, peace and security issues for many years. She is a gender and security sector reform project coordinator at the Geneva Centre for the Democratic Control of Armed Forces (DCAF), where she currently focuses on building the gender capacity of security sector training institutions. She previously managed a project on strengthening the integration of gender into the SSR processes in Liberia and Sierra Leone. Prior to joining DCAF, she coordinated gender, peace and security activities at UN-INSTRAW and worked on gender mainstreaming with the UN Department of Disarmament Affairs. In addition, she is a certified mediator and has grassroots non-governmental organization experience in the areas of domestic violence, sexual assault and refugee support. She holds an MA in conflict resolution from the University of Bradford.

Acknowledgements

This book has grown out of a research project on "The Roles of Women and Children in Post-Conflict Peacebuilding", initially conceived by the two editors of this volume in 2000 as a research activity of the Peace and Governance Programme of the United Nations University (UNU). At that time Albrecht Schnabel was a member of the Peace and Governance Programme, while Anara Tabyshalieva joined it for several months as a visiting research fellow. After securing financial support from UNU and the Asian Women's Fund, the editors assembled a group of contributors and initial author workshops were held in Tokyo and New York to discuss the results of background research and first chapter drafts. Over time the work developed into two book projects, with a changing and growing number of contributors. *Defying Victimhood: Women and Post-Conflict Peacebuilding* is the first volume emanating from this project. The second volume, entitled *Escaping Victimhood: Children, Youth and Post-Conflict Peacebuilding*, will be published later in 2012.

We could not have completed this book without the generous and dedicated support of a number of institutions and individuals. We gratefully acknowledge financial support from UNU, the Asian Women's Fund and the Geneva Centre for the Democratic Control of Armed Forces (DCAF). Albrecht furthermore thanks swisspeace and DCAF for providing institutional support for his work on this project. He wishes to acknowledge the Swiss National Centre of Competence in Research, "North-South Research Partnerships for Mitigating Syndromes of Global Change", co-funded by the Swiss National Science Foundation, and the Swiss Agency for Development and Cooperation and its Transversal Package Project, "Operationalising Human Security for Livelihood Protection" (which he directed), for support in the preparation of this book. We are grateful to Vanessa Farr and Henri Myrttinen for sharing their insights and comments on draft versions of the opening and closing chapters. We thank Kathleen Schnabel and Danail Hristov for proofreading and providing feedback on various drafts of the manuscript. Special thanks go to Marc Krupanski for editorial assistance, helpful comments on the final draft and providing valuable support in copyediting the final round of updates and revisions of the complete manuscript. We thank Yoshie Sawada at UNU's Institute for Sustainability and Peace for superbly and patiently managing the administrative part of the project.

We thank UNU Press, particularly its editor, Naomi Cowan, and her predecessor, Robert Davis, for their continuous encouragement, support and patience during the preparation of this book. We thank Cherry Ekins for her excellent work in copyediting and proofreading the final manuscript, Clive Pyne for assembling a most useful index, and Yoko Kojima and Adam Majoe for guiding and assisting us through the production process. We are grateful for the very helpful and constructive comments of two anonymous peer reviewers, whose ideas have been of great help in revising the initial draft manuscript. We owe a particular debt to many supporters and interview partners in post-conflict societies in Africa, Asia, Latin America and Europe, who willingly shared their insights and knowledge with the contributors to this volume.

Finally, we are grateful to all contributors, who have patiently and with much dedication remained committed to our joint research project. Together we hope that the book will encourage readers to pay increased attention in research, policy design and implementation to the roles women play – or are prevented from playing – in rebuilding societies in the aftermath of violent conflict.

Albrecht Schnabel
Anara Tabyshalieva
Geneva and Huntington/Bishkek
May 2012

Abbreviations

ADB	Asian Development Bank
AFRC	Armed Forces Revolutionary Council (Sierra Leone)
ANC	African National Congress (South Africa)
AWL	Albanian Women's League
BN	Bonuvoni Navovar (Tajikistan)
CAFOB	Collectif des Associations et ONGs Féminines du Burundi (Collective of Women's Associations and NGOs of Burundi)
CBO	community-based organization
CDF	Civil Defense Forces (Sierra Leone)
CEDAW	UN Convention on the Elimination of All Forms of Discrimination against Women
CIVPOL	UN Civilian Police
CNDD-FDD	Conseil National pour la Défense de la Démocratie-Forces pour la Défense de la Démocratie (Burundi)
DCAF	Geneva Centre for the Democratic Control of Armed Forces
DDR	disarmament, demobilization and reintegration
DEVAW	UN Declaration on the Elimination of Violence against Women
ECCD	early childcare and development
ECOMOG	Economic Community of West African States Monitoring Group
EPZ	export processing zone
EU	European Union
FRY	former Republic of Yugoslavia
FYROM	former Yugoslav Republic of Macedonia
GDP	gross domestic product
GWA	Collective of Gatumba Women's Associations (Burundi)
IA	International Alert

ICTR	International Criminal Tribunal for Rwanda
IDP	internally displaced person
LNAP	Liberia National Action Plan
NAP	national action plan
NGO	non-governmental organization
oPt	occupied Palestinian territory
PA	Palestinian Authority
PRSP	poverty reduction strategy paper
RPF	Rwandan Patriotic Front
RUF	Revolutionary United Front (Sierra Leone)
SAPS	South African Police Services
SCR	UN Security Council resolution
SCG	Search for Common Ground
SCSL	Special Court of Sierra Leone
SEA	sexual exploitation and abuse
SFRY	Socialist Federal Republic of Yugoslavia
SLTRC	Sierra Leone Truth and Reconciliation Commission
SSR	security sector reform
SRSG	special representatives of the Secretary-General
TRC	Truth and Reconciliation Commission (South Africa)
UFB	L'Union de la Femme Burundaise (Burundi Women's Union)
UN	United Nations
UNAMSIL	UN Mission in Sierra Leone
UNDP	UN Development Programme
UNFPA	UN Population Fund
UNHCR	Office of the UN High Commissioner for Refugees
UNICEF	UN Children's Fund
UNIFEM	UN Development Fund for Women (now UN Women)
UNMIK	UN Mission in Kosovo
UNMIL	UN Mission in Liberia
UNTAC	UN Transitional Authority for Cambodia
UNTAET	UN Transitional Authority in East Timor
UPRONA	Union for National Progress (Burundi)
USAID	US Agency for International Development
USIP	US Institute of Peace
VPU	vulnerable persons' unit
WHO	World Health Organization

Introduction

1

Forgone opportunities: The marginalization of women's contributions to post-conflict peacebuilding

Albrecht Schnabel and Anara Tabyshalieva

Women have the capacity and commitment to make significant contributions to rebuilding war-torn societies; yet because they are all too often marginalized as a "vulnerable group" or "passive victims", their potential goes unnoticed and underutilized. While no one can argue that they are often on the receiving end of violence and marginalization, they frequently achieve visibility only for their suffering, not for their actual and potential roles as sources, initiators and agents of both conflict and peace. Opportunities for long-term peacebuilding are lost, and sustainable peace and stability are at risk, when a significant proportion of stakeholders in a society's future peace and conflict architecture – half or more of the population – are marginalized and excluded during efforts to heal the wounds of war and build a new society and state. The exclusion of women also distorts our understanding of men's experiences of war and peace, as it tends to protect images of hyper-masculinity and gloss over the vulnerability and suffering of less powerful men.

This is the first of two books that emerged from one common research project on the roles of women and children in post-conflict peacebuilding; the companion volume is entitled *Escaping Victimhood: Children, Youth and Post-Conflict Peacebuilding*. In approaching this as an applied policy research project, we were well aware of the potential problems inherent in focusing simultaneously on women, youth and children: we were not implying an exact similarity between children, youth and adults, but we focused on individual relationships to power. We distinguished adult women and youth/children from adult men, who tend to be the

Defying victimhood: Women and post-conflict peacebuilding, Schnabel and Tabyshalieva (eds), United Nations University Press, 2012, ISBN 978-92-808-1201-5

more powerful members of a society – including post-conflict societies – especially when they belong to the military apparatus and other security, justice, political, cultural and economic institutions. Yet at the same time we recognized that further research would need to be undertaken on male victimization in war, especially through sexual violence, a fairly new field of research that is beyond the scope of these two books.

Defying Victimhood thus offers reflections on key challenges faced by women in post-conflict situations and the decisions that have (or have not) been taken by local, national and international actors to address their needs, contributions and agency in reforming post-war[1] social, political and security institutions. While progress has been made in recognizing these challenges and needs through global, UN-initiated, policy guidance, existing momentum can be maintained and further progress achieved if local and traditional social, economic and political cultures along with external assistance activities become more sensitive and attentive to the post-conflict needs and contributions of women. Not only women but all of society would benefit from such rethinking. Two chapters, including this opening text, provide the thematic and conceptual background and context for the various contributions to the book, which are clustered around four main themes: a focus on post-conflict patterns and changes in women's victimhood and empowerment; examinations of the essential partnership of survival and peace between women and children; national and global efforts to improve women's participation in post-conflict peacebuilding; and experiences and discussions of the need to deconstruct women's roles as victims in political and security institutions.

Drawing on the individual contributions and experiences presented throughout the book, the concluding chapter shows that the post-conflict moment offers a window of opportunity to reconsider and rewrite many of the rules and patterns that have previously governed relations between men and women and between women and society at large. During that period, local, national and international actors can address some of the inequalities and inequities that have not only caused much of the agony endured by women before, during and after war, but might still prevent them from playing a – most rightfully as well as necessary – central and constructive role in consolidating peace and stability in the aftermath.

The contributors to this book draw on comparative and single case studies of post-conflict contexts in different parts of world to offer their insights on how women act as both victims and peacebuilders, to trace the role of women from victimhood to empowerment and to highlight the essential partnership of women and children for ensuring the youngest generation's well-being and survival. Drawing particularly on African cases, they examine national and global efforts to right past wrongs. They also examine the roles of women in political and security institutions. The contributors argue that, for women in post-conflict societies, "defying victimhood" means being recognized as an activist, peacebuilder and – above all – a full participant in post-war social, economic, political and security structures, access to which all too often has unjustly and unwisely been denied.

Before introducing the individual contributions in this volume in the second part of this chapter, we describe the post-conflict peacebuilding context within which the book's discussions take place. We examine definitions of and approaches to peacebuilding more generally, followed by key challenges and opportunities for peacebuilding in the aftermath of conflict. We then discuss the role of women in post-conflict peacebuilding – the suffering that victimizes women and the obstacles to their participating in rebuilding post-war societies and thus acting as agents of positive change. This part of the chapter concludes by reviewing progress made at the level of the United Nations to acknowledge women's active roles as peacebuilders in post-conflict societies – as well as some of the challenges that still exist in turning such intentions into effective practice. As noted above, the chapter then introduces the individual contributions to this book.

Peacebuilding – Definitions and approaches

There is no single set of (typical) peacebuilding challenges – and thus peacebuilding requirements and responses.[2] Moreover, different actors work with different operational peacebuilding concepts. While some governments consider peacebuilding to be about "building market-oriented democracies ... UNDP [UN Development Programme] imagines creating economic development and strong civil societies committed to a culture of nonviolent dispute resolution".[3]

As Lisa Schirch points out in Chapter 2, "peacebuilding relies on relational skills stemming from the fields of conflict resolution and transformation to help people in conflict build relationships with each other". It also "covers a variety of processes, including human rights advocacy and activism, peacekeeping, relief aid, mediation, restorative justice, trauma healing, education, economic development, institution-building, research and many other related processes [that] all help communities build the capacity to prevent and respond to conflict and violence". To meet the demands of such a broad and comprehensive agenda, effective and sustainable peacebuilding depends on the application of "a range of measures targeted to reduce the risk of lapsing or relapsing into conflict by strengthening national capacities at all levels for conflict management, and to lay the foundation for sustainable peace and development. Peace-building is a complex, long-term process ... [that] ... works by addressing the deep-rooted, structural causes of violent conflict in a comprehensive manner."[4]

The Canadian Peacebuilding Network has developed a most useful definition of peacebuilding as guidance for its own conceptual and opera-tional work.[5] As others before and after, it draws a direct link to the term as it was applied by former UN Secretary-General Boutros Boutros-Ghali in his 1992 "An Agenda for Peace", where it is identified as "action to identify and support structures which will tend to strengthen and so-lidify peace in order to avoid a relapse into conflict".[6] As Boutros-Ghali further argued, once peacemaking and peacekeeping have achieved their objectives, "only sustained, cooperative work to deal with underlying eco-nomic, social, cultural and humanitarian problems can place an achieved peace on a durable foundation".[7]

These key activities are still essential components, particularly of post-conflict peacebuilding, a term that will be discussed in the subsequent section and shall be the focus of our book. However,

> Since then, peacebuilding has come to be understood and used as an umbrella concept reflecting a more comprehensive and long-term approach to peace and security including: early warning, conflict prevention, civilian and military peacekeeping, military intervention, humanitarian assistance, ceasefire agree-ments, the establishment of peace zones, reconciliation, reconstruction, institu-tion building, and political as well as socio-economic transformation.[8]

For the Canadian Peacebuilding Network, peacebuilding thus

> identifies and supports relationships, governance modes, structures and systems, and provides capacities and resources to strengthen and consolidate the pros-pects for internal peace in order to avoid a resort to, an intensification of, or a relapse into destructive conflict [and] seeks to mitigate sources of tension that increase the probability or intensity of armed violence [while involving] a range of approaches and transformative processes – for specific contexts or on a larger systemic level – that identify and address both the root causes and ef-fects of violent conflict.[9]

This is a useful approach to a concept that encompasses multiple layers of activity by multiple actors at multiple phases of peace, conflict and violence – and which is thus very difficult to define and delineate for both analytical and practical purposes. However, conceiving peacebuilding as an approach that "emphasizes both the relational and structural elements of violence and conflict" enables one to move beyond "sequential limita-tions of peacebuilding and [take a view that] accommodates both short and long-term approaches and needs ... acknowledges both effects and root causes of conflict, including historical, socio-economic and political elements" and "allows for considerations of the complexities of globalization, including the effects of new 'violence entrepreneurs' and non-state transnational actors".[10] This approach recognizes "the importance of indigenous or local, context-specific mechanisms for resolving conflict, maintaining peace or reducing the likelihood of violence altogether ... highlights the need for country-specific and larger international structural actions to address sources of tension [and] frames peacebuilding as a policy development and policy advocacy tool that may be used to address the consequences of poor development, defence and foreign policy practice".[11]

Such a comprehensive view of peacebuilding necessarily requires one to focus on much narrower aspects of this concept, approach and tool: for instance, one might focus on one particular geographic context, affected community or conflict phase, one particular peacebuilding actor or one specific policy activity or priority. Nevertheless, and this needs to be recognized, no one peacebuilding context (be it in terms of location, phase or actor involved) can be considered in isolation from all other aspects of peacebuilding. This recognition presents considerable challenges to those attempting to make analytical and conceptual sense of peacebuilding as an overarching concept, as well as for those who attempt to translate peacebuilding into a programmatic policy activity with very specific start and end points, in reference to particular peacebuilding providers or recipient communities and in the hope of extracting lessons learned to be applied elsewhere. Peacebuilding is a complex activity that must be broken down into more manageable components, yet always in recognition of each component's specific location within and relevance for the larger peacebuilding "project".

Each peacebuilding activity or actor must be understood and recognized as an element of the larger spatial, temporal and actor-related contexts that determine both the overall conditions that have given rise to peacebuilding needs and the range of strategies, mechanisms and instruments that are required and available to meet those needs. In our book we focus on one particular phase of peacebuilding (post-conflict peacebuilding) and the forgone, actual and potential contributions of one particular peacebuilding actor (i.e. women). The locations of the analysis span the globe, while examinations also engage with a multitude of other peacebuilding actors and phases.

The term "peacebuilding" thus describes a wide range of activities that reduce the destructive forces of everyday conflict and prevent its escalation to violence, at all stages of possible conflict escalation, between individuals, communities and states.[12] Peacebuilding scholars have noted an increase of public attention, academic focus and political and policy commitment on comprehensive peacebuilding activities before, during and after violent conflict. They have observed a "huge upsurge in activity in conflict prevention, conflict management, diplomatic peacemaking and post-conflict peacebuilding activity ... with most of this being spearheaded by the UN itself (but with the World Bank, donor states, a number of regional security organisations and literally thousands of NGOs playing significant roles of their own)".[13] In fact, this book project benefited from such increased attention: it could draw on the insights of experienced researchers and peacebuilding practitioners, was initiated and supported by a UN institution (the United Nations University) and was sustained by applied policy research and training institutions (swisspeace and the Geneva Centre for the Democratic Control of Armed Forces) throughout its completion. Yet despite – and in large part because of – the attention given to conceptual thinking and practical applications of peacebuilding instruments and approaches, we are far from a full understanding and the capacity to apply peacebuilding strategies and techniques to their full potential. As Fisher and Zimina note:

> While the evidence suggests that peacebuilders have made some considerable inroads, despite accompanying ambivalences and confusions ... the peacebuilding community – all those who see themselves as working for peace, justice and development – needs to start getting its own house in order if it is to match up to the intensifying challenges. It needs to have further conversations about "peace writ large" ... Whose peace are peacebuilders working for? Is such work regarded as "transforming" – seeking ultimately to challenge the unsustainable, unjust status quo and bring about profound change towards greater justice and wellbeing? Or is it essentially "technical" peacebuilding, focused on project-bound locations and time-scales and trusting that the bigger picture will look after itself?[14]

Our book addresses one particular flaw in the design and application of peacebuilding, which still stymies efforts to maximize its potential to strengthen, advance and thus *build peace*: the general tendency to underestimate, underutilize and purposely marginalize women's roles in peacebuilding activities at local, national and international levels. In that sense peacebuilding needs to do more to contribute to the "transformation" of society, in the spirit of Fisher and Zimina. While our book focuses mainly on post-conflict peacebuilding activities, many of its lessons and suggestions have similar relevance for peacebuilding activities at all phases of the conflict cycle or, more appropriately, of the *peace and conflict dynamics* that characterize interactions between individuals, communities and their states.[15]

Post-conflict peacebuilding challenges

It is worth noting that, of course, as all routine social interactions are necessarily characterized by disagreements, disputes and competing views and approaches, conflict is part and parcel of everyday life. Without conflict there is no adaptation to changing conditions, no competition for the most constructive adaptation mechanisms, no progress and no ability to meet emerging challenges. In those terms there is no such thing as a post-conflict environment – such a condition would spell the end of adaptation, progress and survival in a constantly changing world. However, if competing ideas and adaptation mechanisms translate into competition for power, authority and resources and cannot be channelled and resolved peacefully and for mutual gain, conflict becomes destructive and makes progress extremely costly; or it halts or reverses it altogether. When we speak of a conflict environment we are referring to a context that is characterized by the existence of violent expressions of conflict and a lack of mechanisms for protection and justice. When we refer to a "post-conflict" context, we are referring to an environment after the formal conclusion of a specific violent and armed conflict, characterized by opportunities for justice, reconciliation, an end to impunity and the building of accountable and responsible forms of democratic governance, which are, among others, the cornerstones of a peaceful society.

In the aftermath of armed violence, post-conflict environments are characterized by a considerable impoverishment of economic, political and social relations between and among groups, individuals and state institutions. Previously existing divisions within society have been exacerbated during times of armed conflict and new fractures have been created. Post-conflict societies are affected by institutional breakdown resulting from weak or non-existent government and civil society institutions. Those institutions possess – at best – limited legitimacy, capacity and authority at a time when restoring a fully functioning system of governance is most critical. A security sector inherited from years of armed conflict poses great risks to internal security and stability: bloated armies with little or no civilian control; irregular, paramilitary and private security forces; vast amounts of arms and ammunition in private and government hands; weak justice institutions; and an environment in which all forms of violence have become normalized. Economic instability and decline, human resource shortage, refugees and displacement, psychosocial trauma, infrastructural damage, landmines and other unexploded ordnance, competing and unresolved territorial claims and a weakened social fabric characterized by a persistent culture of violence create conditions under which conflicts may re-escalate very quickly. This might happen faster, more violently and at greater human cost in a society that has already been weakened by war.[16]

As noted by the High-level Panel on Threats, Challenges and Change, "Deploying peace enforcement and peacekeeping forces may be essential in terminating conflicts but are not sufficient for long-term recovery. Serious attention to the longer-term process of peacebuilding in all its multiple dimensions is critical; failure to invest adequately in peacebuilding increases the odds that a country will relapse into conflict."[17] What should therefore be the main components of a post-conflict peacebuilding strategy that effectively prevents the resurgence of violence? The 2009 report of the UN Secretary-General on peacebuilding in the immediate aftermath of conflict highlights five "recurring priorities": safety and security, including justice and respect for the rule of law; confidence in the political process, through both inclusive dialogue and post-conflict elections; access to basic services such as water and education; a functioning public administration to manage government funds and public records, at a minimum; and economic revitalization, particularly employment creation and infrastructural improvements.[18]

The UN Plan of Action on Peacebuilding, developed by the UN Department of Political Affairs, notes that "Peace-building missions are meant to be temporary catalytic and facilitating mechanisms and are normally small ... Their political responsibilities involve: protection of nascent democratic institutions; crisis management; political mediation; and provision of good offices."[19] These responsibilities are accomplished through "provision of political facilitation and mediation; support to and facilitation of short-term mechanisms for reconciliation and dialogue; political, security and human rights reporting and monitoring; contribution to subregional and regional stability where appropriate and viable; advocacy and sensitization of national actors to human rights, security, democratic and peaceful means of conflict management and the rule of law; and advocacy and the dissemination of information on all aspects of peace-building".[20] Rebuilding war-torn societies is a complex task that involves "a set of physical, social, and structural initiatives"[21] that aim to alleviate direct as well as structural violence in order to bring about both negative and positive peace. As Nick Lewer argues:

> In a negative sense peace can just mean the absence of violence and an acceptance of unbalanced power relationships, inequalities and lack of access to resources which may be associated with such a condition. In this case, the concept of "peace as order" is prevalent. Positive peace, on the other hand, indicates an environment where people strive to *transform* society and communities into fairer and more just places to live. Not only is the "direct" experience of violence tackled, but also the "structural" elements in society which perpetuate

potential sources of conflict. Working for a positive peace means empowering people to become involved in non-violent change processes themselves, to help build sustainable conditions for peace and justice.[22]

Peacebuilding support includes a number of key objectives, as outlined for instance in the 2009 "Report of the Secretary-General on Peacebuilding in the Immediate Aftermath of Conflict":

- Support to basic safety and security, including mine action, protection of civilians, disarmament, demobilization and reintegration, strengthening the rule of law and initiation of security sector reform.
- Support to political processes, including electoral processes, promoting inclusive dialogue and reconciliation, and developing conflict management capacity at national and subnational levels.
- Support to the provision of basic services, such as water and sanitation, health and primary education, and support to the safe and sustainable return and reintegration of internally displaced persons and refugees.
- Support to restoring core government functions, in particular basic public administration and public finance, at the national and subnational levels.
- Support to economic revitalization, including employment generation and livelihoods (in agriculture and public works) particularly for youth and demobilized former combatants, as well as rehabilitation of basic infrastructure.[23]

The meaningful mitigation of a broad range of structural and direct human and national security threats requires the commitment and joint initiative of society, its government and the broader, regional and international communities of state and non-state actors.[24] Peace can be built and consolidated only if all stakeholders are involved in all stages of the process, from the identification of challenges to the implementation of mitigation measures.

Moreover, peacebuilding processes, institutions and activities have to be owned and carried out in large part by all those who will eventually benefit from more political, social and economic stability, predictability, order and justice. While that of course includes the immediate and broader neighbourhood (including the global community), it concerns in the first instance the affected populations. In any society the majority of the population are female, yet women are usually overlooked as contributors in the search for solutions to their society's plight. The cases studies in this volume offer insights into some of the key challenges faced by women in post-conflict situations and the various responses that have (or have not) been instituted by local, national and international actors to address the needs and contributions of women when designing and implementing post-conflict assistance programmes and reforming post-war political and security institutions and systems. If we acknowledge that sustainable peacebuilding rests with the affected society and its people – half or more of whom are female – for peacebuilding efforts to have a long-term and constructive impact it is imperative that international, national, local and traditional social, economic and political cultures change and as a result prioritize the post-conflict needs and contributions of women.

The post-conflict moment – A window of opportunity for change

While marred by destruction, instability, uncertainty and suffering (often extending far beyond state borders), the post-conflict moment offers a window of opportunity to rewrite many rules that previously governed – and misgoverned! – the society. Among these are the rules that determine the relations between men and women, and between women and society at large.[25] This window of opportunity for change can be utilized by local, national and international actors to address some of the inequalities, inequities and injustices that have caused much of the violence endured by women before and during the war, often continuing unabatedly in the post-war period and preventing women from playing a constructive and prominent role in consolidating peace and stability.

Through our book we want to encourage those active in research and those working in the design and application of broader peacebuilding policies at non-governmental, state and intergovernmental levels to take a fresh look at a broader approach to righting the wrongs committed against the supposedly weak in our societies – women and, in the companion volume, children and youth. They have a right to be treated with the respect they deserve as potentially powerful and influential agents of both positive and negative social and political change. Particularly during peace processes in which societies revisit, design and build the structures, institutions, procedures and normative and legal foundations for a new state and society, they must have their voices heard and play an active role in the initiation and implementation of change. Strategies must be designed, supported by proper budgets and capacities, to ensure that such significant social change is possible.

Post-conflict threats to the physical security of women

Cross-cultural studies of post-conflict settings – as well as the experiences reported throughout this book – demonstrate that the risks for women are not simply limited to the context-relevant peculiarities of each post-war situation. Many of the risks described occur across a large number of contexts and are in fact quite predictable and comparable in their intention and their impact: this is why the international community, specifically through the UN Security Council, has been able to develop such a clear set of Security Council resolutions on women, peace and security, which are considered to be applicable in all conflict and post-conflict settings, since the passage of Security Council Resolution (SCR) 1325 in 2000.[26]

Nonetheless, the consequences of conflicts are far from homogeneous and gender-neutral. They differently impact individuals according to gender, age, ethnicity or religious identity, income, social status, level of physical ability (especially for those disabled by war) and geography. For instance, in some cases young women affected by war are stigmatized to a much greater degree than older women, especially in rural areas, while women and girls with physical disabilities, including those resulting from war violence, have little or no hope of ever returning to a semblance of normal life. On the basis of lessons learned from past and ongoing practice, post-conflict initiatives must therefore address a number of priorities, including gender- and age-based violence and the health problems to which it leads, in order to meet the needs of as diverse a group of post-war survivors as possible.

Gender-based violence

Although one might expect levels of interpersonal violence to decrease after war, physical security continues to be of vital concern to women. Rape and sexual harassment, forced pregnancy, marriage, divorce, prostitution and trafficking do not end with the conclusion of peace dialogues or the signing of a formal peace agreement. Such acts of violence all too frequently continue to take place in the context of a traditional culture of shame, post-war insecurity, normalized violence, economic deprivation and poverty (see Chapter 3 in this volume). For example, economic hardship and social marginalization, as well as the peacebuilding economy created by the presence of international actors, almost inevitably increase the rates of prostitution (better characterized, from the perspective of the exploited, as "survival sex") and trafficking in women.[27]

Cultural factors greatly influence how people deal with gender-based violence. Before, during and after conflict, women are more likely to be subjected to sexual violence than men. As a report by the UN Department for Economic and Social Affairs Division for the Advancement of Women argues, "For a woman, there is the added risk of pregnancy as a result of rape. In addition, women occupy very different positions in society to men, and are treated differently because of what has happened to them. Women are frequently shunned, ostracized, and considered unmarriageable. Permanent damage to the reproductive system, which often results from sexual violence, has different implications for women than for men."[28] The same applies to HIV infection rates, which are much higher among women than men, as discussed by Lyn S. Graybill in Chapter 9.

Ann Tickner explains that "In the Rwandan civil war, for example, more than 250,000 women were raped; as a result, they were stigmatized and cast out of their communities, their children being labeled 'devil's children'. Not being classed as refugees, they have also been ignored by international efforts."[29] UNICEF writes that "In Rwanda, rape has been systematically used as a weapon of ethnic cleansing to destroy communities. In some raids, virtually every adolescent girl who survived an attack by the militia was subsequently raped. Many of those who became pregnant were then ostracized by their families and community; some abandoned their babies, other committed suicide."[30] The victims get punished for their suffering by their own communities and families whose support they need most. To cite a further example, "during the Turkish invasion of Cyprus a large number of women were raped. Immediately after the invasion an emergency law was introduced for a short period in which men were allowed to divorce their raped wives (as divorce was legalized in Cyprus only in the 1990s)."[31] Men's "right" to leave "sullied" women was thus entrenched, but little or nothing was done to protect or rehabilitate the women, who were double victims of their society's patriarchal beliefs.

After wars officially end, paramilitary groups may continue to terrorize civilians, among them women, who often become a particular focus of attacks. For instance, in Afghanistan "clashes between Uzbek, Tajik and Hazara militias tend to end up with sexual violence against local women. There is an increasing number of reports of gang rapes and the exchange of women as payment in the settlement of feuds."[32] Similarly, the majority of casualties in recent clashes in southern Sudan are reported to be women and children.[33] Women are always among the largest groups of refugees and returnees. Crimes against women and children have forced families to flee to safer neighbouring countries to protect their daughters and sons.

Women are further threatened by landmines and other unexploded ordnance. Although it is widely recognized that women in particular are affected by the indiscriminate use of anti-personnel landmines, many companies and countries have profited from the sale of these deadly weapons. Mines are cheap to manufacture, but very expensive to remove. As the most affected countries are among the world's poorest, this generates additional challenges. It is estimated that millions of mines have been laid in at least 78 countries and areas not internationally recognized.[34] Afghanistan, Cambodia, Iraq and Sri Lanka are considered among the worst-affected nations in the world. In Afghanistan alone, approximately 70,000 civilians were killed or maimed by landmines during the 1980s and 1990s.[35] Most of the victims were young men and boys, which implies that women are left with specific burdens of care in these countries, as they have to cope with the death or permanent disability of male family members.

In the aftermath of armed conflict, large numbers of small arms remain in the hands of combatants and civilians, threatening society at large and women in particular. The availability of small arms in both conflict and non-conflict contexts is considered to be directly linked to levels of lethal violence – perpetrated by intimate partners, criminals or combatants. As Cukier and Cairns report, 35 per cent of casualties during conflict are civilians, defined as all females and males under the age of 16 and over 50.[36] They note that "If small arms are not removed following the cessation of conflict, interpersonal violence substitutes for violence between warring factions."[37] In addition to continuing spurts of armed violence and increasing armed criminal activity, "worldwide, women are more at risk from violence at the hands of intimate partners in the private sphere of the home [while at the same time] the risk of being murdered by an intimate partner increases with the availability of firearms".[38]

Health problems

War trauma and post-war troubles can trigger an entire range of health disorders. In Afghanistan, long-suffering men and women turn to opium in order to deal with the harsh post-conflict realities.[39] Afghanistan provides the lion's share of the world's opium, and exports both the consumption of and trade in drugs to neighbouring countries in particular. The opium industry, for instance, engages women and men in Iran, Tajikistan and Pakistan who survive by trafficking drugs to Western countries. Traumatized by the war and post-war confusion, many civilians become addicted to drugs, leading to their further marginalization within society.

Sexually transmitted diseases, including HIV/AIDS, are prevalent in the post-conflict environment, affecting in particular women. A UN Population Fund report shows that:

> Armed conflict increases the rate of new infections across affected populations, but women and girls are significantly more likely to become infected than men and boys. A recent post-conflict study in Africa found that the HIV-infection rate of adolescent girls was four times that of adolescent boys. Rape, high-risk behaviour, the inability to negotiate safe sex, and sexual exploitation are risks that have disproportionately impacted women and girls.[40]

Boys and young men are also at risk of rape and sexually transmitted diseases and infections: although affected to a lesser extent than girls and young women, the fact that it happens to boys and youth often receives no attention at all. Indeed, recognition of homophobic violence continues to be one of the greatest taboos in modern war, although its use appears to be increasingly widespread.

Obstacles to women's post-conflict roles

Social integration, economic survival and traditional institutions

Tremendous demographic changes, the collapse of family units, mass killings particularly of the male population, other humanitarian atrocities and massive displacements create a new social environment in which greater social responsibility is borne by women in post-conflict rebuilding. In Afghanistan, for instance:

> The collapse of family structures and the general social fabric of the country during the war is another devastating social impact. The society has become increasingly militarized. Employment opportunities must be developed alongside education opportunities in order to build a civil society out of what is essentially a war economy. Attitudes and values in Afghanistan have become more radical, but the prevailing mores with regard to gender relations, marriage, homosexuality, and adultery have also emerged from the society itself, transformed as a result of the war, and not only because of Taliban policy as international consensus would hold.[41]

As Codou Bop argues, in Rwanda "34 per cent of the households today are headed by women who, in most cases, have lost all (or almost all) their children and must take care of countless orphans left by close relatives or distant dead relatives".[42] Woman-headed and child-headed households are typical features of post-war environments. They represent highly vulnerable families that are in dire need of social and legal protection. Child-headed households face particularly harsh challenges: as Steven Hick notes, "While some communities are supportive, all too many neighbours and relations are ready to exploit orphans and steal their property."[43] Woman- and child-headed households encounter more difficulties and require more protection from state agencies and international organizations than man-headed households. Regrettably, particularly state-led development and assistance programmes tend to be based on stereotypical and traditional perceptions of social responsibilities of men and women. According to Noeleen Heyzer, "The state plans as though men support families when in reality it is men together with women who do so, and frequently it is women who do so alone."[44] War and post-war trauma strengthen ethnic and religious identities, revitalizing long-forgotten ethnic and religious traditions and institutions and evoking neo-traditional beliefs in a purported "golden age" of patriarchal social rule, which tend to enhance archaic forms of gender discrimination.

After war, the situation of young women becomes more complicated due to traditions of shame and restrictions to their freedom. As analysis shows, "the conservative backlash that takes place after war has roots in the older generation's attempt to reassert control and re-establish 'traditions.' In the context of re-establishing livelihood, the older generation finds it particularly important to control young women."[45] At the same time, it is important to facilitate communication between elders and the younger generation for the preservation of positive cultural values and traditions. As adolescents are in a stage of searching for identity, it is imperative that values of their community are preserved. When fathers are absent, "the elders are a special resource in transmitting such values".[46]

In every society there are positive cultural traditions that can mitigate the suffering and obstacles women face in post-conflict settings. For example, local customs of adopting orphans and separated children by relatives, and particularly women family members, tend to be overlooked (and thus are not sufficiently supported) by Western and national aid programmes. In certain cases, encouraging and understanding the cultural context of mutual help can facilitate a less painful return to some sense of normalcy.

External actors' engagement with traditional institutions is a particularly delicate issue in societies that are firmly entrenched in religious beliefs and value systems. For instance, in post-conflict Muslim states such as Iraq, Afghanistan and Tajikistan, external organizations and individuals offering assistance often fail to appreciate the complexity of the culture when engaging with traditional institutions and practice. When gender-sensitive activities are highly politicized, "even modest publicity about a successful program can be a threat to its continuation".[47] On the other hand, Christian religious conservatism has been crippling for women's emancipation in the aftermath of violent conflicts in countries such as Uganda, the Democratic Republic of the Congo, Rwanda and South Sudan.[48] In post-conflict environments harassment and intimidation of women and girls by conservative fanatics from a wide range of religious groups – both locals and outsiders – are considerable threats to their security and involvement in rebuilding society.[49] Moreover, as feminist observers have long pointed out, in many cases donors are the ones who bring more conservative and limiting gender ideologies to the post-conflict society, particularly by systematically excluding women from post-conflict reconstruction, as they know little about women's history of resistance and tend to prefer to work primarily with men.[50]

Justice and the legal status of women

In traditional societies with predominantly oral customary law, the status of women changes during and then again after war. While women take on new responsibilities in times of war, the rapid restoration of "traditional" norms after the war (which, as observed above, may have more to do with controlling women than with restoring tradition!) often leads to renewed discrimination against and marginalization of women. In post-conflict reconstruction, women usually receive less support than many men: while a man wounded by the enemy is seen as a hero, a woman wounded by an enemy who used rape as a tool of war is perceived as a disgrace for the whole community.[51] There is no post-war monument of a raped woman, whereas monuments for dead or wounded men are common. History as a rule does not recognize names of female warriors or women who helped men in a war; if women are recognized, their exact roles may be distorted to reflect gender ideologies rather than what they really did.[52] In post-conflict societies, men and women return to their traditions of gender discrimination, which often become even more intolerant of women's rights than before the war. As Meredeth Turshen observes in the African context, while war erodes some traditional values, it does not erode sexist beliefs, which (not coincidentally) serve the interests of the male-dominated state – whether colonial, apartheid or post-colonial.[53] The legal and social status of women in post-conflict societies often changes quite drastically as a consequence of the war. This happens for instance through the loss of male relatives, legal documents, land and property; the restoration of local ethnic and religious traditions that discriminate against gender; or with the commencement of "state-building" processes which ignore women as citizens with a voice in shaping the institutions that will run their country.

In Muslim countries and those with a sizeable Muslim population, justification of polygamy is becoming a common feature of post-conflict societies. Women tend to marry into the husband's family, leaving behind their own family to live with the in-laws. After the death of the husband, they also, in a sense, become internally displaced persons. Unofficial polygamy in such post-conflict societies is spreading more rapidly as widows have to become second wives to survive and protect themselves and their children. In this context, for example, the National Parliament of Tajikistan has debated the introduction of polygamy and the problem of protecting second wives' rights. As Svetlana Sharipova and Hermine De Soto report in Chapter 7, women in post-war Tajikistan are by no means only passive victims in a male-dominated society, with some of them supporting polygamy to ensure human security for themselves and their offspring. In non-Muslim countries such as Cambodia, too, polygamy reportedly has increased as wars ended, "forcing single women in desperate situations to enter into marital arrangements, both formal and informal, with married men".[54] In post-conflict Muslim societies (Tajikistan, Afghanistan, Chechnya, Sudan and others) polygamy necessitates discussion of the legal protection of women's rights to land and property. In multiple marriages women and their children are often forgotten by both their husbands and the state. Moreover, national administrative systems are often inefficient in dealing with – or challenging – customary law, and few, if any, qualified women lawyers are present to participate in constitutional and other legal reform. As Vanessa Farr notes, in transitional societies such as present-day Egypt, Tunisia and Palestine, women lawyers struggle greatly to get their legal opinions tabled. While surely a delicate issue for international actors as well as national reformers and rights advocates, facilitating local women to debate legal matters is an essential part of post-conflict reconstruction. There are lessons that can be learned from other contexts – the South African constitutional review process, for instance, was effectively informed by feminist lawyers after a tremendous struggle to be heard.[55]

Participation of women in political life

In post-conflict societies women tend to be quite familiar with local traditions but may know very little about their political rights and responsibilities. For example, in post-Soviet Georgia, a country of universal literacy and well-educated women, most displaced women tended to show much greater interest in the everyday economic and psychosocial issues confronting their families and communities than in political questions. A US Agency for International Development (USAID) study found that only five of 105 displaced women surveyed were acquainted with their basic human rights under the UN Declaration of Human Rights and the Convention on the Elimination of Discrimination against Women.[56]

All too often, women are inadequately involved the political decision-making and post-conflict resolution activities of peace processes. However, "as peace processes ... provide a unique opportunity to radically renegotiate the political settlement, the benefits of women's full participation in these processes is significant".[57] Instead, as Castillejo notes, the "experience of being pushed out of public life and back into traditional roles is common for women following the end of conflict".[58] Yet greater participation in peacebuilding and decision-making could lower the risks for women in post-conflict societies to suffer from continued violations (see Chapters 2 and 12 in this volume). As Rose M. Kadende-Kaiser observes in Chapter 5 on Burundi, at the national and local levels female politicians are often more concerned with social, educational and health-care issues than, for instance, with the implementation of peace accords. Yet it is precisely their absence from political processes which ensures that concerns of women are overlooked. For example, a member of the joint commission implementing the peace accords in Angola in the 1990s indicated that, in hindsight, the exclusion of women from the peace process "meant that issues [such] as internal displacement, sexual violence, human trafficking, abuses by government and rebel security forces, and the rebuilding of maternal health care and girls' education were generally ignored".[59] Cukier and Cairns draw similar conclusions about the potential (but unfortunately wasted) opportunities of feeding civil-society-driven arms control initiatives, advocated in large part by concerned and affected women, into official decision- and policy-making processes:

> women account for a higher percentage of victims of gun violence than users of small arms and light weapons; therefore they generally express greater negative attitudes towards weapons than men. They also tend to be more committed to measures created to reduce the misuse and proliferation of guns and gun violence. For these reasons, women have exerted significant influence in many of the movements aimed at reducing the proliferation and misuse of weapons. However, women have also been under-represented in the formal decision-making processes that affect the deployment of weapons as well as their use and control at local, national and international levels.[60]

Drawing on his experience with women's initiatives to establish cross-conflict links with women and men to reduce tension and distrust between former belligerents, John Paul Lederach concludes that "while much of it has gone unnoticed in the long history of the Somali conflict, women have played a far more innovative, constructive, and transformative role in peacebuilding than the sum total of the formal peace conferences of military leaders".[61] Kinzelbach and Hassan observe that "The experience of a gruesome clan-based militia war in the context of a failed state has turned many Somali women into advocates for peace and non-violent conflict resolution."[62] In fact, "Somali men have listened and will continue to listen when women try to keep them from unpacking guns stored at home, or when they demand a cessation of hostilities by singing songs."[63]

According to Ann Tickner, "In the context of a male-dominated society, the association of men with war and women with peace also reinforces gender hierarchies and false dichotomies that contribute to the devaluation of both women and peace."[64] Of course, women of courage everywhere make an important but often unnoticed and unrecognized contribution as peace educators in both their families and their societies. However, such roles should not be unduly romanticized, nor should all women be homogenized as peaceful. Some cases of post-conflict societies, for instance, show that in the name of families and children, or ethnic and religious traditions, some women prefer a mono-ethnic environment or express racial or religious intolerance and ethnic prejudice, while there are many men (also among those in positions of power) who are committed to and practise non-violent approaches to dispute resolution. For instance, as Tickner reports, "A study of Israeli, Egyptian, Palestinian, and Kuwaiti attitudes toward the Arab/Israeli conflict, broken down by sex, found that men and women did not have different attitudes and there was no evidence of women being less militaristic."[65] Moreover, particularly the experience of gruesome gender violence during conflicts makes some women suspicious and intolerant of other ethnic or religious groups.[66]

Missed opportunity finally recognized – Security Council Resolution 1325

The underutilized involvement of women in the maintenance and restoration of peace and security was finally recognized – and thus put on the radar screen of national and international actors – in the discussions preceding and following SCR 1325 on women, peace and security.[67] Since then, several further reports have helped to maintain international humanitarian and political attention to women's contributions as both victims and – increasingly – also powerful actors in determining the dynamics of peace, conflict and stability in their societies. Significant among them are the "2005 World Summit Outcome", which commits member states to eliminating all forms of violence against women and girls;[68] the 2006 SCR 1674, reconfirming and updating various resolutions on the protection of civilians in armed conflict;[69] the 2006 report of the UN Secretary-General entitled "In-depth Study on All Forms of Violence against Women";[70] the 2007 General Assembly Resolution 62/134, "Eliminating Rape and Other Forms of Sexual Violence in All Their Manifestations, Including in Conflict and Related Situations";[71] the 2008 SCR 1820, "Sexual Violence in Conflict";[72] the 2009 report of the Secretary-General on peacebuilding in the immediate aftermath of conflict;[73] and the 2010 report of the Secretary-General, "Women's Participation in Peacebuilding".[74]

These documents are meant to focus UN member states (and in fact all governmental and non-governmental actors that play a relevant role in their societies' efforts at managing peace, conflict and post-conflict trans-formation) on respecting the rights and needs of traditionally yet unjustly marginalized parts of the population. They highlight commitments made in more general terms in previous international legal documents and public statements, including the 1949 Geneva Conventions and the 1977 Additional Protocols,[75] international human rights law (such as the Con-vention on the Elimination of All Forms of Discrimination against Women), the 1994 International Conference on Population and Develop-ment and the 1995 Beijing Declaration and Platform for Action.[76] In Chapter 10 in this book Ancil Adrian-Paul traces the evolution towards SCR 1325, as well as its impact and subsequent developments.[77]

Not all these developments have been considered as evolutionary pro-gress beyond the often poor record of follow-up and implementation, or beyond states' tendency to celebrate and confuse their own written com-mitments with the actual political and social change that should result from these commitments. Particularly, the recent SCR 1820 on sexual vio-lence in conflict has faced some harsh criticism for being one Security Council member's attempt to draw attention away from the larger, deeper and thus more challenging and difficult tasks set out in SCR 1325.

Back to the future? Security Council Resolution 1820

SCR 1820, "Sexual Violence in Conflict", focuses primarily on women as victims of sexual violence in conflict and post-conflict situations (while, for the most part, excluding sexual violence committed against men).[78] Critics fear that the resolution again relegates women to the role of vic-tim, while distracting us from and adding very little in substance and util-ity to the commitments expressed in the original SCR 1325. UNIFEM (now part of UN Women) highlights the following concerns as the main criticisms launched against SCR 1820: the emphasis on sexual violence might risk fracturing SCR 1325, as it portrays women as victims and ob-scures other forms of civilian suffering; by stating that sexual violence "can" constitute a war crime, crime against humanity or constituent act of genocide, SCR 1820 risks diluting existing international law; the focus is limited to the countries on the Security Council's political agenda; the fear of women around the world that producing new resolutions might distract attention away from the full implementation of SCR 1325; the tabling of the resolution was not preceded by a proper consultation pro-cess; and there is too much geographic emphasis on Africa, as other parts of the world experience similar suffering.[79] On the other hand, the propo-nents of the resolution do not agree with these concerns and argue that SCR 1820 should be seen as a constructive expansion of, not a threat to, SCR 1325.[80]

There is of course a danger that follow-up resolutions that expand and possibly even improve on particular points of a preceding resolution are not seen as amendments, but their replacements. The fact that countries which were previously hostile to the implementation of SCR 1325 suddenly appear as champions of SCR 1820 suggests that this resolution may well have been designed to focus on women as traditional victims of conflict, an approach for which sympathetic support can be more easily gathered across diverse political and ideological camps. While this may generate sympathy for the plight of women in armed conflict, it might distract from the urgent need for the type of systematic change demanded by SCR 1325 in the form of promoting women's leadership and full participation in all matters of peace and security.

Challenges for international assistance programmes and missions

International assistance plays an increasingly important role in post-conflict rebuilding. There are many success stories of aid given to governments and local non-governmental organizations, assisting them in offering urgently required support to post-conflict populations. Along with significant progress, international efforts have also been criticized for offering insufficient, inadequate and untimely support. While some of these shortcomings may be rooted in funding constraints or unsuitable and unrealistic mandates, some highly disturbing dynamics of international peacebuilding activities in fact do harm: they increase violence and support exclusionary patterns against women in post-conflict societies. As mentioned earlier, there is a tendency by international and national (often male or male-dominated) expert groups to seek out male counterparts or, in the name of respecting local traditions, to play into the hands of paternalist and discriminating power structures that keep women at the margins of the peacebuilding process. On the other hand, international actors miss out on opportunities to promote and practise inclusive approaches:

> One such example of a missed opportunity is in Kosovo where, despite much rhetoric, the United Nations Mission in Kosovo (UNMIK) conspicuously failed to implement SCR 1325. It did not meaningfully promote women's participation in Kosovan peace processes or give women leadership roles within its own structures. This failure by UNMIK – in a situation where it had enormous influence – resulted in women's representatives being excluded from negotiations on the Comprehensive Proposal for Kosovo Status Settlement. Not only did this mean that the framework for the Kosovan state was established without women's input, but it also created deep mistrust of the international community among women's civil society organisations.[81]

Moreover, the "do-no-harm" principle applies to peace operations' activities in the same way as it applies to humanitarian or development activities: there should not be any negative and harmful consequences to the population as a result of international missions that are meant to bring peace and stability and thus end, not create, violence, as observed by Sumie Nakaya in Chapter 4. For instance, women have increasingly become victims of prostitution following the arrival of peacekeeping forces.[82] In Cambodia:

> The presence of a large number of expatriates, especially UN peacekeepers ... led to a rapid growth in ... prostitution. To meet the demands of the expatriates, many entrepreneurs openly set up brothels, which were soon frequented by local customers as well, institutionalizing the phenomenon. Initially, these brothels imported commercial sex workers from Vietnam and Thailand, but soon they were also recruiting from the countryside.[83]

It is important that peacekeepers and anyone else involved in post-conflict peacebuilding receive meaningful, not merely symbolic, training in international humanitarian law, human rights law, children's rights and gender issues. The training, which should not be a one-off event but repeated periodically, must reflect sensitivity to women's rights and unexpected cultural peculiarities, and be offered by civilian experts on gender equality, social inclusion and health issues. The call for such training is by no means new, but the record is poor in terms of effective, broad-based implementation and subsequent positive change in the behaviour of peacekeepers.[84] International personnel must recognize and experience that in field missions there needs to be zero tolerance of involvement in trafficking of women and girls, and sexual relations with minors and beneficiaries of assistance programmes. Awareness and acceptance of relevant – non-negotiable – standards and norms need to be internalized by all military and civilian staff of the United Nations or a regional organization. These demands were strongly voiced in the recent SCR 1820. After all, "peacekeepers" are sent to and/or invited into a country to bring peace and stability and to reduce, not worsen, the structural and direct violence exerted upon the population. Their mission and purpose, reputation and local acceptance are compromised if they are found to violate and betray those noble objectives.[85]

Over 10 years ago the Brahimi Report (2000) emphasized the need to strive for gender balance in peacekeeping efforts. Its authors argued, for instance, that more female civilian police officers and military observers should serve in UN peacekeeping missions.[86] SCR 1325 specifically demands expansion of "the role and contribution of women in United Nations field-based operations, and especially among military observers, civilian police, human rights and humanitarian personnel".[87] Encouraging examples are the all-female Indian Formed Police Unit despatched to the UN Mission in Liberia in January 2007 and the subsequent all-female Bangladeshi UN police unit deployed in Haiti in June 2010 (see also Chapter 10 in this volume).

Both SCRs 1325 and 1820 call for guidelines, point out that training needs to be developed and applied, and argue that all mission staff should be aware of codes of conduct before they are sent on mission (see also Chapter 13 in this volume). It has become "more widely recognized that women need to be included in peace processes, [and] there should be a parallel effort to integrate women to the senior levels in donor organizations and as facilitators of peace processes".[88] Moreover, gender-sensitive analyses ought to be an integral part of UN reports on peace operations. The UN Secretary-General is thus calling for "more effective measures to track gender funding reports" in response to a review of projects in consolidated appeals for 23 post-conflict countries during 2006–2008, which revealed that only 2.3 per cent of them dealt with gender issues, either by including women as major beneficiaries or by addressing gender-based violence.[89]

Some international agencies have recognized the special needs of women in post-conflict transition, introduced new programmes and expanded ongoing projects. However, increasing the number of players in peacebuilding complicates coordination and leads to duplication and bureaucratization. International and local attempts to stabilize post-conflict societies have therefore been ineffective due to a lack of coordination and a failure to address systematically, across all involved programmes and actors, gender-sensitive issues and the cultural context of gender relationships.

Although the failures of gender-sensitive peacebuilding activities are better known than the success stories, the latter might inspire more meaningful and effective peacebuilding policies and thus need to be studied and analysed to allow international, state and non-governmental actors to build on positive lessons and best practice. This book hopes to make a contribution in this direction.

Women and post-conflict peacebuilding: The debate and its impact on new policy guidance

Until recently, academic and political debates on peacebuilding have not paid much attention to women as a diverse group of agents and actors in peacebuilding processes. As Birgitte Sørensen argued in the late 1990s:

> the most apparent drawback in existing literature on war-to-peace transitions and post-war reconstructions is its remarkably gender-blind perspective. Growing out of disciplines such as international relations, political sciences and economics, a large number of analyses concentrate on macro-issues without distinguishing between men's and women's positions. But even when the focus is shifted to rebuilding activities carried out at the grassroots level, the adoption of inclusive categories such as "people", "the population", or of more narrow technical categories as "refugees", "internally displaced persons", "demobilized soldiers", or "disabled persons", conceals the inherent gender differentiation and the gender specificity of experiences and interests.[90]

In the mainstream literature – and mainstream political debates – this is still the case beyond the occasional declaratory statement. However, such a distorted view of how societies in and after conflict function is counterproductive to effective and lasting peacebuilding.

Sørensen further observed that "Wars and armed conflicts produce a number of new social categories whose identity and status are not easily determined. Among these we find disabled persons, widows, women who have been raped, orphans, and others who in some way challenge existing norms and images of womanhood, wifehood and motherhood."[91] The perceived and experienced vulnerability and disempowerment of women are both results of and reasons for the psychological and social marginalization that are often overlooked in the planning of post-conflict assistance and reconstruction programmes. Women's marginalization and discrimination, often hidden by a culture of shame, ignorance and ingrained sense of exclusion, inhibit their ability to articulate their own needs and claim their rights. This renders peacebuilding efforts insensitive to women and makes them far less meaningful, for them and society overall, than they could be.

However, in recognition of those lost opportunities, more serious engagement with these issues at both academic and policy levels has produced political momentum towards strengthening women's roles in peacebuilding generally and post-conflict peacebuilding in particular. That momentum is building at the level of the United Nations, triggering tangible results among member states, some of which are developing specifically targeted national policy guidance. The following sections will highlight how the United Nations in particular has reflected such new thinking in its own documentation, much of which is meant to guide approaches of all those involved in post-conflict peacebuilding activities, including the United Nations itself, its member states and regional and non-governmental organizations (NGOs).

Good intentions and proclamations: UN initiatives on women, peace and security

In recent years more attention has been paid to gender-sensitive assistance in post-conflict societies, in thought, proclamations, programming and implementation. Increasingly, attention has also been paid to removing obstacles and offering opportunities for women to become active agents within the full range of "positive peacebuilding". For instance, an understanding has developed that resources mobilized for successful post-conflict recovery should be specifically tailored towards women-sensitive strategies and therefore not exclusively benefit men. The 2002 "Report of the Secretary-General on Children and Armed Conflict" emphasized the special needs of girls, as "programmes specifically for girls are often overlooked during post-conflict reconstruction processes designed to foster rehabilitation, peace and stability, including disarmament, demobilization, reintegration, education and vocational training". The report argues that "More explicitly tailored strategies and adequate resources are needed to ensure that girls receive necessary assistance."[92] Increasing attention to women's rights and protection in post-conflict reconstruction by the United Nations, international NGOs and national governments has generated a number of studies that analysed lessons of best and worst strategies and practices, offering specific recommendations to the international community.[93]

Numerous reports and statements of good will, as well as national, regional and international action programmes, have followed – several of which will be referred to and examined in more detail in various chapters of this book. At this point we shall consider evidence of the impacts of such recognition, commitment and good intentions in the UN documents already mentioned in this chapter. The mere existence of those documents and the fact that they are supposed to guide the actions of all 193 UN member states – and as much as possible all other peacebuilding actors – do not mean that they automatically and instantly change prevailing behaviours at international, national and community levels. However, they do indicate that important and long-overdue exercises in international norm-setting are taking place that may have an impact on how the organization itself as well as many of its member states approach peacebuilding interventions both at home and abroad. In this sense, a new peacebuilding practice is hopefully emerging that will promote a form of social engineering through which gender relations in post-conflict societies are realigned. By this means an important aspect of the past injustice that prevented societies from capitalizing on existing but untapped capacities will be overcome.

Let us return to the efforts at the United Nations to guide progress in gender-sensitive and gender-just peacebuilding. There has been formal recognition of the need – and calls on UN member states – to integrate women fully in post-conflict peacebuilding activities. As the United Nations argues, "The increased participation of women within humanitarian, peace-building and peacekeeping operations is crucial if the United Nations goals and mandates regarding gender equality, non-discrimination and human rights are to be realized."[94] SCR 1325 also very specifically calls on the UN Secretary-General "to carry out a study on the impact of armed conflict on women and girls, the role of women in peace-building and the gender dimensions of peace processes and conflict resolution".[95]

SCR 1889 urges UN member states and international and regional organizations:

> to take further measures to improve women's participation during all stages of peace processes, particularly in conflict resolution, post-conflict planning and peacebuilding, including by enhancing their engagement in political and economic decision-making at early stages of recovery processes, through inter alia promoting women's leadership and capacity to engage in aid management and planning, supporting women's organizations, and countering negative societal attitudes about women's capacity to participate equally.[96]

It moreover notes that "women in situations of armed conflict and post-conflict situations continue to be often considered as victims and not as actors in addressing and resolving situations of armed conflict", and stresses "the need to focus not only on protection of women but also on their empowerment in peacebuilding".[97]

The Security Council urges its member states "to ensure gender mainstreaming in all post-conflict peacebuilding and recovery processes and sectors" and member states, UN bodies, donors and civil society "to ensure that women's empowerment is taken into account during post-conflict needs assessments and planning".[98] Furthermore, it requests the UN Secretary-General "in his agenda for action to improve the United Nations' peacebuilding efforts, to take account of the need to improve the participation of women in political and economic decision-making from the earliest stages of the peacebuilding process" and "to submit a report to the Security Council within 12 months on addressing women's participation and inclusion in peacebuilding and planning in the aftermath of conflict".[99] The said report was requested to analyse "the particular needs of women and girls in post-conflict situations", "Challenges to women's participation in conflict resolution and peacebuilding and gender mainstreaming in all early post-conflict planning, financing and recovery processes", "Measures to support national capacity in planning for and financing responses to the needs of women and girls in post-conflict situations" and "Recommendations for improving international and national responses to the needs of women and girls in post-conflict situations, including the development of effective financial and institutional arrangements to guarantee women's full and equal participation in the peacebuilding process."[100]

Establishing new international standards? The UN Secretary-General's report on women's participation in peacebuilding

The UN Secretary-General's report "Women's Participation in Peacebuilding",[101] which was written in response to this request, deserves detailed reflection as it confirms many points raised by the contributions in this book. The report shows that policy discussions – and presumably also policy guidance – may in fact be able to address many of the calls in our book for further and more meaningful inclusion of women in post-conflict peacebuilding. On the other hand, our own studies confirm the validity of the UN report's main arguments and the necessity to follow up on its recommendations. Here we review some of the report's major arguments, before we briefly introduce the individual contributions in this volume.

The Secretary-General's report argues that "Ensuring women's participation in peacebuilding is not only a matter of women's and girls' rights. Women are crucial partners in shoring up three pillars of lasting peace: economic recovery, social cohesion and political legitimacy."[102] However:

> The exclusion of women from the process of designing peace agreements and recovery frameworks means that often, insufficient attention is paid to redressing gender inequalities and addressing women's insecurity; as a result, women's needs go unmet and their capacities remain underutilized. We must transform this vicious circle into a virtuous circle, so that women's engagement in peacemaking brings a gender perspective to post-conflict planning, generating improved outcomes for women and an enhanced capacity to participate in longer-term peacebuilding.[103]

According to the report, there is evidence that this virtuous circle can be achieved, as "In many countries, the application of gender analysis, responses to women's and girls' post-conflict needs and women's engagement in peacemaking and peacebuilding have been mutually reinforcing."[104]

There are pragmatic and easily understandable and communicable reasons for strengthening women's roles in peacebuilding: "Enabling women to contribute to recovery and reconstruction is integral to strengthening a country's ability to sustain peacebuilding efforts. Similarly, efforts to facilitate an increased role for women in decision-making processes must be based on recognition of the fact that peacebuilding strategies cannot be fully 'owned' if half the nation is not actively involved in their design and implementation"[105] and "Women's access to services is constrained by, among other factors, physical insecurity and discriminatory social norms."[106] Thus:

> Removing barriers to all aspects of women's political participation is a matter of fundamental human rights. Women must not be impeded in terms of their ability to vote, join associations, run for office or express their convictions. Neither State nor non-State actors can be permitted to impose restrictions on the free exercise of those rights. Discriminatory laws and policies must be dismantled, and public intimidation of women deterred by security forces.[107]

However, merely symbolic actions or simply increasing the number of women or women-focused programmes will not solve these shortcomings, as the report stresses:

> Women in post-conflict situations are not a homogeneous group, and no woman fits neatly in any one category. Female ex-combatants face unique obstacles when they seek entry into the security forces or return to civilian life. Widows need special assistance. Survivors of sexual and gender-based violence and women and girls with disabilities or HIV/AIDS suffer additional layers of trauma and discrimination, leaving them further marginalized. Displaced women must cope with distinct challenges. Differences of class, region and ethnicity must also be acknowledged.[108]

The United Nations and other peacebuilding actors need to commit themselves to taking a more proactive approach in putting post-conflict interventions on the right path towards empowering women's participation in peacebuilding. Yet, as the report rightly notes, "The existence of guidance material for planners does not mean that post-conflict planning methodologies adequately address gender issues. What matters is the effect on the content of planning documents."[109] For this reason the report calls for a commitment of the "the United Nations system to more systematically institutionalizing women's participation in, and applying gender analysis to, all post-conflict planning processes, so that women's specific needs and gender discrimination are addressed at every stage".[110]

The challenges of translating good intentions into action

Despite the attention given to the analysis of experiences of women in and after armed conflict and commitment to include women and their needs and contributions in peacebuilding interventions, as expressed by "Women's Participation in Peacebuilding", the impact is not satisfactory for those who are meant to benefit from this development. Even in the UN policy documents discussed above, the focus has primarily been on experiences of vulnerable groups and the suffering and injustices perpetrated by the powerful against the weak. Little has been done in terms of research, let alone policy and implementation, on processes, application and the impact of freeing women and men from the grip of – or being relegated to – victimhood.

There are many reasons why international assistance in post-war societies tends to be only modestly effective. While in some cases there is no will to address the plight of women or empower them to contribute positively to peacebuilding efforts, in other cases post-war rebuilding activities are impeded by a lack of knowledge of the local culture and the potential impact of public figures such as religious or grassroots leaders. For instance, in Afghanistan international assistance was hampered by "a lack of understanding and dialogue on the role of culture and religion".[111] Nonetheless, as the above discussion of recent UN reports suggests, international agencies are slowly learning from such experiences and putting greater efforts into understanding cultural peculiarities, contexts and the gendered impacts of the work they do in the aftermath of conflict.

The fact that women are still systematically sidelined and excluded from post-conflict peacebuilding activities defies logic. As noted in the latest policy documents and academic writings, such practice is not only unjust and violates women's rights to participate actively in determining the future lives of their communities, but it also flies in the face of sensible peacebuilding planning and practice. Opportunities are missed to make peacebuilding more relevant for women and for society at large. Prevailing male-dominated ideological, political and cultural preferences still result in the exclusion of women. Real and positive change in peacebuilding practice requires reversing such preferences and ensuring women's inclusion.

Learning from post-conflict contexts: Chapter overviews

The contributions to this book examine five main themes: conceptual frameworks in thinking of women as victims and peacebuilders; experiences of women's victimhood and empowerment in post-conflict situations; the interrelationship of women and children as an essential partnership for both physical and emotional survival and the consolidation of peace across the broader society; examples of national and global efforts to improve the situation of women in the aftermath of violent conflicts; and experiences of women's contributions within political and security institutions of post-conflict societies. Finally, a concluding chapter examines the main challenges, experiences and lessons explored by the individual analyses presented throughout the book, translating them into a number of specific suggestions for evolving academic and policy discourses.

The contributions to the introductory part of the book explore women in post-conflict situations as both vulnerable victims and agents of change. Following these opening lines, in Chapter 2, "Frameworks for understanding women as victims and peacebuilders", Lisa Schirch examines women's experiences of violence and peacebuilding in war and post-war societies. She shows that women face varying degrees of direct, structural, public and private violence in times of peace, times of war and post-war contexts. First, she discusses essentialist and sociological frameworks for understanding gender. She then focuses on the role of women as victims: here, she discusses different types of violence against women, as well as violence in non-war, war and post-war contexts. Schirch then moves on to examine the role of women as peacebuilders. While acknowledging that women do not always positively influence dynamics and processes of peace and conflict, she focuses on their positive capacities and roles as peacebuilders. In her discussion she draws on the fields of biology, sociology and political theory, and on the practice of peacebuilding. She offers brief examples and draws on case studies from around the world, providing snapshots of the complex dynamics of gender, violence and peacebuilding. Schirch argues that a gender-sensitive lens on peacebuilding highlights the urgent need to broaden peacebuilding programming to include the empowerment of women and pay more attention to violence against women in both private and public settings.

From victimhood to empowerment: Patterns and changes

In Chapter 3, "Mass crimes and resilience of women: A cross-national perspective", Krishna Kumar examines major impacts of "mass crimes" on women, suggesting policy measures that should be promoted by the international community to empower women who contribute to post-conflict peacebuilding. As a corollary to Schirch, he argues that women are not passive spectators to mass crimes, but are both active and resilient. They participate in the conduct of mass crimes while trying to keep themselves and their families alive in a context of economic and physical insecurity. Yet they also suffer from the physical and institutional violence inflicted on them – they are clearly affected by mass crime. As Kumar writes, women "are more than silent victims of war crimes; they are survivors". He first defines the nature and types of mass crimes, then identifies their impacts on women and gender relations, and concludes with specific recommendations for the international community. The chapter is based on research he has conducted for USAID in Bosnia, Cambodia, El Salvador, Georgia, Guatemala and Rwanda.

In Chapter 4, "Victimization, empowerment and the impact of UN peacekeeping missions on women and children: Lessons from Cambodia and Timor-Leste", Sumie Nakaya asks which mechanisms sustain violence against women and children in both times of war and times of peace. She examines the issues of violence against women and children in larger institutional contexts that govern their political, legal and social status during their society's transition from war to post-conflict "peace". She shows that institutional frameworks, including the rule of law, determine not only the extent of violence against women and children but also violence in society at large. Additionally, these frameworks determine the extent to which the principles of gender equality and respect for human rights are adopted and implemented. Women, children and gender relations are thus microcosms for broader lessons on the treatment of human rights in a society. Drawing on research about the impact of armed conflict on women and their role in peacebuilding in Timor-Leste and Cambodia, conducted in 2001 as part of a global assessment supported by UNIFEM, Nakaya discusses three main issues: the rule of law, including the reforms of criminal codes, police, the judiciary and civil and family laws; the evolving peacekeeping economy and its impact on sexual exploitation of women and children; and transitional governance at the national level.

Her findings, which are highly instructive even a decade after the initial field research was conducted, show that women and children are inherently vulnerable in the rapid shift towards political and economic liberalization, which still dominates prevailing approaches to post-conflict peacebuilding. By failing to recognize both the potentially destabilizing and negative impact of this peacebuilding approach on non-elite groups such as women, children and other marginalized populations and the need for appropriate safeguarding mechanisms, post-conflict institutional arrangements run the risk of further marginalizing women and girls. They also risk sustaining existing, often patriarchal, structures of power that continue to govern gender relations in many post-conflict societies, particularly at the community and family levels.

In Chapter 5, "Frontline peacebuilding: Women's reconstruction initiatives in Burundi", Rose M. Kadende-Kaiser explores women's approaches to peace activism at the grassroots and at the highest level of political engagement during the Arusha peace talks, which culminated in August 2000 in a peace agreement for post-war Burundi. Along with the main rebel groups, women were excluded from the five-year peace talks. Yet women were still able to carve out a space for themselves. They actively participated in what Kadende-Kaiser calls "frontline peacebuilding". She examines key motivators for peace activism in violent conflict, noting that most – although not all – women are innocent victims of violent conflict. Drawing on research conducted in 1998 and 2000, she reports on two Burundi women's groups that proactively sought an end to ethnic animosities in their communities. She then analyses the challenges and importance of women's participation in the Arusha peace talks, which leads her to conclude that final peace agreements should be considered incomplete if they exclude women's voices.

Throughout the conflict that ravaged Burundi from October 1993, women assumed a leadership role in their communities. With the support of several key mediators and international actors, women were given a chance to take part in the Arusha negotiations as observers. Moreover, they ensured that their recommendations were included in the final agreement. Kadende-Kaiser shows that in Burundi women initiated community-based activities that provided a safe space for honest dialogue across ethnic and gender divides. They shared their wartime experiences with each other in their neighbourhoods, villages or internally displaced or refugee camps. This opened doors for empathy, forgiveness, healing and reconciliation. She finds that those who participated as observers during the Arusha peace talks had their voices heard and the final agreement accommodated their recommendations. She concludes that in a country torn apart by endemic ethnic violence, undermining the importance of women's participation and contributions to peacebuilding betrays a key requirement for durable peace.

Women and children: Essential partnership of survival and peace

In Chapter 6, "Women and children in the post-Cold War Balkans: Concerns and responses", Constantine P. Danopoulos, Konstantinos S. Skandalis and Zlatko Isakovic argue that while no segment of society or age group escapes the trauma of war and its aftermath, women and children are the most severely affected. Yet the two groups are not affected in the same way. While the damage to children is primarily psychological, the impact on women affects their role in society, often intensifying their already subservient social status.

The violent disintegration of Yugoslavia, together with a parallel economic collapse and international isolation, brought great hardship to its citizens. Women and children bore a disproportionate burden of the ethnic cleansing that accompanied the Yugoslav successor wars. Of the over 1.5 million refugees and internally displaced persons generated by these wars, well over half were women and children. Global public opinion was exposed to pictures and stories depicting ethnic cleansing, concentration camps, stories of rape, forced pregnancies, hunger, torture and other forms of violence, affecting Yugoslav people of both sexes and all ages and ethnic or religious backgrounds. Danopoulos, Skandalis and Isakovic identify, explore and analyse the problems facing women and children since the violent conflicts ended in the former Yugoslavia. They offer a brief examination of the Yugoslav conflicts and their victims to help us understand the nature and magnitude of the problems facing women and children. Drawing on field research and conversations with practitioners working for relief agencies, they also offer an assessment of the performance of relief organizations since the fighting formally ended.

In Chapter 7, "Emerging from poverty as champions of change: Women and children in post-war Tajikistan", Svetlana Sharipova and Hermine De Soto situate their analysis in the complex challenges of Tajikistan's post-independence development, characterized by civil war, economic transition, high levels of migration and the re-emergence of traditional religious and patriarchal customs. With the rising poverty that confronts Tajikistan, such changes have dramatically changed Tajik family structures and the position of women and children in both family and society. Sharipova and De Soto employ a gender and social development approach as well as applied anthropological methods to explore how Tajik women and children have been coping with economic and social constraints since the end of the civil war.

Drawing on a social development project conducted by both authors on behalf of the World Bank and the Asian Development Bank, they demonstrate how local women transformed regional conflicts into ongoing community peacebuilding efforts. Sharipova and De Soto describe the social and economic poverty of women, characterized by challenges such as the need to overcome gender inequality; to find jobs with a potential for advancement; to balance work outside the home with almost complete responsibility for the household, children and the elderly; or to secure education opportunities for their children and maintain reasonable health – all of which while overcoming the traditional patriarchal social system and avoiding crime (i.e. trafficking) and violence (i.e. family violence). The project facilitated the empowerment of both women and their children, and was able to inform the World Bank's poverty reduction strategy paper on Tajikistan.

In Chapter 8, "Young mothers as agents of peacebuilding: Lessons from an early childcare and development project in Macedonia", Deborah

Davis shows that, in addition to being victims of violence and dislocation during war, women are an indispensable resource for peacebuilding and social change. She argues that these roles are inextricably linked and part of a purposive tactic: as women are considered the main source of family and community cohesion, the intention of humiliating and degrading women is to disrupt family life and destroy the social fabric at its core.

Davis examines an emergency early childcare and development project in the former Yugoslav Republic of Macedonia, which was implemented by UNICEF and the Albanian League of Women. Its objective was to address the urgent needs of children affected by the ethnic conflict and refugee crisis that followed the break-up of Yugoslavia. The project worked with women who lived in isolated villages and traditional patrilineal families. While lacking social contacts and economic opportunities, they were in constant danger from the possible eruption of inter-ethnic violence. Davis draws lessons from this project, which focused on the facilitation of learning centres for children, where women with different ethnic backgrounds met and, in the process, created a foundation to strengthen inter-ethnic cooperation among their respective families.

Putting good intentions into practice: National and global efforts to right past wrongs

In Chapter 9, "Gender and transitional justice: Experiences from South Africa, Rwanda and Sierra Leone", Lyn S. Graybill discusses how human rights violations committed against women during times of conflict were handled in South Africa and Rwanda in the 1990s, and how Sierra Leone learned from and adapted these models to suit its unique situation. South Africa's Truth and Reconciliation Commission offered a model for restorative justice, while the International Criminal Tribunal for Rwanda offered a mechanism for retributive justice. In 2002 Sierra Leone attempted to set up concurrent post-conflict systems, a truth commission and a special court, to deal with crimes committed during its brutal decade-long civil war. Graybill explores to what extent Sierra Leone managed to improve over these earlier experiences in addressing gender violations.

In a sober conclusion, Graybill argues that the limited successes of all three countries in dealing with gender violations might heighten the continuing violence against women in Africa. She emphasizes that without attitudinal change little will improve in the long run. While it is of course important to recognize that, for instance, rape in times of conflict is repugnant, in the three societies examined this has not been translated into recognition that violence against women in peacetime is equally abhorrent. She argues that the systematic subordination of women and the entrenched social attitudes that preceded periods of conflict have made the notion of "women's bodies as battlefields" acceptable. Even in the post-war period women's bodies continue to be sites of struggle. Graybill cautions that without the implementation of gender equality – and the necessary attitudinal change to respect women as equals – violence against women will continue to pervade societies even after conflict subsides, and will likely erupt on a massive scale if intra-state conflict reignites.

In Chapter 10, "Empowering women to promote peace and security: From the global to the local – Securing and implementing UN Security Council Resolution 1325", Ancil Adrian-Paul traces the resolution's evolution from a civil society initiative to a resolution of the Security Council and, beyond that, to its implementation through national action programmes. She first reflects on the global campaign called Women Building Peace: From the Village Council to the Negotiating Table, which was initiated and run by International Alert and over 200 organizations worldwide, before reflecting on follow-up activities in the immediate aftermath of the adoption of SCR 1325, highlighting strategies and tactics that were used and lessons that can be learned. Drawing on her involvement in both the Women Building Peace campaign and the design of a subsequent implementation programme in Liberia, she examines the Liberia National Action Plan to draw lessons learned from both creating and implementing SCR 1325. She also offers policy and research recommendations for those continuing to work on and with SCR 1325 and its follow-up resolution, SCR 1820.

Adrian-Paul shows us that SCR 1325 recognizes the negative experiences women face in conflict situations, while it also – perhaps more importantly – represents a landmark in the recognition of women's contributions to the maintenance of peace and security. It acknowledges their specific needs and concerns during and after armed conflict, and that they are not merely victims but also have agency and are involved in active peacebuilding in informal grassroots diplomacy in conflict zones. Thus SCR 1325 speaks directly to the main message of this book – the need to look at women (and children, as other chapters and this book's companion volume argue) beyond their suffering as victims, as active agents in making and breaking peace. From this perspective, she argues, SCR 1820 refocuses the international community's attention mainly on the victimization of women in violent conflict and thus represents a step backwards.

SCR 1325 was adopted following concerted advocacy and other initiatives by civil society organizations, UN agencies and member states in recognition of the fact that women have generally been excluded from the formal reconciliation, reconstruction and peacebuilding processes in post-war transformations. A decade after its passing there has undoubtedly been progress, with a number of initiatives being taken by the United Nations, its member states, regional and subregional institutions and civil society organizations, yet, as Adrian-Paul argues, its implementation has been slow and sporadic.

Deconstructing victimhood: Women in political and security institutions

In Chapter 11, "State-building or survival in conflict and post-conflict situations? A peacebuilding perspective on Palestinian women's contributions to ending the Israeli occupation", Vanessa Farr shows that women's lack of participation in debates about the future of the Palestinian state might derail their efforts to become more relevant and influential actors in the post-conflict and state- and society-building future of Palestine. Despite their important contributions to the liberation struggle over many generations, for fear of becoming politicized women's organizations avoid discussions on hard issues of national liberation and are mostly absent from the current state-building discourse. Farr offers a focused analysis of Palestinian women's groups in the prolonged Israeli military occupation of Jerusalem as an entry point for considering larger Palestinian statehood questions, drawing on field research that examined the work of a diverse range of Palestinian women's organizations, how they view and contribute to the politics they encounter in their everyday lives and how they prioritize their activities in an increasingly difficult operating environment. An analysis of this research reveals that the Palestinian women's liberation struggle, like the national one, is forced to confront ever-changing obstacles, risks and challenges, with limited success.

Despite their long experience of participating in the struggle for Palestinian liberation, Jerusalem-based women's organizations currently lack a national strategy for the emancipation of women within the state-building process and do not effectively influence the high-level political discussions of the day with clearly articulated opinions on a number of key challenges, including the restoration of human rights through a just end to the Israeli military occupation and the achievement of Palestinian sovereignty and independence, inclusive state-building, citizenship rights, gender-equitable institutional reform, social transformation, demilitarization and peacebuilding. The limited yet steady contributions made by women's peacebuilding strategies might not translate into real political gains in the post-conflict period if they remain at their current marginal levels of organization. Farr also points to the need for the donor community to recognize and overcome its tendency to disempower, even if not intentionally, women's organizations, and develop more effective funding responses that value and encourage women's public political participation now and as a basis for the future.

In Chapter 12, "Women's participation in political decision-making and recovery processes in post-conflict Lebanon", Kari H. Karamé argues that while women are active in most functions during armed conflicts, both civilian and military, and while most activists in peace movements are women, they are usually marginalized from the decision-making levels in the post-conflict peacebuilding process. Moreover, without women present at the peace negotiation table, the experiences they gained during the war and the capacities they developed will not be taken into consideration in the planning and construction of the future. Karamé examines the war in Lebanon and the difficult post-conflict situation in the country as the background for a reflection on the main obstacles to women's participation in public decision-making, found in Lebanon's patriarchal culture and political and electoral system. She also discusses the effect of the almost total absence of women in setting political priorities for the reconstruction process. Karamé notes the general assumption that women and men have different priorities in politics, with women's entrance into the political arena changing the nature of the political agenda itself. This affects policies on reproductive health and choice, nutrition, families and equality in education and work, which are among the topics that women have introduced and advocated in national and international policy forums. As other contributors argue in this book, these questions should not be framed only as "women issues", as they are of great importance for the well-being of society as a whole. Karamé suggests that limited participation of women in political decision-making necessarily has an impact on the state's priorities in the post-conflict rebuilding process, with negative consequences for women and other marginalized and disadvantaged individuals.

In Chapter 13, "Combating stereotypes: Female security personnel in post-conflict contexts", Kristin Valasek argues that reconstruction, peacebuilding and development initiatives in post-conflict environments often fail to include women in post-war security institutions. Discourses framing women in post-conflict contexts only as either victims or peacebuilders reinforce such failure by ignoring the multiplicity of roles played by women, including in the provision of security and justice. Currently, very few women serve in post-conflict security institutions, including the armed forces, police, intelligence, border management, justice system, prisons, traditional security and justice providers and private security companies. This severely limits the effectiveness and accountability of security institutions in terms of operational and representation requirements. It also impedes normative compliance with national, regional and international standards and commitments.

Valasek discusses the link between peacebuilding, disarmament, demobilization and reintegration (DDR), security sector reform (SSR) and feminist theories, before offering a rationale for strengthening the participation of women within security sector institutions. She then provides information on how to overcome common challenges to the increased participation of women, including cultural norms and stereotypes, lack of education, discrimination, sexual harassment and sexual violence. She concludes with practical recommendations on how to increase women's recruitment, retention and advancement in post-conflict contexts. Drawing on personal experiences in Liberia and Sierra Leone, she suggests that post-conflict DDR and SSR processes in particular offer useful and critical entry points for increasing women's presence in post-conflict security institutions.

In the concluding Chapter 14, "Defying victimhood: Women as activists and peacebuilders", we return to some of the main issues relevant to the debate on reconsidering and "righting" the roles, contributions, rights and responsibilities of women in post-conflict peacebuilding. We also offer brief assessments of the main findings and recommendations developed in the case studies for those active in the worlds of academic enquiry and policy work to advance the position of women in post-conflict peacebuilding. As we did not impose a rigid template on the contributors, the chapters do not all address a common set of questions and their authors' approaches and considerations may be tailored to their specific cases. Consequently, the concluding chapter does not merely focus on a comparative analysis of the individual chapter contributions, but reflects on some of the most significant findings and messages expressed throughout the volume by drawing on the analysis and arguments presented by any one or more of the chapters. These reflections also serve to highlight the relevance of the international policy debates and calls for international peacebuilding policy change reviewed in the first part of this opening chapter. In our concluding comments we attempt to bridge academic and empirical with more policy-oriented and prescriptive argumentation. We point to areas that need further reflection, study and action in both academic and practical terms. The concluding chapter thus speaks about the debate and practice of boosting women's participation in post-conflict peacebuilding.

Notes

1. For the purposes of this chapter we use the terms "post-war" and "post-conflict" interchangeably. Neither "war" nor "conflict" follows specific definitions regarding numbers of battle-deaths or duration. The terms refer to the aftermath of armed conflicts,

marked by either one-sided victories or formal or informal agreements as to the con-clusion of organized armed violence, defining a moment of negative peace. Post-conflict contexts tend to be characterized by the continuation of low-level, latent conflict and significant levels of social, political and economic instability as well as direct and struc-tural violence, the results of and responses to which are described in more detail later in this chapter.

2. For a discussion of peacebuilding approaches see Schirch, Lisa (2004) *The Little Book of Strategic Peacebuilding*, Intercourse, PA: Good Books. As Biersteker notes, "There is no strong consensus on the definition of peacebuilding, let alone the best practices for achieving it." See Biersteker, Thomas J. (2007) "Prospects for the UN Peacebuilding Commission", *Disarmament Forum* 1, p. 39.

3. Barnett, Michael, Hunjoon Kim, Madalene O'Donnell and Laura Sitea (2007) "Peace-building: What Is in a Name?", *Global Governance* 13(1), pp. 35–58. See also Tschirgi, Neclâ (2004) "Post-Conflict Peacebuilding Revisited: Achievements, Limitations", paper presented at WSP International/IPA Peacebuilding Forum Conference, New York, 7 October.

4. Department of Peacekeeping Operations/Department of Peace Support (2008) "United Nations Peacekeeping Operations: Principles and Guidelines", United Na-tions, New York, available at http://pbpu.unlb.org/pbps/Library/Capstone_Doctrine _ENG.pdf. This and other definitions are cited in an excellent overview of the peace-building debate: Chetail, Vincent (2009) "Introduction: Post-Conflict Peacebuilding – Ambiguity and Identity", in Vincent Chetail (ed.) *Post-Conflict Peacebuilding: A Lexicon*, Oxford: Oxford University Press, pp. 1–33.

5. See Peacebuild (2008) "Strategic Directions January 1, 2008 to December 31, 2012", January, Canadian Peacebuilding Network, Ottawa, pp. 3–4.

6. Boutros-Ghali, Boutros (1992) "An Agenda for Peace: Preventive Diplomacy, Peace-making and Peace-keeping", Report of the Secretary-General pursuant to the state-ment adopted by the Summit Meeting of the Security Council on 31 January 1992, UN Doc. A/47/277-S/24111, 17 June, United Nations, New York, para. 21.

7. Ibid., para. 57.

8. Peacebuild, note 5, p. 4. Peacebuild drew its definition from Casey, Claire, Nilanj Desai and Benedikt Franke (2005) "Peacebuilding: An Overview. Conflict Management Toolkit", Johns Hopkins University School for Advanced International Studies, Wash-ington, DC, available at www.sais-jhu.edu/cmtoolkit/approaches/peacebuilding/index. html; Malek, Cate, Michelle Maiese and Heidi Burgess (undated) "Peacebuilding", Conflict Resolution Information Source, available at www.crinfo.org/CK_Essays/ck _peacebuilding.jsp.

9. Peacebuild, note 5, pp. 3–4.

10. Ibid., p. 4.

11. Ibid.

12. For a discussion of conflict prevention and peacebuilding activities along various stages of conflict see Schnabel, Albrecht (2010) "Mainstreaming Human Rights in Responding to the Conflict Cycle: The Role of NGOs", in Omar Grech and Monika Wohlfeld (eds) *Human Rights and the Conflict Cycle*, Msida: Mediterranean Academy of Diplomatic Studies, University of Malta, pp. 83–114. See also Chapter 2 in this volume.

13. See Evans, Gareth (2007) "Conflict Prevention: Ten Lessons We Have Learned", Feb-ruary, International Crisis Group, Toronto, available at www.crisisgroup.org/home/ index.cfm?id=4653&l=1, cited by Fisher, Simon and Lada Zimina (2009) "Just Wasting Our Time? Provocative Thoughts for Peacebuilders", in Beatrix Schmelzle and Mar-tina Fischer (eds) *Peacebuilding at a Crossroads? Dilemmas and Paths for Another*

Generation, Berghof Handbook Dialogue Series No. 7, Berlin: Berghof Conflict Research, p. 12.

14. Fisher and Zimina, ibid., p. 13.
15. Wohlfeld, Monika (2010) "An Overview of the Conflict Cycle", in Omar Grech and Monika Wohlfeld (eds) *Human Rights and the Conflict Cycle*, Msida: Mediterranean Academy of Diplomatic Studies, University of Malta, pp. 13–32; Schnabel, note 12.
16. On peacebuilding challenges see Newman, Edward and Albrecht Schnabel (eds) (2002) *Recovering from Civil Conflict: Reconciliation, Peace and Development*, London: Frank Cass (also published as a special issue of *International Peacekeeping* 9(2)); Ball, Nicole (1996) "The Challenge of Rebuilding War-torn Societies", in Chester A. Crocker, Fen Osler Hampson with Pamela Aall (eds) *Managing Global Chaos: Sources of and Responses to International Conflict*, Washington, DC: US Institute of Peace Press, pp. 615–616; International Peace Institute (2009) "Peacebuilding", IPI Blue Paper No. 10, Task Force on Strengthening Multilateral Security Capacity, New York.
17. United Nations (2004) "A More Secure World: Our Shared Responsibility", Report of the Secretary-General's High-level Panel on Threats, Challenges and Change, United Nations, New York, para. 224.
18. United Nations (2009) "Report of the Secretary-General on Peacebuilding in the Immediate Aftermath of Conflict", UN Doc. A/63/881-S/2009/304, United Nations, New York.
19. United Nations (2002) "Women, Peace and Security", study submitted by the Secretary-General pursuant to Security Council Resolution 1325 (2000), United Nations, New York, para. 206, available at www.un.org/womenwatch/daw/public/eWPS.pdf. The report cites UN Department of Political Affairs/UN Development Programme (2001) "Report of the Joint Review Mission on the United Nations Post-conflict Peacebuilding Support Offices", 20 July, United Nations, New York, p. 11.
20. United Nations, ibid.
21. Maiese, Michelle (2003) "Peacebuilding", Beyond Intractability: A Free Knowledge Base on More Constructive Approaches to Destructive Conflict, available at www.beyondintractability.org/bi-essay/peacebuilding/.
22. Lewer, Nick (1999) "International Non-Governmental Organisations and Peacebuilding – Perspectives from Peace Studies and Conflict Resolution", Working Paper 3, Centre for Conflict Resolution, Department of Peace Studies, University of Bradford, p. 2, available at www.brad.ac.uk/acad/confres/assets/CCR3.pdf. See also ibid.
23. United Nations, note 18.
24. See Schnabel, Albrecht (2008) "The Human Security Approach to Direct and Structural Violence", in *SIPRI Yearbook 2008: Armaments, Disarmament and International Security*, Oxford: Oxford University Press, pp. 87–96.
25. For further elaboration on post-conflict peacebuilding as a second chance for conflict prevention gone wrong see Schnabel, Albrecht (2002) "Post-conflict Peacebuilding and Second-generation Preventive Action", *International Peacekeeping* 9(2), pp. 7–30.
26. United Nations (2000) "United Nations Security Council Resolution 1325: Women, Peace and Security", S/RES/1325 (2000), 31 October, available at www.uneca.org/daweca/conventions_and_resolutions/Res%201325.pdf.
27. Kumar, Krishna (2000) "Aftermath: Women and Women's Organizations in Postconflict Societies: The Role of International Assistance", USAID Program and Operations Assessment Report No. 28, July, USAID Center for Development Information and Evaluation, Washington, DC, p. 15, available at http://pdf.usaid.gov/pdf_docs/PNACG621.pdf; Friesendorf, Cornelius (ed.) (forthcoming) *Strategies against Human Trafficking:*

The Role of the Security Sector, Geneva and Vienna: Geneva Centre for the Demo-cratic Control of Armed Forces/Austrian National Defence Academy.

28. United Nations (1998) "Sexual Violence and Armed Conflict: United Nations Re-sponse", April, UN Department of Economic and Social Affairs, Division for the Ad-vancement of Women, New York, available at www.un.org/womenwatch/daw/public/w2apr98.htm.

29. Tickner, J. Ann (2001) *Gendering World Politics: Issues and Approaches in the Post-Cold War Era*, New York: Columbia University Press, p. 50.

30. UNICEF (1996) "Children in War: The State of the World's Children", UNICEF, New York, available at www.unicef.org/sowc96/3torrape.htm.

31. Karamé, Kari with Gudrun Bertinussen (2001) "Gendering Human Security: From Marginalization to the Integration of Women in Peace-building", Fafo Report 352, NUPI Report No. 261, Fafo Institute for Applied Social Science/Norwegian Institute of International Affairs, Oslo, p. 42, available at www.fafo.no/pub/rapp/352/352.pdf.

32. *The Economist* (2002) "A Liberated Nation, Except for Women", *The Economist*, 14 November, available at www.economist.com/node/1446952.

33. Kagumire, Rosebell (2011) "Women Dream of Independence", *IPS*, 13 January, avail-able at http://ipsnews.net/news.asp?idnews=54116; Martin, Ellen (2010) "Gender, Violence and Survival in Juba, Southern Sudan", HPG Policy Briefs 42, November, Overseas Development Institute, London, available at www.odi.org.uk/resources/docs/6230.pdf.

34. For updated information on mines and mine action see "Landmine Monitor", Inter-national Campaign to Ban Landmines, Ottawa, available at www.lm.icbl.org; Geneva International Centre for Humanitarian Demining, available at www.gichd.org.

35. *IRIN* (2008) "Afghanistan: Landmines, UXO Kill, Maim Hundreds in 2007", *IRIN*, 21 January, available at www.irinnews.org/report.aspx?ReportID=76344.

36. Cukier, Wendy and James Cairns (2009) "Gender, Attitudes and the Regulation of Small Arms: Implications for Action", in Vanessa Farr, Henri Myrttinen and Albrecht Schnabel (eds) *Sexed Pistols: The Gendered Impacts of Small Arms and Light Weapons*, Tokyo: United Nations University Press, p. 20.

37. Ibid.

38. Ibid., p. 21.

39. Tulwasa, Parween (2003) "Desperate Women Seek Solace in Drugs", Afghan Recovery Report No. 43, 10 January, Institute for War and Peace Reporting, London, available at www.iwpr.net.

40. UNFPA (2001) "The Impact of Armed Conflict on Women and Girls", paper presented at consultative meeting on Mainstreaming Gender in Areas of Conflict and Recon-struction, Bratislava, 13–15 November, p. 3.

41. Asia Society and Carnegie Council on Ethics and International Affairs (2001) "Build-ing Peace and Civil Society in Afghanistan: Challenges and Opportunities", report of symposium on Building Peace and Civil Society in Afghanistan: Challenges and Op-portunities, New York, 17 May and Washington, DC, 18 May, p. 6, available at www.carnegiecouncil.org/resources/articles_papers_reports/706.html/_res/id=sa_File1/706_afghanistan_report.pdf.; UN Development Fund for Women (2008) "Women and Men in Afghanistan: Baseline Statistics on Gender", available at www.unhcr.org/refworld/docid/4a7959272.html.

42. Bop, Codou (2001) "Women in Conflicts, Their Gains and Their Losses", in Sheila Meintjes, Anu Pillay and Meredeth Turshen (eds) *The Aftermath: Women in Post-conflict Transformation*, London and New York: Zed Books, p. 27.

43. Hick, Steven (2001) "The Political Economy of War-affected Children", in Alan W. Heston and Neil A. Weiner (eds), Jede L. Fernando (special ed.) *Children's Rights, The*

Annals of the American Academy of Political and Social Science, London: Sage Publications, p. 113.

44. Heyzer, Noeleen (1994) "Introduction: Market, State and Gender Equity", in Noeleen Heyzer and Gita Sen (eds) *Gender, Economic Growth and Poverty*, New Delhi: Asian and Pacific Development Centre, p. 17.

45. Meintjes, Sheila, Anu Pillay and Meredeth Turshen (2001) "There Is No Aftermath for Women", in Sheila Meintjes, Anu Pillay and Meredeth Turshen (eds) *The Aftermath: Women in Post-conflict Transformation*, London and New York: Zed Books, p. 13.

46. Norwegian Refugee Council, Redd Barna (Save the Children Norway) and UN High Commissioner for Refugees (1999) "Protection of Children and Adolescents in Complex Emergencies", conference report, Oslo/Hadeland, 9–11 November 1998, p. 46, available at www.unhcr.org/cgi-bin/texis/vtx/home/opendocPDFViewer.html?docid =3ae690200&query=protection.

47. Strand, Arne, Karin Ask and Kristian Berg Harpviken (2001) "Humanitarian Challenges in Afghanistan: Administrative Structures and Gender and Assistance", report, Chr. Michelsen Institute – Development Studies and Human Rights, Bergen, p. 24, available at www.cmi.no/pdf/2001/Reports/rapport%20R%202001-4.PDF.

48. We are grateful to Vanessa Farr for sharing this observation.

49. See, for instance, Al-Ali, Nadje (2007) "Iraqi Women – Four Years After the Invasion", *Foreign Policy in Focus*, 19 March, available at http://towardfreedom.com/home/content/view/999/1/. This phenomenon of a conservative gender roll-back in society is of course not restricted only to Muslim post-conflict societies, but also occurs in other religious contexts, such as in Catholic Timor-Leste, Hindu Nepal and Buddhist Cambodia.

50. We are again grateful to Vanessa Farr for this insight.

51. While female rape victims are seen as a disgrace, the existence of male rape victims is often completely denied. For analyses of male rape in conflict and post-conflict situations see Dolan, Chris (2009) *Social Torture: The Case of Northern Uganda, 1986–2006*, New York and Oxford: Berghahn Books.

52. See Farr, Vanessa (2002) "Gendering Demilitarization as a Peacebuilding Tool", BICC Paper 20, Bonn International Center for Conversion, June, p. 10.

53. Turshen, Meredeth (2001) "Engendering Relations of State to Society", in Sheila Meintjes, Anu Pillay and Meredeth Turshen (eds) *The Aftermath: Women in Post-conflict Transformation*, London and New York: Zed Books, p. 83.

54. Kumar, note 27, p. 17.

55. We thank Vanessa Farr for sharing this observation.

56. Buck, Thomas with Alice Morton, Susan Allen Nan and Feride Zurikashvili (2000) "Aftermath: Effects of Conflict on Internally Displaced Women in Georgia", Working Paper No. 310, September, Center for Development Information and Evaluation, USAID, Washington, DC, pp. 9–10, available at http://pdf.usaid.gov/pdf_docs/PNACJ947.pdf.

57. Castillejo, Clare (2011) "Building a State that Works for Women: Integrating Gender into Post-conflict State Building", FRIDE Working Paper No. 107, Madrid, March, p. 3, available at www.fride.org/publication/896/building-a-state-that-works-for-women:-integrating-gender-into-post-conflict-state-building.

58. Ibid.

59. Steinberg, Donald (2009) "Peace Missions and Gender Equality: Ten Lessons from the Ground", OSCE Round Table on Gender and Security, Vienna, 11 March, available at www.crisisgroup.org/en/publication-type/commentary/peace-missions-and-gender-equality-ten-lessons-from-the-ground.aspx. See also Koyama, Shukuko (2009) "Just

a Matter of Practicality: Mapping the Role of Women in Weapons for Develop-ment Projects in Albania, Cambodia and Mali", in Vanessa Farr, Henri Myrttinen and Albrecht Schnabel (eds) *Sexed Pistols: The Gendered Impacts of Small Arms and Light Weapons*, Tokyo: United Nations University Press, pp. 329–355.

60. Cukier and Cairns, note 36, p. 43.

61. Lederach, John Paul (2002) "Building Mediative Capacity in Deep-rooted Conflict", *Fletcher Forum of World Affairs* 26(1), p. 96; see also Kinzelbach, Katrin and Zeinab Mohamed Hassan (2009) "Poems against Bullets? The Role of Somali Women in Social Gun Control", in Vanessa Farr, Henri Myrttinen and Albrecht Schnabel (eds) *Sexed Pistols: The Gendered Impacts of Small Arms and Light Weapons*, Tokyo: United Nations University Press, pp. 356–389.

62. Kinzelbach and Hassan, ibid., pp. 386–387.

63. Ibid., p. 387.

64. Tickner, note 29, p. 59.

65. Ibid.

66. See women's experiences in the case studies featured in Farr, Vanessa, Henri Myrt-tinen and Albrecht Schnabel (eds) (2009) *Sexed Pistols: The Gendered Impacts of Small Arms and Light Weapons*, Tokyo: United Nations University Press.

67. United Nations, note 26.

68. United Nations (2005) "2005 World Summit Outcome", UN Doc. A/RES/60/1, 24 October, United Nations, New York, para. 116.

69. United Nations (2006) "UN Security Council Resolution 1674", UN Doc. S/RES/1674, 28 April, United Nations, New York, available at http://daccess-dds-ny.un.org/doc/UNDOC/GEN/N06/331/99/PDF/N0633199.pdf?OpenElement.

70. UN General Assembly (2006) "In-depth Study on All Forms of Violence against Women: Report of the Secretary-General", UN Doc. A/61/122/Add.1, 6 July, United Nations, New York.

71. UN General Assembly (2008) "Eliminating Rape and Other Forms of Sexual Violence in All Their Manifestations, Including in Conflict and Related Situations", Resolution adopted by General Assembly, UN Doc. A/RES/62/134, 7 February, United Nations, New York, available at www.undemocracy.com/A-RES-62-134.pdf.

72. United Nations (2008) "UN Security Council Resolution 1820: Sexual Violence in Conflict", UN Doc. S/RES/1820, 19 June, United Nations, New York.

73. United Nations (2009) "Report of the Secretary-General on Peacebuilding in the Immediate Aftermath of Conflict", UN Doc. A/63/881-S/2009/304, 11 June, United Nations, New York, available at http://daccess-dds-ny.un.org/doc/UNDOC/GEN/N09/367/70/PDF/N0936770.pdf?OpenElement.

74. United Nations (2010) "Women's Participation in Peacebuilding, Report of the Secretary-General", UN Doc. A/65/354-S/2010/466, 7 September, United Nations, New York, available at www.betterpeace.org/files/SG_Report_Womens_Participation_in _Peacebuilding_A.65.354_S.2010.466_7Sept2010.pdf.

75. For these documents see www.icrc.org/eng/war-and-law/treaties-customary-law/geneva-conventions/index.jsp.

76. UN International Conference on Population and Development, Cairo, 5–13 September 1994, available at www.iisd.ca/cairo.html; Beijing Declaration and Platform for Action, Fourth World Conference on Women, 15 September 1995, available at www.unesco.org/education/information/nfsunesco/pdf/BEIJIN_E.PDF.

77. See also Cockburn, Cynthia (2007) *From Where We Stand: War, Women's Activism and Feminist Analysis*, London: Zed Books, particularly the chapter on "Achievements and Contradictions: WILPF and the UN", pp. 132–155; DCAF (2011) "Women, Peace and Security: From Resolution to Action – Ten Years of Security Council Resolution 1325",

DCAF, Geneva, available at www.dcaf.ch/DCAF/EZ/Publications/Women-Peace-and-Security-from-Resolution-to-Action-Ten-Years-of-Security-Council-Resolution-1325.

78. United Nations, note 72.
79. Anderson, Letitia (2008) "Security Council Resolution 1820", PowerPoint presentation, UNIFEM/Stop Rape Now, New York, 18 July, slides 13–14, available at www.stoprapenow.org/uploads/advocacyresources/1282164625.pdf.
80. Ibid.
81. Castillejo, note 57, p. 3.
82. United Nations (1996) "Impact of Armed Conflict on Children, Report of the Expert of the Secretary-General, Ms Graza Machel, Submitted Pursuant to A/RES/48/157", UN Doc. A/51/306/26, August, United Nations, New York, para. 98. See also Aoi, Chiyuki, Cedric de Coning and Ramesh Thakur (eds) (2007) *Unintended Consequences of Peacekeeping Operations*, Tokyo: United Nations University Press.
83. Kumar, Krishna, Hannah Baldwin and Judy Benjamin (2001) "Profile: Cambodia", in Krishna Kumar (ed.) *Women and Civil War: Impact, Organizations, and Action*, Boulder, CO: Lynne Rienner Publishers, p. 45.
84. Aoi, de Coning and Thakur, note 82.
85. For further information and practical guidance see Bastick, Megan and Kristin Valasek (eds) (2008) *Gender and Security Sector Reform Toolkit*, Geneva: DCAF/OSCE/ODIHR/UN-INSTRAW; Organization for Economic Co-operation and Development (2007) *OECD/DAC Handbook on Security System Reform and Governance*, Paris: OECD.
86. Bouta, Tsjeard and Georg Frerks (2002) *Women's Roles in Conflict Prevention, Conflict Resolution and Post-Conflict Reconstruction: Literature Review and Institutional Analysis*, The Hague: Netherlands Institute of International Relations, Clingendael, Conflict Research Unit, p. 157, available at www.clingendael.nl/publications/2002/20021100_cru_bouta.pdf.
87. United Nations, note 26, para. 4.
88. Karamé with Bertinussen, note 31, p. 37
89. United Nations (2009) "Strengthening of the Coordination of Emergency Humanitarian Assistance of the United Nations", Report of the Secretary-General, UN Doc. A/64/E/2009, United Nations, New York, para. 59; United Nations (2010) "Strengthening of the Coordination of Emergency Humanitarian Assistance of the United Nations", Report of the Secretary-General, UN Doc. A/65/82-E/2010/88, 25 May, United Nations, New York.
90. Sørensen, Birgitte (1998) "Women and Post-Conflict Reconstruction: Issues and Sources", WSP Occasional Paper No. 3, June, War-torn Societies Project, UN Research Institute for Social Development, Geneva, p. 44, available at www.unrisd.org/unrisd/website/document.nsf/0/631060b93ec1119ec1256d120043e600/$FILE/opw3.pdf.
91. Ibid., p. 37.
92. UN Security Council (2003) "Report of the Secretary-General on Children and Armed Conflict", UN Doc. S/2002/1299, 26 November, United Nations, New York, p. 5. For subsequent reports see the website of the Office of the Special Representative of the Secretary-General for Children and Armed Conflict, available at www.un.org/children/conflict/english/securitycouncilwgroupdoc.html.
93. For some early studies see Bouta and Frerks, note 86; Kumar, note 27; International Alert (2003) *Gender Mainstreaming in Peace Support Operations: Moving Beyond Rhetoric to Practice*, London: International Alert; Wood, Bernard (2001) "Development Dimensions of Conflict Prevention and Peace-building: An Independent Study Prepared for Emergency Response Division", June, UNDP, New York; Norwegian Refugee Council, Redd Barna (Save the Children Norway) and UN High Com-

missioner for Refugees, note 46. For a more recent study see Denov, Myriam (2007) "Girls in Fighting Forces: Moving Beyond Victimhood", report prepared for government of Canada through Canadian International Development Agency, available at www.crin.org/docs/CIDA_Beyond_forces.pdf.

94. United Nations, note 19, para. 15.
95. United Nations, note 26, para. 16.
96. United Nations (2009) "UN Security Council Resolution 1889", UN Doc. S/RES/1889 (2009), 5 October, United Nations, New York, p. 3.
97. Ibid., p. 2.
98. Ibid., p. 4.
99. Ibid.
100. Ibid., p. 5.
101. United Nations, note 74.
102. Ibid., para. 7.
103. Ibid., para 8.
104. Ibid., para. 9.
105. Ibid., para. 11.
106. Ibid., para. 22.
107. Ibid., para. 40.
108. Ibid., para. 12.
109. Ibid., para. 31.
110. Ibid.
111. Karim, Farahnaz and Gregory Hess (2001) "Thinking about Aid Management and Peacebuilding in Afghanistan", Peacepath Discussion Paper, November, Peacepath Consulting, Rome, available at www.institute-for-afghan-studies.org/Afghan %20Reconstruction/Peacepath%20Afghn%20DP.pdf.

2

Frameworks for understanding women as victims and peacebuilders

Lisa Schirch

Each week, women around the world suffer abuse at the hands of their partners, resist rape by soldiers, watch their children die of starvation and lack of healthcare, work in sweatshops, undergo female genital mutilation and are tortured for their political activities. At the same time, women organize groups for change in their communities, send human rights reports to organizations around the world, act as relief providers and peacekeepers, organize dialogues and build relationships across the lines of conflict, lead or receive training to build their capacity in the skills of peacebuilding and teach their children how to handle differences without violence. Women are both the victims of violence and the builders of peace. Yet there is no universal female experience of violence, and the differences in women's capacity for peacebuilding are vast.

This chapter looks specifically at women's experiences of violence and peacebuilding in war and post-war societies. Women face varying degrees of direct, structural, public and private violence in times of peace, times of war and post-war contexts. The chapter offers a variety of frameworks for understanding gender, different types of violence against women and women's capacities and roles as peacebuilders, drawing on the fields of biology, sociology and political theory and the practice of peacebuilding. Examples from around the world provide snapshots of the complex dynamics of gender, violence and peacebuilding. A gender-sensitive lens on peacebuilding highlights the urgent need to broaden programming to include the empowerment of women and attention to violence against women in both private and public settings.

Defying victimhood: Women and post-conflict peacebuilding, Schnabel and Tabyshalieva (eds), United Nations University Press, 2012, ISBN 978-92-808-1201-5

Frameworks for understanding gender

Understanding the differences between men and women is increasingly known as "gender analysis". Gender analysis lays the foundation for understanding the forms of violence women experience in peace, war and post-war contexts. It also provides a lens for understanding women as peacebuilders, and why peacebuilding itself is a gendered activity.

One set of theories asserts that there are major biological and psychological differences between men and women. Another set asserts that differences between men and women result from cultural socialization. Both purport to explain the gendered nature of conflict, violence and peacebuilding.

Essentialist theories: Differences between men and women are biological

Some theories suggest biological differences affect the "essential" nature of males and females, thus shaping their approaches to conflict and peacebuilding. Biological facts spawn a wide range of conclusions about men's and women's roles in violence and peacebuilding. Because females can bear children, some essentialists see women as being more protective of life. Some believe women are more "natural", more emotional, more bound by relationships and less suitable because of all this to serve as leaders in making either war or peace. Yet others who take an essentialist approach look at women's biology and capacity to reproduce, and conclude that females are superior and more peaceful than men. They argue the nature of politics would change for the better if women were in leadership roles.[1]

Essentialists see men as more ready and able to use violence to protect their families and communities. These conclusions are based on physical observations, such as the fact that males usually have more upper-body strength and a higher level of the hormone testosterone, which is linked by some researchers to violent behaviour. Some essentialists believe biological differences between males and females justify unequal social relations, with males holding more leadership positions and decision-making power than females. Essentialist approaches differ in concluding whether women should be involved in leadership for either conflict or peacebuilding. While some essentialists glorify what they see as the qualities of women, others laud the essential qualities of men. These theories rarely lead to an embracing of the diversity among and between men and women.

Sociological theories: Differences between men and women are created

The field of sociology makes a distinction between sex, the biological differences between males and females based on genes and physical characteristics, and gender, the socially learned behaviour and expectations that distinguish masculine and feminine social roles. While not denying the biological differences between men and women, the field of sociology places much more emphasis on how the environment shapes men and women in the process of socialization. Human beings are not born as "men" or "women". Masculinity and femininity must be learned, rehearsed and performed daily. Boys and girls experience strong social pressure to learn and practise different ways of communicating, acting, thinking and relating according to an idealized image of what it means to be a "man" or a "woman". Individuals establish their status as real men and real women by performing, demonstrating and acting out gender roles. Peterson and Runyan argue that "gender comes to matter in what we wear, eat, and drink; what entertainment and activities we prefer; how we approach risk-taking and dependence; and how we measure intelligence, courage, and leadership".[2] Figure 2.1 details examples of stereotypical gender roles in many (but not all) parts of the world.

A man's or woman's sex and gender identity is shaped by other identities such as race, class, age, nation, region, education, religion, etc. Gender expectations for men and women vary according to context. There are different expectations for men and women in the home, marketplace or government office. Gender roles are dynamic; they are constantly pro-

Masculine	Feminine
Aggressive	Passive
Competitive	Cooperative
Rational	Irrational/emotional
Express power through violence	Express power through relationships
Independent	Dependent/interdependent
Strong/steady	Weak/compassionate
Leaders	Submissive followers
Income earners/family providers	Child raisers/housekeepers

Figure 2.1 Sociological approaches to gender difference

duced, reinforced and reinvented in every culture. Gender roles shift along with social upheaval. In times of violent conflict, men and women face new roles and changing gender expectations. While grouping or stereotyping men and women into distinct gender role categories is still widely appealing, from a sociological point of view there is a "gender spectrum", and everyone in every culture performs both feminine and masculine roles at various points in their lives.

Difference matters

There is growing agreement that both biological and sociological differences are important to the study of gender, particularly as it affects violence and peacebuilding.[3] In particular, what matters about the biological and social differences is that often individuals, communities, businesses, religions and government structures value men and masculinity more than women and femininity. Such preferential treatment of men and maleness finds its expression in "sexist" behaviour and patriarchal systems and structures of power. Sexism can be seen in the exclusion of women from leadership roles in business, governmental, cultural and religious institutions. It is also the attitude that allows women's bodies to be physically abused, raped or used as tools of advertisement. Women in every culture experience sexism, although in vastly different ways and to different degrees. Women wearing the *burqa* in Afghanistan may look with just as much pity at male influence over Western women in their tight skirts and high heels as vice versa.

Sexism leads to the prevalence of violence against women. All violence is a denial of a person's human right to physical safety, respect and dignity. The term "violence" includes public and private, and structural and direct forms of denying people their human needs and rights. All violence is also about power. People decide to engage in violence when they feel they have the right – and the power – to meet their own needs at the expense of the needs of others. Some people have an "internalized superiority" that leads them to believe they are entitled to more power and rights than others. Other people have an "internalized inferiority" that gives them the sense they are entitled to less than other people. This "psychodynamic" of superiority and inferiority plays an important role in many important "ism" conflicts, including racism, classism and sexism. While oppression takes different shapes, the relational patterns between races, classes and sexes are strikingly similar.

Hierarchical social structures rank the value of different types of people and give those at the top of the social ladder a sense of superiority and cultural permission to meet their needs at the expense of others lower in the hierarchy. Some cultures of the world today grant men

Examples of hierarchies					
Men over women	Adults over children	Masculine over feminine traits	White people over people of colour	Wealthy over poor	One ethnic or religious identity group over another

Figure 2.2 Hierarchical beliefs and structures

permission to meet their needs at the expense of women and afford permission for adults to meet their needs at the expense of children, for example. The hierarchies in Figure 2.2 reflect what some people believe about the "natural" order of relationships between human beings and how they influence economic, political, religious, cultural and other structures in societies.

Structural violence institutionalizes these hierarchies by making it more difficult for those groups on the bottom to attain higher education or leadership roles in business and government, or even find housing and a job. Direct forms of violence such as crime, civil war or terrorism are expressions of these hierarchies at the national and international levels, as some groups fight to maintain their superiority while others fight to gain power or equalize relationships.

Violence is a form of communication that transmits messages between people or groups of people in these hierarchies. White people who create structures that discriminate against people of colour communicate their internalized superiority and their power to enforce inequalities. Groups branded as "terrorists" around the world use violence to express their deep resentment against perceived economic, political and cultural domination. Men who engage in violence against women communicate to women that they should keep in their place below men. Women who engage in child abuse communicate that they have power over children. The hierarchy of value placed on the lives of men over women and masculine over feminine characteristics creates the context where a society can accept, or at least not actively oppose, massive violence against women.

Women as victims

Women experience numerous types of violence, "from the bedroom to the battlefield".[4] This section describes a variety of analytical frameworks for examining different forms of violence against women.

Type of violence against women

The 1993 UN Declaration on the Elimination of Violence against Women (DEVAW) defines it as "any act of gender-based violence that results in, or is likely to result in, physical, sexual, or psychological harm or suffering to women, including threats of such acts, coercion, or arbitrary deprivation of liberty, whether occurring in public or private life".[5] There are a variety of different frameworks for categorizing types of violence against women. Frequently, scholars and activists such as the authors of DEVAW refer to public and private violence, as detailed in Figure 2.3.

A second framework identifies distinctions between direct violence and structural violence (see Figure 2.4). Direct violence inflicts direct, physical harm. Structural violence refers to deaths and disabilities that result from systems, institutions or policies that discriminate against some people.

A World Health Organization (WHO) report on violence against women documents the types, frequency and consequences of such violence around the world. The report classifies violence against women throughout the life cycle, as seen in Figure 2.5.[6]

Public	Private
Physical, sexual and psychological violence occurring in public settings, such as rape, sexual abuse, sexual harassment, intimidation at work, school or other public space, trafficking in women, forced prostitution, etc.	Physical, sexual and psychological violence occurring in the home setting, including battering, sexual abuse of children, marital rape, incest, female genital mutilation, etc.

Figure 2.3 Public and private violence against women

Direct violence	Structural violence
Domestic violence; female genital mutilation; rape; torture; injury due to landmines; warfare	Social sanctioning of men and women who deviate from their gender roles; sexual harassment; sexist humour; providing more education, food and opportunities to boy children than to girls; feminization of poverty (greater numbers of women in poverty); inadequate healthcare; unequal pay for equal work; glass ceilings and limits to female leadership

Figure 2.4 Examples of direct and structural violence against women

Phase of life	Type of violence
Pre-birth	Sex-selective abortion; effects of battering during pregnancy
Infancy	Female infanticide; physical, sexual and psychological abuse
Childhood	Child marriage; female genital mutilation; physical, sexual and psychological abuse; pornography; malnutrition
Adolescence and adulthood	Dating and courtship violence; economic coercion by "sugar daddies" in return for university tuition; sexual assault; honour killing; dowry killing; incest; sexual abuse in the workplace; prostitution and pornography; trafficking in women; intimate partner violence; marital rape; homicide; psychological abuse; abuse of women with disabilities; abuse of widows and single mothers; forced pregnancy, contraception, sterilization or abortion
Elderly	Forced "suicide" or homicide of widows for economic reasons; sexual, physical and psychological abuse

Figure 2.5 Violence against women throughout the life cycle

For the purposes of this chapter and this book, it is helpful to put forth yet another framework for understanding violence against women in non-war, war and post-war contexts.

Non-war violence against women

Women experience many types of violence in societies that are not fighting wars. Some of this violence is structural, meaning that economic, political, religious and other structures and policies inhibit women's ability to meet their human needs. The UN Development Programme uses a gender development index to identify the disparity in standards of living between men and women within each country. This difference has been shrinking in many countries since the 1970s. However, while structural violence against women may be slowly subsiding, statistics still show a large gap in the quality of life for men and women.[7]

The concept of the "feminization of poverty" reflects the growing number of statistics showing that, increasingly, poverty has a feminine face.[8] In general, women work more, rest less and are paid less than men.

In both developing and industrial countries, two-thirds of women's work is unpaid. Women in the developing world face serious economic exploitation as the majority of workers in "export processing zones" (EPZs), also known as sweatshops. EPZs are designed to provide cheap labour to foreign companies in tax-free and often union-free areas. In countries like the Philippines, Mexico, Malaysia, Taiwan and Sri Lanka, women hold over 80 per cent of the jobs in EPZs.[9] Many people in EPZs work long hours and only make subsistence wages that mean living in slums without running water, electricity, healthcare or education for children.

Female poverty correlates with female illiteracy and lack of women's leadership. Almost two-thirds of the world's illiterate are women.[10] Without formal education, it is very difficult to gain economic and political power. Women are underrepresented in the governments of every country. In most countries, women make up less than a quarter of elected officials and are severely restricted from holding administrative and managerial positions in the economic sphere.

In addition to these structural forms of violence, many women face astounding levels of direct violence even when there is no declared "war" in their countries. Over 90 million women and girls are "missing" worldwide, according to statistics that show the actual number of women and girls in the world compared to the number of females expected in birth rates.[11] Women "disappear" because of murder, kidnapping or trafficking against their will. In some countries, female infanticide and feticide (selective abortion of female foetuses) account for the millions of "missing" females in a population. In many traditional societies, parents consciously or unconsciously prefer male children. Boys are thought to be worth more economically, socially and in relation to social status than girls. Parents and communities more often encourage boys to pursue higher levels of education than girls, boys are given less work in the home and parents attend to boys' physical needs with more resources than for girls.

Females suffer from sexual violence at much higher rates than males. They also face the added burden of potential pregnancy. Some rape victims may have restricted choices in marriage opportunities or even be killed to escape the shame brought on the family. According to the WHO, an estimated 100–140 million girls and women worldwide have undergone female genital mutilation.[12] In addition to the loss of sexual pleasure, women's health and lives can be seriously damaged in the process.

Violence by men against women is a greater cause of injury and death than traffic accidents and malaria combined.[13] Examples of domestic violence include direct physical abuse such as kicking, biting, slapping, trying to strangle, burning, throwing acid in the face, stabbing and shooting women.

In addition, domestic violence is committed as a means to inflict psychological pain. Psychological or mental violence includes verbal abuse, harassment, confinement, lack of physical and financial freedom and attacks on the self-confidence and integrity of a woman. The WHO report includes a descriptive statement from a victim of psychological violence:

> The body mends soon enough. Only the scars remain but the wounds inflicted upon the soul take much longer to heal. And each time I re-live these moments, they start bleeding all over again. The broken spirit has taken longest to mend; the damage to the personality may be the most difficult to overcome.[14]

Chronic forms of violence against women are serious issues for anyone concerned about building peace at the community or national level. A gender analysis of conflict and violence must include a discussion of these everyday experiences of women. The silent ongoing war against women and girls, even in times of public peace, likely has an impact on the stability and resiliency of a community to respond to war and post-war crises.

Wartime violence against women

War brings about a variety of changes, many of which have direct effects on women. Each stage of war brings a unique set of challenges for women and exposes a different sexual dimension to wartime violence.

First, pro-war propaganda often cultivates the connection between masculinity and violence. Military language is gendered. It connects killing and winning to masculinity; and losing and/or using non-violence or negotiation to a loss of masculinity or being feminine. Research suggests that the link between masculinity and violence increases domestic violence and acts of rape during war.[15]

Second, as militaries begin to mobilize, their soldiers' sexual violence increases. As men (and some women) are forced or volunteer to leave their families to serve their countries or join armed movements seeking political change, normal avenues for expressing healthy sexual relationships between men and women decrease. In turn, there is an increase in the commercial sex trade, adult and child prostitution, HIV/AIDS and unwanted pregnancies.[16] Over 2 million women are trafficked as sex slaves each year, mainly in war zones. Female sex slaves are raped, forced to cook and ordered to walk in fields or roads with landmines to clear the path for soldiers.[17]

Third, as men abandon their families to serve the larger needs of the community or nation, women take on male roles and occupations while trying to care for their families with fewer resources to meet their basic needs. War causes shortages of food, water and other resources. Women left in charge of caring for extended families may face increased difficulty in meeting the family's basic needs. Some women may be forced to offer sex for sheer survival, exchanging their bodies for food, shelter or protection.[18]

Fourth, sexual violence against women can become a weapon of war. The lowered concern for human rights during warfare and the widespread availability of weapons exposes civilians, particularly women, to mass rape, military sexual slavery, forced prostitution, forced pregnancies and other efforts to conquer the enemy's territory metaphorically by sexually violating the enemy's women.[19] Women suffer ongoing consequences of this sexual violence. Prostitutes and rape victims experience social stigmatization, physical and mental trauma, sexually transmitted illnesses, unwanted pregnancies and ill treatment including beatings or death to restore the family's honour.[20] Pregnancy from rape creates new generations that may, along with their victimized mothers, be seen as "part enemy" by their communities. Women may also experience persecution specifically for the political or military activities of their male relatives or members of their ethnic or identity group, or due to their own activities. In addition to suffering more human rights abuses than men, women are often legally or culturally restricted from reporting human rights violations, which in turn makes them more susceptible to these.

Fifth, rapid social change during war often destroys the few existing protections against violence against women. During war, traditional and state structures may collapse. Traditional or legal forms of authority that prevented, limited or dealt with domestic and public forms of violence against women may disappear, leaving women more vulnerable to violence. Underlying cultural acceptance of violence against women may become more outwardly acceptable without legal structures in place. The frustration some men feel over new gender roles for women and their own inability to protect their families may lead to increased rates of domestic violence. Some may reinforce cultural identity through the revival of traditional practices used to control women, such as female genital mutilation. Others may increase their use of drugs or alcohol during war to escape the feelings of humiliation or trauma associated with war. Increased alcohol and drug abuse often leads to increased rates of domestic violence against women.[21]

Post-war violence against women

In recovering from war, societies literally have to reconstruct their physical, political, economic and cultural infrastructure. Post-war reconstruction is a time for dreaming big about how to change a society so that it has the capacity to solve future problems without again resorting to violence and war. It is also a time of dashed hopes, as people's high expectations for change may not meet the grinding pace of real progress. More often than not, women's hopes and dreams of a less violent and more peaceful life are shattered. Post-war processes affect women in a variety of ways.

First, peacekeeping operations that are designed to prevent violence in the post-war period often actually perpetrate violence against women. Military peacekeeping often fails to protect women from sexual violence by warring parties and may in fact pose further threats to women, who may be victimized by peacekeeping forces, particularly when peacekeeping operations lack a substantial female presence or leadership. Research on the effect of peacekeepers on local populations in Cambodia and Sierra Leone found widespread (including forced) prostitution and the spread of HIV/AIDS among local women.[22]

Second, reconstruction programmes have far too few resources to help women, particularly survivors of wartime rape. There is a lack of funding, training, support services and coordinating networks.[23] Reconstruction programmes often neglect to support gender equality, and intentionally or inadvertently reinforce pre-war forms of structural violence that give priority to male employment, male education, male healthcare, etc.[24] Reconstruction funds often target demobilization programmes that give young men land allocations, financial assistance and education at the expense of programmes that would assist women, such as trauma healing and rape crisis centres.[25]

Third, women are often absent from peace talks that create post-war reconstruction plans and designate post-war leadership. Since women are greatly underrepresented politically in non-war contexts, it is not surprising that they are also left out from political decisions made in war and post-war situations. At best, women are overlooked and neglected as important stakeholders in peace settlements. At worst, men forcibly resist efforts by women's groups to gain access to the decision-making arena. In Burundi, Somalia, Sudan and Liberia, for example, women achieved a small proportion of seats only after repeated pleas and lobbying by UNIFEM (the UN Development Fund for Women) and other international organizations backed demands from local women's groups.

During war, some revolutionary movements embrace a feminist agenda that empowers women and provides equal opportunity to both women and men in education and leadership. In Nicaragua, Mozambique and Eritrea, for example, liberation movements articulated the relationship between women's rights and greater democracy. While some movements did grant women new rights after succeeding in gaining political power, women's groups have been largely disappointed with the limited nature of revolution in terms of achieving gender equality in leadership. Male leaders in many social movements, such as the US civil rights movement, saw a focus on gender as diverting attention from the larger political issues of racial equality.[26] In other places, such as Afghanistan, warring groups agree on little besides the continued discrimination of women.

In those cases where violent conflict has led to real change in gender hierarchies, such as in Sri Lanka, some women feel uneasy about their new roles. While women may have had more freedom to explore new responsibilities and decision-making power during violent conflict, they did so under the stress and trauma of war, without the satisfaction of having *chosen* these new roles. Women may be ambivalent about this empowerment, which can leave them with a sense of resentment and guilt about their new freedoms.[27]

Fourth, post-war transitional justice processes such as the Truth and Reconciliation Commissions in South Africa and Sierra Leone pose unique challenges for addressing gender-based and sexual violence. Some women feel that public trials where victims face their offenders are not safe for women to speak about sexual crimes. It is difficult for women to testify about the crimes committed against them during war because of cultural barriers to talking about sexual violence as well as the threat of further violence against those who are prepared to tell the truth of what happened to them during war.[28] Some communities may revictimize women for speaking about sexual crimes, since in many places the *victim* of rape is held responsible and accountable for not resisting rape to the point of death.

Women as peacebuilders

Frameworks for understanding women's victimization in war and post-war contexts need to be held together with efforts to document and include women as peacebuilding actors. This section examines arguments for including women in peacebuilding, women's capacity for and roles in peacebuilding, and why the full range of types of violence against women discussed in the first section should be included more fully in the wider field of peacebuilding.

Conflict prevention and peacebuilding efforts seek to prevent, reduce, transform and help people recover from violence in all forms, even structural violence that causes disparity in wealth or education between groups – which in turn can lead to polarization and conflict.[29] By addressing a conflict's root causes, peacebuilding addresses the social conditions that foster an "unstable peace" and may lead to violent conflict. Peacebuilding relies on relational skills stemming from the fields of conflict resolution and transformation to help people in conflict build relationships with each other. Peacebuilding covers a variety of processes, including human rights advocacy and activism, peacekeeping, relief aid, mediation, restorative justice, trauma healing, education, economic development, institution-building, research and many other related processes that all help communities build the capacity to prevent and respond to conflict and violence.

Why women need to be involved in peacebuilding

Women and men are not essentially peaceful or warlike. Men and women make decisions to engage in war or peacebuilding based on their own assessment of their best interests. Yet when women want to be involved in peacebuilding, they often meet resistance from men and other women who believe women's gender roles should not include public leadership. Men currently hold the seats in most peace talks due to their dominance in government and economic spheres.[30] Women, on the other hand, are now making the case why it is important for them to be involved during all stages and activities of peacebuilding. The discussion of including and encouraging women as peacebuilders often faces the challenge of needing to "prove" that women make a difference when they are involved in peace processes. Women scholars and community leaders make a variety of arguments to legitimate women's participation. Figure 2.6 summarizes some of the arguments as to why women should be involved and included in peacebuilding. The following subsections explore these arguments in more depth.

Women's capacity for peacebuilding

In the struggle to find equal representation and inclusion of women in peacebuilding processes, a great deal of current energy and research seeks to determine how women "make a difference" in peacebuilding. Women's advocates sometimes fall into the trap of arguing that women are somehow "naturally" more peaceful than men. While essentialist theories of women's "natural capacity for peacebuilding" still get cheers and nervous laughter from crowds of both progressive and conservative men and women, they leave significant questions unanswered. Understanding women's capacity for peace requires a more complex understanding of the social construction of gender and its interaction with ethnic, class and other forms of identity.

Women are not equally peaceful. When mobilized as members of an ethnic group or nation that feels threatened, many women actively support war and violence against others. In *Women Warriors: A History*, Jones argues that women throughout history have led armies, created

1. The tasks of peacebuilding are simply too great and too complex to leave decision-making solely to a few select male leaders. Peacebuilding requires the participation of the whole of society.
2. Women represent half or more of every community and should have a voice and active role to play in peacebuilding. Peacebuilding is by definition an inclusive process that seeks to empower people to take personal responsibility for fostering peace.
3. Both men and women play roles in escalating violence. Peacebuilding requires both women and men to become aware of how gender roles impact on violence and peace.
4. Women and men are socialized differently. Because many women grow up being encouraged to care for and build relationships with others, these skills can often assist in the process of peacebuilding.
5. Women have different experiences in their lives because of their gender roles. Women's concerns and perspectives are unique and cannot be represented by male leaders.
6. Since women are the central caretakers of families in many cultures, everyone suffers when women are oppressed, victimized and excluded from peacebuilding. The centrality of women to family and communal life makes their inclusion in peacebuilding essential.
7. Women have unique social networks in many communities. These networks can be vital for disseminating information and garnering participation in peacebuilding processes.
8. Sexism originates from the same set of beliefs that foster racism, classism and ethnic and religious discrimination; the belief that some people are inherently "better" than others. Since peacebuilding aims to end discrimination of all types against any group of people, women's empowerment and gender equality should be seen as inherent to the process of building peace.
9. UN Security Council Resolution 1325 calls on the international community to realize the inclusion of women in all peacebuilding processes.

Figure 2.6 Reasons for women and men to be partners in peacebuilding

women's battalions, passed as male soldiers, rallied the troops as symbolic leaders and defended family and community structures in the absence of men.[31] He argues that women have displayed the same bloodthirsty and courageous leadership in times of war as men. Women also play powerful roles in mobilizing their sons, husbands and fathers to fight. Peterson and Runyan claim that even women who do not fight directly play significant roles in supporting wars. Governments argue that protecting women in places such as Afghanistan is a major reason for waging war, while ignoring the fact that war itself hurts and kills women. Women are often tasked with putting life back to normal during and after wars. They play important symbolic roles in mourning the loss of soldiers and produce new lives to replace those who died.[32] Gender identities exist alongside ethnic, religious and class identities. Women may be encouraged to fight an opposing ethnic group or an enemy of their state. This helps to explain the mixed ways women respond to war, with some supporting it and others working for peace.

Even in non-war situations, women contribute to a culture of violence. Both sexes are guilty of woman and child abuse. Since women often have the primary responsibility to shape their children into gender roles, some play a significant role in encouraging males to be violent to prove their masculinity. In northern Kenya, some mothers acknowledge that they urge their sons to steal cattle and kill young men from opposing tribes so they can prove their masculinity and be initiated into manhood. Women in elite economic and social groups often discriminate against and oppress other women whom they consider to be placed lower than themselves in the social hierarchy.

Women draw on skills, assets and capacities that are available to them in oppressive systems, and harness these for productive use in peacebuilding. Within a patriarchal framework, women's capacities for peacebuilding differ from men's in at least four ways: how women are socialized; which concerns and issues they bring to peacebuilding; which social networks they are part of; and how their gender identities allow them to do some peacebuilding activities that are denied to men.

Socialized for peace

Research suggests that both men and women have the capacity for the full range of peacebuilding skills. Women are not, by nature, more advantaged or disadvantaged at building peace than men. Yet there are plenty of qualitative data suggesting that more women tend to exhibit more collaborative conflict behaviours than men, and more men demonstrate competition, aggression and violence than women.[33] Both essentialist and sociological theories can explain the tendency for men to be less cooperative and more aggressive than women.

Women, according to essentialist theorists, have had to develop nonviolent alternatives to problem solving because of their relative lack of physical strength compared to men. Sociological theories offer a more complex analysis: many women are socialized and socially restricted to find power through relationships *with* others rather than through power *over* others in traditional political or economic structures. Many families,

religions, educational institutions and other community structures encourage or force female children to be less aggressive and more compas-
sionate to the needs of others than male children. If girls learn that they
gain recognition and social rewards for playing their culturally determined roles as women by demonstrating these skills and characteristics,
they are more likely to show empathy, compassion and communication,
and in turn excel at the sophisticated social skills needed for peacebuilding. The socialization process in many cultures also puts pressure on boys,
on the other hand, to be tough and willing to fight or use violence to
prove their manhood. Some may not develop social skills to communicate and express empathy appropriately to others, and therefore may
lack these assets needed in peacebuilding.

Concerns about ending all forms of violence

A second approach to understanding women's capacity for peacebuilding
centres on how the experience of oppression and marginalization shapes
their concerns about conflict. Women's identities are complex, and shaped
by multiple layers of race, class, religion, age and education, among
others. The experience of oppression – in many cases multiple oppres-
sions of race, class and gender – may give some women a unique perspective on the need to treat all people with respect.

Yet not all women are interested in advocating peace. In some situations, women appear to put their national, ethnic, religious or class identity above their gender identity and solidarity. For example, some Israeli
and Palestinian women do not relate at all to women of the opposing
group. Others, however, feel they have more in common with other women
who are tired of war and the violence that destroys their lives, and thus
intentionally build relationships across the lines of conflict to oppose
those male leaders on both sides who may escalate threats and violence.

Research on women's roles in peacebuilding identifies the trend for
some women to raise a wider set of issues than male representatives in
peace processes because they see the effects of violent conflict in both
public and family settings, including the ways in which public violence
and domestic violence against women and children are connected.[34]
Peace agreements in Northern Ireland and Burundi were significantly affected by the presence of women's groups and their wider agenda for
peace. Peterson and Runyan claim that even a small increase in the
number of women in formal politics has had significant effects on the
types of issues discussed at the highest levels of government. They argue
that women in public office are more likely to incorporate all forms of
human rights, economic and environmental justice, a broader concept of
human security and a commitment to putting gender equality at the forefront of all initiatives and policies.[35]

Links to women's networks

Infusing all social networks with the values, skills and knowledge of peacebuilding is essential to developing a grassroots capacity for peace. In societies where men and women work and socialize in separate places, they develop distinct social networks. In many cultures, women's domain is in the market, in religious groups, among other mothers and, increasingly, in the medical and counselling professions. If information about peacebuilding programmes is circulated only through male social networks, women will not have the knowledge required for active participation. Moreover, the failure to include women's networks in peacebuilding programmes can restrict the ability of leaders to gain the consent and support needed to implement peace agreements.

Mobilizing around the ideology of womanhood

Women living in patriarchal cultures often find their greatest strength while performing their traditional roles as mothers, wives, sisters and daughters. The paradoxical logic of patriarchy condones or ignores private and structural forms of violence against women, while prohibiting public violence against or repression of women. While mobilizing ideal or archetypal visions of womanhood may not address the problem of patriarchy and ongoing oppression, it allows some women to harness their collective strength as women for peace.

As women tend to have less authority and political power, they may be seen as more neutral or even irrelevant to political conflict. In turn, they may be granted permission to be involved in activism and demonstrations as opposed to male or mixed groups. In her study of women's peace activities, Ferris notes that women's leadership is often categorized as "volunteer" or as an extension of their caretaking roles as mothers and wives rather than describing their activities in terms of political power or professional peacebuilding.[36]

Hanan Ashrawi, a leading spokeswoman for Palestinians, explains why women are effective activists against Israeli occupation: Palestinian women "were aware of the ingrained sexism of the soldiers, which largely prevented them from firing at women".[37] By using traditional notions of motherhood and womanhood, women may gain both protection and licence to intervene in conflicts without violent retribution. As primary caretakers of children, a mother's concern for her children is perceived by many to be "natural". If a woman's son or daughter is abducted by the military, she may be seen as a more legitimate and authentic advocate for their release because she is seen to be responding in her role as mother rather than participating in a political act. In some situations, particularly in Latin American countries like Chile, Argentina and Guatemala, mothers who organized and demonstrated for the release of their children from military governments were able to deliver a clear message to the international community about their situation without immediate crackdowns by the government. While violent repression was delayed due to the cultural respect for mothers within most Latin American societies, it did in the end require great sacrifice from the women, who were eventually brutalized and killed for their courageous acts. However, the delay in silencing the activist mothers allowed them to mobilize world attention, something other activist groups had not been able to do.

Women's identities as mothers, sisters, wives and daughters of men who fight and/or die in war may also contribute to their ability to find common ground with women from different sides of a conflict. Women in Northern Ireland, former Yugoslavia, Somalia, Cyprus, Israel, Palestine and Colombia developed active relationships across the lines of conflict to share common experiences and joint understandings of the conflict, and proposed solutions to their leaders and governments.

While the stereotype that women are not political may allow them to "get away with" more activism than men, when it comes to negotiating peace settlements and redesigning social structures the stereotype may lead men to exclude women from these essential steps. Women's groups are strategizing about how they can raise awareness of their political contributions in humanitarian and human rights activism while at the same time drawing strength from the stereotype that women are less likely to scramble over others for political power.

In Somalia, women from different clans developed an innovative approach to assert political power using their identities as women. There are five main clans in Somalia, and each sent representatives to the negotiations to end the war during the 1990s. Women were not chosen to represent any of the clans, so they decided to form a "sixth clan of women". This sixth clan then chose its own representatives and sent them to the negotiations. Women's roles in Somalia made their presence at the peace table particularly important. Many Somali girls are given by their fathers in marriage to men from another clan. When clans fight each other, women find themselves as bridges between their fathers and brothers in their clan of origin and their husbands and sons in the new clan. Some women serve as channels of communication and conciliation between warring clans because of these bridged relationships.

Women's roles in peacebuilding

There are four main categories of peacebuilding activities. The map of peacebuilding in Figure 2.7 shows the four circles of activity: advocating for structural change; reducing direct violence; transforming relationships; and building structural capacity.[38] Peacebuilding includes immediate or crisis responses to violence, such as waging conflict non-violently and creating programmes to reduce violence. Intermediate and long-term forms of peacebuilding seek to address the underlying causes of conflict, help people recover from trauma and create sustainable structures that bring justice and peace through building relationships. A survey of women's roles in peacebuilding highlights the ways women address the problems of violence in their communities through activities in each category (see Figure 2.7).

Women advocating for structural change

Women use advocacy for structural change in situations where those in power impose their will on others and are not willing to negotiate or

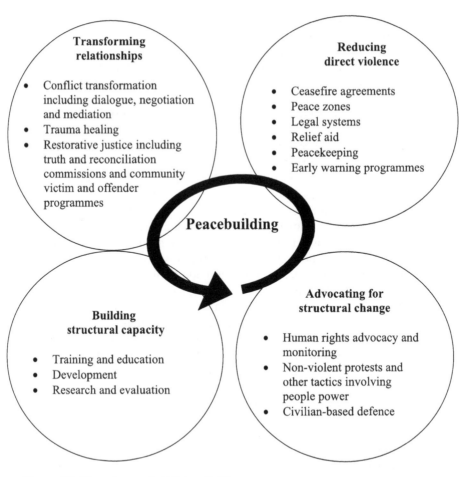

Figure 2.7 Map of peacebuilding activities

engage in dialogue. Like other social movements, women use policy advocacy and non-violent tactics to raise public awareness of violence, promote human rights and increase power for groups wanting peaceful social change.

There are examples of women's groups demonstrating and organizing for peace in virtually every country.[39] One example is the Women in Black movement that began in Israel in 1987. Each Friday, mostly Jewish women would gather in Jerusalem's busiest intersections during rush hour wearing black clothes to symbolize mourning, and stand in silence to oppose the Israeli occupation of Palestine. The Women in Black movement has been spreading around the world. In 1991 a Women in Black group began in Belgrade, Serbia, to denounce the victimization of civilians throughout the Balkans. In the weeks before the 2003 US-led war on Iraq, Women in Black joined together in silent protest against the impending war in cities around the world. Today, Women in Black is a global network of women who organize and demonstrate to resist war, violence and militarism wearing black and silently standing in public places. In addition to these women-led non-violent campaigns, women are often the majority in mixed-sex activism such as the US civil rights movement and the recent protests against global economic injustice. A global women's advocacy movement brought about UN Security Council Resolution (SCR) 1325, which mandates women's participation in peacebuilding and continues to have an impact on women's efforts to build structural capacity for change.

Women reducing direct violence

The second category of peacebuilding includes a set of activities primarily aimed at reducing direct forms of violence and addressing the immediate needs of victims in times of crisis at the individual, community and national levels. In war and post-war contexts, women play active roles in helping victims of violence. In many cultures, women's groups are known for their charity work to provide food and clothing for people in crisis. Shelters operated by and for women are essential in times of crisis for domestic violence survivors and their children. The Medica Women's Therapy Center in Bosnia-Herzegovina is an example of the kind of service needed around the world by female victims of war. Medica's all-female staff work with rape victims and women traumatized in the war to provide for their psychological, physical and social needs.[40]

Civilian and military forms of peacekeeping seek to reduce violence during and after wars. Women also play important roles in peacekeeping. In the Philippines, women gave birth to the concept of "peace zones", a form of civilian peacekeeping. Peace zones aim to create safe spaces for civilians during war. Villages, cities or regions negotiate with armed groups to make it illegal for anyone to carry a weapon within the boundaries. Women initiate this process to keep their families safe in the midst of war. Peace zones separate civilians from military fighting, creating safety and reducing trauma for all those inside them.[41]

Research documents that a "critical mass" of women in UN peacekeeping missions seems to correlate with increased success in other forms of peacebuilding, such as formal peace talks. It also focuses attention on human rights and gender issues in the code of conduct for peacekeepers and contributes to an environment of compassion, non-violence, listening, learning, stability and morality in the peace process. In addition, substantial numbers of women peacekeepers in a force correlate with increased confidence and trust among the local population, improved ability to use dialogue and negotiation to diffuse potentially violent situations in the local context, and the transformation of discriminatory views and stereotypes of women in the host country.[42]

Early warning programmes identify activities that indicate people are preparing for war and collect data about these indicators from many people in many different places and levels of society. They then analyse the data and determine the possible best- and worst-case scenarios to allow mobilization of support and resources for addressing underlying conflict issues. Women and women's groups are important data collectors and analysers. In many conflicts, women may notice the sale of gold jewellery in the marketplace and recognize that this means other women are selling their gold so their husbands can buy weapons in preparation for war. A woman collecting firewood in the forest may see men going to the hills to plan violent attacks. Or she may see truckloads of arms enter her community at night, hear rumours of war in the marketplace or sense a growing hatred among ethnic groups and political exclusion.[43]

Women transforming relationships

The third category of peacebuilding includes a variety of high-level and grassroots efforts to build relationships that heal trauma, address the root causes of conflict and strengthen or rebuild community relationships. Relationship-building processes set the stage for open communication, so individuals and groups can identify their needs and create solutions that meet these needs.

The process of coming to terms with a history of war and violence, healing trauma, transforming conflict and doing justice requires "truth telling" at the family, community and national levels. Women require special, protected spaces to tell their particularly personal truths of rape and sexual violence. In South Africa's truth and reconciliation process, for example, women demanded that the Truth and Reconciliation Commission hold women-only hearings to allow women to speak more freely about their rape and torture.[44]

As noted earlier, when women are involved in high-level peace processes they can have a substantial impact on the quality and tone of the process. Women at the peace table are often perceived to be less concerned with political ambition and personal agendas, and instead more focused on ensuring that women's human security needs are met.[45] Groups of women have creatively pushed their way into many formal peace talks around the world.[46] Women bring a unique set of priorities to peacebuilding processes, often with a far greater emphasis on the impacts of public violence on women and children.[47]

At the grassroots level, women are often the first to reach across the lines of conflict to others in the enemy camp. Women in Northern Ireland, Israel/Palestine, former Yugoslavia, Rwanda, Burundi and many other places have risked their lives to meet with other women across the lines of conflict. In *The Space Between Us: Negotiating Gender and National Identities in Conflict*, Cynthia Cockburn details the phenomena of cooperation and communication between women of polarized ethnonational groups. Women in these collaborative projects do address differences between them, yet seek constantly to renegotiate the terms of solidarity to affirm their common ground. Women create joint organizations with shared decision-making to help overcome the tensions and differences that arise in their work. Cockburn argues that women's groups have a wider influence and create models and foundations for coexistence, development and peace by engaging differences creatively and democratically.[48]

Women building structural capacity for peace

The final category of peacebuilding includes long-range plans for structural change. Capacity-building includes all forms of education and training, particularly peace and human rights education; political, economic and social development; demilitarization programmes, including reintegration of armed groups and arms control agreements; and research projects to evaluate existing programmes and develop new models for sustainable democratic societies. All these activities aim to build the capacity of individuals, communities and/or states to prevent and respond to further violence. In this category of peacebuilding, women help create capacity, especially in post-war contexts, to address violence against women and establish gender equality.

At the local level women conduct training to build the long-term capacity of women to be active decision-makers in their families, communities and nations. Women have been active in promoting peace education through school systems. They have also begun training programmes for adult women. For example, the West African Network for Peacebuilding conducts workshops specifically for women so that they can be active participants in all types of peacebuilding projects.[49] In India, the Panchayati Raj campaign trains and equips women to run for political office in response to national legislation imposing a quota of 33 per cent women in local government positions.

At the national and international levels, a variety of women's groups have developed an impressive array of global initiatives. Such groups have successfully put violence against women and women's contribution to peacebuilding on the international diplomatic agenda. Most states have signed and ratified the UN Convention on the Elimination of All Forms of Discrimination against Women (CEDAW), designed as a set of principles to guide state policy to ensure that women and men are treated equally. The UN Fourth World Conference on Women's Platform for Action on Violence against Women proposes to take CEDAW a step further by encouraging all governments, employers, unions and community and youth organizations to create policies and procedures to eliminate sexual harassment and discrimination. It calls for community-based education programmes to raise awareness about violence against women and the personal and social effects of violence in the family and community, and give information on how to solve problems without violence and available community services for addressing violence.

The WHO project on Elimination of Violence Against Women has created one of the most thorough efforts to document rates of violence against women in each country.[50] With its eye towards gender inequality in development, the World Bank increasingly highlights the disparity in the quality of life between men and women. A World Bank policy report, entitled *Engendering Development*, details a number of strategies to address this disparity, including reforming discriminatory institutions, strengthening women's voice and equalizing economic development for men and women.[51]

UN SCR 1325 has spawned a flurry of international activity to document, advocate for and guide women's participation in peacebuilding. International Alert, the Initiative for Inclusive Security and the Gender Action on Peace and Security programmes aim to mainstream the issue of women, peace and security in the international arena through awareness-raising activities, influencing international policy and building partnerships between women's organizations around the world. The goals are to give women and women's organizations the support and resources they need to build peace, end impunity for crimes committed against women, particularly refugees, and increase the number of women in the planning and implementation of all phases of peacebuilding.[52]

In addition, a variety of research reports have begun developing a set of benchmarks, quota systems, action plans and a global legislative agenda on violence against women and women's roles in peacebuilding to raise awareness and create expectations about women's participation, and institutionalize progress in these areas. Gender Action for Peace and Security has developed a set of recommendations for more fully involving and integrating men into efforts to promote SCR 1325 at the national level.[53]

Conclusion: Mainstreaming gender in peacebuilding

This chapter began by examining how biological and sociological ideas about gender translate into an environment where widescale violence against women is accepted as normal in times of peace, war and post-war. Understanding the complex concept of gender and the extent of violence against women in non-war contexts provides frameworks for examining their experience of violence and peacebuilding in war and post-war contexts.

There are plenty of road signs pointing the way forward to reduce and prevent violence against women and increase their participation in peacebuilding. Placing equal value on male and female lives and experiences is the first step in creating an environment that is serious about ending violence against women. In war and post-war contexts, addressing such violence requires three key steps to help mainstream gender into the peacebuilding agenda (Figure 2.8): gender analysis, the goal of gender equality and gender inclusion in peacebuilding.

First, the tools of gender analysis need to infuse every peacebuilding programme. Conflict analysis and assessment tools are important guides to all peacebuilding planning. All too often, peacebuilding analysis leaves out the significant differences between male and female experiences and

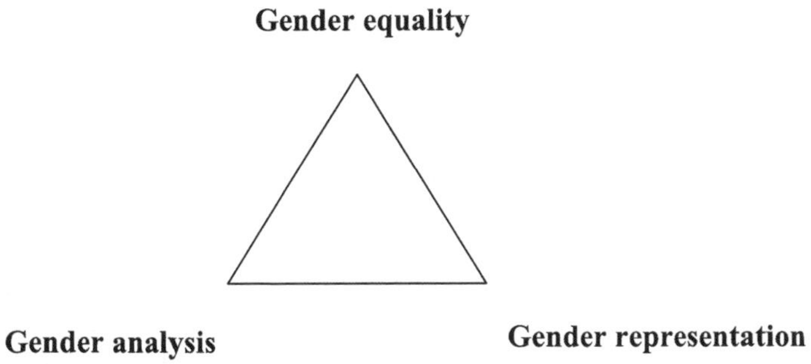

Gender equality

Gender analysis   **Gender representation**

Figure 2.8 Three key steps to mainstream gender in peacebuilding

roles. Gender analysis requires gender-disaggregated data about how war affects men and women differently; gender roles of men and women in local cultures, including the division of labour and resources; needs of women from different economic classes, religions, ethnic groups and ages; and how women are included in all peacebuilding processes from relief aid distribution, peacekeeping programmes and grassroots dialogue to formal peace talks. Infusing a gender analysis into peacebuilding requires concrete action.

UNIFEM's independent experts' report on the impact of armed conflict and the role of women in peacebuilding calls for a truth commission on violence against women. The commission could focus world attention and action on the unique experiences of women in non-war, war and post-war contexts. It also calls for specific analysis and coordinated action on trafficking of women and children, particularly during war, and domestic violence.[54]

Creating gender units within UN programmes was among the first generation of attempts at gender mainstreaming in peacebuilding, as detailed in Chapter 4 in this volume. The presence of trained gender advisers for all peacebuilding organizations and staff, in addition to training in and opportunities for gender analysis by other staff, can help institutionalize a shared responsibility for ongoing gender analysis of all programmes. There is evidence that gender analysis leads to changes in programming. Gender analysis training among police in Cambodia, for example, resulted in new police initiatives to address domestic violence and sex trafficking.[55]

Second, the goal of gender equality needs to be embraced by all peacebuilding actors as a central value framework. Peacebuilding grows out of the values of human rights and democracy. It recognizes the close relationship between the ability for people to meet their basic needs and the presence of a just peace. While peacebuilding is careful to ensure equal treatment of people from different ethnic and religious groups, gender equality is often ignored.

Gender equality refers to the goal of equal opportunities, resources and respect for men and women. It does not mean that men and women become the same, but that their lives and work hold equal value. Gender equality will take shape in different ways according to local cultures and religions. Peacebuilding programmes demonstrate their commitment to gender equality when it becomes integral to every aspect of peacebuilding and not relegated to one or two programmes for women. Because women and men do not have equal access to opportunities, resources and respect in most communities, peacebuilding programmes need to take affirmative action to ensure that these patterns are broken. Funders need to urge recipient organizations to include women at every level of their staff and board, and ensure that these women have the support of other women and women's organizations and are not just token representatives put in place to look good but keep quiet.

Third, women and women's organizations need to participate in every stage and activity of peacebuilding alongside men and male-led organizations. Both women and men need representation in all aspects of peacebuilding. Because of the patriarchal context that discriminates against women and women's experiences, women's groups require ongoing opportunities to analyse and articulate the forms of violence women experience. Women-only spaces are important forums to build bridges between women from different identity groups, collect information about the types and effectiveness of current programmes to address violence against women, and set priorities and strategies for addressing this violence. Women-only forums do not aim to exclude men; rather they create a safe space for discussion of highly personal forms of violence and the unique perspectives of women that are often excluded in mixed-sex forums.

For example, the Kenya Women's Peace Forum meets regularly to evaluate and discuss how national policies and events affect women. During the 2002 election, women's groups played important roles in organizing themselves to support women candidates and create a relatively violence-free election.[56] Local women leaders and organizations need to have access to and active relationships with all peacebuilding actors so that their analysis and ideas can be communicated and their efforts coordinated with other peacebuilding activities.

Over the last 10 years the international community has made significant progress in mainstreaming gender in peacebuilding through gender analysis programmes, focusing on gender equity and institutionalizing gender inclusion. But the road ahead is still long. While there is a committed network moving this agenda forward, widespread ignorance of gender, refusal to address violence against women and obstruction of women's peacebuilding efforts still exist.

Notes

1. Montagu, Ashley (1953) *The Natural Superiority of Women*, New York: Macmillan; Elshtain, Jean Bethke (1987) *Women and War*, New York: Basic Books.
2. Peterson, V. Spike and Anne Sisson Runyan (1999) *Global Gender Issues*, Boulder, CO: Westview Press, p. 37.
3. Taylor, Anita and Judy Beinstein Miller (eds) (1994) *Conflict and Gender*, Cresskill, NJ: Hampton Press.
4. Cockburn, Cynthia (1998) *The Space Between Us: Negotiating Gender and National Identities in Conflict*, New York: Zed Books.

5. United Nations (1993) "Declaration on the Elimination of Violence against Women", UN Doc. A/RES/48/104, 20 December, UN General Assembly, New York.

6. World Health Organization (1997) "Violence against Women Information Pack: A Priority Health Issue", WHO Women's Health and Development Programme, Geneva; Ellsberg, Heise (2005) *Researching Violence against Women: A Practical Guide for Researchers and Activists*, Geneva: World Health Organization, p. 10.

7. UNDP (2007) *Human Development Report 2007/8, Gender Development Index*, New York: UN Development Programme.

8. Moghadam, Valentine M. (2005) *The "Feminization of Poverty" and Women's Human Rights*, Paris: UNESCO.

9. Seager, Joni (1997) *The State of Women in the World Atlas*, New York: Penguin Books, p. 69.

10. Ibid., p. 74.

11. Ibid., p. 35.

12. World Health Organization (2010) "Female Genital Mutilation", Fact Sheet No. 241, February, available at www.who.int/mediacentre/factsheets/fs241/en/index.html.

13. World Health Organization, note 6, p. 4.

14. World Health Organization (1998) "Elimination of Violence against Women Executive Report", WHO, Geneva, available at www.who.int/violence_injury_prevention/vaw/endvaw.htm.

15. UN Division for the Advancement of Women (1998) "Sexual Violence and Armed Conflict: United Nations Response", April, available at www.un.org/womenwatch/daw/public/w2apr98.htm.

16. Enloe, Cynthia (1989) *Bananas, Beaches, and Bases: Making Feminist Sense of International Politics*, London: Pandora, pp. 84–92.

17. UNIFEM (2002) "Women, War, and Peace: Executive Summary", Independent Experts' Assessment on the Effect of Armed Conflict on Women and the Role of Women in Peacebuilding, Progress of the World's Women, UNIFEM, New York, p. 5.

18. Woroniuk, Beth (1999) "Gender Equality & Peacebuilding: An Operational Framework", April, Canadian International Development Agency, Ottawa, available at www.cida-ecco.org/CIDARoadMap/RoadMapEnvoy/documents/GE%20and%20Peacebuilding.pdf.

19. UN Division for the Advancement of Women, note 15.

20. Pankhurst, Donna and Sanam Anderlini (2000) *Mainstreaming Gender in Peacebuilding: From the Village Council to the Negotiating Table*, London: International Alert.

21. World Health Organization, note 6, p. 8.

22. UN Division for the Advancement of Women (2000) "The Role of Women in United Nations Peace-Keeping", *Women2000*, December, available at gopher.undp.org:70/00/secretar/dpcsd/daw/w2000/1995-1.en.

23. World Health Organization, note 14, p. 15.

24. Sorensen, Birgitte (1998) "Women and Post-conflict Reconstruction: Issues and Sources", War-Torn Societies Occasional Paper, WSP, Geneva, available at www.unrisd.org/wsp/op3/toc.htm.

25. Ibid.

26. Ibid., p. 12; Randall, Margaret (1992) *Gathering Rage: The Failure of Twentieth-Century Revolutions to Develop a Feminist Agenda*, New York: Monthly Review Press.

27. Manchanda, Rita, Bandita Sijapati and Rebecca Gang (2002) "Women Making Peace", in *Strengthening Women's Role in Peace Processes*, Kathmandu: South Asia Forum for Human Rights.

28. Pankurst and Anderlini, note 20.

29. Schirch, Lisa (2004) *The Little Book of Strategic Peacebuilding*, Intercourse, PA: Good Books. See also Chapter 1 in this volume.
30. Anderlini, Sanam Naraghi (2007) *Women Building Peace: What They Do, Why It Matters*, Boulder, CO: Lynne Rienner Publishers.
31. Jones, David (1997) *Women Warriors: A History*, Washington, DC: Brassey's.
32. Peterson and Runyan, note 2, p. 117.
33. Keashly, Loraleigh (1994) "Gender and Conflict: What Does Psychological Research Tell Us?", in Anita Taylor and Judi Beinstein Miller (eds) *Gender and Conflict*, Cresskill, NJ: Hampton Press.
34. See Anderlini, Sanam Naraghi (2000) *Women at the Peace Table*, New York: UNIFEM; Marshall, Donna Ramsey (2000) *Women in War and Peace: Grassroots Peacebuilding*, Washington, DC: US Institute of Peace; McKay, Susan and Dyan Mazurana (2000) "Raising Women's Voices for Peacebuilding: Vision, Impact, and Limitations of Media Technologies", International Alert, London, available at www.international-alert.org/women/media.pdf; El-Bushra, Judy (2000) "Transforming Conflict: Some Thoughts on a Gendered Understanding of Conflict Processes", in Susie Jacobs, Ruth Jacobson and Jennifer Marchbank (eds) *States of Conflict: Gender, Violence and Resistance*, New York: Zed Books, pp. 66–86.
35. Peterson and Runyan, note 2.
36. Ferris, Elizabeth (1993) *Women, War, and Peace*, Uppsala: Uppsala Life and Peace Institute.
37. Anderlini, note 34, p. 23.
38. Schirch, note 29.
39. McAllister, Pam (1988) *You Can't Kill the Spirit: Stories of Women and Nonviolent Action*, Philadelphia, PA: New Society Publishers; McAllister, Pam (1991) *This River of Courage: Generations of Women's Resistance and Action*, Philadelphia, PA: New Society Publishers.
40. Cockburn, note 4.
41. Mitchell, Christopher and Susan Allen-Nan (eds) (1997) "Zones of Peace", *Peace Review* 9(2), special edition.
42. UN Division for the Advancement of Women, note 22, p. 12.
43. Schmeidl, Susanne with Eugenia Piza-Lopez (2002) *Gender and Conflict Early Warning: A Framework for Action*, London: Save the Children.
44. Marshall, note 34, p. 21.
45. Anderlini, note 34.
46. Anderlini, Sanam Naraghi (2001) *Women, Peace and Security: A Policy Audit from the Beijing Platform for Action to United Nations Security Council Resolution 1325 and Beyond, Achievements and Emerging Challenges*, London: International Alert, p. 20.
47. International Alert (2008) "Integrating Women's Priorities into Peacebuilding Processes: Experiences of Monitoring and Advocacy in Burundi and Sierra Leone", report of civil society workshop, London, 25–29 February.
48. Cockburn, note 4.
49. Ekiyor, Thelma (2001) "Women in Peacebuilding: An Account of the Niger Delta Women", in *From the Field*, 3rd edn, Accra: West African Network for Peacebuilding, available at www.wanep.org/wanep/attachments/article/107/tp_women_in_peacebuilding.pdf.
50. World Health Organization, note 14, p. 16.
51. World Bank (2001) *Engendering Development Through Gender Equality in Rights, Resources, and Voice*, Washington, DC: World Bank.
52. See Chapter 10 in this volume.

53. Gender Action on Peace and Security (2007) "Report on Involving Men in the Implementation of UN Security Council Resolution 1325 on Women, Peace and Security", GAPS, London, available at www.gaps-uk.org/docs/GAPSreport_Involving_Men_in_SCR_1325_Implementation.pdf.
54. UNIFEM, note 17, p. 6.
55. Ibid., p. 70.
56. For instance, on 17 January 2003 the Women's Peace Forum organized a meeting in Nairobi on "Women and the 2002 Elections".

Part I

From victimhood to empowerment: Patterns and changes

3

Mass crimes and resilience of women: A cross-national perspective

Krishna Kumar

The purpose of this chapter is to examine major impacts of "mass crimes" on women and suggest policy measures that the international community can promote to empower women in contributing to post-conflict peace-building.

Two premises that inform the chapter need to be made explicit here. First, contrary to the popular stereotype, women are not passive specta-tors to mass crimes. The imagery of women as silently bearing their miseries and misfortunes in the face of such crimes is belied by past ex-perience. Extensive fieldwork conducted by USAID (the US Agency for International Development) in countries as diverse as Bosnia, Cambodia, El Salvador, Georgia, Guatemala and Rwanda shows that women are ac-tive and resilient.[1] They often participate in the conduct of mass crimes, struggle to keep themselves and their families alive in the midst of conse-quent economic and physical insecurity, and contribute to the recovery and reconstruction of affected societies. This does not mean they are not affected by mass crimes or do not suffer from the physical and institu-tional violence inflicted upon them. It simply means that they are more than silent victims of war crimes; they are survivors.

Second, the purpose of all efforts – local, national and international – after mass crimes should not be simply to alleviate the misfortunes in-flicted upon women, but to transform existing gender relations on a more egalitarian course. This normative premise is important because the post-conflict era often provides opportunities for making structural changes in economic, political and even social spheres. For example, when a new

Defying victimhood: Women and post-conflict peacebuilding, Schnabel and Tabyshalieva (eds),
United Nations University Press, 2012, ISBN 978-92-808-1201-5

constitution is written or an old one revised, women's rights can be enshrined in it. If far-reaching changes are being made in macroeconomic policies, many barriers to women's employment and access to productive resources can be eliminated. The problem of unequal access to education for girls and women can also be tackled at this stage. Although with varying degrees of success, in the past national and international actors in many post-conflict societies have seized the opportunity to push for changes in gender relations to establish a better social and economic order.

The chapter is divided into three sections. The first explains the nature and types of "mass crimes", while the second identifies their impacts on women and gender relations and women's resilience to these crimes. The last section presents recommendations for the international community.

The nature and types of "mass crimes"

As conceptualized here, "mass crimes" denote large-scale physical, psychological and structural violence inflicted upon people intentionally or unintentionally, directly or indirectly, by the state or any organized group. Such mass violence is generally, although not exclusively, inflicted during broader periods of intra- and inter-state conflicts. The primary focus of this chapter is on various types of mass crimes usually committed during violent conflicts: mass killing, massacres and genocides; mass rapes and sexual abuse; intense physical and psychological deprivation; and uprooting of populations.

Mass killing, massacres and genocides represent the most obvious type of mass crimes. In intra-state conflicts, belligerent parties intentionally inflict violence on the civilian population. According to some estimates, up to 95 per cent of the casualties in civil wars have been civilians, which alters a country's demographic composition and social relations.[2] While the state-supported ethnic cleansing in Bosnia and Rwanda is well known, the systematic killing and maiming of innocent people by belligerent groups in Afghanistan, Congo, Guatemala and Liberia are often overlooked. The situation is slightly different in inter-state conflicts, where warring parties are obliged to follow international norms to minimize direct harm to the civilian population. Although these norms are never fully enforced or practised, they nonetheless exist and circumscribe combatants' behaviour. For example, in the 2003 invasion of Iraq, the US forces took pains to avoid civilian casualties, although they were not always successful.

Mass rapes and sexual abuse of women as a tactic of warfare are another example of mass crimes perpetuated by warring groups. In Bosnia and Rwanda rape has been an essential tactic of ethnic cleansing. Women were raped, often in the presence of their spouses, parents or other family members, to humiliate and terrorize members of particular ethnic groups. In Rwanda women were forced to have sex with military personnel as "payment" for victory or were raped by men of the enemy groups in revenge. Security forces in El Salvador and Guatemala abused young women suspected of rebel sympathies.[3] Little information exists on the extent of abuse, as victims hide the crimes and suffer silently because of associated shame and humiliation. Conservative estimates of rape victims ran in the thousands in Bosnia, El Salvador, Guatemala and Rwanda. During the Rwandan conflict, researchers estimate that more than 5,000 women were impregnated through rape.[4] Many of them are now raising the children fathered by those who killed their spouses or family members. Little is known about these mothers or their children, but their social and psychological suffering remains largely under-researched. Guatemala's Commission for Historical Clarification recorded the testimony of thousands of abused women, but hesitated to delve deeply into issues of rape.[5]

Intense physical and psychological deprivation inflicted on a populace by violent conflicts represents a category that may be problematic in operationalization. Most if not all wars result in mass hunger, intense psychological stress and physical insecurity, particularly in war and post-conflict zones. During civil wars in Angola, Cambodia, Ethiopia and Liberia mass starvation was more common than is generally acknowledged. In war and post-war areas people – especially ailing mothers, children and the elderly – are unable to get access to elementary medical treatment, resulting in death or long-term disabilities which worsen the deep physical and psychological insecurities that people experience.

The *uprooting of populations* is also an important category of "mass crimes". In major conflicts, wanton destruction, physical insecurity, disruption in livelihood and shortages of food force people to flee from their homes and communities and seek refuge in other parts of the country or in neighbouring countries. In the aftermath of genocide, 2 million citizens fled from Rwanda across the borders to adjacent countries. In Cambodia the Khmer Rouge forced all city dwellers to relocate to remote rural areas with no physical and institutional structures to sustain them, which resulted in death or malnutrition. Massive displacement of people also took place in Bosnia, El Salvador, Georgia and Guatemala.

The displacement of populations imposes suffering and deprivation. The overall situation of those who migrate abroad is generally better than that of internally displaced persons, as the former often come under the protection of international donor agencies. They are settled in refugee camps that provide food and shelter. In contrast, the internally displaced usually receive scant international assistance and are on their own. Some become burdens on their reluctant friends and relatives, who themselves lack resources to survive during war and violence.

Effects on and consequences for women

The mass crimes described above profoundly affect women and gender relations. Their impacts and consequences can be discerned in the identities, family relationships, economic activities and political participation of women exposed to them. However, the effects on an individual are circumscribed by factors such as age, ethnicity, social and economic status, the nature and duration of conflict and the social and political milieux.

Psychological trauma and physical health problems

Mass crimes leave undeniable marks on women's psyches. Referring to the predicament of Mayan women in Guatemala, anthropologist Green wrote: "Women's bodies have become repositories of the painful experiences they have been unable to articulate as a result not only of being silenced but also because of the non-narratability of atrocious experiences."[6] Unfortunately this statement also applies to Bosnia, Cambodia, El Salvador and Rwanda. In all these countries, war-related mass crimes have traumatized women and children in particular. The psychological trauma of the victims of rape and other forms of sexual abuse is compounded by their social isolation. Often they are ostracized by their own families, friends and community. Newbury and Baldwin quote from the testimony of a Rwandan at the Fourth World Conference on Women at Beijing:

> Raped women are doubly punished by society. First, judicial practice does not grant them redress for rape as long as graphic evidence is not brought out into the open. Second, from society's point of view there is little sympathy, for at the moment men and children died without defense, these women used the sex card, selling their bodies to save their lives ... Thus they are judged from all sides, and even among their families they are not easily pardoned. Even worse, people reproach them for having preferred survival through rape.[7]

For example, rebel militia in Liberia, Sierra Leone and Mozambique abducted young women and kept them as sexual slaves. When the conflict was over, these women were abandoned by the militia. Because of the social stigma, their families and communities did not accept them back. The guilt and shame of the victims of sexual violence prevent them from seeking outside help, including medical assistance, without which they suffer chronic gynaecological problems. In Guatemala, Mayan women who witnessed violence or lost family members have suffered from psychological and physical ailments (*tristeza*) such as "chronic headaches, gastritis, chest pains, visual problems, respiratory infections, and psychological manifestations such as recurring dreams and nightmares, sadness, and depression". As Garrard-Burnett noted:

> "Tristeza" is also manifested in more amorphous physical ills such as "mournful heart" and sleep disturbances from nightmares and other types of compelling dreams. In the case of Maya victims in particular, disturbing dreams have a special significance, since dreams are considered to be a form of communication with the ancestors and are a rich reservoir of cultural interpretation.[8]

The truth is that the psychological wounds of mass crimes, although often invisible, continue to affect victims' attitudes, perceptions and behaviours throughout their lives. In many war-torn countries such as Bosnia, Cambodia and Rwanda, women continued to experience high levels of stress and anxiety in their daily lives and display typical signs of trauma, including depression, listlessness, chronic fatigue, anguish, psychological disabilities and recurrent recollections of traumatic incidents. Despite severe emotional trauma, these women demonstrated remarkable resilience and courage in surviving. Their sufferings often remained unvoiced, however, and were sometimes expressed through abusive relationships with their spouses or children. Most of these women continued undertaking their normal responsibilities, and this clinging to routine work may have helped them to cope with the trauma. Interestingly, in post-Soviet Georgia internally displaced women appeared to adjust better than their male counterparts. Although men became passive and moody, women took outside work to feed their families. Some attributed the women's behaviour to their nurturing nature. Others suggested that their comparatively low status within the family led women to be more willing than men to take on work below their skill level.[9]

Family roles and relationships

A common effect of many mass crimes is a growth in numbers of households that are headed by single women, as men are killed, disabled, imprisoned or away fighting. Although rare before the war in Cambodia, women-headed households constituted between 25 and 30 per cent of all families in the late 1990s. In the Ixcan region of Guatemala, women-headed households were not uncommon before the conflict, but their proportion increased during the war and later constituted an estimated 30–50 per cent of all households. In such households the traditional division of labour between men and women is blurred, with women assuming traditionally male roles – disciplining male children, building or repairing houses, dealing with community leaders and government officials, and fulfilling religious and social obligations. Most importantly, they have to feed and support their families singlehandedly.

The emergence of single-woman-headed households has significant implications for existing gender relations. Because these women play traditional male roles, they indirectly undermine existing gender stratification. Often they are treated by their male counterparts with greater consideration than traditional housewives or woman workers. In many cases they serve as role models for young women dissatisfied with their present status. The self-images of women who are heads of households improve, as they pride themselves on their struggles and achievements. In a comparative analysis of female heads of households in Cambodia and Sri Lanka, van der Wijk found:

> The women heads of households in both countries also experience positive elements in their changed roles. On a personal level women feel empowered by their increased capacity of planning activities in combination with nurturing children. They derive strength and confidence from doing it all themselves. Cambodian women said that they felt happy after establishing a good business in which they had made money and some enjoyed the freedom of handling the finances. The positive perceptions were more strongly emphasized by Cambodian women, while Sri Lankan women felt more strongly about the fact that their work left them with no time to themselves.[10]

The workload of women also increases during and after violent conflicts, as they have to assume greater economic and social responsibilities in view of growing poverty and hardships. These additional responsibilities, however, do not necessarily result in a corresponding decline in their household chores. They have to continue to perform tasks such as cooking, washing clothes and caring for children as well as spending more hours on farm work or other jobs. In Bosnia, Cambodia and Guatemala the workload of women drastically increased in the aftermath of mass crimes. In Georgia, many internally displaced women who started working in the informal sector to feed their families complained that their unemployed spouses refused to seek work and wasted their meagre resources on cigarettes or vodka.[11]

The growth in the number of orphans and unaccompanied children[12] also adds to their burden. Many children lose their parents during mass crimes; others are separated from their families during conflict and forced migration. Still others are abandoned by their parents because of severe economic or psychological stress. The burden of raising these children often falls on extended families or even neighbours, with women shouldering most of the responsibilities. In Rwanda the rapid exodus of hundreds of thousands of people created thousands of unaccompanied children. Women throughout the country immediately volunteered to care for them, in part as a protection of their ethnic group's future.

The experience of Cambodia and Rwanda also indicates that demographic imbalance caused by war crimes can contribute to a decline in the status of women in the family. For example, Judy Ledgerwood suggested that the traditional status of women was adversely affected by the surplus of "women of marriage age" in Cambodia.[13] Because of the post-conflict demographic imbalance, men found themselves in a better bargaining position. They have been able to offer lower bride prices, and easily divorce their spouses and find new wives. Faced with this situation, many women preferred to become second or third wives rather than remain unmarried.

There is some anecdotal evidence that mass crimes contribute to an increased incidence of domestic violence. For example, high rates of domestic violence against women have been reported in post-genocide Cambodia. A survey conducted in 1996 found that 16 per cent of women respondents were physically abused by their husbands, and half of them sustained injuries. In another survey, the Cambodian Women's Crisis Center noted that more than 27 per cent of women were battered by a member of their household, usually the spouse. In focus groups conducted by a USAID team, participants indicated that wife and child beating have become widespread in the country.[14] Many factors offer at least a partial explanation for this phenomenon. The genocide and prolonged conflict resulted in the institutionalization of a subculture of violence that condones family abuse. Under such situations, violent behaviour was seen as natural, and not aberrant. As both men and women were traumatized by the genocide, they were unable to control their tempers. The decline in women's status made them more susceptible to physical abuse by their spouses.

Expanded horizons and limited choices of exiles

Mass migration and settlement of refugees in camps tend to have some positive consequences for gender equity. They undermine traditional roles and relationships, as both men and women are exposed to new social and cultural environments. Often it is the first time in their lives that these refugees have stepped outside their villages or towns. As they struggle to carve a new life in unfamiliar surroundings, the hold on tradition declines, creating new opportunities for change.

Refugee camps increasingly provide educational and vocational activities for women, men and children. Literacy classes are held. Some camps even encourage women to acquire vocational training in the occupations traditionally assigned to men. For example, in Honduras, Salvadorian women refugees received training in camps in shoemaking, carpentry and mechanics, although only men were supposed to acquire such skills in their own country. Refugee camps now encourage women to assume administrative and technical responsibilities in the management of camp activities, which redefine their traditional roles. Camps also provide healthcare and family planning services. Some women find employment opportunities within or outside camps and are able to keep a part of the wages themselves.

Finally, many camps hold programmes to educate women about their rights. For example, in Honduras and Mexico camp officials organized workshops to raise gender awareness among women refugees. The camp personnel emphasized that women had the same rights and abilities as men. Often women officials become role models for the refugees. For example, because most workers in the camps in Honduras and Mexico were women, "the refugee population as a whole became familiar with seeing women in roles other than wife and mother".[15] One interesting feature of the Mexican camps for Mayan women was the presence of women's organizations, which became the major vehicles for the incorporation of women in the community. These organizations "promoted women's rights to be heard, to be educated, to organize, and to participate in the community".

Describing the impact of camps for refugees from El Salvador and Guatemala, Fagen and Yudelman observe:

> The conditions in the refugee camps for Guatemalans in Mexico, as for the Salvadorians in Honduras, obliged men and women to take on the new roles that broke with the traditions of their native villages. Like their Salvadorian counterparts, the Guatemalan women reported significant changes due to the refugee experience. And in a similar fashion, they learned that they had options apart from being wives and mothers.[16]

The authors add:

> Refugee women learned a wide range of new skills, including literacy, Spanish language (in the case of Guatemalans) and productive trades. They engaged for the first time in community activities and worked collectively. They made political contributions that were valued by the community as a whole, and in the process became more self-confident, aware of their rights, and more assertive.[17]

Thus the overall result of the refugee experience in camps is that the intellectual and social horizons of women expand. Many women become aware of their rights and responsibilities, and acquire new skills and attitudes.

The problem arises when women refugees return home at the end of hostilities. In most cases they are forced to revert back to their traditional life. Male members of the family, who were willing to tolerate new roles for women in camp life, want them to resume their traditional gender-based responsibilities and duties. For example, once the conflict ended in El Salvador and Guatemala, the spouses of the women refugees insisted that women focus on home and not on social and political issues. Moreover, women encounter social and economic barriers in using their acquired skills. Limited employment opportunities, for example, exist for vocationally trained women. Many girls are unable to go to school because of gender stereotyping, insecurity and the shortage of schools or long distances to get to them. The old social structures reproduce themselves, largely undermining the positive effects of the refugee experience. Thus despite their expanded skills and visions, the choices remain limited for female former refugees. This often causes some bitterness and frustration, especially among young and educated women, who feel constrained and marginalized in a restored gender order.

Despite these problems, some changes are always visible in the lives of these women. Often they learn the value of sanitation and family planning. Some learn to read and write, which enables them to interact better with government officials and other workers. Others find outside employment. For example, Mayan women who learned Spanish in Mexican camps were able to move to cities and find new employment. In both El Salvador and Guatemala, refugee women's experiences are likely to change the futures of their children. There are already indications in both cases that the younger returnees who came of age in the camps are seeking alternatives to traditional female roles.[18] Many Cambodian women refugees assumed major roles in running non-governmental organizations (NGOs) as a result of their training in camps on the Thai border.[19]

Increased poverty and its consequences

A major consequence of mass crimes is increased poverty and a sharp deterioration in the standard of living of the people. For example, in Bosnia, Cambodia, Mozambique and Rwanda poverty levels significantly increased after violent conflicts. There is also some evidence indicating that the number of women living in poverty increased disproportionately in many recent wars.[20]

The consequences of poverty are usually worse for women. Cultural, social and economic factors work to their disadvantage. Because women traditionally nurture their family, they usually sacrifice their own welfare for that of other family members during economic adversity. Moreover, since men control most of the assets, the household allocation of food and resources tends to be biased towards them. Consequently, there are proportionately larger reductions in nutrient intake for women than for men.[21] In addition, the health and education needs of girls receive less priority than those of boys in many families.

The economic conditions of three categories of women – returning refugees, single-woman-headed households and women dependent on public subsidies – tend to worsen during and after mass crimes.

The economic plight of women refugees usually aggravates on their return. While they live in refugee camps, they receive food and shelter and enjoy access to basic health and education facilities. But after repatriation they are generally on their own, with less consistent and often greatly reduced outside assistance. For example, repatriated Rwandan women faced enormous problems on their return. Their homes were either taken or destroyed. Often their lands had been appropriated by unscrupulous relatives or other farmers. As Hutus had participated in the genocide of the Tutsi population, Hutu women and their families were also suspects in the eyes of the government. It took years before they could settle down peacefully.

Single-woman-headed households also face serious economic and social constraints, resulting in extreme poverty. A major constraint is the lack of property rights over lands previously owned by parents or spouses. For example, in Cambodia, Mozambique and Rwanda widows had difficulty in acquiring legal rights to the land owned by their husbands. Until very recently, Rwandan women could not inherit land and property under customary law. Consequently, thousands of war widows were deprived of legal ownership of their husbands' or parents' farms. The situation was different in Cambodia, where laws provided for the legal ownership of land, but widows encountered obstacles in gaining legal possession because of their low social status and the indifference of local authorities. In Guatemala women had difficulty exercising newly legislated land ownership and inheritance rights because of institutional negligence, pervasive machismo and ignorance of their own rights.[22]

Women-headed agricultural households, particularly those headed by widows and divorcees, often lack the resources to purchase seeds, pesticides, fertilizers and starter livestock. Women farmers also experience shortages of farm labour. Lacking the resources to hire workers, they often have to depend on the generosity of their relatives and friends, which is not always forthcoming. In Guatemala, because Mayan women were not encouraged by tradition to cultivate corn, many had to force their young sons to perform the necessary work. In addition, new women farmers find it difficult to get technical advice on agricultural operations.

Agricultural extension services do not exist in most cases; even when available, they rarely reach women farmers. Finally, lacking the capacity to transport goods to bigger markets, women farmers often have to sell their agricultural surplus locally, thus depriving them of a fair price for their produce. The cumulative result is the abject poverty of these households in subsistence economies.

A substantial number of women-headed households do not own land or other assets. Women heading such households work as landless labourers or sharecroppers. They receive minimal compensation for their hard work and barely manage to feed their families. In urban areas most women work in the informal sector, carving out a living mainly through petty trading. Since many women lack the requisite skills, experience and education, only a small portion can secure employment in organized industrial and service sectors. The economic conditions of these households remain precarious in view of the desperate economic circumstances of post-conflict societies.

The last category is composed of poor women who depend on public subsidies. They often suffer when conflict begins and resources are relocated for military purposes. Their conditions still worsen during the post-conflict transition as a result of macroeconomic reforms. International financial institutions generally insist on economic stabilization through monetary and fiscal discipline, resulting in cuts in social expenditure. Although such reforms are essential for putting the economy on a sound footing, they impose heavy sacrifices on vulnerable groups, particularly women. The social safety-net programmes funded by the international community are usually not sufficient to make up the loss.

Expansion of public roles

Like their male counterparts, women participate in mass crimes. For example, former Serbian president Biljana Plavsic and Pauline Nyiramasuhuko, the former minister of family and health affairs in Rwanda, have been indicted for crimes against humanity. Nyiramasuhuko has also been accused of exhorting Hutus to rape Tutsi women. In Cambodia, El Salvador, Mozambique, Rwanda and Sri Lanka women joined militia and even participated in mass crimes. In many wars women have played supporting roles in military operations by running and managing auxiliary services such as health and intelligence operations. In addition, they have provided both moral and material support for many conflicts in the name of ideology or ethno-nationalism by organizing public meetings and marches, raising funds and mobilizing public opinion.[23]

Women also become active at the community level to provide relief to vulnerable populations during and after war crimes. For example, women in Bosnia-Herzegovina managed schools and daycare facilities and over-saw voluntary health services in seized communities. Women participated in the distribution of food aid in Rwanda. In El Salvador they founded organizations to press for the release of political prisoners and provide relief to families of the victims of political repression. In many recent civil wars women became more engaged in churches, schools, hospitals and private charities, usually volunteering their services.

Women can even take charge of local political institutions in the absence of men. This happened in El Salvador, where a substantial number of women were elected mayors: between 1985 and 1988, 33 out of 262 mayors (12.6 per cent) were women.[24] Because the women had organized themselves before the peace accords and the formation of political parties, when the conflict ended they were successful in obtaining seats in parliament. After the fall of the Pol Pot regime in Cambodia, women's representation in village councils drastically increased. Other countries, like Lebanon and Mozambique, witnessed a similar phenomenon. However, there are also instances when conflict had an adverse impact on women's public participation. For example, with the breakdown of political authority in Somalia, political power passed into the hands of clan elders. Councils of elders, which replaced government officials and party functionaries, consisted of males only and thus deprived women of any say in community affairs.[25]

In many recent civil wars women founded grassroots women's organizations to help victims of the conflict. Such organizations assisted the most vulnerable: the traumatized, sexually abused, destitute and widowed. Examples include Medica Zenica, which provided medical and psychological assistance to sexually abused women in Bosnia, Samiti, which helped destitute women in Bangladesh, and Koka, a Georgian co-operative farming society founded on the principle of mutual help. Micro-enterprise groups, although founded to provide group credit, also fall into this category.[26]

Mass crimes profoundly affect the status, roles and responsibilities of women and existing gender relations. They often create new opportunities for promoting gender equity and changes in the existing gender stratification. Yet there is some evidence that once violent conflicts are over, there is a retreat of women from public life. Barring the case of outstanding women leaders, most women who had assumed leadership positions during conflict revert back to their traditional roles. Three factors contribute to such retrenchment. First, the stress produced by mass crimes tends to generate nostalgia for traditional social and political orders in which women assumed marginal roles in public life. Second, women who shouldered heavy public burdens in addition to their family responsibilities become physically and emotionally exhausted and feel relieved to give up their social and political activism. Finally, men tend to assert their authority once they are free from war.

In lieu of a conclusion: Recommendations to the international community

The observations in this chapter can be summarized in the form of a number of recommendations that should be given particular consideration by the major multilateral and bilateral agencies involved in post-conflict reconstruction and peacebuilding.

Develop innovative, low-cost approaches to treat traumatized women and children

As discussed earlier, women are traumatized by war crimes and their psychological wounds continue to haunt them. The international community has supported some modest programmes for dealing with psychological trauma in Bosnia, Cambodia and Rwanda. These programmes included training local caregivers, teachers and health workers to identify the symptoms of trauma, establishing mental health programmes in hospitals and developing counselling services in health centres. But such programmes usually reached only a small fraction of the suffering women, and no precise information is available about their effectiveness. A major obstacle to the treatment of traumatized women is that counselling is very labour-intensive and therefore costly. Poor countries have neither the resources nor the institutional infrastructure to provide it on a large scale.

Therefore, the international community and national actors should support efforts to develop low-cost indigenous approaches to deal with psychological trauma. One possible approach is to use deep-rooted religious beliefs and value systems to provide solace to suffering women. For example, in Cambodia traumatized women often went to Buddhist pagodas to derive relief by meditation. In many tribal areas in Africa local healers have been able to help traumatized women and children. In Angola efforts were made to help child soldiers and traumatized boys by performing traditional rituals to exorcise bad spirits. Another approach is to help form women's groups where women can share their problems and experiences and provide psychological support to each other.

Focus on women's physical security

The decline of social control, disintegration of the community, poverty, unemployment, presence of demilitarized soldiers and ineffectiveness of law enforcement agencies tend to increase lawlessness and violence in post-conflict societies. Although all strata of society suffer, women and children are undoubtedly the worst victims. The international community has given scant attention to this problem.

Therefore, it is imperative that bilateral and multilateral agencies, international organizations and NGOs devise and implement programmes that can enhance physical security for women and children. Such programmes could include security sector reforms, greater representation of women in police forces and judicial processes, training for security staff on women's rights, establishment of peace committees to prevent the eruption of violence and special interventions for vulnerable youth.

Promote micro-credit programmes

The experience of post-conflict societies indicates that micro-enterprises serve both humanitarian and developmental goals, albeit to a limited extent. They provide livelihood to a large number of people and alleviate the urgent problems of hunger and malnutrition. Micro-credit programmes funded by the international community have usually been successful. Although not specifically targeted at women, most of the credit has gone to them. They have enabled poor, widowed, single heads of households and abused women to survive in the aftermath of mass crimes.[27]

An additional benefit of micro-credit programmes is that many women's groups formed to provide collective surety for loans develop attributes of support groups. Since the members share similar backgrounds and experiences, they are better able to relate to each other. The informal interactions in these groups have therapeutic value and mitigate inter-ethnic tension. In Rwanda, Newbury and Baldwin found that women's groups included both Tutsi (victims of genocide) and Hutu (the ethnic group responsible for genocide) members, helping each other to rebuild their shattered lives.[28]

Enforce women's human rights

Although in the aftermath of mass crimes human rights are universally emphasized and appropriate legal and regulatory frameworks are established, past experience indicates that women's rights are not rigorously enforced by law enforcement agencies. This has been particularly the case in those tradition-bound societies where women did not enjoy equal social and political rights. Therefore, the international and local communities should support additional measures to enforce women's human rights. They can fund programmes that create awareness about human rights through radio, television and print media. If and when possible, they can help establish comprehensive reporting systems to document abuses of women's human rights and support survivors in seeking redress for the crimes committed against them. Finally, they can support special training activities for law enforcement agencies so that they are in a better position to enforce women's rights.

Support implementation of property rights reforms for women

Women's lack of access to agricultural land and other productive assets is a major problem in post-conflict societies. As mentioned earlier, women are often denied legal rights to land and other resources owned by their dead husbands, fathers or other close relatives. Consequently, widows and single women are unable to engage in many productive activities, thereby suffering abject poverty and deprivation.

The international community has been pushing for property rights for women in post-conflict societies, and should continue these efforts. It should press not only for constitutional and legislative reforms but also for their implementation. It should support initiatives designed to build public support for women's property rights and actions to help resolve bureaucratic inertia and resistance.

Foster women's organizations

The international community has supported women's organizations in post-conflict societies both to channel humanitarian assistance and to empower women. Past studies have shown that in many countries, such as Bosnia, Cambodia, El Salvador and Rwanda, women organizations have played an important role in rehabilitating women victims of mass crimes and promoting women's economic and political rights.[29] In Afghanistan women's organizations have been providing a multitude of services that would otherwise be unavailable in many rural areas, running independent girls' schools, income-generation programmes, healthcare training and legal aid clinics. In fact, "These organizations are often the only place where women can go for support, education, protection, shelter or to escape violence, forced marriages and other threats."[30]

The international community should continue with greater vigour its policy of fostering women's organizations as an integral part of its efforts to rehabilitate and reconstruct post-conflict societies. It should adopt a policy of direct funding to women's community-based organizations so they can help female victims of war crimes as well as contribute to gender equality.

Promote political participation of women

Post-conflict societies offer openings for women's political participation. Often democratic constitutions are adopted, providing equality between men and women. Such constitutions also provide a legal framework for women's participation in the political arena. Because of their increased involvement in public life during conflict, some women not only acquire leadership skills and experience but also become aware of their political rights and responsibilities.

The international community has provided modest assistance in the past to encourage women to participate in political affairs. It should increase such assistance, and consider developing additional programmes to facilitate greater representation for women in post-conflict elections, assist women candidates in subsequent elections on a non-partisan basis and support women's advocacy organizations engaged in promoting women's participation in local and national affairs.

Notes

1. The data and information for this chapter were collected during the course of a six-nation study on women and women's organizations in post-conflict societies which the author directed for the US Agency for International Development. The study involved fieldwork in Bosnia, Cambodia, El Salvador, Georgia, Guatemala and Rwanda. The results are published in Kumar, Krishna (ed.) (2001) *Women and Civil War: Impact, Organizations, and Action*, Boulder, CO: Lynne Rienner, available at http://pdf.usaid.gov/pdf_docs/PNADO649.pdf.

2. Organisation for Economic Co-operation and Development (1999) *Guidance for Evaluating Humanitarian Assistance in Complex Emergencies*, OECD/DAC Working Party on Aid Evaluation, Paris: OECD.

3. This finding has been emphasized in numerous studies and investigations. For example, see Stephen, Lynn, Serena Cosgrove and Kelley Ready (2000) "The Impact of Conflict on Women", paper by commissioned by USAID Center for Development Information and Evaluation, Washington, DC; Garrard Burnett, Virginia (2000) "Gender and Violence in Guatemala", paper commissioned by USAID Center for Development Information and Evaluation, Washington, DC.

4. Kumar, Krishna (2001) *Aftermath: Women and Women's Organizations in Postconflict Societies*, Washington, DC: USAID.

5. Garrard Burnett, note 3.

6. Green, Linda (1994) "Fear as a Way of Life", *Cultural Anthropology* 9(2), pp. 227–256.

7. Kumar, Krishna (2001) "Civil Wars, Women, and Gender Relations: An Overview", in Krishna Kumar (ed.) *Women and Civil War: Impact, Organizations, and Action*, Boulder, CO: Lynne Rienner, pp. 5–78, available at http://pdf.usaid.gov/pdf_docs/PNADO649.pdf. See also Kumar, Krishna (2000) "Aftermath: Women in Postgenocide Rwanda", Working Paper No. 303, USAID, Washington, DC.

8. Garrard Burnett, note 3.

9. Kumar (2001), note 7.

10. van der Wijk, Dieneke (1997) "The Human Side of Conflict: Coping Strategies of Women Heads of Households in Four Villages in Sri Lanka and Cambodia", report for Oxfam UK Gender and Learning Team, London.

11. Buck, Thomas with Alice Morton, Susan Allen Nan and Feride Zurikashvili (2000) "Aftermath: Effects of Conflict on Internally Displaced Women in Georgia", Working Paper No. 305, USAID, Washington, DC.

12. The term "unaccompanied children" refers to those who have lost their parents during the fighting or while migrating. Children are not considered orphans unless it is known that their parents have been killed.

13. Ledgerwood, Judy (1996) "Politics and Gender: Negotiating Conceptions of the Ideal Woman in Present Day Cambodia", *Asia Pacific Viewpoint* 37(2), p. 139.

14. All these studies and findings are cited in Kumar, Krishna, Hannah Baldwin and Judy Benjamin (2000) "Aftermath: Women and Women's Organizations in Postconflict Cambodia", Working Paper No. 307, USAID, Washington, DC.

15. Fagen, Patricia Wess and Selly W. Yudelman (2001) "El Salvador and Guatemala: Refugee Camps and Repatriation Experience", in Krishna Kumar (ed.) *Women and Civil War: Impact, Organizations, and Action*, Boulder, CO: Lynne Rienner, p. 81. See also Vázquez, Norma (1999) "Refugee and Returnee Women: Skills Acquired in Exile and Their Application in Peacetime," Project Report, Promoting Women in Development Program, El Salvador, November.

16. Fagen and Yudelman, ibid., p. 86.

17. Ibid.

18. Ibid., p. 92

19. Kumar, Baldwin and Benjamin, note 14.

20. Ibid.

21. Dercon, Stefan and Pramila Krishnan (2000) "Vulnerability, Seasonality and Poverty in Ethiopia", *Journal of Development Studies* 36(6), pp. 25–53.

22. Garrard Burnett, note 3.

23. This is highlighted by several published and unpublished studies referred to in Kumar, note 4.

24. Stephen, Cosgrove and Ready, note 3. Also Ready, Kelley, Lynn Stephen and Serena Cosgrove (2001) "Women's Organizations in El Salvador: History, Accomplishments, and International Support", in Krishna Kumar (ed.) *Women and Civil War: Impact, Organizations, and Action*, Boulder, CO: Lynne Rienner, pp. 183–203. These details are also given in Kumar, note 4.

25. Kumar, note 4.

26. Morton, Alice, Susan Allen Nan, Thomas Buck and Feride Zurikashvili (2000) "After the Turmoil: Women's Organizations in Postconflict Georgia", Working Paper, USAID/CDIE/Development Alternatives, Washington, DC.

27. Kumar, note 4.

28. See Newbury, Catharine and Hannah Baldwin (2001) "Confronting the Aftermath of Conflict: Women's Organizations in Postgenocide Rwanda", in Kumar Krishna (ed.) *Women and Civil War: Impact, Organizations, and Action*, Boulder, CO: Lynne Rienner, pp. 97–128.

29. Case studies on the role of women's organizations in Bosnia, Cambodia, El Salvador, Georgia, Guatemala and Rwanda are presented in Kumar, note 1.

30. Womankind Worldwide (2008) "Taking Stock Update: Afghan Women and Girls Seven Years On", Womankind Worldwide, London, February, available at www.womankind.org.uk/wp-content/uploads/2011/02/taking-stock-final-proof-14-Feb-08.pdf.

4

Victimization, empowerment and the impact of UN peacekeeping missions on women and children: Lessons from Cambodia and Timor-Leste

Sumie Nakaya

The paradox of post-conflict reconstruction – the concurrent empowerment and victimization of women – is not unique to Cambodia and Timor-Leste. The post-conflict peacebuilding process involves both institutional reform and social readjustment to the legacies of civil war, which also defines post-war gender relations. While this chapter focuses on the role of the United Nations in Cambodia and Timor-Leste, with a particular focus on peacekeeping missions, its implications are relevant to other transition contexts. The author travelled to Cambodia and Timor-Leste in July 2001 to assess the impact of armed conflict on women and their correlative role in peacebuilding as part of a global assessment supported by the UN Development Fund for Women (UNIFEM). In extensive consultations on gender issues with civil society, legislators, government officials and representatives of multilateral and bilateral donors, it was agreed that violence against women and children had emerged as one of the most pressing issues in both Cambodia and Timor-Leste.

In Timor-Leste, despite the massive mobilization and empowerment of women's groups for the first democratic elections in July 2001, the continued prevalence of violence against women and children was evident.[1] Since 1975 the Indonesian military and militias have reportedly raped, tortured and assaulted women and girls on a massive scale, although irreplaceable data indicating such atrocities were destroyed during the heightened conflict in 1999.[2] Many women were abducted and brought to military-run brothels, or taken as "local wives" by military members, while spouses of prominent leaders of the independence movement were

Defying victimhood: Women and post-conflict peacebuilding, Schnabel and Tabyshalieva (eds), United Nations University Press, 2012, ISBN 978-92-808-1201-5

targeted for punishment and surveillance.[3] In April 2002 UNICEF reported that although political and social violence had plummeted since 1999, child abuse and commercial exploitation had increased – mostly conducted by young males who perpetrated sexual exploitation and assault, including roughly 60 per cent of the reported cases involving children.[4]

In Cambodia the sheer extent of sexual violence and exploitation indicated the disadvantaged status of women and children in the post-conflict society. Reported incidents of rape increased 30 per cent from 1999 to 2000.[5] There were an estimated 14,000 sex workers throughout the country, and 35 per cent of commercial sex workers in Phnom Penh brothels were children under 18 years old.[6] The majority of children were forced into the sex industry – of those 45 per cent were sold by abductors, 50 per cent by family members and 5 per cent by boyfriends.[7] The lowest age of sex workers rapidly declined from 18 (October 1992) to 15 (April 1993), coinciding with the arrival of the UN peacekeeping mission. By 1995 minors (12–17 years old) comprised about 31 per cent of the sex workers in Phnom Penh and 11 other provinces; in Takeo, almost 50 per cent of sex workers were below the age of 17.[8]

Two contrasting portraits of women emerged in Timor-Leste. The first was positive: Timorese women won 26 per cent of the seats in the Constituent Assembly in July 2001, despite a lack of electoral gender quotas. The second, however, was more troublesome: domestic violence continued to be pervasive and nearly 40 per cent of all reported crime in 2001 involved violence against women and girls, such as rape, attempted rape and sexual assault.[9] Similarly, in Cambodia domestic violence had become endemic. According to a survey carried out by the Project against Domestic Violence in 1996, one in every six women in Cambodia had been a victim of domestic violence, with the rates higher in areas where the Khmer Rouge engaged in intense fighting.[10]

In both Cambodia and Timor-Leste changing gender roles in post-war households and the failure of states to provide educational and socio-economic opportunities marginalized women and children, in part reversing the leadership role women played during the war as the head of a household or the primary source of income. For instance, before the peace process began in Cambodia, the majority of workers in state industrial enterprises – 7,000 of 11,000 – were women, due in part to the absence of men during the war.[11] In contrast, in 1998 women constituted only 21 per cent of all government and state enterprise workers.[12] According to a Cambodian female senator:

> During war, more men were killed than women. Men had to witness, or even help the Khmer Rouge kill others. Now these men are back at home, extremely

frustrated and traumatized, with no jobs and no "status" at home. They beat their wives. Who are the victims here?[13]

Faced with the magnitude of sexual violence and exploitation, civil society groups in Cambodia and Timor-Leste mobilized social support networks, provided shelter and medical and psychological care for the survivors and raised awareness of women's and children's rights and gender equality. Their governments, too, took measures to curb domestic violence and trafficking. Yet violence against women and children continued to flourish in these war-ruined societies and appeared intractable.

What mechanisms sustain violence against women and children in both times of war and times of peace? This chapter attempts to capture a multiplicity of responses to such violence in larger institutional contexts governing the political, legal and social status of women and children in a transition from war to "peacetime". Institutional frameworks, such as the rule of law, determine not only the extent of prevailing violence against women and children, but also violence in society at large and the extent to which the principles of gender equality and respect for human rights are adopted and implemented.

Institutional variables include the role of international interventions, as international involvement in transitional reforms has a critical effect on the emerging political, legal and social structures of war-torn countries. The United Nations has increasingly assumed the administration of transitional processes, as in the UN Transitional Authority for Cambodia (UNTAC) and the UN Transitional Authority in East Timor (UNTAET). In Cambodia and Timor-Leste, in the absence of a legitimate, functioning government, the UN administration was delegated sovereign powers for a mandated period to carry out critical steps towards the consolidation of peace and the establishment of stable, democratic governance. In this process, security sector reforms that encompassed "the deployment of well-trained police officers, closer military cooperation, a more sustained focus on judicial reconstruction and conceptualizing law and order issues"[14] were immediate and critical tasks to restore law and order and create conducive environments that would enable institution-building. In this regard, the performance of the United Nations, particularly in the area of law enforcement, "invariably affects not only the credibility of the UN mission and the image of local law enforcement agencies but also the security of the local population".[15]

International interventions in the transitional period have other advantages. First, international administration of local authority can generally represent high human rights and gender equality standards in accordance with international benchmarks, including the Convention for the Elimination of All Forms of Discrimination against Women (CEDAW) and the Beijing Platform for Action. Second, as the international administration becomes the *de facto* government, it can exercise influence in the design of the state system, thereby advocating gender equality in constitutional, legislative, judicial and electoral reforms. The establishment of a gender affairs unit in UNTAET largely achieved these goals by mainstreaming gender perspectives in the UN mission planning and management and interim national decision-making process at the Transitional National Council[16] (see Chapter 10 in this volume for the background to gender mainstreaming in peacekeeping and Security Council resolutions). However, the conduct of peacekeepers in both Cambodia and Timor-Leste largely discredited the legitimacy of the operations in the eyes of the local populations because of the association of the mission with the proliferation of sexual exploitation of local women and children.

This chapter focuses on institutional variables, including the rule of law and reforms of criminal codes, police, the judiciary and civil and family laws; the peacekeeping economy and its impact on sexual exploitation of women and children; and transitional governance at the national level. The two case studies highlight that women and children are inherently vulnerable in the rapid shift towards political and economic liberalization which characterizes the prevailing approach to peacebuilding. In the words of Roland Paris:

> A single paradigm – liberal internationalism – appears to guide the work of international agencies engaged in peacebuilding. The central tenet of this paradigm is the assumption that the surest foundation for peace, both within and between states, is market democracy, that is, a liberal democratic polity and a market-oriented economy. Peacebuilding is in effect an enormous experiment in social engineering ... This paradigm, however, has not been a particularly effective model for establishing stable peace. Paradoxically, the very process of political and economic liberalization has generated destabilizing side effects in war-shattered states, hindering the consolidation of peace and in some cases even sparking renewed fighting.[17]

Without recognizing the potentially destabilizing and negative impact of prevailing peacebuilding models on marginalized groups such as women, children and other disadvantaged populations, and thereby the need for safeguarding mechanisms, post-conflict institutional arrangements run the risk of further limiting participation of women and children and sustaining the existing (and often patriarchal) structure of power which continues to govern gender relations in many post-conflict societies, particularly at the community and family levels.

Rule of law

The rule of law is the first and foremost, although not the only, step to combat violence against women and children and a culture of impunity. The establishment of an effective judiciary is a priority for both peace maintenance, in which a functioning criminal justice system is the core feature of law and order,[18] and the observance and implementation of statutory laws guaranteeing the rights of women and children. Gender equality and the protection of women and children in the rule of law encompass gender-sensitive reforms of basic and fundamental laws, including the constitution, criminal law and civil and family law, as well as post-war justice, such as war crimes tribunals.

Constitutional reform

Both East Timorese and Cambodian constitutions use progressive language with regard to human rights and gender equality.[19] For instance, the East Timorese constitution includes a provision protecting children born outside of marriage and recognizes the citizenship of children born of rape by Indonesians or parented by international peacekeeping personnel.[20] The Cambodian constitution mandates specific attention to rural women, protects domestic workers with equal pay and provides maternity leave from work. These gender-sensitive provisions are due in large part to women's participation in the respective constitutional drafting processes. In Timor-Leste a coalition of national and international organizations such as Oxfam, the UNTAET Gender Affairs Unit and UNIFEM established a gender and constitution working group, which reviewed various constitutional models from Portugal, Indonesia and Japan, among others, from a gender perspective and involved local women in consultations. Subsequently, Timorese women formulated a charter of women's rights, which was included in the constitution.[21] Similarly, in Cambodia UNIFEM supported consultations among women from all social and economic backgrounds on gender-specific dimensions of the constitution.

In both constitutions, however, the citizenship of minority women and children remains ambiguous. The East Timorese constitution does not permit dual citizenship,[22] thereby excluding from the definition of "original citizens" Indonesian migrants to Timor-Leste, including women and children trafficked from Indonesia to Timor-Leste prior to 1999.[23] Similarly, the Cambodian constitution limits the definition of citizenship to "Khmer citizens of both sexes", and treats the ethnic Vietnamese and Chinese merely as "residents".

Penal codes

Legal systems in Cambodia and Timor-Leste, other than as embodied within their constitutions, were in a state of flux as a result of multiple coexisting legal traditions. This legal pluralism involved traditional customary laws that substituted for the collapse of the judiciary during war, colonial/foreign laws and varying approaches adopted by the United Nations.[24] In Timor-Leste there were three officially operating laws: Indonesian laws, including the Indonesian penal code, which were designated as a basic legal framework by UNTAET; UNTAET regulations, including the Transitional Rules of Criminal Procedures; and a broad set of international laws introduced by UNTAET, including CEDAW and the Convention on the Rights of the Child. This arrangement was introduced to avoid a legal vacuum in the initial phase of the transitional administration, and was made in consultation with local lawyers who had obtained law degrees and training in the Indonesian legal system.[25] However, it was done without thorough review, clarification or systematization of the three different legal systems, in part due to UNTAET resource constraints that prevented it from undertaking a comprehensive assessment of those legal gaps within its limited duration.[26]

For most day-to-day matters, particularly in criminal offences, the Indonesian laws continued to apply, despite the antagonism and mistrust among local populations towards any state apparatus of Indonesian origin. Although UNTAET maintained that Indonesian laws were only applicable when consistent with international human rights laws, some of the UNTAET-issued regulations were themselves contradictory to the Indonesian-based framework, thereby creating confusion and at times arbitrary application of different normative and implementation standards.[27] For instance, the Indonesian penal code did not provide adequate protection of women and children from sexual violence and exploitation. It defined sexual offences as "crimes against decency" and criminalized adultery,[28] but it did not recognize marital rape and attempted assault as crimes,[29] nor did it treat domestic violence as a distinct crime. It did not regulate sexual crimes committed by the state, either.[30] UNTAET decriminalized adultery in 2001, but did not address other aspects of criminal laws on sexual violence.

In addition, UNTAET permitted the continued use of alternative justice mechanisms at the local level.[31] In cases of sexual and domestic violence, these traditional justice mechanisms were commonly used at the *suku* (clan or subvillage) and village levels. Disputes at the community level, including reports of violence against women, were often resolved through mediation and compensation, such as the payment of dowry to the victim's family, agreed among village chiefs/elders and men representing the families of the victim and offender.[32] Traditional definitions and treatment of violence against women and children are often incompatible with international standards. As a result, as Amnesty International's report on the justice systems in Timor-Leste notes, "The chronic delay in establishing an effective criminal justice system by UNTAET has reinforced an existing lack of confidence in formal justice systems and contributed to a continued reliance on alternative forms of justice [with the result that] ... Traditional justice and other informal mechanisms are being applied inconsistently without effective monitoring by, or full integration into, the formal judicial system."[33]

Similarly, Cambodia's legal system remained problematic. With UNTAC's civilian mandates including the supervision of judicial reforms and law enforcement, French and American lawyers were contracted to draft a far-reaching set of criminal justice provisions compatible with criminal justice systems in liberal democracies. Adopted in September 1992, the Supreme National Council Decree on Criminal Law and Procedure, or the so-called UNTAC penal code, provided a 75-article basic framework of criminal justice. In January 1993 the Cambodian government adopted its Law on Criminal Procedure, which applied concurrently with the UNTAC penal code.[34] The relationship between the two sets of criminal procedures remained ambiguous, and early enactment of a code of criminal procedure and a penal code was urgently needed to synthesize the two laws. According to the Human Rights Task Force on Cambodia:

> The essential legal and other structures and process to maintain the rule of law are still very weak and subverted by endemic corruption at all levels ... the National Assembly – plagued by political in-fighting – has yet to pass critical laws that can effectively protect and promote the rights of women and children ... Some of these laws [pre-UNTAC French law, the UNTAC penal code and the 1993 law], particularly those relating to women and children, are either weak in terms of clear implementing provisions, contradictory to each other, or not consistent with basic human rights principles.[35]

The new penal codes did not criminalize domestic violence and marital rape, although Cambodian women's groups had lobbied vigorously to change this through legislation since 1994. The bill they helped introduce was still pending. More troubling, however, was that the latest draft of the penal code even proposed to reduce the minimum sentence for rape to one to five years from five to 10 years under the 1992 UNTAC penal code. Neither the penal code nor the code of criminal procedures had yet passed.[36] In lieu of structural reforms of legal mechanisms, local women's groups organized a self-help system, providing local police officers with gender training and organizing workshops for community leaders to raise awareness on violence against women and children.[37]

Consequently, in both Cambodia and Timor-Leste the inconsistent and incoherent adoption of different legal norms and traditions created a great deal of confusion among local populations, as well as national and international law enforcement officials, and placed onerous burdens on the scarce resources of local legal structures. In Cambodia courts preferred to rely on the 1993 law, ignoring the greater protections afforded to defendants in the 1992 UNTAC penal code.[38] Despite its support for CEDAW, the Convention on the Rights of the Child and other international human rights instruments, UNTAET seemed content to accept the role of traditional justice forms for "minor crimes", without defining what constituted a minor crime.[39] UN Civilian Police (CIVPOL), entrusted to restore and maintain law and order until the local police services were fully established, were not familiar with the complex mix of various legal jargons, had received no training on the substance of these laws and did not know which laws to apply under varying circumstances.[40] In some instances, including those involving rape, CIVPOL deferred to traditional law and no attempt was made to charge the case formally under Indonesian law or UNTAET rules.[41] Language barriers, lack of competence and professional misconduct also undermined CIVPOL's efficacy.[42]

In response to the growing criticism concerning the lack of protection of women and children, UNTAET established vulnerable persons' units (VPUs) within CIVPOL, first in Dili and subsequently in other districts. VPU Dili had female officers and translators dedicated to responding to violence against women and children, and worked with the women's group Fokupers to provide shelter and psychosocial support to survivors of sexual violence. During the author's field research in July 2001, there were two survivors with cases under investigation referred to Fokupers by VPU Dili. In other districts, however, women rarely knew of the VPU and often one CIVPOL officer was simply appointed as a VPU focal point.[43]

Civil and family law

Reforms of civil codes and family law also faced considerable delay. The task of reforming civil and family law was complicated by the breakdown of family institutions during the war. In Cambodia in particular, the Khmer Rouge sought to undermine family unity by the mass movement of urban populations to rural areas, which separated many families. It also did so by encouraging people to spy on their own families and promoting mass marriages. The breakdown of social fabric, the psychological effects of violence and oppression and the lack of community-based support systems during the conflict accounted for widespread violence within families in post-conflict Cambodia, leaving few solutions available to abused women and children. Existing civil and family laws in Cambodia and Timor-Leste not only made divorce difficult, but also provided few civil remedies in cases of divorce based on domestic violence.[44]

In Cambodia the 1989 Law on Marriages and the Family called for reconciliation as an initial and ongoing response to divorce requests. Court officials were required to dissuade a person from seeking divorce.[45] Divorce requests based on domestic violence were covered under the provision of "cruelly beating" (Article 39), thereby implicitly permitting some degree of violence before a strong-enough claim for a divorce request could be made.[46] Similarly, the Indonesian Marriage Law (1974) provides that divorce shall be carried out only before a court of law and only after the court has endeavoured to reconcile the parties. Domestic violence falls under "cruelty or mistreatment endangering life", suggesting that lesser, non-life-threatening violence is acceptable.[47] Although divorce may be the only viable option to escape domestic violence, these legal barriers constrained women from seeking divorce. Many women, without prospects of remarriage, gaining sufficient income or receiving state support, ultimately chose to stay in their marriage despite violence against themselves and their children.

War crimes tribunals and truth and reconciliation commissions

The pursuit of post-war justice strengthens the sense of justice and confidence in the rule of law, if the process is carried out properly. Legal proceedings on crimes committed during the war should always promote transparency and accountability, improve the local rule of law and contribute to collective memory in national catharsis and further reconciliation.[48] Post-war justice thus often focuses on a restorative approach that prioritizes the restoration of relationships rather than inflicting punishment.[49] For instance, psychologists at Cambodia's Center for Social Development argued that trials could help the Cambodian population (up to 30 per cent of whom still suffer from post-traumatic stress disorder) deal with their personal wounds.[50] For the same reason, however, if improperly and inadequately planned and conducted, the pursuit of post-war justice could undermine trust in the rule of law and result in a culture of impunity.

After long and painful negotiations, in January 2001 Cambodia's National Assembly adopted the Law on the Establishment of Extraordinary Chambers in the Courts of Cambodia for the Prosecution of Crimes Committed during the Period of Democratic Kampuchea. At the insistence of the Cambodian government, the court took the form of a hybrid trial in which the Cambodian judges constituted the majority of decision-makers. Now, sexual violence could be prosecuted as a crime against humanity, as a breach of the Geneva Convention, or as homicide, torture or persecution under the 1956 Cambodian penal code. However, the trial was intended only for senior leaders of the Khmer Rouge, many of whom had already been granted amnesty for surrendering to the government. Moreover, the efficiency and impartiality of the trial were questioned by international legal experts in light of the scarce resources of the Cambodian judicial institutions and the lack of judicial independence from state interventions.

Timor-Leste began investigating and prosecuting "serious crimes" in the District Court of Dili, which involved cases of genocide, crimes against humanity, war crimes, torture and certain violations of the Indonesian penal code – including murder and sexual violence – that had taken place in 1999.[51] However, the Serious Crimes Unit, comprising predominantly international judges and staff, "was viewed with much anger by East Timorese jurists, who felt that they had been excluded from the process and that the atrocity cases, which they had previously been dealing with, were being taken away from them by the international community".[52] Furthermore, the Serious Crimes Unit did not try "lesser" crimes and crimes committed prior to 1999, which included a large number of cases involving rape, sexual slavery and sexual assault of women and children perpetrated by Indonesian military and militias.

In search of a workable alternative, the East Timorese proposed the Commission for Reception, Truth and Reconciliation in Timor-Leste, which was established by UNTAET in July 2001 (Regulation 2001/10). Unlike the Serious Crimes Unit, the commission was headed by seven national commissioners and staffed by East Timorese, with the logistical support of a small number of international technical advisers.[53] The commission was intended to address lesser-offence crimes by seeking truth and facilitating grassroots reconciliation. For the survivors of sexual violence, this truth and reconciliation commission was a better venue for legal redress and remedies.

Peacekeeping economy

The arrival of large-scale peacekeeping missions corresponded to an increase in sexual violence and the exploitation of women and children in two ways. First, the presence of large, foreign, externally supplied missions created an inflationary economy that was particularly destabilizing in poor countries such as Cambodia, where such an economy had become "infamous for the rapid development of dual economies that had colonial overtones".[54] The economic boom that exclusively centred on construction, trade and the service sector aimed at foreign consumption in Phnom Penh relegated women to being the primary employees in restaurants, bars, hotels and shops. Job security was non-existent, as peacekeeping economies tend to be unsustainable and bound to downsize dramatically once the international presence ends. In Timor-Leste the Dili-centred emergence of a US$-based economy in one of the world's poorest nations created a considerable urban-rural disparity. Although UNTAET officials recognized the impact of UNTAET's eventual withdrawal on the local economy – and on women employees in the service sector – no concrete response had been developed.[55]

Vulnerability and exploitation of women and children in a peacekeeping economy are exacerbated by the failure of peacekeeping missions to provide skills training, stable income-generating jobs, education and community development in rural areas. With the World Bank pushing for downsizing the civil service, Cambodian women, even those with education and public service experience, found it difficult to get employment in the government sector. UNTAC also failed to recruit local women in the peacekeeping mission. For instance, November 1992 figures showed that only 10–15 per cent of the 6,000 Cambodians employed by UNTAC were women, and no woman occupied one of UNTAC's top 10 positions or served as their deputies.[56] In contrast, UNTAET and its national counterpart, the East Timor Transitional Authority, made a systematic effort to recruit women for at least 30 per cent of all positions. As of August 2001 the 30 per cent goal was reached in the departments of education, health and foreign affairs.[57]

Peacekeepers reportedly exploited local women and children sexually. For instance, with the arrival of UNTAC, the number of sex workers in Phnom Penh alone leaped from 6,000 in 1991 to 20,000 by the end of 1992, which was in large part attributed to the fast-growing demand for such services by international UNTAC personnel.[58] As a token of numerous complaints of rape and sexual exploitation by peacekeepers, 170 people signed a letter to the special representative of the Secretary-General complaining of sexual exploitation and harassment by UNTAC and calling for measures to redress sexual harassment, convene an advisory committee on gender and ensure the immediate and widespread dissemination of codes of conduct. In response, UNTAC set up an office to handle complaints. With the departure of UNTAC, the number of sex workers decreased to the range of 4,000–10,000 in 1993. In Timor-Leste two members of the Pakistani army engineer battalion were sent home in disgrace after being found guilty of "inappropriate behaviour" involving East Timorese women. Several Jordanian soldiers were expected to face charges at the local court after a UNTAET investigation concluded that strong grounds for prosecution were found over alleged sexual misconduct.

The sexual exploitation of women and children within the peacekeeping economy is premised on an illegal war economy that generally develops during the war, "partly as a result of people's coping strategies and sometimes based on smuggling and/or drug production, trafficking, or on extraction of natural resources".[59] In Cambodia the Khmer Rouge completely prohibited voluntary migration, trafficking and prostitution. The trafficking and exploitation of non-Cambodian children, most of whom (85–95 per cent) were Vietnamese, began after the fall of the Khmer Rouge. Cambodia became a hub for sending, transiting and receiving trafficked women and children, and it was widely believed that high-ranking officials in border control, customs, police and internal affairs were involved in the trafficking and prostitution businesses that were run by both Khmers and Vietnamese.

Until 2002 the United Nations did not have clear, coherent policies that could guide or regulate staff interaction with local populations. It also did not have a permanent mechanism in place to monitor, investigate and prosecute charges against peacekeeping personnel. Although voluntary codes of conduct were established for peacekeepers – but not for civilian personnel in peacekeeping missions or humanitarian and development aid workers – the sanctioning of conduct of UN peacekeeping troops is left to the military courts or judicial systems of the sending states. The maintenance of professional conduct within each mission varied depending on the level of gender sensitivity of the mission leadership at the highest level. UNTAET's relative success in gender mainstreaming was owed in large part to the leadership of the special representative of the Secretary-General, Sergio Viera de Mello, who maintained regular consultations with local women's groups and took steps in August 2001 to revoke the diplomatic immunity of peacekeepers when evidence of rape was confirmed.[60]

In early 2002 the UNHCR (Office of the UN High Commissioner for Refugees) and Save the Children UK released a study on "Sexual Violence and Exploitation: The Experience of Refugee Children in Liberia, Guinea and Sierra Leone", which featured accusations by children and adolescents in refugee and IDP (internally displaced person) camps of sexual exploitation and violence against them by mainly male, locally hired aid workers as well as UN peacekeepers and other males with authority and/or resources.[61] In response, the UN Inter-Agency Standing Committee established the Task Force on Protection from Sexual Exploitation and Abuse in Humanitarian Crises, which developed a plan of action, including new codes of conduct and core principles on the prevention of sexual exploitation and abuse.

Governance

Although recent international peacebuilding interventions are largely guided by liberal internationalism, according to which transitions to democracy and a market economy are the major areas of institution-building, gender-insensitive planning and management of this process can easily undermine instead of promoting women's empowerment. In Cambodia democratization reduced the number of women in decision-making. During the Vietnamese occupation, women occupied 21 of 117 seats (18 per cent) in the National Assembly and five seats (23 per cent) in the 21-member Central Committee.[62] The 1993 elections saw only seven women (5 per cent) in the 122-member National Assembly. None of the ministers was a woman. This happened despite the fact that women constituted 56 per cent of registered voters and 58 per cent of actual voters.[63] Women constituted approximately 0.5 per cent of village chieftains, with no women at the district or provincial levels.[64] Five years later, in the 1998 National Assembly elections, women received only 8.2 per cent of the vote; in 2003 they won almost 18 per cent in the National Assembly.[65] After the 2008 election women represent 21 per cent in the National Assembly.[66]

Women's political empowerment and participation are not ends unto themselves, but part of the post-conflict democratic process in which decision-making power is transferred primarily from those who were waging war to every citizen on a basis of equality. Contributions to this process stem not only from the fact that women constitute a sizeable constituency, if not the majority, but also because they have intimate knowledge of the diverse and complex needs of war-affected families and communities. Women and girls constitute the majority of single heads of household, and they know and represent the needs of the families and communities they had cared for during times of war. Thus the participation of women from all kinds of backgrounds – refugees, IDPs, mothers, widows, girls, minority and/or indigenous groups – is critical for structural and social transformations during peace negotiations and post-conflict reconstruction. Yet women continued to be marginalized in post-war decision-making structures due to gender-discriminatory policies, attitudes and behaviours that pre-date the conflict.

One of the common safeguards that are considered to increase women's representation in the electoral process is the introduction of quotas. Statutory quotas require parties to recruit a certain number of women candidates. These quotas might be specified by the constitution or national legislation such as an electoral law. Informal quotas might be voluntarily adopted by political parties.[67] In Cambodia, women's groups participating in the UNIFEM-supported consultations prior to the 1993 elections demanded the introduction of a 30 per cent quota, which was rejected by the political leadership.

Similarly, in Timor-Leste women's groups demanded the introduction of quotas for the July 2001 elections, but the National Council (an interim legislative body preceding the Constituent Assembly) passed the electoral regulation without reference to the proposal. During the intensive negotiations between the council and several women's groups, UNTAET did not forcefully intervene in favour of quotas, as UNTAET's Political Affairs Division and the UN Department of Political Affairs in New York were reluctant to set a precedent for UN policies supporting quotas. According to East Timorese women and other sources, UNTAET's Political Affairs Division even lobbied against the quotas, particularly as they concerned the National Council. A prominent East Timorese member of the Constituent Assembly summarized the views of East Timorese women as follows:

> We experienced threats from UNTAET's Electoral Affairs Division; at one stage, there was a threat that they would pull out and they would not run the elections in Timor-Leste. They were also telling us that they thought the inclusion of quotas would detract from free and fair elections because it would force political parties to choose certain types of candidates. The electoral affairs division of UNTAET asked the election assistance division in New York for their comment on this issue. The response was that UNTAET has exclusive responsibility for holding free and fair elections in Timor-Leste and while some countries do have quotas for women and other groups, other democratic countries vehemently oppose quotas. This would include members of the Security Council. Electoral quotas for women or any other group do not constitute international best practice for elections.[68]

To promote gender equality in post-conflict reconstruction, women also called for establishment of a national women's machinery. In Cambodia the Ministry of Women's and Veteran's Affairs was established in 1995, replacing the Cambodian Women's Association, a gender wing of the Vietnamese-installed government. In Timor-Leste heated discussions took place concerning the future location of the equivalent of UNTAET's Gender Affairs Unit after the July 2001 elections. The Gender Affairs Unit was part of the Transitional Authority's National Planning Office, and some argued that the gender office should be part of the Ministry of Justice. Ultimately, an adviser of equality position was created, concurrently with an adviser of human rights, reporting directly to the chief of cabinet. The efficacy of these offices, however, continued to be challenged by the lack of budgetary and operational capacity to reach out to their constituency (women in rural areas), and the lack of authority to influence national law-making and budgetary processes. For instance, the Ministry of Women's Affairs in Cambodia received only 0.12 per cent of the national budget in 1994. The ministry's failure to pass domestic violence legislation since 1994 also indicates its lack of political weight in the National Assembly.

As such, gender equality and the respect and protection of human rights are part of improving governance that is based on transparency and accountability. However, the development of civil society in Cambodia and Timor-Leste is focused mostly on the delivery of social services, rather than political reforms. This was the case particularly in Cambodia, where the July 1997 coup reinstated patrimonial decision-making and inherited traditional social structures, and replaced the outcomes of the 1993 UNTAC elections.[69] The trend towards service delivery, including among women's groups, reflected the preferences of foreign donors. Major bilateral donors tend to offer support to humanitarian and development non-governmental organizations (NGOs), rather than those involved in good governance or "politics". Donors also tend to collaborate with NGOs in the delivery of public goods, rather than strengthening the capacity of the government apparatus, due in part to widespread governmental corruption and inefficiency.[70] On the other hand, government inefficiency partly results from a lack of financial and operational support. Due to lack of financial resources in the public sector, some local officials are attracted to cooperate with foreign-funded NGOs. This was the case of Cambodia's Ministry of Women's and Veteran's Affairs, although Minister Mo Sochua, who established the first women's NGO, Khemara, in 1993, was widely respected by women's groups and donors alike for her leadership and personal devotion. Similarly, in Timor-Leste the new government was under pressure from international financial institutions to reduce the size of its civil service and public expenditures. As a result, most assistance to the survivors of sexual violence and exploitation was delivered by local women's groups funded and trained by international donors and NGOs. The need for training and strengthening of the civil service in the areas of health and education, on the other hand, received less attention.

Steps forward

To women and children, the "post-war" period brings new threats from unresolved communal and domestic violence, from international peacekeepers and from the contest between the new international standards and traditional or patriarchal law that may be discriminatory against women and children. The UN "nation-building" interventions in Cambodia and Timor-Leste demonstrated that women and children continued to receive inadequate protection under the rule of law, decision-making and the peacekeeping economy. The ambiguity of the United Nations regarding its policy on electoral quotas highlights the incoherent and inconsistent character of international gender interventions.

Since 2002 attention has focused heavily on the plight of Afghan women and their participation in the reconstruction of Afghanistan. Owing in large part to international advocacy and pressures, women gained 160 seats among the 1,451 members of the Emergency Loya Jirga, a tribal council held in June 2002. The UN Mission in Afghanistan included a gender adviser and the interim government established a ministry of women's affairs. These steps taken in Afghanistan were largely a replica of the Timor-Leste and Cambodian cases. Yet much remains to be learned from women's experiences in Timor-Leste and Cambodia, particularly from the challenges caused by the incoherent introduction of international human rights standards and the lack of consolidation with national and local judicial structures; the fact that political and economic liberalization was not accompanied by protection of vulnerable groups, including women and children; and the weak capacity of the state apparatus, which resulted in heavy reliance on civil society organizations for social service delivery.

Furthermore, the establishment of gender units in peacekeeping missions or national political architecture, although intended to enhance gender equality in international and national decision-making processes, may in fact marginalize the issues related to women and children by creating a weak agency without adequate authority, capacity and expertise, but which alleviates the responsibility of all other relevant institutions to take the needs of women and children into account within their mandates and activities. Thus bureaucratic institutionalization of gender issues is not a solution in itself and supplementary measures need to be explored, including mandatory and regular "gender audits" involving budgetary, personnel and operational performance reviews from a gender perspective and recruitment of a gender specialist in a senior position in every department of UN missions and interim/post-conflict governments. The donor community bears the responsibility for translating token policies of women's empowerment and gender equality into institutional and programmatic arrangements to make tangible impact. However, such initiatives also require local and national ownership, thereby synthesizing universal human rights standards and the principle of gender equality with local and national norms and processes.

On the part of the United Nations, its approaches to post-conflict institutional reforms have generally been *ad hoc*, inconsistent and incoherent. To address this gap, some policy-makers long ago proposed "justice packages" for peace operations,[71] which focus on the establishment of a functioning criminal justice system as a crucial priority if the gains of a peacekeeping operation are to be consolidated and a relapse into conflict avoided. No viable government or social order could be built without them, according to the advocates of justice packages, while there will be situations where only the United Nations is capable of delivering them.[72] On the other hand, the portability of justice packages should be designed in relation to the existing customary and national legal/normative frameworks. The unilateral introduction of international standards, even for a transitional period, may create more confusion, inaccessibility of legal proceedings and a tendency to revert to customary practices for more speedy resolutions of conflict, as the cases of Timor-Leste and Cambodia have demonstrated.

In terms of gender-specific challenges of international human rights frameworks, a normative gap remains in the treatment of domestic violence in international human rights instruments. While sexual violence is now recognized in the statute of the International Criminal Court as a war crime and crime against humanity, domestic violence is not distinctively recognized *per se* as prosecutable under international criminal law.[73] As a result, the definition of domestic violence in national criminal justice systems remains ambiguous in many countries, including Timor-Leste and Cambodia. While UNTAET recognized the increase of domestic violence as a societal issue, its response in January 2002 to launch a nationwide advocacy campaign against domestic violence fell short of fulfilling a need for relevant legislation.[74] On the other hand, the Vienna-based UN Commission for Crime Prevention and Criminal Justice issued a resolution in 1997 to enhance gender equality in the area of criminal justice systems, which was approved by the General Assembly in December. This resolution and its annex provide guidance on a wide range of issues, including criminal procedures, police powers, sentencing and corrections and victim support and assistance.[75] They should be considered for implementation in UN transitional administrations.[76]

The promotion of governance, including democratization, transparency, accountability and civil society development, requires a regional and international approach. In Cambodia many of the trafficked children came from southern Viet Nam. Despite local and international efforts to rescue and repatriate them, Vietnamese children were repeatedly sold into the sex industry. Such regional, illicit trade often pre-dates peace processes, as UNTAC failed to engage and disarm the Khmer Rouge partly because of the involvement of Thai military in illegal mining and logging in the Khmer Rouge-controlled border areas. Hence the early engagement of neighbouring countries from peace negotiations onwards is crucial for the prevention of trafficking in women and children. Similarly, much of Timor-Leste's reconciliation and reconstruction has depended on relations with Indonesia, particularly West Timor. International involvement in peacebuilding thus needs to develop regional and international approaches that take into account the political, legal, social and economic development of neighbouring countries.

Notes

1. This chapter is largely informed by interviews with women's groups during the author's field research in Cambodia and Timor-Leste in July 2001 and desk review of literature and UN and NGO reports. Thus the brunt of the analysis presented here draws on the years 1999–2002. While being a historical case study, its observations and findings are still very relevant for today's debate on the same issues.
2. One form of systematic violence against women during the occupation was the Indonesian national population control programme, Program Keluarga Berencana (KB), which reportedly conducted forcible injection of young women with hormonal contraceptives. KB birth control programmes were often run by military members, therefore coercively, with the consent of the predominantly Catholic Timorese women. Medical Aid for East Timor (undated) "Conditions for Women in East Timor", available at www.aideasttimor. org/women.html.
3. United Nations (1999) "Situation of Human Rights in East Timor, Note by the Secretary-General", UN Doc. A/54/660, 10 December, United Nations, New York, available at www.unhchr.ch/Huridocda/Huridoca.nsf/TestFrame/6fae6dad5614a51 c80256865005b729a?Opendocument. Also Oxfam Community Aid, cited in Nakaya, Sumie (2011) "Women and Gender Issues in Peacebuilding: Lessons Learned from Timor-Leste", in 'Funmi Olonisakin, Karen Barnes and Eka Ikpe (eds) *Women, Peace and Security: Translating Policy into Practice*, New York: Routledge, pp. 155–169; Medical Aid for East Timor, ibid.
4. *UN News Service* (2002) "Child Abuse Emerging Problem in East Timor, UNICEF Reports", 25 April, available at www.un.org/apps/news/story.asp?NewsID=3484&Cr =timor&Cr1=.
5. Asia Human Rights Commission (2001) "A Sharp Increase in Cambodian Rape Cases", *Asia Human Rights News*, 2 March, available at www.ahrchk.net/news/mainfile.php/ ahrnews_200103/1478/.
6. Ministry of Planning (1998) *Cambodia Human Development Report 1998: Women's Contribution to Development*, Phnom Penh: Ministry of Planning, Kingdom of Cambodia, p. viii.
7. Human Rights Task Force on Cambodia (1996) "Cambodia: Prostitution and Sex Trafficking: A Growing Threat to the Human Rights of Women and Children in Cambodia", *Human Rights Solidarity* 6(4), November, available at www.ahrchk.net/hrsolid/mainfile. php/1996vol06no04/219.
8. Ibid.
9. UNTAET (2002) "Chief Minister, SRSG Speak Out Against Domestic Violence", UNTAET Daily Briefing, 22 January, Dili, available at http://members.pcug.org.au/ ~wildwood/02jandv.htm.
10. Nelson, Eric and Cathy Zimmerman (1996) "Household Survey on Domestic Violence in Cambodia", August, Cambodia Ministry of Women's Affairs/Project against Domestic Violence, Phnom Penh. This, the first and the largest quantitative survey of domestic violence in Cambodia, covered six provinces and Phnom Penh, representing approximately 59 per cent of the Cambodian population. An increase in domestic violence was

also noted by the United Nations: Economic and Social Council, Commission on Human Rights (2001) "Advisory Service and Technical Cooperation in the Field of Human Rights, Situation of Human Rights in Cambodia", Report of the Special Representative of the Secretary-General for Human Rights in Cambodia, Mr Peter Leuprecht, submitted in accordance with Resolution 2000/79, UN Doc. E/CN.4/2001/103, 24 January, United Nations, New York, available at www.unhchr.ch/Huridocda/Huridoca.nsf/0/398c15c0b96a37a2c1256a2b005123d6/$FILE/G0110508.pdf.

11. Kumar, Krishna, Hannah Baldwin and Judy Benjamin (2000) "Aftermath: Women and Women's Organizations in Postconflict Cambodia", Working Paper No. 307, USAID, Washington, DC, p. 3.

12. Ministry of Planning, note 6, p. viii.

13. Interview in the Senate, 16 July 2001.

14. Ong, Kelvin (2000) "Policing the Peace: Towards a Workable Paradigm", IPA conference report, November, International Peace Academy, New York, p. 2, available at www.ipacademy.org/media/pdf/publications/pdf_report_policing.pdf.

15. Ibid.

16. Gender Affairs Unit (2001) "Report to the Department of Peacekeeping Operations on the Implementation of Security Council Resolution 1325", 25 May, UNTAET, Dili.

17. Paris, Roland (1997) "Peacebuilding and the Limits of Liberal Internationalism", *International Security* 22(2), p. 56.

18. Plunkett, Mark (1998) "Reestablishing Law and Order in Peace-Maintenance", *Global Governance* 4, January–March, p. 66.

19. Cambodia is a signatory of the UN Convention on the Rights of the Child and the Convention on the Elimination of All Forms of Discrimination against Women, and the East Timor Transitional Administration has requested the UN High Commissioner for Human Rights to assist in ratification and implementation of relevant international human rights laws.

20. Interview with Milena Pires, member of the Constituent Assembly and long-time gender specialist and advocate, 11 March 2002, in Helsinki.

21. *La'o Hamutuk Bulletin* (2001) "Campaign to Support Women's Rights in the Constitution", *La'o Hamutuk Bulletin* 2(5), available at www.etan.org/lh/pdfs/bullv2n5.pdf.

22. See Constitution of the Democratic Republic of East Timor, entered into force 20 May 2002, "Section 3 (Citizenship)", available at www.etan.org/etanpdf/pdf2/cnen0202.pdf.

23. The US State Department noted unconfirmed reports of trafficking of women and children from Indonesia to Timor-Leste. US State Department (2002) "Country Reports on Human Rights Practice 2001: East Timor", 4 March, US State Department Bureau of Democracy, Human Rights and Labor, Washington, DC.

24. In both Cambodia and Timor-Leste legal pluralism also hampers already scarce capacity of local legal sources. In Timor-Leste the lack of translators and locally trained legal professionals familiar with Indonesian laws as well as international humanitarian law has delayed the proceedings of courts established by UNTAET. When UNTAC designed Cambodian political and legal systems to be based on liberal democratic principles, the numbers of surviving legal professionals who had been trained under French rule and had some familiarity with the new UNTAC systems were estimated to be only between six and 10. Most of the Khmer lawyers had been trained in Vietnamese laws based on the socialist model, which limits rights of speech, press and assembly and lacks independence of the judiciary.

25. Strohmeyer, Hansjoerg (2001) "Policing the Peace: Post-conflict Judicial System Reconstruction in East Timor", *UNSW Law Journal* 24(1), p. 174.

26. Judicial System Monitoring Program (2001) "East Timor's New Judicial System", *La'o Hamutuk Bulletin* 2(6/7), pp. 6–7.
27. Fox, James J. (2002) "Assessing UNTAET's Role in Building Local Capacities for the Future", in Hadi Soesastro and Landry Haryo Subianto (eds) *Peace Building and State Building in East Timor*, Jakarta: Centre for Strategic and International Studies, pp. 39–58.
28. Linton, Suzannah (2001) "Cambodia, East Timor and Sierra Leone: Experiments in International Justice", *Criminal Law Forum* 12(2), p. 211.
29. Halliday, Kate (2001) "Women and Justice", *La'o Hamutuk Bulletin* 2(3), p. 7.
30. Commission on Human Rights, UN Economic and Social Council (1999) "Integration of the Human Rights of Women and the Gender Perspective: Violence against Women", report of the special rapporteur on violence against women, its causes and consequences, Ms Radhika Coomaraswamy, Addendum, "Mission to Indonesia and East Timor on the Issue of Violence against Women (20 November–4 December 1998)", UN Doc. E/CN.4/1999/68/Add.3, 21 January, United Nations, New York, available at http://daccess-dds-ny.un.org/doc/UNDOC/GEN/G99/103/19/PDF/G9910319.pdf ?OpenElement.
31. Amnesty International (2001) "East Timor: Justice Past, Present and Future", 27 July, Amnesty International, London, available at www.unhcr.org/refworld/pdfid/3c29def60.pdf.
32. *La'o Hamutuk Bulletin* (2002) "An Assessment of the UN's Police Mission in East Timor", *La'o Hamutuk Bulletin* 3(1), p. 3. In one rape case, a perpetrator gave nine water buffaloes to the victim's family.
33. Amnesty International, note 31, p. 41.
34. Amnesty International (2002) "Kingdom of Cambodia: Urgent Need for Judicial Reform", AI Index ASA 23/04/2002, Amnesty International, London, available at www.unhcr.org/refworld/pdfid/3deb63334.pdf.
35. Human Rights Task Force on Cambodia, note 7.
36. A draft of a code of criminal procedures was prepared by the Ministry of Justice and sent to France to be revised by French magistrates in 1998. United Nations (1999) "Report of the Secretary-General on the Role of the Office of the United Nations High Commissioner for Human Rights in Assisting the Government and People of Cambodia in the Promotion and Protection of Human Rights", UN Doc. E/CN.4/1999/100, United Nations, New York.
37. Case study from UNIFEM (2001) "Forging Institutional Partnership", in *End in Sight*, New York: UNIFEM.
38. Ratner, Steven and James Abram (2001) *Accountability for Human Rights Atrocities in International Law: Beyond the Nuremberg Legacy*, Oxford: Oxford University Press, p. 271.
39. Amnesty International, note 31.
40. *La'o Hamutuk Bulletin*, note 32.
41. Ibid.
42. Suhrke, Astri, Arve Ofsta and Are Knudsen (2002) *A Decade of Peacebuilding: Lessons for Afghanistan*, Chr. Michelsen Institute, Bergen, 2 April, p. 32. Also author's interviews in Timor-Leste, 10–16 July 2001.
43. Interviews in districts of Occussi and Alieu, 11–12 July 2001.
44. Levi, Robin S. (1998) "Cambodia: Rattling the Killing Fields", in Leni Marin, Helen Zia and Esta Soler (eds) *Ending Domestic Violence: Report from the Global Frontlines*, San Francisco, CA: Family Violence Prevention Fund.
45. Zimmerman, Cathy (1996) *Plates in a Basket Will Rattle: Domestic Violence in Cambodia*, Phnom Penh: Project against Domestic Violence, p. 172.

46. Ibid.
47. Government of Indonesia, Department of Information (1975) "Introduction to Law of the Republic of Indonesia Number 1 of the Year 1974 on Marriage", 5 November, available at www.law.emory.edu/ifl/.
48. Marks, Stephen (1999) "Elusive Justice for the Victims of the Khmer Rouge", *Journal of International Affairs* 52(2), p. 3.
49. Lambourne, Wendy (1999) "The Pursuit of Justice and Reconciliation: Responding to Genocide in Cambodia and Rwanda", paper presented at International Studies Association Annual Convention, Washington, DC, February, p. 4.
50. Chandrasekaran, Rajiv (2000) "Cambodians Want Justice but Fear Genocide Trials", *Washington Post*, 17 April, p. A1.
51. Linton, note 28.
52. Ibid., p. 214.
53. For more on the commission see its homepage at www.easttimor-reconciliation.org/index.htm.
54. Suhrke, Ofsta and Knudsen, note 42, p. 12.
55. Interview with chief of administration, Dili, 10 July 2001.
56. Arnvig, Eva (1996) "Women, Children and Returnees", in Peter Utting (ed.) *Between Hope and Insecurity: The Social Consequences of the Cambodian Peace Process*, Geneva: UNRISD.
57. *La'o Hamutuk Bulletin* (2001) "Employment of Women in the East Timor Transitional Administration", *La'o Hamutuk Bulletin* 2(5), p. 4, available at www.laohamutuk.org/Bulletin/2001/Aug/bullv2n5.pdf.
58. Human Rights Task Force on Cambodia, note 7.
59. Suhrke, Ofsta and Knudsen, note 42, p. 35.
60. ETAN (Reuters) (2001) "UN Peacekeepers in East Timor Face Possible Sex Charges", 3 August, available at www.etan.org/et2001c/august/01-4/03unpeac.htm. Also interviews with Milena Pires, Sherrill Willington, head of Gender Affairs Unit, and women's groups in Timor-Leste, 10 July 2001.
61. UNHCR and Save the Children UK (2002) "Sexual Violence and Exploitation: The Experience of Refugee Children in Guinea, Liberia and Sierra Leone", February, available at www.alnap.org/pool/files/825.pdf.
62. Some scholars suggested that the regime promoted women in commune solidarity groups because men were reluctant to serve in these groups, as officeholders received no salary. Kumar, Baldwin and Benjamin, note 11.
63. Ministry of Planning, note 6.
64. Marcus, Rachel (1996) "Cambodia Case Study", *BRIDGE* II(35), Institute of Development Studies, University of Sussex, p. 4.
65. European Union Election Observation Mission (2008) "Kingdom of Cambodia, Final Report, National Assembly Elections, 27 July 2008", 13 October, p. 38, available at http://aceproject.org/ero-en/regions/asia/KH/cambodia-final-report-national-assembly-elections.
66. UNDP Cambodia (2010) "Concerted Efforts Needed to Bring More Cambodian Women into Parliament", 14 September, available at www.un.org.kh/undp/pressroom/events/concerted-efforts-needed-to-bring-more-cambodian-women-into-parliament.
67. Matland, Richard E. (2005) "Enhancing Women's Political Participation: Legislative Recruitment and Electoral Systems", in Julie Ballington and Azza Karam (eds) *Women in Parliament: Beyond Numbers*, Stockholm: International Institute for Democracy and Electoral Assistance, p. 99, available at www.idea.int/publications/wip2/upload/WiP_inlay.pdf.
68. Interview with East Timorese member of Constituent Assembly.

69. Speech by Frederik Z. Brown, evaluator of Asia Foundation projects in Cambodia, Asia Society, 23 September 1997, available at www.asiasociety.org/speeches/brown.html.
70. Interview with donors in Phnom Penh, 17 July 2001.
71. Plunkett, note 18, pp. 61–79; Carothers, Thomas (1998) "The Rule of Law Revival", *Foreign Affairs*, March/April, pp. 95–106.
72. Gareth Evans, cited in Carothers, ibid.
73. Meanwhile, the 1992 recommendation issued by the CEDAW Committee, which supplements the 1979 CEDAW by correcting a previous lack of treatment for sexual violence, urges states to adopt legal measures, including penal sanctions, civil remedies and compensatory provisions, to protect women against all kinds of violence, including violence and abuse in the family.
74. United Nations (2002) "Report of the Secretary-General on the United Nations Transitional Administration in East Timor for the Period from 16 October 2001 to 18 January 2002", UN Doc. S/2002/80, 17 January, United Nations, New York, available at http://daccess-dds-ny.un.org/doc/UNDOC/GEN/N02/215/64/PDF/N0221564.pdf ?OpenElement.
75. United Nations (1998) "Crime Prevention and Criminal Justice Measures to Eliminate Violence against Women", resolution adopted on 12 December 1997 by the UN General Assembly, including annex on "Model Strategies and Practical Measures on the Elimination of Violence against Women in the Field of Crime Prevention and Criminal Justice", UN Doc. A/RES/52/86, 2 February, United Nations, New York, available at www.unfpa.org/gender/docs/52-86.pdf.
76. International Centre for Criminal Law Reform and Criminal Justice Policy (1999) "Model Strategies and Practical Measures on the Elimination of Violence against Women in the Field of Crime Prevention and Criminal Justice", ICCLRCJP, Vancouver.

5

Frontline peacebuilding: Women's reconstruction initiatives in Burundi

Rose M. Kadende-Kaiser

Burundi signed a peace accord on 29 August 2000, two months before the UN Security Council adopted Resolution 1325 on women, peace and security. Burundi is among the 185 countries that are signatories to the Convention to End All Forms of Discrimination against Women (CEDAW), thus committing the government to a gender-sensitive approach to peace and security. This represents a radical shift from the way politics was conducted during the five-year peace talks in Arusha, Tanzania, that denied women's right to equal participation.[1] But despite this act of political exclusion, women were able to carve out a space for themselves, and took part in what I define in this chapter as "frontline peacebuilding".

Throughout the conflict that started in October 1993, women assumed a leadership role in their communities. Not only did they organize to bring former neighbours displaced by the war back together, but they were also able to develop the skills needed for engaging their male counterparts during the Arusha peace talks that culminated in the peace agreement signed in August 2000. With the support of several key mediators and the international community, particularly the UN Development Fund for Women (UNIFEM, now known as UN Women), women were given a chance to take part in the Arusha negotiations as observers. Together, the participants in the peace talks sought to achieve an end to the war and recognition of the importance of power sharing, not only between all key political parties but also between men and women.[2]

This chapter explores women's approaches to peace activism at the grassroots as well as the highest level of political engagement. In Bu-

Defying victimhood: Women and post-conflict peacebuilding, Schnabel and Tabyshalieva (eds), United Nations University Press, 2012, ISBN 978-92-808-1201-5

rundi, women initiated community-based activities that provided a safe space for honest dialogue across the ethnic divide. In their neighbourhoods, villages and even camps for refugees and internally displaced persons (IDPs), women were able to express among themselves feelings of hurt and accounts of gruesome experiences, which opened doors for empathy, forgiveness, healing and reconciliation. Those who participated as observers during the Arusha peace talks had their voices heard and ensured that the final agreement accommodated women's recommendations. In a country torn apart by endemic ethnic violence, undermining the importance of women's participation and contributions to peacebuilding at both levels would have left out key ingredients for durable peace.

This chapter is based on analysis of primary sources, including one-on-one interviews and focus group discussions with more than a dozen organized women's groups in post-conflict Burundi.[3] Initial interviews with individual women and focus groups were conducted in 1998. Follow-up research was carried out in June and July 2000, following a workshop in Burundi's capital, Bujumbura, funded by the US Institute of Peace (USIP) and organized to highlight women's approaches to conflict management.[4] Secondary source data obtained through desk research provided the framework for understanding women's roles in peacebuilding in Burundi and beyond. I have kept in contact with many of the women who participated in the 2000 workshop; some of them, as well as others whom I met during the time I returned to Burundi to work in 2009 and 2010, remain actively involved in efforts aimed at fostering post-conflict community cohesion and reconstruction.

The first section of the chapter highlights the many ways women become victims of violent conflict and their relevance to the case of women in Burundi in the aftermath of the civil war that started in 1993. The next section explores key motivators for peace activism in violent conflict. The bulk of the analysis, however, is reserved for exploring women's peacebuilding initiatives in post-conflict Burundi. Case studies of two Burundi women's groups that proactively sought an end to ethnic animosities in their communities by developing activities aimed at mutual support, forgiveness, healing and reconciliation are presented. The third case study analyses the challenges and importance of women's participation in the Arusha peace talks, and concludes that final peace agreements are incomplete if they exclude the voice of women.

This chapter does not intend to highlight all the roles that women played during the war in Burundi. Indeed, many women and children joined the war effort and fought in the army and militias. Many girls were forced to fight as child soldiers, while others were forced to provide for and sustain male relatives who served in the army or had joined "militias".

While these roles are critical to a full appreciation of the ramifications of the ethnic conflict in Burundi and are discussed briefly in the following section, this chapter focuses primarily on women's peace and post-conflict reconstruction initiatives. Experiences of women who were instrumental in the creation of various women's groups for peace provide the necessary data for a deeper understanding of the gendered nature of reconstruction and frontline peacebuilding in Burundi.

War victimization

Women and girls suffer greatly during war and its aftermath. They are victims of rape, forced to work as servants to militias and often left to care for the wounded, orphans and the elderly. Armed groups from all sides of the Burundian ethnic conflict repeatedly subjected women and girls to violent atrocities that included rape and other physical and psychological abuses. Many rape victims became pregnant and were forced to bear a new generation, ostracized in their communities and serving as a constant reminder to the rape victim of the identity of the rapist. This kept the trauma of violence fresh in the minds of many rape victims. A 2007 report by Amnesty International provides a detailed account of rape prevalence in Burundi, including testimonies from victims. On average, 25 women were raped per week during a three-year period between 2004 and 2006. In addition to feelings of shame and ostracism in their communities, victims require psychosocial and medical services that are not readily available, especially for adult women who fear reprisal should they take a public stance against the rapist. Rape also contributed greatly to the spread of the deadly HIV that causes AIDS. According to Amnesty International, "the threat of rape often forced families to sleep away from their homes at night. Certain categories of women, including women living alone, widows, internally displaced women and refugee women, were particularly vulnerable. Other women were targeted as they searched for firewood or water."[5] Rape has far-reaching consequences, causing ill health, alienation and dislocation of women and families in both war and peacetime.

The war forced many families to seek refuge in IDP and refugee camps and put a heavy burden on them due to the loss of loved ones killed prior to or at the time of displacement, material loss including land and other assets, and physical and psychological injuries. By 2003, 10 years after the war had started, 44 per cent of households in camps were under the responsibility of a female head.[6] Men had died, disappeared or were directly involved in the fighting and therefore gone from home during most of the war. The increased number of female heads of households in

Burundi is an indication of the greater loss of male lives in wartime, leading to a prevalence of widows in the country.[7] When men's traditional roles as heads of household, providers and protectors of the family could no longer be fulfilled, women had to step in to protect surviving members of their families. Many of these women were traumatized and unprepared for these new responsibilities. Recognizing the gendered nature of displacement, several studies have explored experiences of and coping mechanisms employed by IDPs.[8]

Abuse and health risks in refugee camps

Those in refugee camps were exposed to new challenges and different forms of abuse committed against them by male relatives, other men in the camps and, at times, local authorities. While in times of "peace"[9] women are also subjected to different forms of violence, in wartime the situation is even worse.[10] Women and girls suffered from gender-based violence, including rape, health and food insecurity, and other deprivation. In some cases men prevented women from gaining direct access to humanitarian aid. Human Rights Watch confirms that "when Burundi women fled the internal conflict there, they expected to find safety and protection in the refugee camps. Instead, they simply escaped one type of violence in Burundi to face other forms of abuse in the refugee camps in Tanzania."[11] Violence and attacks also target those in IDP camps, as the International Committee of the Red Cross reports.[12] Often men assumed domination, undermining women's search and felt need for safety, provision and protection.

In addition to gender-based violence, women in camps lacked access to basic sanitation and healthcare services. Refugee International laments the deplorable conditions in the camps for the "250,000 Burundians ... displaced from their homes in Bujumbura Rural Province".[13] The refugees lacked proper housing, clean and sufficient water and latrines, resulting in the contamination of new camps by human waste and an increased risk of diarrhoea, dysentery and cholera. Due to poor harvests, landmines and continuing insecurity in the country, food security was unachievable in the camps.[14]

Some women who fled in search of safe havens moved in with relatives, a choice that on the surface seems preferable. However, as one member of the local organization United Against Hunger noted, those hosted by relatives were often "packed in tiny rooms, with a mother forced to share a room with older boys and girls as well as small children ... In some cases, family members have to take turns sleeping, as they cannot fit in the one room dedicated to them by their host."[15] So staying with a host family is not necessarily a viable option for many displaced families. In addition to health risks resulting from lack of basic means of survival, lack of sleep leads to fatigue and general ill health among IDPs without adequate shelter.[16]

Women's access to land and job insecurity

Customary laws in Burundi restrict women's rights to land and property ownership. As a result, women constitute the largest number of victims of unresolved land grievances. Women are often chased away from their husbands' ancestral property by male and female in-laws after their husbands have been killed or disappeared, even if they are legally entitled to the property. Women's access to land and property remains the greatest challenge for displaced populations, as it does for the government of Burundi. Lack of access to land has a direct impact on economic security as well as the physical and psychological welfare of the family.

Due to inflation in the country, wages have become so insignificant that even most civil servants can no longer rely solely on their monthly salaries, which are barely enough to cover two weeks of living expenses. Parents are constantly in search of additional sources of income, working long hours or in multiple jobs in an effort to supplement their meagre revenues and ensure the survival of their children. In a country where resources have become scarce, the displaced population had limited opportunities for competition on the job market. The World Food Programme and the UNHCR (Office of the UN High Commissioner for Refugees), along with several non-governmental organizations (NGOs), provided food assistance to these vulnerable communities to enable them to survive critical periods of deprivation.

Changes in social and professional status

Life in refuge leads to changes in family roles and professional status for women. Even with adequate education, many are unable to find appropriate employment in their areas of competence in the refugee or IDP camps. Table 5.1, created by Sabine Sabimbona, a Burundian lawyer, widow and active member of the Collective of Women's Associations and NGOs of Burundi (CAFOB), illustrates the effects of the war on 100 displaced women in Burundi.[17]

The greatest impact was felt by farmers and those who made handicrafts. As many had no other skills that would enable them to survive and remain active in camps, they ended up joining those who prior to the war had no occupation. The number of those with no occupation grew from 1.6 per cent before the war to 30.5 per cent in camps during the war.

Table 5.1 Distribution of 100 displaced women aged 15 and above according to current professional activity in camps and before the crisis

Activity	In camps	Before the crisis
Farming	61.4	87.3
Handicrafts	0.6	1.0
Public employee	0.9	0.9
Private employee	0.5	0.5
No occupation	30.5	1.6

Destroying hopes for a better future, unemployment was one of the factors leading to increased frustration and anger, keeping the trauma of war alive in the minds of those in camps. Unemployed men also tended to be more violent.

Peace activists, peace movements and frontline peacebuilding

This research builds on current studies on peace movements and "frontline"[18] peacebuilding that seek to challenge assumptions that women are passive beneficiaries of peace efforts, rather than active agents of peace. It places Burundi women's peace activism in the context of other organized women's groups that have used non-violent means to bring about necessary change.[19] Peace movements are led by men and women concerned with the immediate and long-term effects of war. These activists are influenced, as Ho-Won Jeong notes, by "a variety of traditions, motivated by a range of concerns and guided by diverse strategies".[20] They operate at the highest level of political establishments, as well as at the grassroots. Among them are physicians who raise public awareness of the dangers of nuclear war by warning of its medical consequences; politicians who work for the legislation of disarmament and arms control; artists who express a moral voice for peace and the environment; scientists who question the wisdom of new weapons; and many others who contribute to the public outcry against violence and oppression in large or small ways.[21] They also include grassroots women's groups which employ moral persuasion and other subtle but effective methods that lead to conflict transformation and create the foundation for sustainable peace.

As social phenomena, peace movements benefit from the support of "ordinary people who nurture ideas, initiatives and motivation for peace as well as a commitment to the prevention of war or the abolition of the war system".[22] Women emerge from ordinary circumstances, but as a result of war they are able to reach extraordinary achievements on the peace front. In small and big ways, women have been able to carve out a niche for themselves as they build the foundation for durable peace.[23]

Burundi women's political activism

Organized Burundi women's groups did not emerge from a strong tradition of political activism, with the necessary skills and capacity to operate as free and independent political agents. In post-colonial Burundi in the early 1990s, L'Union de la Femme Burundaise (UFB – Burundi Women's Union) was the only umbrella organization that mobilized for women's political participation and networking. Prior to the 1990s, UFB members worked alongside the Union for National Progress (UPRONA), the single political party in power from the late 1950s until the democratic elections of June 1993 that brought the Front for Democracy in Burundi to power. UFB was formed to encourage and engage women in national policy-making and to support UPRONA through grassroots civic education.

The assassination of the democratically elected president, Mechior Ndadaye, by renegade members of the army in October 1993 triggered a civil war that lasted over a decade, killing more than 300,000 people. The Conseil National pour la Défense de la Démocratie-Forces pour la Défense de la Démocratie (CNDD-FDD) is the party in power today, following a mediated agreement between major political parties that participated in the Arusha peace talks in 1998–2000.[24] The peace agreement resulted in all parties calling upon their members and supporters to stop the fighting, and power sharing between most of the active political parties. Democratic elections in 2005 brought Pierre Nkurunziza of CNDD-FDD to power for a five-year term. During the period between the 2005 and June 2010 elections, widespread violence had generally stopped across most of the country.[25] However, women and children continued to face sporadic acts of violence following the contested 2010 elections. A positive outcome of the war was the emergence of a new wave of women peacemakers who were eager to play an active role in community rebuilding and national reconstruction.

Empathy towards the tragedies of others was a major driving force for women leaders, who developed initiatives aimed at supporting widows, orphans and youth at risk, often irrespective of their ethnic backgrounds. These grassroots initiatives focused on humanitarian aid, self-help and dialogue. They opened doors that enabled women from one group to reach out to those from another. Fundraising efforts enabled them to buy and distribute food items, blankets and clothing, and to rebuild schools and homes that were destroyed during the war. Active membership in women's associations protected many from the isolating experience of loss and ensuing traumas of violence. It also helped them to focus on healing and enhanced their ability and willingness to move on as they contributed to productive efforts aimed at rebuilding their lives and communities.[26]

Organizations also formed on the basis of interpersonal affinity and regional identity. For example, some groups found it more practical to look after the needs of the displaced in their home town or village. Hence the women of Gatumba joined together to improve the living conditions of all the people who took refuge in Gatumba after 1993. The Association des Femmes de Kinama (Association of Women from Kinama), the Association des Femmes de Rusaka (Association of Women from Rusaka), Dufashanye Kinindo (Let's Help One Another Kinindo) and the Union des Femmes pour le Developpement de la Province Ngozi (Women United for the Development of Ngozi Province) were all geographically oriented. They were concerned about the welfare of people in a particular region of the country or a specific neighbourhood of the capital city.[27] These and a number of other newer associations offering mutual support and post-conflict community development are still active today.

Others aim to support a vulnerable or at-risk group, including the Association des Veuves du Burundi (Association of Burundi Widows), Appui aux filles descolarisees, concerned with supporting girls and young women who dropped out of school, the Association of Women Heads of Households and the Society for Women and AIDS in Africa Burundi. A common denominator for all these is that they target a particular disadvantaged group and seek resources for improving living conditions for that group. There are others that are committed to direct peace and development efforts – the names they chose for their organizations reflect this commitment. These include the Association de Femmes Eprises de Paix (Association of Women Dedicated to Peace), Association des Femmes Burundaises pour la Paix (Association of Burundi Women for Peace) and Femmes pour la Paix, l'Equite et le Developpement (Women for Peace, Equality and Development). New organizations continue to form. The Women Allies Peacebuilders Network is one of the newer groups: its aim is to create "better coordination in regards to civil society initiatives related to the advocacy and monitoring of peace and security issues, specifically UNSCR 1325 and 1820".[28]

Most of these associations are affiliated with the Collectif des Associations et ONGs Féminines du Burundi (CAFOB), whose membership was estimated at 52 in 2007. It was formed after the civil war began in 1993, to address the needs of women and children in post-conflict Burundi. CAFOB started with only seven members in 1994 and rapidly grew to serve as the main umbrella women's organization in the country. It coordinates the activities of all registered members and is the major national women's organization in charge of monitoring and lobbying on behalf of women as it contributes to grassroots peacebuilding and reconstruction initiatives. As Sabine Sabimbona noted in reference to the *raison d'être* of CAFOB, women were "convinced that they would be stronger if united".[29] CAFOB also lobbied for women's participation in the formal peace process in Arusha. The umbrella organization engaged Burundi politicians and other mediators in the peace process and was officially recognized for the important role it played in peacebuilding. A major achievement of this lobbying was women's appointment to official roles in the transitional and the democratically elected governments.

Frontline peacebuilding in Burundi

Victimization has not stopped women from active involvement in peace efforts at the grassroots level and in seeking a voice at the highest level of political engagement during the Arusha peace talks. This section examines the strategic roles of these two levels of involvement in the movement towards peace and reconciliation in Burundi. Conscious of the impact the war continues to have on them, and of the important role they need to play in post-conflict reconstruction, women organized themselves and developed initiatives aimed at community survival and national healing. In a 23 October 2002 statement to the UN Security Council, Burundi parliament member Sabine Sabimbona said that women's associations representing different groups united for peace at a time when men were hostages of "ethnic ghettos".[30] Feedback from attendees at the USIP-funded workshop in 2000 revealed that elite, educated, urban women tended to be the most visible activists, linking local organizations with the international communities through fundraising activities, training workshops and peacebuilding conferences. There were also poor but visionary displaced women who formed their own associations independently from urban elites. However, they tended to focus most of their energy on survival rather than broader political participation. The forces that most effectively strengthen the peacebuilding and reconstruction efforts will have to cut across not only ethnic but also class differences.

This wave of post-conflict women's activism is driven by two categories of women. The first group includes women at the front line, working hard to improve living conditions of survivors and their families, seeking resources needed for self-help and at times risking their lives to ensure that war does not erode the common thread that, prior to the war, held communities together. I place the grassroots women's initiatives and political activists who participated in and contributed to the Arusha peace agreement in this first group. These are the peace activists without whom the face of post-conflict Burundi would look quite different today. The second category comprises those who believe that peace can only be achieved through the presence of deterrent force or waging war. Thus some women have joined the army or police force, or are working alongside the "rebel" and militia groups, seeking to restore peace and stability often through violent means. The focus of the rest of the chapter is on efforts made by the first category, who contributed to grassroots peacebuilding using subtle, non-violent but effective means to restore trust and build community clusters committed to non-violence, dialogue and reconciliation.

Mobilizing for peace and survival

At the grassroots level, women developed productive activities that contributed to the survival of their families and communities. These are women who, prior to joining the peace movement, primarily lived in IDP or refugee camps or with relatives, but maintained a feeling of isolation that held them hostage to the trauma of loss and violence they had experienced prior to forced displacement. Having lost trust in communal life, many were reluctant to join community-based organizations. However, they soon discovered that joining others with similar problems gave them opportunities to share experiences of war and trauma of violence and rediscover a sense of community among war victims. Hence several organizations were born, and membership was dominated by IDP and returning refugee women. Women's initiatives included identifying and joining other families in safe havens, as a way of preventing the temptation to respond to violence through retaliation. In these communities, women organized themselves and developed cooperative farming or basket weaving, engaged in music, dance and informal peace discussions and shared resources and ideas. They developed income-generating activities such as keeping a vegetable garden, animal husbandry or arts and crafts production and sale.

Despite many limitations, women have a great capacity for survival. Women's groups that formed in post-conflict Burundi exhibited strong resilience and a shared commitment to active involvement in peacebuilding. Women were aware that real peace (or "positive peace") could not be achieved without their direct involvement and without taking into account their interests and needs. As one woman interviewed during field research in July 2000 stated: "Recognizing the level of suffering that the war has brought to us widows and orphans should be a precondition for engaging in genuine peace talks."[31]

Several women political activists were resolute in their decision to take part in formal peace negotiations, recognizing that women have an equal stake in the outcome of the political processes that would bring an end to the war and pave the way for lasting peace.[32] Those who participated in the Arusha peace talks also had opportunities to attend conflict transformation conferences and training workshops that built their capacity for negotiation and peacebuilding and enabled them to be better equipped for active participation in the talks. One of the three case studies below discusses the role and achievements of women during these peace talks.

The experiences of Duhozanye and Gatumba women's associations

This subsection looks at three women's groups which contributed to grassroots peacebuilding and made an impact on the peace process in Burundi. First, I discuss the efforts of Gatumba women's groups through an analysis of interviews conducted with 21 group leaders. The Collective of Gatumba Women's Associations (GWA) represents mainly elementary school teachers and educators who sought to provide educational opportunities to youth affected by the civil war. Second, I reflect on the initiatives of Duhozanye, an organization founded by an officer of the Women's Peace Center, a project of Search for Common Ground (SCG), a Washington-based organization with an office in Bujumbura, Burundi. SCG developed or supported various grassroots peace initiatives around the country and influenced some staff members to develop and implement other peace projects on their own. Duhozanye worked both in the capital city, Bujumbura, and in the north of the country in the province of Kayanza. It was instrumental in renewing hope by facilitating peaceful cross-ethnic interactions and bridging a gap that had been reinforced by inter-ethnic violence in the country. Third, this subsection examines women's search for full participation in the Arusha peace talks.

These organized women's groups were part of the frontline peace movement. They engaged in successful activities that contributed to the physical, psychological and economic welfare of their members and surrounding communities. Many groups included Hutu and Tutsi women who joined with the intention of reaching out to the "other" or maintaining bonds that had existed before the outbreak of the war. Duhozanye and another association called Twishakira Amahoro (All We Want is Peace), which brought together residents of two ethnically segregated neighbourhoods of Musaga-Busoro, both on the southern outskirts of the capital city, gained national recognition for their successful efforts in bridging the ethnic gap. Duhozanye and the GWA, which I discuss in detail, express the importance of informal peace initiatives led by grassroots women's groups in the country. The all-party observers at the negotiation table represent the partial success of these grassroots groups at influencing the formal peace process.

Case 1: Standing up for children: Key motivation for inclusive peace in Gatumba

Building on Sara Ruddick's *Maternal Thinking*,[33] this discussion examines the extent to which women's activism is focused on the welfare of children in wartime. The GWA sought to prevent further deterioration of the living conditions of children growing up amid insecurity. Does this mean that women – and mothers in particular – are more interested in children's security and well-being than men? In *Maternal Thinking*, Ruddick suggests that socialization processes, rather than innate qualities, influence men's and women's knowledge of and interests in war or peace. She concludes that women are not any more peaceloving than men. However, in the case of Burundi, as one woman explained:

> In situations of scarcity, men tend to leave the house and disappear so that they do not have to face the anguish of having nothing to offer starving children. Mothers will stay around, trying to figure out what to do. Thus, women tend to stay closer to their children and will not run away even during times of extreme scarcity. They are there with the children regardless of whether or not they have something to offer. Women are always home with children.[34]

The story of a Congolese member of the GWA, who fled violence in her home town of Bukavu in eastern Democratic Republic of the Congo and took refuge in Gatumba, seems like *déjà vu*, indeed a clear caricature of displacement as it applies to women in most troubled parts in the world. Her story exhibits bravery, empathy and activism. She was able to relieve pain and suffering along the journey to an unknown destination as she became a refugee in Burundi. In response to my question as to why women have been more willing to engage in grassroots peace activism than men, she said that women "suffer more than men during wartime". As I enquired more about what she meant by this, she explained:

> When we fled from Zaire [Democratic Republic of the Congo], for example, you know we also had conflict in Zaire, it was very difficult for us. You know us women, you have to think about how to carry all the children, may be four of them or five, you start looking for your husband and can't find him, you don't know where he went. You, as the mother, are left on your own to take the children when you flee. It is very difficult. I know from my own case that it was very difficult and I was lucky because when I left, we were going towards Bubembe. I was carrying a basket with powdered milk and a little bit of cooking oil. And I remembered to bring a small pot along with a cooking spoon. I wanted to make sure that as soon as I got there [somewhere safe], my children

wouldn't die from hunger. When I arrived there, these were so useful, and I was able to help so many other people, who were able to borrow my plate and pot. When I ran into someone with a stomach ache, I was able to give him/her a little bit of milk and they would feel better. When a kid was so hungry that she couldn't walk anymore, I would prepare a little milk and would give it to her and they were able to keep moving. This is why it is so difficult for women because they can't leave children behind. They are always passionate about their children.[35]

This testimony demonstrates that the main motivating factors behind her acts of charity were empathy and a concern for the welfare and survival of children fleeing from eastern Congo to Burundi, across the western border. Many Burundi children are orphans (*udupfuvyi*),[36] after having lost one or both parents. The war and the HIV/AIDS pandemic have forced thousands of children on to the streets, and their number is continuously on the rise. The fortunate ones, few in number, have been adopted by extended families with sufficient resources to meet their basic needs. Women's activists for children's rights and welfare recognized that "attending school is the only hope for a better future for these children".[37] Otherwise, they turn to robbery:

They are heading down the wrong path. They spend all day roaming the streets, playing in the dirt, you look at them and feel sorry for them and then you ask yourself, what can I do to help? The task is overwhelming. There are too many of them, they spend the night in public bars, or out in the open. We need help so that we can teach them at least basic literacy.[38]

Women also feared that without prospects for a brighter future for these children, peace and security will continue to be in jeopardy in the country.

Organized teachers of the Gatumba district sought to educate displaced children despite the lack of adequate schools in the new location. Schools have either been destroyed or were non-existent to begin with. Therefore, until teachers and school administrators were able to secure financial support to fix schools or build new ones, professional careers could be halted. The women of Gatumba were proactive in seeking outside funding to keep the only school in their new location open after it was destroyed during the war. As one woman explained:

we have approached the United Nations Children's Fund [UNICEF] and they have helped, by providing free notebooks for children whose parents were the most dispossessed and this has helped a lot. This past year, we were only able to secure funds to support those who have nothing; those who cannot even afford to buy their own clothes and walk around in rags. But there are many others who cannot afford educational materials.[39]

For the principal, who called herself the "director of the school that everyone is lamenting, a school built out of sticks and worn-out tents", the challenge was twofold.[40] First, the state of the school was deplorable. The materials used for reconstruction were the cheapest available on the market, and were non-durable and wore out within a year. Some of the walls were made of thin wood and branches woven together to build classrooms. The principal took it as her responsibility, every summer, to raise resources needed to fix dilapidated structures.

The principal also had to manage public relations concerns with parents of children ready to enrol in first grade at a school where space and capacity were already greatly overstretched. As the existing classrooms were inadequate for those already registered, she had a moral dilemma, wondering whether it would be more strategic to fix existing rooms before admitting a new cohort of students. The alternative would be to admit new students and leave everyone to deal with an inadequate learning environment.

While school principals are usually respected members of their communities, heading a school for displaced populations in post-conflict Burundi was not an enviable position to be in. Tension between her and parents who placed unrealistic expectations on her was almost unavoidable. Parents wanted their children registered regardless of the circumstances. At the time of the interview in summer 2000, the school had 12 "classrooms", mostly unfinished – some lacking a wall, others with a half-covered roof. Approximately 1,050 children had registered for the six levels of elementary school. With the support of most of her teachers, who were committed to taking part in fundraising meetings for the school, and by raising public awareness about the needs of children in Gatumba, the principal was hopeful.

What does peace mean for the GWA? Genuine (or positive) peace generally encompasses the absence of organized and unorganized violence, including wife battering, rape, child abuse and street killings. Many studies that now seek to draw a distinction between positive and negative peace indicate that indirect violence, repression and other conditions that reduce people's quality of life, freedom of choice and fulfilment need to be eliminated before positive peace can be achieved.[41] For the Gatumba women, positive peace would mean that children are being raised in families and parents or guardians have the necessary means to support their children's education. This would result in better safety for children, as they would spend less time on the streets, where they are often at risk of abuse, and more time gaining the skills and knowledge that prepare them for a brighter future as adults.

Women do not limit their expectations to the achievement of formal peace accords and ceasefire agreements. Women's interests look deeper into the fundamentals of human rights, focusing on the combination of negative and positive peace. Having experienced direct and indirect violence, psychological trauma or human and material losses incurred during the civil war, women understood all too well that meeting basic needs and bridging various fault-lines cutting across ethnic, regional or political affiliations were not only the most practical ways to peace, but also secured their very survival. This is not to say, however, that women were the only ones concerned with peace or the only victims of war. Men did suffer greatly, and some were forced to take proactive roles in war simply because of their traditional roles as family heads and protectors. In fact, if we agree with Sara Ruddick, we realize that the dominant understanding of war and peace, which remains dichotomous and split along gender lines, is problematic. If "a boy is not born, but rather becomes, a soldier", then the practice of violence in men is a learned process. To go to war, men (and women) have to learn to "control fears and domestic longings".[42] Examining women's roles throughout the conflict, and their dominant coping mechanisms during the transition period, one comes to the conclusion that women's roles in conflict and peacebuilding were greatly influenced by their positions as mothers and family caretakers. The majority of the Hutu and Tutsi women with whom the author interacted longed for peace and did not take a proactive role in support of war efforts after its outbreak in 1993. They simply lacked the capacity to control the war's outcomes.

For the women of Gatumba, peace meant that they were able to sleep comfortably without being woken up by night shootings in the neighbourhood or surrounding communities. As one woman explained, "if they could spend a couple of nights sleeping through the night, then things were getting better". But they were not complacent about the renewed sense of security. In fact, many attributed recent progress towards "peace" to the fact that the army was always around, guarding the area against potential attacks. For them, having "quiet nights" in their neighbourhood was a first step towards the attainment of peace. However, positive peace, which refers to "the absence of indirect and structural violence", was still absent in much of the country. For the GWA, positive peace also meant addressing the needs of IDPs and returning refugees whose land had been misappropriated. Representatives of the GWA expressed the hope that eventually a national action plan will take into account the needs of these two groups of displaced populations.

While a ceasefire is often a precondition for productive peace talks, many women viewed the ceasefire as only a step towards a broader goal, increased safety for all, as well as the establishment of a fair and just system that would give displaced populations access to their property once they returned to their original homes. Although the majority of those who fled to Gatumba were Hutu, individual associations were sometimes ethnically mixed or serving Hutu, Tutsi and ethnically mixed children in the schools. The GWA did succeed in serving the children of the three communities at the local school, bringing humanitarian support to orphans and children whose parents were most destitute, regardless of their ethnic background or social status as either locals, IDPs or returning refugees. A ceasefire alone only leads to negative peace. It is a crucial first step to bringing an end to violent killings. If implemented successfully, it opens up doors for positive peace, expressed through the achievement of fundamental human rights and access to basic education, food and healthcare for all, including returning refugees and IDPs. The GWA's activities aimed at healing the wounds of war by supporting orphans, widows and local authority efforts to minimize violence in the community. Their ultimate goal was to achieve positive peace.

Peace built on a strong foundation yields the eradication of extreme poverty, and respect for private property and the rule of law. This would effectively prevent *ubusuma* (robbery), so prevalent in Gatumba that night shootings were often committed by robbers rather than rebels or the army. Through the rule of law it would be possible to combat robberies on people's farms effectively so that farmers would no longer be targets of killings. Peace would also mean that people could return to their original homes and regain access to their property instead of being forced to move to other locations assigned to them by the same local governmental authorities that lacked the will or capacity to return individual property to its legal owner.

For a Rwandan member of the GWA, a holistic approach to peacebuilding will also reserve room for spiritual healing, a belief in and fear of God and respect for God's creation. To her, peace could be achieved "if people truly feared God and saw every human being as sacred". Finally, peace requires "true leadership exhibited in the manners in which those who are involved in the Arusha peace process will stop looking after their own self-interests and start addressing the needs of the poor who are among the worst victims of the current conflict".[43]

Case 2: Duhozanye and mutual empathy in peacebuilding

The organization Duhozanye was started by an officer at the SCG Women's Peace Center, who recognized the divisive effects of the war on natives of her home region of Kayanza, in the north of the country. She decided to invite Hutu and Tutsi women who were natives of Kayanza and resided in the capital city to discuss possibilities of forming a joint association. The reaction was positive from all who attended the initial meeting. As the women organized discussion groups and developed peace and fundraising activities, they determined that their efforts would have a stronger impact if they involved relatives in the rural areas who had been forced to move away as a result of the ethnic conflict. They organized an initial visit to their home village and challenged parents and relatives to follow their example. Their ultimate goal was for Hutu and Tutsi of that particular region of the country, in rural and urban areas, to recognize that both groups had suffered atrocities at the hands of the "other" group. Duhozanye, which means "let's console one another", was founded on this recognition of the "other's pain". Its mission was to help its members engage in trauma healing and reconciliation processes through grassroots development initiatives. Most of the activities were conducted on local farms, where Hutu and Tutsi women met and grew various farm produce as they shared stories about their losses, pain and suffering. Women were able to discuss their concerns as they took part in creating a shared space, open and accepting of cross-ethnic support.

Under direct guidance and support from the Women's Peace Center, and as a major programme of SCG, Duhozanye became part of a genuine women's movement that would be successful in renewing peaceful ties across the ethnic lines for all its members. Its efforts were duplicated in other parts of the country. In Bwambarangwe, in Kirundo province across the Rwandan border, for example, regional subcommittees of women's associations decided to implement a series of initiatives aimed at welcoming back displaced members of their communities who resided miles away. With logistical and material support from the Women's Peace Center and local authorities, they initiated an official visit to the IDP camp, carrying with them a message of peace, unity, forgiveness and reconciliation. Representatives of the women's groups expressed regret over what had happened since 1993. They also made it clear that, for the most part, women had no say in how the war had been carried out. As one woman stated, "we are here to ask for your forgiveness, to express our love for you. We miss you. Living by ourselves has not been good for us. We have thought hard about the current situation and have decided to come and ask for your forgiveness. We want to live together again."

Throughout the speeches delivered by women's representatives on the day of the visit, the message of forgiveness prevailed. Indeed, if it were up to the women, one could imagine a peaceful return of all the displaced of this particular location to their original homes. But we know that other factors, including the overall political situation in the rest of the country, affected the overall implementation of the women's will for and interest in restoring peace. The war moved around as the army followed rebel groups across the country. As long as the government was unable to control violent attacks committed by rebel groups and the army, the success of peace initiatives by the civilian population remained superficial at best. Nonetheless, one can hope that the wider the range of people who join this grassroots peace movement, the higher the chance of eventually reaching a peaceful settlement of the Burundi conflict as elected officials learn to represent the interests of their constituents.

Indeed, Duhozanye (and other women's groups supported by the Women Peace Center around the country) would not have been possible had local government authorities, as well as male partners in the family and the community, not cooperated to ensure a successful and well-coordinated visit between the rural and urban groups and women from the village and those in IDP camps. Coordination and cooperation between all interested parties are essential in successful implementation of peace initiatives.

Although Duhozanye and its partners in the north of the country cannot prevent violence initiated by non-members, they have created trust and hope that could be emulated by the future generations whose parents remain committed to peaceful inter-ethnic communication. Once people were actively involved in these associations, the discourse shifted from a focus on the victim/self and perpetrator/other frame of mind to the recognition that both groups were victims and needed healing. Recognition that not all members of one's group were innocent and did indeed commit atrocious acts against the other was part of a process that enabled the innocent "other" to engage in healing and forgiveness. It is a conscious act that recognizes that many members of the other group were also victims.

The initiator of Duhozanye said that as groups came together and openly shared their thoughts and feelings the outcome was "beautiful", as Hutu and Tutsi, children and adults alike, recognized and appreciated the importance and symbolism behind inclusiveness. Members made a conscious decision to join Duhozanye, knowing what it represented. As they joined, they brought their families along, contributing to the reinforcement of the peace movement across ethnic and intergenerational lines. Indeed, if the movement towards peace is to be sustained, the need for a new generation of Burundians committed to preserving a culture of peace is essential – while the opposite would be suicidal.

Case 3: Mobilizing for political inclusion: The Arusha Peace Accord

Formal and informal meetings between the major warring factions took place during most years of the conflict: some were held in Burundi, while others were held in countries including Gabon, South Africa, Tanzania and Italy.[44] All these meetings aimed at bringing most, if not all, the conflict parties to the negotiation table. Mediation strategically targeted various groups at different times in the process. The ultimate goal was to involve Burundians in developing mechanisms for non-violent conflict transformation and reach an agreement regarding the way forward. Such an agreement would restore the rule of law in Burundi.

Despite this goal of political inclusiveness, the formal peace process failed to encourage participation of non-formal actors, the level at which the majority of women operate. Yet as war and catastrophes are gendered phenomena, an inclusive analysis of war and peace actors needs to account for men's and women's roles. Building a "house of peace"[45] requires mutual support and cooperation between parties involved in such an effort at the grassroots, mid-range and top levels of leadership. Women's voices and open participation were ignored throughout much of the peace talks that eventually led to the agreement signed in August 2000. As women were not leaders of any political party, their inclusion did not seem to be anyone's priority.

For almost three years women tirelessly lobbied for inclusion in and active contribution to the peace process. Their efforts were manifested in different arenas. At a conference held in Addis Ababa in November 1997 on "Best Practices in Peace Consolidation and Non-violent Methods of Conflict Resolution", the six Burundi women's representatives shared their concerns regarding the impact of the economic embargo imposed by regional countries on the civilian population in Burundi with other female participants, among them former Ugandan vice-president Speciosa Kazibwe and minister of women's affairs in Rwanda Aloisea Inyumba. Although the sanctions were not removed until January 1999, the crucial role played by women in facilitating this cross-national discussion on the plight of Burundians as a result of the embargo could not be ignored.

This was part of the initial efforts marking many women's unwavering commitment to peace and reconstruction as they sought to be heard at the highest levels of political involvement. With firm encouragement from former South African president Nelson Mandela, the Mwalimu Nyerere Foundation and UNIFEM, women had the opportunity to attend the All-Party Conference that took place on 17–20 July 2000 in Arusha, Tanzania. This conference gave the participants the opportunity to discuss the impact the war had had on women in general, and determine how they could benefit from the peace process and the role they could play during this process.[46]

Many men were reluctant to allow women to participate during the early phases of the negotiations. Indeed, as Imelda Nzirorera, then interim director of the Center for the Promotion of Human Rights and Genocide Prevention, explained, "from the beginning on, men were not pleased with our presence. They would say, 'we do not understand why you need to be here. You should be at home. Peace is a men's issue.' "[47] Eventually women were allowed to attend as observers, with no right to take part in formal discussions.

Although only included as observers in the talks, without becoming signatories to the Arusha Peace Accord, women were able to make written contributions on crucial issues that were debated in formal meetings, leading to the drafting of the peace agreement that was signed on 28 August 2000. It is important to note that many of the recommendations women made in their capacity as observers were included in the final document. This was possible despite many factors that hindered progress for women's peace initiatives, including insufficient material support to such efforts; underrepresentation in decision-making; feminization of poverty; the weight of tradition, which undermines women's roles; overall low levels of education (70 per cent of Burundian women are illiterate); and a lack of solidarity expressed by many men.

Nonetheless, as Swanee Hunt and Cristina Posa argue, women are crucial to inclusive security: "Every effort to bridge divides, even if unsuccessful, has value, both in lessons learned and links to be built on later. Local actors with crucial experience resolving conflicts, organizing political movements, managing relief efforts, or working with military forces bring that experience into ongoing peace processes."[48] As Hunt and Posa conclude, "We can ignore women's work as peacemakers, or we can harness its full force across a wide range of activities relevant to the security sphere: bridging the divide between groups in conflict, influencing local security forces, collaborating with international organizations, and seeking political office."[49] It would indeed be remiss to ignore Burundi women's contributions to peacebuilding and reconstruction. Despite all attempts at political exclusion, women found ways to create spaces for themselves, and to make their voices heard. They made conscious efforts to renew relationships at the community level, and were involved in cross-national and international lobbying.

Conclusion

This chapter demonstrates how women's grassroots efforts contributed to peacebuilding at local and national levels through the peace process. Productive activities were fostered by a realization that the sole reliance on male relatives for peace and security does not guarantee women's and families' survival. The Burundian women's peace movement operates in a fragile post-conflict environment characterized by a number of obstacles that stand in the way of durable peace and security, including the lack of basic means of survival for many war victims due to economic pressures; inflation and limited sustained productivity among those who have not returned to their original homes since the war started in 1993; loss of years of schooling and productivity by youth at risk; and continued political instability.

This movement therefore needs to be strengthened through continuous efforts at the local, national and international levels. Support at the three levels would enhance the capacity of women peace activists and their constituents on both sides of the ethnic divide to reach a level of maturity and a sense of security that a genuine peace movement deserves.

Women's experiences of extreme deprivation and physical and psychological abuse, as well as forced relocation during periods of violent conflict, explain why it is in their best interest to support a peaceful settlement of differences and seek an end to war. Burundi women took a proactive role searching for peace in the one arena where they are least considered to be a threat – the grassroots level. Women's survival was dependent on their creative abilities to form coalitions across ethnic lines, driven by the fact that they played a critical role in family survival. Thus they turned their misfortunes and victimization into opportunities for strengthening the women's peace movement, which needs to be supported at all levels to create a lasting impact in Burundi and the entire Great Lakes region.

Despite the trauma of war and violence, women were less inclined than men to resort to destructive measures, including violent retaliation. Instead, many devised practical approaches to survival, contributing (albeit informally) to peacebuilding. Many of the women's associations were formed by those who decided to focus on reclaiming their own sense of identity, reviving dormant skills and engaging in a number of activities that were conducive to personal healing and economic productivity. As peaceful responses to structures of oppression and violence, these associations sought productive means of survival in the hope that the war would soon end. There was a need among many to change their mindset, focusing less on individual traumas (*kwiyibagiza amagorwa babonye, ivyo baciyemwo kuko benshi usanga ari impunzi* or "forcing oneself to forget one's traumas, what one has been through because as you know most of them are refugees") and needs due to loss of human lives and material possessions (*kugirango barabe ko bokwiyibagiza ubukene bwabo* or "so that they can force themselves to focus less on extreme poverty"). Women decided to come together to identify ways in which they could best support each other. Culturally sensitive trauma healing, forgiveness and reconciliation programmes proved to be very helpful and need to be developed and strengthened at all levels in similar situations, from the grassroots to the top level of political leadership, to ensure that people are not trapped in a cycle of hatred and violence. Some women at the grassroots demonstrated that they were gifted with an innate quality of forgiveness. Mutual support was necessary at many different levels. For some, a search for internal peace and a sense of commonality away from the isolating experiences of war motivated their decision to join organized groups. For others, associations served as forums for information exchange, enabling women to place their personal tragedies within broader contexts while seeking mutual support. As one woman said, the association became the new context in which women could explore creative ways to ensure their survival and create a new sense of stability in a very unstable environment. They simply wanted to improve their living conditions and move on.

Women did not wait for safety and security to be assured before they engaged in these activities. This chapter therefore credits the women at the forefront of the peace efforts, specifically those who risked their lives and were involved in filling a void and communicating across ethnic lines at a time when the country had devolved into separate ethnic camps for Hutu and Tutsi. The survival strategies employed by Burundi women were often so subtle that even well-intentioned and informed practitioners and academics may have failed to recognize their critical role in peacebuilding. Women's creative, practical and non-violent approaches to peacebuilding enabled them to focus less on "victimization" and more on survival and reconstruction initiatives, which strengthened women's capacity as effective peace players. Frontline women's peace activism and reconstruction efforts are often the only hope in post-conflict societies where governments are unwilling or unable to address issues that are critical to the survival of women, their children and society overall.

Notes

1. For a detailed analysis of why many were sceptical about the peace process, see "Burundi Peace Process Fatally Flawed", *Sunday Times*, Johannesburg, 21 July 2003, available at http://allafrica.com/stories/printable/200307210048.html.
2. See Rehn, Elisabeth and Ellen Johnson Sirleaf (2002) *Women, War, Peace: The Independent Expert Assessment*, New York: UNIFEM, p. 78.
3. My work with these groups began during summer 1998 when I returned to Burundi to visit my family and see first-hand the impact of the war in the country. I had initially left Burundi to go to the United States for graduate studies in January 1991. I returned almost two years later in December 1992 for a one-month visit. At this time, in spite of evidence that political change was taking shape, I did not anticipate the turn that politics took soon after I returned to the United States in mid-January 1993. The assassination of the democratically elected president in October 1993 came as a shock, and the

ensuing violence that took hold of the country for over 10 years left many wondering about the future of peace in Burundi. I returned to Burundi in July 1998 to visit my family again. At this time I was resolved to find signs of hope in this country's quest for peace. I was initially intrigued by the internally displaced women's willingness to join ethnically mixed voluntary associations at a time when the country was still deeply divided along ethnic lines. My meeting with these women was instrumental in my attempt to spend more time trying to uncover the factors that motivate women to seek peace in times of war. I continue to learn about women's peacebuilding efforts around the world, and this chapter seeks to ensure that a record is kept of Burundi women's voices and contributions to peacebuilding.

4. Funded by USIP, this workshop brought together representatives from more than 20 women's organizations based in and around Burundi's capital, Bujumbura.

5. Amnesty International (2007) "Burundi: No Protection from Rape in War and Peace", October, Amnesty International, London, p. 7, available at www.unhcr.org/refworld/docid/470b304f2.html. Also see Rehn and Sirleaf, note 2, pp. 49–60, for a detailed account of the prevalence of rape in war and its impact on women.

6. See www.oxfam.org.uk/landrights/Buruten.rtf.

7. This is the case in post-genocide Rwanda. It also applies to other conflict areas, whether current or historical, including Guatemala and Argentina for example, and refers to the wives of the disappeared.

8. See for example Cohen, Roberta and Deng M. Francis (1998) *Masses in Flight: The Global Crisis of Internal Displacement*, Washington, DC: Brookings Institution Press; Refugees International (2001) "Towards a More Effective Response to Internal Displacement", 8 June, available at http://reliefweb.int/sites/reliefweb.int/files/reliefweb_pdf/node-81902.pdf.

9. I put peace in quotes because "positive" peace, as I define it later in the chapter, means the absence of structural violence in addition to the absence of war ("negative" peace), which is another approach to peace.

10. See Lisa Schirch's discussion on violence against women in wartime and peacetime in Chapter 2 in this volume.

11. See Human Rights Watch (2000) "Seeking Protection: Addressing Sexual and Domestic Violence in Tanzania's Refugee Camps", 1 October, Human Rights Watch, New York, available at www.unhcr.org/refworld/docid/3ae6a8720.html.

12. International Committee of the Red Cross (2004) "Burundi: Help for the Victims of Attack on Gatumba Refugee Camp", 15 August, available at www.icrc.org/Web/Eng/siteeng0.nsf/htmlall/63WMM8.

13. Smith, Steven (1999) "Burundi: At the Brink of Humanitarian Tragedy", *Refugees International*, 12 October, available at http://reliefweb.int/node/54120. For a detailed account of challenges refugees in general and women in particular experience in camps in Tanzania see Human Rights Watch (2000) "Seeking Protection: Addressing Sexual and Domestic Violence in Tanzania's Refugee Camps", October, available at www.hrw.org/legacy/reports/2000/tanzania/.

14. After the successful elections in 2005, many families that had spent years in refugee camps started returning home in Burundi, only to face different types of challenges, including lack of a home, employment and means of survival.

15. Author's interview with a representative of the local NGO United Against Hunger, Bujumbura, Burundi, July 2000.

16. It was shocking to meet women in 2009 and 2010 still living as IDPs in different parts of Burundi, including in remote areas of Buhiga in central Burundi and Muyinga and Ngozi in northeast and northern Burundi respectively. While some were too poor to afford rebuilding their homes, others did not feel safe enough to return home. Durable

peace will not be achieved until all Burundians can feel safe in their homes and have the opportunity and resources needed to participate in rebuilding their lives and to contribute to national reconstruction.

17. Sabimbona, Sabine (1998) "The Problems of Displaced and Returnee Women Faced with Current Land Tenure Policies in Burundi", paper presented at inter-regional consultation, Kigali, February, p. 3, available at www.google.ch/url?sa=t&rct=j&q=Sabine +Sabimbona%2C+table&source=web&cd=1&ved=0CCMQFjAA&url=http%3A%2F %2Fwww.oxfam.org.uk%2Fresources%2Flearning%2Flandrights%2Fdownloads %2Fburuten.rtf&ei=CKkkT5DjM4eWOsrpmcII&usg=AFQjCNGeB-2Scc7vdWebg 9fJNAavhDFQ9A&sig2=FkQgxyNH0gcVmR5_ArJqmQ.

18. For various discussions on what it means for women's activist roles on the front line see Waller, Marguerite R. and Jennifer Rycenga (eds) (2000) *Frontline Feminism: Women, War and Resistance*, New York: Garland Publishing.

19. Several cases studies are referred to in Marshall, Donna Ramsey (2000) *Women in War and Peace: Grassroots Peacebuilding*, Washington, DC: USIP; Rehn and Sirleaf, note 2.

20. See Jeong, Ho-Won (2000) *Peace and Conflict Studies: An Introduction*, Aldershot: Ashgate, p. 358.

21. Ibid., p. 337.

22. For a detailed discussion see ibid.

23. Burundi women proactively sought to take an active role in the Arusha peace process. After much lobbying internally and with international support, they were finally included as observers.

24. The peace talks were followed by a series of ceasefire talks that culminated in the handover of power in 2003 from President Pierre Buyoya to his successor, Domitien Ndayizeye, who then led the transitional government until the democratic elections of 2005. For details see Centre for International Cooperation and Security (2008) "Disarmament, Demobilisation and Reintegration (DDR) and Human Security in Burundi", July, University of Bradford, available at www.ddr-humansecurity.org.uk/images/ DDR%20DESK%20REVIEW%20BURUNDI.pdf.

25. Sporadic violence was common in the months preceding the June 2010 elections and continues to bring instability to villages and communities in and around rural Bujumbura. Attacks have become frequent, particularly targeting known supporters of the party in power, but also unfortunately creating threats to users of the public transport system to and from the capital city. According to public opinion, the attackers are members of a coalition of supporters of several opposition party leaders who seek to destabilize the party in power and are ready to use any means to remind the current leaders that in their opinion the elections were rigged. These include members of the Palipehutu, the last rebel group to give up fighting and which, after the signing of the Arusha Peace Accord, continued to call for a renegotiation of the signed agreement and claim more seats for the Hutu ethnic group in the government. In May 2009 the Palipehutu left the Kibira forest where they had been launching attacks on surrounding villages and users of the public transport system.

26. The peace movement in Burundi emulates efforts achieved in other parts of the world where women made their mark through contributions to peace processes, as well as in post-conflict reconstruction. Specific cases include the Peace People and the Northern Ireland Women's Coalition in Northern Ireland, and the Madres de la Plaza de Mayo in Argentina, where women were able to make a successful transition "from protesters to politicians".

27. Kinama and Kinindo are neighbourhoods of the capital city. Ngozi is a major province in the north and Rusaka is a region in the centre of the country.

28. For details see Global Network of Women Peacebuilders at www.gnwp.org/members/ women-allies-peacebuilders-network.

29. Statement of Sabine Sabimbona of the Collective of Women's Associations and NGOs of Burundi, CAFOB, to the UN Security Council Arria Formula on the Implementation of Security Council Resolution 1325, 23 October 2002, in NGO Working Group on Women, Peace and Security Resolution 1325 (2002) "Two Years On Report", 31 October, available at www.peacewomen.org/assets/file/SecurityCouncilMonitor/Debates/WPS/ WPS2002/Statements/ngowgtwoyearson.pdf.

30. Ibid.

31. Interview with a female member of an organization that brought together internally displaced women of diverse regional backgrounds to find ways to survive and achieve peace through economic productivity. The founder and president, an officer at the Adult Literacy Center in Bujumbura, was instrumental in creating a healing and open environment for all the members.

32. See Chapter 2 in this volume for nine reasons why men and women need to partner to achieve lasting peace. The same reasons apply to the case of Burundi.

33. Ruddick, Sara (1989) *Maternal Thinking: Toward a Politics of Peace*, Boston, MA: Beacon Press.

34. Interview with a teacher and GWA member, July 2000.

35. Interview with a Congolese GWA member, July 2000.

36. Children may be considered orphans in Burundi when the family's primary breadwinner has died. Often children who have lost their fathers are considered orphans because they are no longer assured of their right to property inheritance.

37. Interview with a GWA member, July 2000.

38. Interview with an elementary school teacher and GWA member, July 2000.

39. Ibid.

40. Ibid.

41. See Galtung, Johan (1969) "Violence, Peace, and Peace Research", *Journal of Peace Research* 6(3), pp. 167–191; Jeong, note 20; Brock-Utne, Birgit (1985) *Feminist Perspectives on Peace and Peace Education*, New York: Pergamon Press; Chapter 2 in this volume for a distinction between positive and negative peace.

42. For a detailed analysis see Ruddick, note 33, p. 145.

43. Interview with Rwandan GWA member, July 2000.

44. For a detailed account of mediation efforts to end the Burundi crisis see for example Hara, Fabienne (1999) "Burundi: A Case of Parallel Diplomacy", in Chester Crocker, Fen Osler Hampson and Pamela Aal (eds) *Herding Cats: Multiparty Mediation in a Complex World*, Washington, DC: USIP, pp. 139–158.

45. See Lederach, John Paul (1997) *Building Peace: Sustainable Reconciliation in Divided Societies*, Washington, DC: USIP, p. 37.

46. It was around this time that the UK-based organization International Alert launched the Women Building Peace: From the Village Council to the Negotiating Table global campaign, which eventually led to the October UNSC Resolution 1325. For further details of the aim of this campaign, and follow-up efforts by International Alert, see www. womenpeacesecurity.org/about/international-alert.html.

47. See de Silva Burke, Enid, Jennifer Klot and Ikaweba Bunting (2001) *Engendrer la paix: Réflexion sur le processus de paix au Burundi*, New York: UNIFEM, p. 7.

48. See Hunt, Swanee and Cristina Posa (2001) "Women Waging Peace: Inclusive Security", *Foreign Policy*, May/June, available at www.swaneehunt.com/articles/FP _InclusiveSecurity.pdf.

49. Ibid.

Part II

Women and children: Essential partnership of survival and peace

6

Women and children in the post-Cold War Balkans: Concerns and responses

Constantine P. Danopoulos, Konstantinos S. Skandalis and Zlatko Isakovic

The wars that accompanied the violent disintegration of Yugoslavia caused a plethora of traumatic and long-lasting economic, social, physical and psychological disruptions for its citizens and often those of neighbouring societies. Although the physical damage may become less visible with the passage of time, the psychological, mental and societal wounds are much harder to heal. While no segment of society or age group escaped the trauma, women and children are the most severely affected. Yet the two groups are not affected the same way: as Nadine Puechguir-bal asserts, if we are to "have a better picture of the social and political flux within societies", we need to "change language and talk about gender perspectives instead of using fossilized categories like *women-and-children*".[1] During the wars and their aftermath the burden of caring for children and the elderly rested increasingly on the shoulders of women. Decreasing budgets and reduced government spending on social needs compound the problem. These tasks and responsibilities rarely disappear with the end of the fighting, and in some cases can even intensify. Displacement, rape, unwanted pregnancies and other forms of violence during these wars are compounded by psychological trauma, community and spousal rejection, economic hardships, prostitution and discrimination that follow the termination of the fighting. Chris Corrin speaks for many when she describes the Kosovo situation: "women tend to make up the majority of targeted civilian casualties of war but are not just victims of war, as their contributions and commitment to peace and reconstruction testify".[2]

Defying victimhood: Women and post-conflict peacebuilding, Schnabel and Tabyshalieva (eds), United Nations University Press, 2012, ISBN 978-92-808-1201-5

Krishna Kumar's conclusions are remarkably similar: "civil wars profoundly affect women's personal well-being, their status and role in the family, their access to economic resources, their political participation and their attitudes and perceptions".[3] Puechguirbal concurs, stating that "women have access to resources, but if they do not have control over these resources, they remain dependent".[4] Julie A. Mertus is even more direct, asserting that in wartime women are likely to "suffer more from human rights violations than men will".[5]

Although different, war-related damages to children are equally pervasive and arguably emotionally more lasting. Children are more vulnerable, and the sight of combat, loss of parents, lack of adequate nutrition and removal from schools lead to devastating physical, developmental and psychological consequences. In a report entitled "We the Children", UNICEF recognizes the immediate and long-term deleterious legacies of pre- and post-war economic, social and psychological difficulties for children:

> There are stages in life when children are capable of growing by leaps and bounds – physically, intellectually and emotionally. They are also particularly vulnerable at these stages to risks that lead to stunted growth, failed learning, trauma or death. If a child's cycle of growth and development is interrupted, this often becomes a lifelong handicap.[6]

The report makes clear that "children are the most severely affected". Poverty and other war-related hardships strike "at the very roots of their potential for development – their growing minds and bodies".[7]

International and indigenous non-governmental organizations (NGOs) and UN-related relief agencies are cognizant of the vulnerability of women and children in war-torn environments and design their intervention strategies accordingly. The well-known and highly experienced NGO activist Andrew S. Natsios identifies five general sets of humanitarian situations that are likely to stimulate relief organizations to intervene: deterioration or collapse of state authority; widespread abuses generated by ethnic or religious conflict; severe food shortage; economic collapse; and mass population dislocation of people looking for food or seeking to escape violence and death.[8] The world economic crisis that arose in 2008 is likely to intensify the plight of war-affected women and children.

The violent disintegration of Yugoslavia, coupled with a parallel economic collapse and international isolation, brought untold and ongoing hardships on the citizens of that troubled land. As in other fratricidal and inter-state conflicts, women and children bore and continue to bear the brunt of the legacy of ethnic cleansing and the Bosnian (1992–1995) and Kosovo (1999) wars that followed. Of over 1.5 million refugees and internally displaced persons (IDPs), well over half were women and children. World public opinion was exposed to pictures and stories depicting ethnic cleansing, concentration camps, rape, forced pregnancies, hunger, torture and other forms of violence, touching Yugoslav people of both sexes and all ages and ethnic or religious background. To many NGOs and UN-related relief agencies the situation in Yugoslavia displayed the criteria for humanitarian intervention identified by Natsios, and they eventually moved to alleviate the plight of the affected.

Even though the fighting has stopped and a modicum of uneasy peace has returned to the Yugoslav successor states, the suffering has not ended, despite the efforts of international and newly formed indigenous NGOs and other relief agencies. Thousands are still displaced, poverty is pervasive and the emotional and psychological wounds have yet to heal. As during the fighting, women and children continue to bear the brunt of the pain and misery in the post-war environment. This chapter will identify, explore and analyse the problems facing women and children since the guns fell silent in the former Yugoslavia. It also assesses the record and performance of local and international NGOs and other relief agencies. A brief look at the Yugoslav conflict and its victims helps us understand the nature and magnitude of the problems facing women and children, as well as assess the performance of relief-providing organizations since the fighting formally ended.[9]

Yugoslavia's violent disintegration

The creation of the People's Republic of Yugoslavia, later renamed the Socialist Federal Republic of Yugoslavia (SFRY), by Marshal Josip Broz Tito and his victorious communist partisans came on the heels of the Second World War and a failed inter-war attempt at south Slav unity. The SFRY was a religiously, ethnically and culturally diverse entity held together by the force of Tito's personality as well as the unique neutralist posture it maintained in the Cold War environment. American aid, coupled with freedom of movement and access to Western markets and financial capital, enabled Yugoslav citizens to enjoy considerable economic prosperity and social and cultural freedom.

Tito's edifice consisted of six republics (Bosnia-Herzegovina, Croatia, Macedonia, Montenegro, Serbia and Slovenia) and two autonomous regions within Serbia (Kosovo and Vojvodina). Ethnicity anchored on religious background formed the basis of ethnic group identity. The cumbersome collective/rotating presidency Tito established and his death in 1980 left a leadership vacuum, with no one institution or individual with sufficient authority to tackle the country's mounting problems. By the late 1980s, as the federal government began withering away, authorities at the republic level filled the void. The parallel relaxation of Cold War tensions affected the Yugoslav landscape. The weakening of the Soviet Union eclipsed the threat that served as a catalyst of unity among the republics following the 1948 Tito-Stalin split. Similar considerations prevailed on American policy-makers to downgrade the importance of Yugoslavia to Western security calculations. Washington was too preoccupied with the Gulf War, and the European Union (EU) proved unable or unwilling to help check the thickening clouds of ethnic nationalism among Yugoslavia's constituent republics.

Yugoslavia came unglued when Slovenia bolted from the federation in 1991, followed by Croatia soon after. The Serb government, dominated by Slobodan Milošević, made only a token effort to prevent Slovenia's secession. The short but destructive war that followed Croatia's secession in 1991 generated thousands of refugees and IDPs, and accompanying atrocities. An uneasy ceasefire left most territorial disputes intact, and the two countries fought a second round in 1995, resulting in additional expulsions, including 250,000 Serbs expelled from Krajina by Croatia.

Bosnia was an even more difficult matter. Burgeoning ethnic nationalism destroyed initial efforts by the three groups (Croats, Serbs and Muslims) to work out a power-sharing agreement. The three-year war that followed caused more casualties and generated more refugees and human suffering than the Serbo-Croatian wars. The war in Bosnia turned ethnic cleansing into a household term throughout the world. The 1995 Dayton Accords brought an uneasy peace to Bosnia and the rest of former Yugoslavia. It called for the refugees and IDPs to return home. Although some heeded the advice, many did not. It is estimated that by the end of 1996 "more than one million Bosnian refugees and displaced persons remained [and remain] in other parts of former Yugoslavia or elsewhere in Europe".[10]

The Dayton Accords did not end the Yugoslav drama, however; the Kosovo problem simmered and blew up in 1999. The mass exodus of Kosovar Albanians, partly as a result of the NATO bombing that followed, created more suffering and additional refugees and IDPs. With the United Nations taking administrative control of Kosovo, the majority of the refugees returned to their destroyed homes. However, almost the entire Serb population of the province – about 200,000 people – were displaced and joined other IDPs in rump-Yugoslavia, with virtually no prospect of return. After formal fighting stopped, secessionist tendencies in the area still simmered, raising the possibility of still more refugees and IDPs.

UN relief agencies and American, European and other international NGOs sought to assist the nearly 5 million refugees and IDPs generated by the various stages of the conflict in Yugoslavia. Although there are no official statistics, Mertus cites what she considers reliable data and asserts that "women and children were disproportionately affected by the displacements. As in most refugee and displaced populations, an estimated 80 per cent of the displaced population were women and children; over half of the families had at least one pregnant or nursing woman."[11]

Although somewhat late in coming, the response of international humanitarian organizations was considerable. At the height of the Bosnia war more than 300 NGOs and UN organizations had offices in Sarajevo and other major cities. UNICEF, Médecins Sans Frontières, Care, the Red Cross and a variety of other international humanitarian organizations moved in to provide food, medical care and other forms of assistance to the needy. Some attempted to help with long-term needs, such as psychological trauma, education, fostering economic opportunity and helping establish indigenous NGOs and civil society in the post-war environment. Despite enormous structural, cultural, economic and other difficulties, their efforts made a difference to the lives of those affected, especially the most vulnerable: women and children.

Yet the role of NGOs and UN agencies in helping to create a civil society capable of addressing the needs of women and children in the Yugoslav successor states in the post-war period appears to have been limited. UNICEF reported in 2000 that in post-war Yugoslavia "women have remained unsafe even in the sanctuary of their own homes". The same document concludes that children and young people are equally "affected as direct victims or witnesses of violence", unemployment, drug abuse, trafficking and other forms of organized crime.[12] Despite the fact that the more visible effects have dissipated, the psychological and emotional dramas linger on. What is the nature of the problems facing women and children in post-war Yugoslavia, and what explains the inability of NGOs to build sustainable structures to deal with these problems?

Women in the post-war environment

Even though the guns are now silent, social and economic conditions in some Yugoslav successor states are appalling, with no prospects for immediate improvement. The majority of IDPs ended up in Serbia, Bosnia-Herzegovina, Montenegro and Croatia. Slovenia was largely unaffected. It is estimated that about half of IDPs and refugees still live with relatives or in dilapidated and cramped government-provided quarters. This is especially true of those who ended up in Serbia and Montenegro. More than two-thirds of them are women and children. A sample of official and other statistics paints a bleak picture. Compared to a decade earlier, in

1999 the former Republic of Yugoslavia's (FRY) GDP was only half its previous size, the former Yugoslav Republic of Macedonia's (FYROM)[13] was 71 per cent and Croatia's 77.5 per cent. Bosnia-Herzegovina reported that in 2000 the per capita GDP "stood at only $1,000, which was approximately half of the pre-war level".[14] Only Slovenia posted a gain of 7.5 per cent during the same period. Official unemployment data provide little comfort, either: in 1997 the registered unemployment rate for the FRY stood at 26 per cent and in Croatia and FYROM 18 and 42 per cent, respectively. Unofficial statistics indicate much higher rates of unemployment: in Bosnia and Kosovo it was estimated to be close to 70 per cent. UNICEF documents that "over 60 per cent of the population of FRY was estimated to be living below the poverty line and in Croatia the figure was some 20 per cent". The report concludes that "increasing poverty and falling incomes have pushed many people into the burgeoning black or informal economy for survival. Many have emigrated, adding to the brain drain."[15]

Interviews with on-the-ground observers Monika Kleck and Nila Kapor-Stanulovic confirm the dismal state of affairs. Kleck reports that "there are many families without any income [and] living, health, nutrition and other conditions are absolutely poor". Kapor-Stanulovic concurs: "unemployment, uncertainty for the future and the breakdown of the social and health insurance systems" have a devastating effect on the population. Those employed in the burgeoning black market – and there are many – have virtually no rights at all.[16]

Women and children are severely affected by the economic slump and its implications. Data indicate that employment conditions for women have deteriorated in the last decade. In their work Kapor-Stanulovic and David report that in the FRY women's average income is 20–40 per cent lower than that of men. Moreover, 50–60 per cent of all unemployed persons are women.[17] Many of these are widows or single mothers who have shouldered the exclusive responsibility of caring for their children and often their parents or in-laws. Ian Smillie's work lends further support to these observations:

> Gender is an especially important area of concern. Women may have been protected from violence in some emergencies, but in many they have been targeted and in most the burden for children and for the care and feeding of their families has increased.[18]

Yet a host of societal and cultural considerations work against needy women. Citing a report by the UN Commission on the Status of Women, Mertus feels that "affected women face discrimination in access to relief supplies and are included in only token numbers in decision-making humanitarian work".[19] A US State Department human rights country report on Bosnia finds evidence that "women have been discriminated against in the workplace in favor of demobilized soldiers".[20] A report by the Swedish-based Kvinna till Kvinna Foundation points to a gender bias in Kosovo, especially in rural areas.[21] Similar situations prevail in Serbia, FYROM and Croatia.

In addition to economic and employment-related problems, women face equally devastating psychological, social and family problems. During the various Yugoslav wars, soldiers engaged in systematic and widespread rape of women of rival ethnic backgrounds, involving thousands of Muslim, Croat, Kosovar and Serb women. Although the exact number of victims may never be known due to lack of reliable data, an estimated 20,000–70,000 women endured sexual assault during the Bosnian and other wars. Raping women appeared to be a deliberate part of the war strategy, with the aim of ethnic cleansing. According to the United Nations, ethnic cleansing is a deliberate and coordinated attempt to render "an area ethnically homogeneous by using force or intimidation to remove persons of given groups from the area".[22]

In traditional patriarchal societies in the Balkans, rape and impregnation of women of rival ethnic groups are believed to produce future soldiers who would carry on the ultra-nationalist dream of domination, since the child's nationality is derived from its father. Todd A. Salzman encapsulates this deeply held cultural myth as follows:

> In the Balkan patriarchal society, the family name passes on through the male, regardless of religion or ethnicity. Even though biologically the child shares an equal amount of genetic material from the male and female, this does not overcome the sense that a child born from rape by a Serb will always be considered Serbian.[23]

Despite the fact that the Serb side was widely blamed as the perpetrators of sexual violence against women, Salzman further notes that "the Serbs were not the only group who accept this myth" and other Yugoslav ethnic groups are guilty of similar acts.[24]

The same traditional masculine considerations hamper women's social and psychological status long after the war is over. Two broad groups have been observed among affected women of all ethnic groups in postwar Yugoslavia. Fearful of shame, dishonour and stigmatization, an unknown but presumed large group of raped women chose not to share their ordeal with family or friends, or seek professional counselling. The majority of women in this group are those who did not become pregnant or terminated the pregnancy without their family or community ever finding out. Salzman points out that "All these factors tend to dissuade women from talking about their experiences with friends as well as seeking psychological counselling."[25] Reporting on the situation in Kosovo, Kvinna till Kvinna found that "due to fear of being evicted from families, women are very reluctant to come forward even when they need psychological help due to the consequences of the rapes".[26] But psychological and other research shows that lack of openness and sharing of traumatic experiences "hamper[s] the ability to heal emotionally, physically and psychologically".[27] Women with untreated traumas experience difficulty in employment as well as in community and personal relationships.

The second group consists of women whose experience with sexual violence is known to the community. Their burdens are similar to those afflicting the first group, but in some respects are more pronounced. Balkan patriarchal attitudes tend not to perceive raped women as innocent victims. This creates an environment of suspicion that "stigmatize[s] rape survivors rather than rapists". As Sharlach argues, "When a woman's honor is tarnished through rape, the ethnic group is also dishonored. To restore its honor, the ethnic group may ostracize or expel the raped girl or woman."[28] Kvinna till Kvinna found that Kosovar women who were encouraged to talk to the press about their ordeal faced condemnation upon their return home. The report is disarmingly clear:

> It was worse for women who had visible wounds and bruises and immediately got a microphone in the face with questions as to whether she had been raped. As the refugees returned to Kosovo, so did the silence about the raped women. Incidents started to be reported about women having been thrown out by their families.[29]

Lisa Sharlach refers to this treatment as "the second rape",[30] and feels that it further complicates rehabilitation efforts. Increased prostitution and trafficking of women for the purpose of sexual exploitation are but a few of the undesirable consequences. Moreover, the arrival of UN peacekeeping soldiers led to an increase in the number of brothels in Kosovo, as happened earlier in Bosnia.

These developments and cultural/societal attitudes impact negatively on family relationships, leading to increased divorce and domestic violence. Azza Karam argues that "The existence of violence has been associated with increasing levels of violence in the society as a whole and this sometimes translates into increasing incidence of domestic violence."[31] Yugoslavia's experience supports her point. Citing interview data, Salzman argues that "one of the recurring concerns is that if [raped women's] husbands found out about the rape, [they] would not take them back or they may be violently abused, or in some cases killed". He notes that the Helsinki-based International Federation for Human Rights reported in

2000 that about 30 per cent of women in Bosnia were victims of domestic violence. Such attitudes and practices appear to plague the Muslim, Orthodox and Catholic communities of the former Yugoslavia.[32] Sharlach is correct when she asserts that rape causes "serious physical and/or mental injury to the survivor and [can] destroy the morale of her family and ethnic community. Rape is difficult to prove, there is no corpse left as evidence and war crimes tribunals and domestic courts seldom prosecute soldiers for rape."[33] Mertus adds that in the former Yugoslavia "legal prohibitions and cultural mores often constrain women from reporting sexual violence or from receiving the assistance needed".[34]

Violence and war created space for ultra-nationalistic and socially conservative views to reassert themselves. The rise of religion added to the androgenic Balkan milieu. Such attitudes continue to be dominant in the post-war environment. Yugoslav women, who had made steady civil, political and social gains in the pre-1990 era, now find themselves on the sidelines. Their political influence and power have declined, and with them the ability to influence policy-making. This is particularly true in rural areas. The loss is reflected in the absence of women from decision-making positions.[35] The US State Department report on human rights in Bosnia agrees with Mertus's assessment that few women hold positions of responsibility.[36] Croatian women work in low-level and low-paying jobs and are first to be laid off when employers seek ways to reduce payroll expenses.[37] Kvinna till Kvinna is equally direct, stating that Albanian Kosovar women are "excluded from the closest circles of decision-making".[38] Under the circumstances it is not surprising that "women's needs and potential contributions are marginalized, not regarded as a vital ingredient in all reconstruction processes".[39]

Children in the post-war chaos

Children in Yugoslav successor states also feel the after-effects of war. The severity of the economic crisis has an equally devastating and arguably more profound impact on them, impeding their health, physical and mental growth, education and safety. A 2001 UNICEF report encapsulated their plight: "the economic collapse was having a profound impact on both parental and state capacities to provide for children and as a result on the welfare status of children".[40] Indicators abound. Infant (one year of age and younger) mortality per 1,000 live births in 1997 stood at 16.3 in FYROM, 14.3 in the FRY and 8.2 in Croatia. At 35 per 1,000, Kosovo had the highest infant mortality rate in Europe.

Even though official data indicate that over 95 per cent of children attend primary school, the situation on the ground is less rosy.[41] Monika

Kleck provides eyewitness testimony, reporting that severe shortage of books, structurally unsafe buildings and other problems keep many children, especially girls and Roma children, away from school. The situation in Kosovo has improved since the UN force moved in and managed to bring calm to the territory. Most Kosovar Albanians have returned to their homes, schools are once again functioning and medical and other services have returned to a state of normalcy. Yet the psychological and social effects of the war on women and children linger on.

Ethnic background, gender and patriarchal cultural traits appear to play a role as well. Girls and children of Roma background post much higher non-attendance and dropout rates. For example, evidence indicates that nearly all Roma children attending Croatian schools drop out by the eighth grade. The dropout rate for girls in Kosovo is 34 per cent.[42] While there are no reliable data, it appears that the percentage of girls removed from school by their parents was lower before the war. Corrin lists four factors that explain the unusually high dropout rates among girls: "Security – fear of being attacked or raped; poverty – boys are chosen above girls who are useful to work at home or on land; unwillingness – often girls did not want to go because of a lack of encouragement at home or school; age – reflecting the fear girls in their late teens will be too old to find marriage partners."[43]

Ethnically based segregation and discrimination are also a problem, particularly in Bosnia's complex ethnic tapestry. The US State Department's human rights report on that country is both troubling and revealing: students in minority areas frequently face a hostile environment in schools that do not provide an ethnically neutral setting. At times minority children are barred from attending school. Students of different ethnic groups may share the school building, but attend class on different floors or use the same facility in shifts without ever actually interacting with other students or teachers of a different ethnic group.[44]

Displaced, maimed and disabled children and those of non-dominant (minority) ethnic groups are having an even more difficult time. Albanian Kosovar youngsters who were used as child soldiers during the Kosovo conflict and their Roma counterparts engaged by the Serbian paramilitaries are equally affected. A UNICEF report on Yugoslavia states that "as at end-April 2000, there were 218,129 IDPs registered [in FRY], of which 81,894 were children". The report continues that this "in absolute terms is the largest such population in any European country", and points to the "profound effect on society, public services and the national economy that is likely to endure for years to come". Citing research data, the document states that such experiences have devastating and long-term consequences on the children themselves: "of those exposed to severe war trauma, 62% exhibited symptoms of mental suffering and 35% were in need of professional psychiatric support. None have had normal lives."[45] Unexploded mines have claimed the lives or limbs of many children. For example, in Bosnia since the end of the war "nearly 17,000 children were killed, 35,000 wounded and over 1,800 permanently disabled". In war-torn countries in the area, including Bosnia, "social services for children are in extremely low supply. Children with disabilities lack sufficient medical care and educational opportunities."[46]

Children born as a result of rape/forced impregnation are the worst hit. Although there are no statistics on the number of such children, circumstantial evidence indicates that there are several thousand scattered across various parts of former Yugoslavia, especially Kosovo, Bosnia and Croatia. Owing to the view that the father's ethnic background determines the child's ethnic identity, these children are in dire straits. They are discriminated because of their perceived ethnic status and carry the stigma associated with rape by a male of a hostile ethnic group. It is hard to know how many of these youngsters have ended up in orphanages or are roaming the streets of various communities. These children have the dubious distinction of not being wanted by their natural mothers, who in a desperate effort to be accepted by society disown the flesh of their flesh. The future of these unwanted, if not despised, children is in doubt and very little is known about their situation.

Relief efforts: A balance sheet

Evaluating the effectiveness of relief agencies and NGOs in post-war Yugoslavia is neither easy nor judgement-free. If one sticks to the data and the unsolved problems affecting women and children, an observer is led to the inevitable conclusion that the relief effort has been a colossal failure. The many ills afflicting women and children in Yugoslav successor states, years after the guns have fallen silent, provide ample ammunition to support an unflattering view regarding the performance of relief organizations. One could also postulate that these problems would have been a lot worse had it not been for the relief efforts of international and local NGOs and UN agencies. UNICEF, the Red Cross and Red Crescent, Médecins Sans Frontières and many intergovernmental organizations and international NGOs provided food, medical and other types of much-needed aid and technical assistance. While some help came from Muslim countries like Saudi Arabia, the bulk of the funding as well as relief-providing organizations came from the United Nations, the European Union, the United States and a number of other countries.

Centres for abused women were set up in Sarajevo, Brcko and other Bosnian towns to provide psychological and other much-needed assistance. Their number has declined in recent years due to financial difficulties and seeming lack of urgency, but many are still functioning today. The same can be reported in Kosovo. In other words, the relief effort had both successes and failures. The truth lies somewhere in the middle and the performance and effectiveness of these organizations are mixed, containing both successes and failures. This section identifies and analyses the achievements and shortcomings of relief organizations in the post-Yugoslav context.

As pictures of famished and haggard people made the nightly news in the early part of 1992, a plethora of international NGOs and UN relief agencies stepped in to provide food, medical care and other types of help to thousands of refugees and IDPs. Only when they got to the ground did the relief organizations realize the enormity of the crisis and the challenges facing them. Despite much experience and ample warning, "the international community was unprepared" for the Kosovo face of the Yugoslav tragedy.[47] Although somewhat tardy and lacking in coordination, the response became substantial and concerted when the Bosnia conflict became full blown. A similar pattern occurred later during the Kosovo crisis. A multitude of NGO volunteers fed and comforted numerous hungry and suffering women and children, as well as men. Help ranged from milk to medical and psychological care. It is estimated that more than 4,000 lives were saved during the height of the Yugoslav crisis thanks to the relief provided by Médecins Sans Frontières, Caritas, UNICEF and a host of other UN-connected agencies and NGOs. The same was true in Kosovo, when about 1,000 Kosovar refugees were flown to and accommodated in different parts of the world, including distant Australia. And although not every child's life was saved and not every woman's psychological and other needs were met, the fact remains that despite the magnitude of the task, relief organizations provided much-needed help at a very critical moment. One can only speculate how many lives were saved by the heroic efforts of NGO volunteers from around the world.

Much has occurred since NATO intervened in mid-1999 to reverse ethnic cleansing in Kosovo, Yugoslavia's last war. Kosovo has achieved independence, Slovenia became a full-fledged EU member and Montenegro peacefully left the federation with Serbia in 2006. Once-recalcitrant Serbia has taken steps to refurbish its image and cooperated with the international community to bring to justice some of those accused of gross human rights violations, such as Milošević and, more recently, Ratko Mladić. Progress can be noticed on the economic front as well. Although badly trailing EU members, Serbia's per capita GDP reached nearly $11,000 in 2010. Montenegro's is a bit less and FYROM came close to $9,500. Wealthier republics like Croatia and Slovenia have done even better: the former's GDP stands at $17,700 and the latter's at $28,400.

With $6,600 and $2,500 respectively, Bosnia-Herzegovina and Kosovo lag behind and still depend on international handouts.

Despite improvement, unemployment and infant mortality remain stubbornly high. In 2009, for example, infant mortality in FYROM stood at 17 per cent, in Serbia 14 per cent, Montenegro 10 per cent and Croatia 8 per cent. The latest data (2010) show that nearly 20 per cent of Serbs, 18 per cent of Croats, 33 per cent of FYROM citizens and 27 per cent of those living in Bosnia-Herzegovina were unemployed. The percentage of those living below the poverty line has followed a similar trajectory. The last available data (2007–2008) showed that 17 per cent of Croats, 29 per cent of FYROM's citizens, 25 per cent of inhabitants of Bosnia-Herzegovina and 35 per cent of Kosovars had difficulty obtaining enough food and other essentials. There are signs that the ongoing world economic crisis has worsened the situation. Citing survey data, Mark Baskin and Paula Pickering report that "throughout the successor states, citizens identify unemployment as the most important problem facing their countries. Poverty and corruption vie for second place."[48]

Yet even though fighting has formally ended and there are signs of economic improvement, the post-war situation for women and children remains critical. In a 2009 report, the Office of the UN High Commissioner for Refugees (UNHCR) stated that "well over 800,000 refugees and IDPs were still seeking durable solutions by returning home".[49] It is in the post-war arena that the performance of NGOs and other relief agencies falls short. Shortage of funds and critical humanitarian needs in the Congo and other parts of Africa, Afghanistan and other trouble-spots caused a large number of relief organizations to pull out of Bosnia, Kosovo and other war-torn parts of former Yugoslavia shortly after the guns went silent. Although with reduced budgets, UNICEF and other UN agencies remain and continue to provide services, while many American and fewer EU-based NGOs pulled out. Severe needs elsewhere led to the removal and reassignment of the most experienced staff, even among those NGOs that decided to stay. In our interview and correspondence Kapor-Stanulovic observed: "The effectiveness of NGOs [still operating in former Yugoslavia] has been low due to limited budgets and lack of experienced staff." She also reports that "UNHCR programs have been of high quality, but do not target women and children specifically, rather they serve the refugees in general." The experiences of the other interviewee, Kleck, are almost identical. In other words, relief organizations receive fairly high marks when it comes to delivering immediate, emergency help, but seem not to do as well in ameliorating problems once the fighting is over.

Without a doubt, lack of funding, pressing needs elsewhere and personnel shortages are important contributing factors, as is the eclipse of the pressure generated by international news coverage. These elements only tell a small part of the story, however. Unlike emergency assistance, long-term effectiveness depends on the "capacity-building" success/failure of relief organizations. According to Sue Lautze and John Hammock, "capacity-building is any intervention designed to reinforce or create strengths upon which communities can draw to offset disaster-related vulnerability".[50] The development of a civil society and building local relief capabilities are essential to long-term success. In Smillie's estimation, "one way to reduce conflict or to regain stability in a postconflict situation is to strengthen civil society". However, "support for civil society writ large – clubs, trade unions, NGOs, welfare societies and self-help groups – may not do much for democracy unless these organizations are explicitly committed to their own independence from government, and more broadly to principles of pluralism, democracy and human rights".[51]

Further elaborating on the crucial role of local capability and civil society, Peter Morgan states that capacity-building "is the ability of individuals, groups, institutions, organizations and societies to identify and meet development challenges over time ... It sets the strengthening or development of individual organizations in a much broader framework of sectoral or national efforts to improve development capabilities."[52]

To be effective, local organizations must possess "organizational autonomy". Julie Fisher identifies a number of factors that are key to organizational autonomy: clear and self-conscious organizational commitment to autonomy; diversified financial support enabling the organization to act "independently of any single donor, including the government"; well-developed grassroots ties to the community; experienced and well-trained staff; and strong managerial expertise and strategic knowledge.[53]

According to Ian Smillie, the ability of international NGOs to help local capacity-building is anchored on three essential elements: "training, timing and the capacity of those who would build capacity in others". Although important, textbook knowledge cannot substitute for practical training. In practice, capacity-building "boils down to giving the intended beneficiary a training program". Time and timing are equally vital. In Smillie's mind, "the most effective kinds of capacity building take time and short-term efforts applied on a piecemeal basis have limited impact". But capacity-building is neither simple nor quick; rather, it is a lengthy process requiring commitment and may take up to 15–20 years. Finally, the capacity to build capacity is arguably the single most important limitation. Smillie's assessment is critical: international NGOs' "capacity to build capacity is limited". A shortage of adequate funding, lack of time and preparation and a host of other organizational and personal problems involving the field workers themselves are among the contributing factors. Relief workers are often "young, overworked, operating in high-stress situations, and subject to sudden reassignment, [and] few are equipped or mandated to gain a deep understanding of communities in conflict, whether local civil society organizations or NGOs".[54]

Andrew Natsios's assessment is equally revealing. In his mind, relief organizations "are seriously over committed in coping with demands placed on them". Describing the onerous responsibilities and tribulations of aid workers, he states:

> The emotional toll that these emergencies are taking on relief staff cannot be calculated quantitatively, but it is significant. This has meant that NGOs and UN organizations are increasingly sending inexperienced staff to the field to run massive operations that even seasoned managers would find intimidating. This work is not a nine-to-five, Monday to Friday job.[55]

Out of necessity or design, NGOs neglect problems of national governance and instead tend to concentrate on village or neighbourhood problems. In so doing, "they produce patches of green in barren landscapes, patches that are usually small, fragile and usually unconnected to each other".[56] As a result of the enormous difficulties and lack of the necessary capacity-building mechanisms, NGOs often fail to help empower local organizations to alleviate the plight of women and children in post-conflict environments: "capacity building, or the way it has been managed, has in many cases resulted in the opposite of what was intended".[57] Lack of cooperation on the part of weak and authoritarian governments, which often view with suspicion local and international NGOs, complicates the situation even more.

The difficulties facing NGOs in delivering long-term relief to women and children by helping to build the capacity of indigenous organizations is exemplified by the situation in post-war Yugoslavia. Many international relief agencies left the scene when the fighting subsided. Those who stayed appear to prefer cities and not the countryside. Kleck's observation is instructive: "many NGOs work in the bigger towns and reach women and children, but not those in the villages". Funding for psychological work has declined substantially and emphasis is placed on providing micro-credit and other short-term projects, such as hairdressing, sewing and English lessons. Kapor-Stanulovic asserts that "most NGO programs have been of limited duration and reach". In her view, "the main drawback is total lack of coordination among international NGOs". Although valuable, these efforts lack coordination and consideration of possibilities for success. As Corrin argues, such "piece-meal, short-term projects cannot substitute for longer-term development plans for offering support and training to local women".[58]

These and other ills have hampered the ability of international NGOs to help build local capacity; it may very well be their single most enduring failure. Despite their proliferation, local NGOs seem to be unable or unwilling to help alleviate the plight of women and children in Bosnia and other affected parts of former Yugoslavia. Lack of and/or competition for funding and organizational autonomy, weakness in managerial and other expertise, as well as absence of clear vision and purpose are some of the ills afflicting local NGOs. For example, the numerous women's and other NGOs that mushroomed in Bosnia after 1996 "were quick to fall into competition with each other, vying for donor attention and funding. [Many were given] basic project funds for a year, a little training perhaps and then set adrift in a sea of jargon about sustainability."[59] Biljana Vankovska's assessment is almost identical: in the former Yugoslavia, she argues, "civil society manifests an extraordinary proliferation of NGOs and other forms of organization that remind us of the appearance of mushrooms after the rain". Yet their small size and other deficiencies force these newly created entities to engage in "grant hunting, mostly from foreign sources".[60] Under the circumstances, "nearly every women's NGO in Bosnia today relies on international sources of support".[61] The authors' own field research adds credence to these observations.

Besides funding, local NGOs manifest additional impediments in capacity. The majority of them tend to be phantom organizations devoid of direction and goals. Smillie and Todorovic argue that in Bosnia "few developed out of community spirit and many [operate] without boards of directors or anything resembling the sort of constituency that Western NGOs take for granted".[62] Vankovska offers a similar if not more devastating view:

> Local NGOs are nothing but "one man/woman shows" created with no intention and/or power to make a real impact on the societal/political sphere. For an NGO to be [officially recognized], all that is necessary is a relatively good education, English proficiency and an attractive name (usually centered on democracy, peace-building or human rights).[63]

In addition to indigenous weaknesses, Smillie and Todorovic, Vankovska and other analysts call attention to the lack of capacity of international NGOs and funding organizations. Miroslav Hadzic's comment is indicative: "Not the least contribution to the silent and concealed antagonism among the [local] NGOs was provided by the donor foundations themselves with their lack of clear-cut criteria and support procedures."[64]

Finally, inability or unwillingness of local and even international NGOs to establish and maintain their autonomy from governmental authority has impeded their capacity to provide relief to women and children in post-war zones, especially in male-dominated societies like Yugoslavia. In traditional patriarchal societies females are often in the background and a host of cultural and religious norms prompt women not to share or publicize a problem. In such settings women are also responsible for the welfare of their children. Revealing a child's problem indicates irresponsibility on the part of the mother and is looked down upon by the community. Under the circumstances, NGOs are often in the dark as to where and what the needs are. Again, the evidence is overwhelming. Vankovska is not alone in her assessment; she argues that the sensitive nature of the situation in former Yugoslavia prompts many international organizations to "prefer to work with the consent of host governments". This usually involves teaming up with a local NGO. Because of a lack of experience of civil society organizations in the post-communist Balkans, the "perfect local partner" tends to be "a phantom NGO, established either by the ruling regime or by the former supporters of the overthrown dictatorial regime who have just re-written their CVs and have put on attractive labels (such as Atlantic Club of ...)".[65]

Civil society and local capabilities have a long distance to travel in post-war Yugoslavia, and so does relief for the war's hardest-hit victims: women and children. Taking their cues from a US Agency for International Development study, Baskin and Pickering recently concluded that in former Yugoslavia "ordinary citizens remain dissatisfied and even view local NGOs as promoters of Western agendas and sources of support for opportunistic leaders. Civil societies remain dominated by organizations that promote narrow group interests rather than focusing on crosscutting problems."[66]

Concluding comments: Teach(ing) to fish

This chapter looked at the plight of women and children after the Yugoslav wars and assessed the role of NGOs and UN-related relief agencies in providing assistance to those affected. Over 20 years, international and national actors have done outstanding work on integrating women's and children's priorities into post-conflict recovery in the Balkans. However, the data reveal that the situation of women and children has improved less than desired, despite efforts of UN agencies, EU and US organizations and local and other relief bodies. The magnitude of the post-conflict reconstruction in combination with cultural and religious norms and gender-discriminating practices militate against placing the priorities of women and children at the forefront of the agenda of international and local relief organizations. Lack of adequate resources relative to needs, high turnover among the largely volunteer and overworked personnel, and increasing donor demands for expensive and time- and fund-consuming records and unhelpful interference on the part of host governments impede the performance of relief agencies.

As the Balkans case makes clear, the relief agencies are forced to choose between giving people fish or teaching them to fish. Societal considerations as well as funding and other pressing issues facing NGOs and UN relief agencies force them to concentrate on immediate and visible problems at the expense of long-term capacity-building efforts that could empower the affected to care for themselves and improve their lives. Yet these agencies provide much-needed relief that saves the lives of those affected by war and its aftermath. In sum, the findings of this chapter regarding the effectiveness of NGOs and other relief organizations lend credence to Natsios's thesis that "even the most charitable assessment must conclude that their responses have had mixed results".[67]

The international and national agencies could improve their effectiveness by concentrating on women's involvement with mainstream activities in politics, the economy and social life. One example is teaching women and children practical and job-related skills. The Balkans experience indicates that the limited efforts at teaching and training such skills have empowered some women to take the first step towards independent survival. One sees a number of women-owned shops in Sarajevo, Belgrade and other cities and communities. NGOs should encourage skills training to help women and young people starting and running small businesses. Providing small interest-free loans to qualified women in post-war environments may be worth pursuing. A few such efforts have been made, but not enough resources have been committed to make a noticeable difference. The international donor community and Northern/Western NGOs should set aside some resources for long-term solutions that can only come about through empowerment of women and children. Finally, there is a need for more studies to assess and analyse the long-term effects of the Yugoslav wars on the victims and society, and to develop multilateral approaches aimed at fostering meaningful participation of Balkan women and children in mainstream political, economic and social life.

Notes

1. Puechguirbal, Nadine (2004) "Women and Children: Deconstructing a Paradigm", *Seton Hall Journal of Diplomacy and International Relations* Winter/Spring, p. 15.
2. Corrin, Chris (2001) "Post-Conflict Reconstruction and Gender Analysis in Kosovo", *International Feminist Journal* 3(1), p. 79.

3. Kumar, Krishna (2001) "Civil Wars, Women and Gender Relations: An Overview", in Krishna Kumar (ed.) *Women and Civil War: Impact, Organizations and Action*, Boulder, CO: Lynne Rienner, p. 25.
4. Puechguirbal, note 1, p. 8.
5. Mertus, Julie A. (2000) *War's Offensive on Women: The Humanitarian Challenge in Bosnia, Kosovo and Afghanistan*, Bloomfield, CT: Kumarian Press, p. 3.
6. Quoted in Yugoslav Child Rights Centre (2001) "Annual Report", Yugoslav Children's Rights Centre, Belgrade, p. 8.
7. Ibid.
8. Natsios, Andrew S. (2001) "NGOs and the UN System in Complex Humanitarian Emergencies: Conflict or Cooperation?", in Paul F. Diehl (ed.) *The Politics of Global Governance: International Organizations in an Interdependent World*, Boulder, CO: Lynne Rienner, p. 389.
9. In addition to many primary and secondary sources, the authors had extensive personal correspondence with two people who were directly involved with relief efforts in former Yugoslavia: Monika Kleck, who is associated with a Bosnian NGO (Prijateljice) and the Freudenberg Foundation; and Nila Kapor-Stanulovic, UNICEF's officer for psychological rehabilitation in Serbia, Montenegro and FYROM, who also worked for the World Health Organization in the early 1990s.
10. Smillie, Ian and Goran Todorovic (2001) "Reconstructing Bosnia, Constructing Civil Society: The Disjuncture of Convergence", in Ian Smillie (ed.) *Patronage or Partnership: Local Capacity Building in Humanitarian Crises*, Bloomfield, CT: Kumarian Press, p. 26.
11. Mertus, note 5, p. 39.
12. UNICEF (2001) *Ten Years of Child Rights in Yugoslavia, 1990–2000: A Review*, Belgrade: UNICEF, p. 9.
13. The internationally recognized official and full name of Macedonia is Former Yugoslav Republic of Macedonia.
14. US Department of State (2001) "Bosnia and Herzegovina, Country Reports on Human Rights Practices", Bureau of Democracy, Human Rights, and Labor, US Department of State, Washington, DC, p. 3, available at www.state.gov/g/drl/rls/hrrpt/2001/eur/8236.htm.
15. UNICEF, note 12, p. 3.
16. Conversations with Monika Kleck and Nila Kapor-Stanulovic.
17. Kapor-Stanulovic, Nila and Henry P. David (1999) "Former Yugoslavia and Successor States", in Henry P. David with assistance of Joanna Skilogiannis (eds) *From Abortion to Contraception: A Resource to Public Policies and Reproductive Behavior in Central and Eastern Europe from 1917 to the Present*, Westport, CT: Greenwood Press, p. 310.
18. Smillie, Ian (2001) "Capacity Building and the Humanitarian Enterprise", in Ian Smillie (ed.) *Patronage or Partnership: Local Capacity Building in Humanitarian Crises*, Bloomfield, CT: Kumarian Press, p. 13.
19. Mertus, note 5, p. 1.
20. US Department of State, note 14, p. 24.
21. Kvinna till Kvinna (2001) *Getting it Right? A Gender Approach to UNMIK Administration in Kosovo*, Stockholm: Kvinna till Kvinna, p. 10.
22. Salzman, Todd A. (1998) "Rape Camps as a Means of Ethnic Cleansing: Religious, Cultural and Ethical Responses to Rape Victims in the Former Yugoslavia", *Human Rights Quarterly* 20, p. 354.
23. Ibid., pp. 364–365.
24. Ibid.

25. Ibid., p. 370.

26. Kvinna till Kvinna, note 21, p. 19.

27. Salzman, note 22, p. 370.

28. Sharlach, Lisa (2000) "Rape as Genocide: Bangladesh, the Former Yugoslavia and Rwanda", *New Political Science* 22(1), p. 19, available at www.tandfonline.com/doi/pdf/10.1080/713687893.

29. Kvinna till Kvinna, note 21, p. 19.

30. Sharlach, note 28.

31. Karam, Azza (2001) "Women in War and Peace-building: The Roads Traversed, the Challenges Ahead", *International Feminist Journal of Politics* 3(1), p. 24.

32. Salzman, note 22, pp. 371–372.

33. Sharlach, note 28, p. 90.

34. Mertus, note 5, p. 13.

35. Ibid., p. 50.

36. US Department of State, note 14, p. 24.

37. US Department of State (2001) "Croatia, Country Reports on Human Rights Practices", Bureau of Democracy, Human Rights, and Labor, US Department of State, Washington, DC, p. 17, available at www.state.gov/g/drl/rls/hrrpt/2001/eur/8240.htm.

38. Kvinna till Kvinna, note 21, p. 13.

39. Corrin, note 2, p. 92.

40. UNICEF, note 12.

41. Ibid., p. 7.

42. Corrin, note 2, p. 90.

43. Ibid.

44. US Department of State, note 14, p. 25.

45. UNICEF, note 12, p. 86.

46. US Department of State, note 14, p. 25.

47. Mertus, note 5, p. 44.

48. Baskin, Mark and Paula Pickering (2011) "Former Yugoslavia and Its Successors", in Sharon L. Wolchik and Jane L. Curry (eds) *Central and East European Politics – From Communism to Democracy*, 2nd edn, Lanham, MD: Rowman & Littlefield, p. 301.

49. Cited in ibid., p. 284.

50. Sue Lautze and John Hammock, quoted in Smillie, note 18, p. 17.

51. Ibid., pp. 13–15.

52. Peter Morgan quoted in ibid., p. 16.

53. Fisher, Julie (1998) *Non Governments: NGOs and the Political Development of the Third World*, West Hartford, CT: Kumarian Press, p. 78. A similar conclusion was reached by Cooley, Alexander and James Ron (2002) "The NGO Scramble: Organizational Insecurity and the Political Economy of Transnational Action", *International Security* 27(1), pp. 36–39.

54. Smillie, note 18, pp. 17–21.

55. Natsios, note 8, p. 403.

56. Ibid., p. 398.

57. Smillie, note 18, p. 9.

58. Corrin, note 2, p. 86.

59. Smillie and Todorovic, note 10, pp. 28–32.

60. Vankovska, Biljana (2002) "Western Civil-Society Employment and the Lessons Learned from the Balkans", paper presented to DCAF workshop on Promoting Civil Society and Good Governance: Lessons for the Security Sector, Prague, 15–16 April.

61. Mertus, note 5, p. 31.

62. Smillie and Todorovic, note 10, p. 28.

63. Vankovska, note 60, p. 5.
64. Hadzic, Miroslav (2001) "(In)Ability of the Local NGOs to Influence Law-Making Process: Between Lack of Will and Lack of Knowledge", in *Legal Framing of the Democratic Control of Armed Forces and the Security Sector: Norms and Reality/ies*, Belgrade: DCAF/Center for Civil-Military Relations, p. 179.
65. Vankovska, note 60, p. 9.
66. Baskin and Pickering, note 48, pp. 298–299.
67. Natsios, note 8, p. 389.

7

Emerging from poverty as champions of change: Women and children in post-war Tajikistan

Svetlana Sharipova and Hermine De Soto

Conventional logic maintains that any country in post-conflict transition faces difficult challenges. However, the magnitude of Tajikistan's challenges in its post-independence development has been striking. Civil war, economic transition, high levels of migration and a re-emergence and invention of religious and patriarchal traditions have dramatically changed the Tajik family and the position of women and children.[1] Following the collapse of Soviet rule, men gained power in almost all the important new institutions of society, while women's access to power in these institutions was curtailed. Further, the increased and multidimensional aspect of poverty that confronted Tajikistan had the most dramatic effect on women and children. Employing a gender and social development approach, combined with applied anthropological methods, this chapter explores how Tajik women and children have been coping with economic and social constraints after the civil war (1992–1997).

In this chapter, gender is understood as the cultural definition of behaviour defined as appropriate to different sexes in a given society at a given time. It is a set of cultural roles. The social development approach employed here is based on the definition that social development transforms exclusionary institutions and, as such, promotes gender inclusion, better growth, better development projects and better quality of life. Most of the empirical data presented were collected by the authors, assisted by a local research team. Qualitative and quantitative research tools, techniques and primary and secondary data included anthropological fieldwork and participant observation in various regions in Tajikistan

Defying victimhood: Women and post-conflict peacebuilding, Schnabel and Tabyshalieva (eds),
United Nations University Press, 2012, ISBN 978-92-808-1201-5

(Sharipova intermittently from 1997 to 2011; De Soto intermittently from 1999 to 2006). In-country primary data collection was undertaken by the authors for poverty studies, gender analyses, rural social assessments, needs assessments, country social analyses, monitoring and evaluation and, finally, implementation of a women's empowerment project. Secondary data included desk and literature reviews of development projects and reports, as well as relevant academic work. While most of the primary data presented here were collected between 2000 and 2005, revisits and recent World Bank development research indicate that social change has been slow and has not significantly altered the socio-economic landscape in Tajikistan.[2] By presenting a specific social development project, the final part of the chapter demonstrates how local women transformed regional conflicts into ongoing community-level peacebuilding efforts (see also Chapter 14).

In brief, the problems that Tajik women face in the post-socialist and post-conflict era are many: overcoming poverty and gender inequality; finding jobs that present opportunities for advancement; balancing work outside the home with almost complete responsibility for the household, children and the elderly; obtaining education for children; maintaining reasonable health; resisting male dominance over women and children in the family and the extension of male dominance over women in society in general; and avoiding crimes committed against women (such as trafficking and gender-based violence).[3] Children in particular are affected by issues that affect their mothers, as their lives are so intertwined. For example, the impact of poverty on a child's education (lack of teachers, books, schools) is exacerbated when a parent requires a child to drop out of school to help supplement the household income.

Tajikistan's poverty reduction strategy paper (PRSP),[4] the Voices of the Poor poverty study[5] and the country social analysis "Social Dimensions of Resource Flows in Education: Role of Formal and Informal Institutions in Tajikistan"[6] were analysed in depth for the purposes of this study. These and other resources are cited throughout this chapter.

The government of Tajikistan initiated a comprehensive PRSP with the goal of improving living standards and dealing with the socio-economic problems of the country. In general, PRSPs describe a country's macro-economic, structural and social policies and programmes to promote growth and reduce poverty, as well as associated external financing needs. PRSPs are prepared by governments through a gender-mainstreaming participatory process involving civil society, non-governmental organizations (NGOs) and development partners such as the World Bank, the International Monetary Fund, the UN Development Programme and the Asian Development Bank (ADB), among others. The concept of bringing gender issues into the mainstream of society was established as a global strategy by these multinational organizations in order to promote gender equality. In brief, mainstreaming a gender perspective is the process of assessing the implications for women and men of any planned action, including legislation, policies and programmes in any area and at all levels. It is a strategy for making the concerns and experiences of women as well as those of men integral parts of the design, implementation, monitoring and evaluation of policies and programmes in all political, economic and societal spheres, so that women and men benefit equally and inequality is not perpetuated. Thus the ultimate goal of gender mainstreaming is to achieve gender equality.

To ensure the inclusion and participation of both Tajik women and men in the PRSP process, the government supported a gender-sensitive qualitative Voices of the Poor study. The study was carried out jointly by the World Bank, ADB and a Tajik research team.

To understand the different impacts of poverty on women, men and children after the war and ensure that the PRSP was informed by the different voices of poor women and children, as well as men, the authors and the research team carried out consultations with three focus groups selected for interviews in each *rayon* (administrative district). Each focus group comprised 8 to 10 people, with one group of men, one of women and one of children. Given the cultural barriers to women participating with a formal voice in Tajikistan, these separate sessions proved to be an effective technique to ensure their active participation.

Tajikistan's political and economic background

The political landscape in Tajikistan has been rocky since its independence in 1991, in contrast to the stable regimes that have predominated in the other former Soviet republics in Central Asia.[7] The country has had to grapple with far more than the conventional problems of economic and social change in transitioning from one system to another, because the challenge of transforming Tajikistan into a new nation-state was thwarted in 1992 by a brutal civil war that lasted for five years.[8] The elements that triggered the war arose out of a complex mix of regional, ethnic and religious differences that had been suppressed during the Soviet era.[9] "The civil war in Tajikistan is an extreme case of the region's intra-ethnic disintegration, where the primacy of regional, clan, and opposing political interests have resulted in a national tragedy."[10] Prior to the Soviet collapse in 1991, relationships between the most important clan/kinship, ethnic and religious factions were crucial in the allocation of power and resources in Tajikistan. With the Soviet disintegration and the loss of 40 per cent of GDP in subsidies, competition for scarce resources became intense. The enormous loss of resources stoked the fires of clan, ethnic and religious differences and competition, leading to the eruption of civil war.[11]

In the past, mounting economic problems and other tensions in and between some of these subnational regions provided fertile ground on which the conflict developed. The imbalances in power distribution and the inability of the state to balance the needs of different sections of the population and forge unity and an overarching national identity from these disparate and potentially conflicting groups significantly contributed to the conflict.[12]

The civil war was fought between various alliances based on these subnational ties, which therefore deeply affected the social conditions in various war-torn districts of the country. Neighbourhoods fell apart and entire villages were forcefully displaced or driven into exile depending on their alliances and allegiances. The civil war lasted five years, until a UN-brokered peace agreement in 1997 paved the way to national reconciliation. Tajikistan's experience in ending the brutal civil war and integrating opposition factions into its government has won deserved praise.[13]

Wherever civil war and conflict occur, especially with a consequent economic collapse, there is a huge impact on all members of society, but especially on women and children. In Tajikistan, one undisputed fact was the war's heavy toll on the lives and well-being of women.[14] Not surprisingly, men comprised the vast majority of those killed in the conflict. This resulted in an estimated 20,000 widows and 55,000 orphans. Additionally, more than 40,000 homes were destroyed. Of the 200,000 refugees who fled, mainly to Afghanistan, Iran, Pakistan and Russia, more than half were women and children. About 100,000 citizens eventually returned from abroad and about 80 per cent of internally displaced persons also returned to their pre-war residences.[15]

Historical background on the roles of women

Under the Soviet system, women in Tajikistan were emancipated from the "enslavement" of household duties and brought into the labour force.[16] However, in everyday life it appears that traditional gender roles and socialization reproduced gender-specific activities at home and at the workplace, and a contradiction existed between a public image of equality and a private reality of heavier responsibilities due to a heavier workload within the home.

Efforts were also made to include women in political and administrative processes. Unions were organized for women, and the members were allotted approximately one-third of government positions, although they were rarely appointed to senior posts.[17] Even though these unions allowed women to become involved in politics, the groups were organized *for* women rather than *by* women. In Soviet states political organizations were not independent as negotiating agents of interest groups and mediators between political parties and the state; rather, socialist organizations were part of the official party, which represented in theory and practice the socialist Soviet state.[18]

While women were important contributors in the labour force, the Soviet system also promoted their reproductive and motherhood roles through social and financial rewards: a safety net of steady employment, pensions and maternity benefits, including maternity leave for up to three years, a generous allowance for each child and access to state-supported nurseries, kindergartens and after-school programmes. Such policies, it was hoped, would assist in lifting women's double burden at the workplace and in the domestic sphere. In addition, mothers with the largest families were rewarded with titles such as "Hero Mother" (for bearing and raising 10 or more children), "Mother Glory" (for seven to nine children) and "Medal of Maternity" (for five to six children). Women who won such awards were entitled to early retirement and special pensions.[19] However, with the collapse of the socialist system, most women lost both their jobs and all the socialist welfare benefits.

Poverty is not a new phenomenon in Tajikistan. Before independence, Tajik per capita income was one of the lowest among the Soviet republics and the percentage of people living in poverty was one of the highest. To a large extent, this was the result of an economic policy that virtually ignored the comparative advantages of the country and its regions, including abundant water and mineral resources, significant agricultural and industrial potential and a large labour force. The civil war in Tajikistan had and continues to have an enormous human, social and economic impact in terms of poverty, death, displacement and trauma suffered by the people. The increased poverty that now confronts Tajikistan has had the most dramatic effect on women and children. This chapter focuses on the impact and great burden of poverty on women and children after the war, and their resilient responses to these challenges.

As in many post-conflict societies, women and children in Tajikistan were extremely vulnerable to exploitation and abuse. Women suffered extensively, which directly impacted children because their well-being is intrinsically linked to that of their mothers. The civil war, the disintegration of the Soviet Union, severe drought and suboptimal implementation of economic reforms have impoverished many households in Tajikistan, depriving communities of local cultural, political and economic institutions as well as their former social cohesion.

Tajikistan is one of the poorest countries in Asia, and about 80 per cent of its households considered themselves poor in the immediate aftermath of the civil war. Since most of those who died during the civil war were male heads of household, their widows generally had to assume this position. Women have also lost husbands through natural death (illness, accident), official and unofficial divorces (traditional religious divorce) and migration. Female-headed households represent 21 per cent of all households, and these households are the poorest.[20] The Voices of the Poor study indicates that women – especially in single-woman-headed households – experience unemployment rates of 70–95 per cent in post-conflict areas.[21] About 38 per cent of these women-headed households are in urban areas, while 62 per cent are in rural venues. Tajikistan is more than 70 per cent rural, and poverty is most prevalent in rural communities.

In addition to being materially poor, women-headed households have lost a sense of community, hope and confidence due to the post-conflict situation in the country. As a result, social cohesion within communities has decreased considerably, creating more distrust, instability and tension. Describing the psychological dimension of their poverty, members of poor households say that life on the fringe of economic survival is made worse by acute uncertainty, hopelessness and despair.

Gender perspectives on poverty: Challenges and survival strategies

The focus group discussions demonstrated that although women and men share some similar poverty indicators, they really have, for the most part, very different perspectives on poverty and strategies to cope with its numerous challenges.[22]

Women and men alike perceived indicators of poverty as being shortages of food, clothing and money; high unemployment rates; high incidence of diseases; rising illiteracy; and uncertainty about the future. In addition, both focus groups were concerned about the lack of electricity, water and irrigation systems. However, rural men believed the main reasons for poverty were the lack of employment, land for farming and access to irrigation.

Women viewed the civil war as a major cause of poverty. They described poverty as not being able to provide both short- and long-term consumption items for their children. As stated, in some *rayons* many women became war widows and consequently female heads of households, and were perceived by both women and men as the most vulnerable sufferers in Tajikistan. Most men expressed the belief that women's workloads had increased tremendously because women now had to look for work in both the formal and informal economy while continuing to take care of the domestic chores, the children and the elderly.[23]

The impact of poverty on women's and children's health is dramatic, both regarding general health issues (lack of money for doctors, poor health facilities, etc.), but especially in family planning and reproductive health, which affect these groups the most.

As noted earlier, under Soviet rule women enjoyed a host of social benefits which helped to support their families. With the diminishing prospects for female employment these employment-related benefits have diminished as well, representing a major contributor to female poverty,[24] despite the hard labour that goes into growing commercial crops on their household plots. With old certainties (such as allowances, job security and benefits) now removed, a secure income is no longer guaranteed.[25]

One study cautions that women's formal labour market participation has fallen less than men's, with the result that their share in the total labour force has risen over the last decade. Still, women remain concentrated in the lowest-paid sectors of agriculture, education and health where the wages are now at a level insufficient to live on.[26] Women and children are the majority of workers in the cotton fields, labouring throughout the whole cycle of cotton production from weeding to harvesting. If women find work in agriculture or education, they are paid the lowest wages.

Women's efforts are further thwarted by the decollectivization of *kolkhozes* (Soviet collective farms) and the land redistribution process. Many women were excluded from obtaining land under the new *dehkan*[27] farms. Land laws require that those applying for land have the necessary knowledge, qualifications and agricultural experience to use it. Whether or not it is intended by lawmakers, some of those who manage land distribution at local levels use this requirement to exclude many women from the process. Female-headed household applications are often denied on the grounds that they lack the capable manpower.

However, women do not seem to face significantly greater barriers to self-employment. The majority of women are now self-employed, including family businesses. Women are engaged much more than men in the informal economy, buying and selling produce and selling the products of their sewing, clothing repairs, embroidery and knitting.[28] Other money-making activities include cultivating small household plots and trading small imported goods. Setting up a stand in local bazaars, many women sell food and other household produce, or resell food products from rural producers.

There is thus reason to believe that in formal employment, discrimination causes women to be less successful at securing jobs, career promotion and opportunities to improve their qualifications, while they are often the first to be let go during personnel reductions. In addition, male corporate interests stand guard over the most prestigious jobs. Applications from males are considered long before those from women, and generally men are hired. Only rarely do women become top managers. Women are also forced out of those fields of economic activity where efforts bring the greatest success in the form of high income, social status and prestige.[29]

Social poverty – Women, gender and society

There are many examples of women's limited social power that directly affect their level of poverty. This section addresses some of these major issues that women currently face, including unequal social relationships within marriage, forced family separation due to husbands who migrate to find work, crimes by women and violence against women.[30]

There is a growing awareness that the need to address gender inequalities is more imperative now during Tajikistan's transition. Urgent actions need to be taken to prevent Tajik women from losing all the advances gained under the Soviet system. That system had institutionalized various social rights and welfare policies[31] under which women had been the key recipients of the major benefits, including free education, guaranteed employment, state childcare centres and food subsidies.[32] Furthermore, at least on paper, women enjoyed equal rights with men.

In Tajikistan's short history as an independent state, the country has joined all major international conventions and declarations on women's rights and put in place a legal system to protect these rights.[33] The "National Plan of Actions for Advancement of Women for the Years 1998–2005" was adopted in 1998. The presidential decree "On Advancement of Women" was adopted in 1999. Another provides education quotas for poor rural women. These measures contain solid provisions intended to change the disproportionate representation of women and men in different levels of society. Furthermore, the measures create foundations for the development of gender-oriented and gender-balanced policy. However, most legislation is written in the masculine grammatical form, "leading observers to believe that the language itself, while formulating legislative acts and an expository legislative style as a whole, has a dominant tendency to identify women through men".[34]

While there is recognition that there is no *de facto* gender discrimination in regard to political rights, there are limitations on women exercising their rights as compared to men. For example, during the armed conflict women's role in politics was non-existent because then, more than ever, men monopolized the political arena. Therefore, women were not closely involved in the national reconciliation process. However, in 1994 with the support of international organizations, a new type of women's socio-political activity appeared in which women began to resume political activism and found their niche in the non-governmental sector. There are currently more than 120 women-based NGOs. At the outset, these NGOs were mainly involved in providing humanitarian assistance. Now they tend to focus their activities on issues that directly affect women. They call for women to have partnerships with the authorities in order to improve their situation and, ultimately, achieve executable equal rights and equal opportunities. Some of these NGOs make efforts to get involved in the gender expertise of the legislative acts, while at the same time lobbying for their interests at different levels in civil society. For example, the Women and Family Legislation project participants held roundtable discussions with parliamentarians and developed specific proposals for amendments to improve the well-being of women and children.[35]

However, their level of political and legal sophistication admittedly remains minimal, despite a gradual increase in women's participation in the post-conflict reconstruction of society.[36] Yet in spite of the resurgence of interest in women's issues and renewed activity of women's NGOs, the impact on the majority of women remains low. A strong voice is needed to develop social partnerships, or new ways of working together for everyone, but especially between the state and civil society, in order to achieve equality between men and women.[37]

Unequal social relationships within marriage

Contrary to the Soviet vision, efforts at equal labour market participation did not bring about gender equality, because women's progress in obtaining equality in the public arena was not matched in the household. Men were seen as the main breadwinners and there was little pressure on them to absorb an equal share of household responsibilities, while women were seen as mothers and wives first, primarily responsible for nurturing the hearth and household. Gender roles and male dominance in society and family remained unchanged, the abysmal economy took its toll and women were left to assume the double burden of productive and nurturing activities, performing long hours of unpaid work at home in addition to their paid contribution in the labour market.[38]

A survey conducted in 1998 found that women spent an average of 6.3 hours a day on unpaid work, compared with 3.3 hours for men (rural women spent 7 hours on unpaid work, while rural men spent 5.8 hours).[39] Both rural and urban women spent more time on cooking, cleaning and laundry, while rural men spent time on their private plot (2 hours), and urban men on other tasks. Further, rural women spent more time on housework than urban women because their access to utilities such as water, electricity and gas was limited or non-existent.[40] Many women, particularly in rural areas, also lacked access to simple domestic appliances; for example, 20 per cent did not have a washing machine. In urban areas women had less leisure time than men, while rural women had the least amount of leisure time of all.

Quite often economic hardships and reduced production have led to an increase in hidden unemployment, i.e. when workers are listed as employees of an enterprise but are actually forced to take prolonged unpaid leave. As a result many men leave their families to work in other countries, such as Russia, Kazakhstan and Turkmenistan, while family responsibilities fall squarely and heavily on women's shoulders, thus exacerbating their workload.

The resurgence of polygamy

Although Tajikistan is 95 per cent Muslim, it is legally a secular state, with a constitution that guarantees equality to all citizens regardless of nationality, race, sex, language, religion, political views and social and property status. The country's cultural traditions and national customs, suppressed during the Soviet era, enjoyed a resurgence during the civil war and have had both positive and negative effects on society. On the positive side, community tradition encourages people to assist family members in difficult situations. However, religious orthodoxy has resulted in the revival of polygamy; marriage of young girls; restrictions on education for girls and women; limitations on women's behaviour and freedom of movement, especially in rural areas; and prejudice against widows, divorced women and women who choose to remain unmarried.

Since 1992, when polygamy was outlawed in Tajikistan, there have been no existing official data on how many people are involved in polygamous relationships. In 1999 the parliament discussed this troubling trend as part of a debate on the need to draft a family code.

A culturally pervasive and widespread view in Tajikistan is that the man is the breadwinner in the family, thus making the woman dependent on her husband. This opinion was formed because women are chiefly responsible for running the household, and this activity cannot be measured in economic terms. Women with a low level of education are particularly vulnerable to this economic dependency. The low economic and social status of some women is leading to a resurgence of polygamy, which has been viewed by many as a form of social poverty alleviation.

However, it is not only poverty and unemployment that contribute to this practice. The resurgence of patriarchal views and gender-discriminatory interpretation of religious norms is a major contributor to the idea that men may have two or more wives. This view is clearly given credence by a *surah* from the Qur'an, which states: "Get married to two, three, four wives if you can be fair to all of them. And if you cannot, marry only one."[41] Yet there is a current lack of meaningful understanding of the obligations inherent in polygamy, and the issue of fair treatment remains elusive. Consequently, in its effort to draft a family code, the parliament acknowledges that polygamy is a sign of a moral crisis and devaluation of family relationships. As available evidence suggests, some women believe that the major cause of poverty is that their husbands have several wives.[42]

Women sometimes support polygamy in the hope that it will serve as a form of protection for themselves and their children. Meanwhile, there is an increasing concern for the escalating vulnerability of second wives and their children – who have no legal status or protection under the law. In Tajikistan, there are two levels of marriage. A *nikoh* is a marriage that is sanctified by a religious ceremony and is without state registration. The contemporary civil marriage is registered with state officials, providing a legal status. The type of marriage entered into determines the legal status of wives and children.[43] Case studies focused on the extent and nature of post-war polygamy reveal that a woman who becomes a second or third wife in the belief that she and her children will be supported by her husband finds that quite the opposite is true. Since a woman who has married in a *nikoh* is not registered as a legal wife, she is not eligible to receive the protections of spousal and child support, as well as an equitable division of marital assets. However, there is an increasing trend whereby a man who deserts his sole wife, although married only by *nikoh*, may have her petition for support and bill of divorce recognized legally, as if she were a wife in a registered marriage. The rationale follows that the court may assume the husband has purposely refused to register the marriage so that, if he chooses to desert his wife, he will not be charged as a registered husband with continuing marital support. However, it is unlikely that women who are subsequent wives in a polygamous marriage would be offered that consideration by the courts.

Crimes by and against women

Women's lives changed rapidly in the post-Soviet and post-conflict social and economic climate of Tajikistan. As described earlier, the devastation of the civil war altered the structure of the household and diminished the status accorded to motherhood, while fiscal difficulties led to economic hardship and inability to find work. These circumstances increased the potential for some women to commit crimes, be drawn into criminal enterprises or be forced by gangs to carry out their criminal purposes, such as drug trafficking, to make a living. It is unfortunate that increasing numbers of women have become involved in the trade in illegal drugs entering Tajikistan from neighbouring Afghanistan. Seduced by easy money, these women discount the possibility of being discovered and caught and therefore willingly take risks.

According to some observations, the number of female prisoners housed in a women-only facility in the north of the country during the Soviet era was no greater than 50, of whom only about five were Tajiks. Currently the situation has changed. There are 432 female inmates in this facility, half of whom are ethnic Tajiks.[44] The most common crimes committed by these women are drug trafficking and murder; 255 out of the 432 inmates were convicted for drug-related crimes.[45] However, some of the women did not actually commit the crimes, but willingly took responsibility for crimes committed by their husbands or sons.

Crimes against women, specifically the trafficking of women and children, in Tajikistan (as well as in other countries of Central Asia) have grown with alarming speed. According to the US State Department's 2011 "Trafficking in Persons" report, many trafficked women and children are illegally transported to Russia, the United Arab Emirates, Saudi Arabia, Kazakhstan and within Tajikistan.[46] Most come from the poorest families and suffer from psychological trauma, loss of social position, family disavowal, loss of self-respect and a deterioration of health. Their vulnerability is exacerbated by poverty, unemployment, labour migration and their work in the informal economy where they are exposed to illegal activities such as prostitution and the drug trade. Tajikistan is the principal drug-trafficking channel from Afghanistan to the countries of the Commonwealth of Independent States and Eastern Europe, and the lawlessness created by this situation puts women at high risk of sexual exploitation by recruiters and criminals, particularly in areas without strong traditional and religious influences. Recruiters tend to prey on women who are young and impoverished; these women fall victim more easily to false promises, kidnapping or fictitious marriages and are more desperate to feed their families.

Violence against women

During the civil war women were subjected to pernicious forms of violence, including rape, torture and verbal abuse.[47] The most vulnerable were refugees and women who remained in post-conflict areas, where un-controlled militants perpetrated the mass raping of women after the sei-zure of inhabited localities, as either revenge or punishment. However, information is insufficient regarding the number of women who were subject to violence, i.e. beating and sexual abuse, including in family situ-ations, as a result of military action.

About 87 per cent of women in Tajikistan experience family violence.[48] Although actions that cause bodily injury are violations of the criminal code, it is difficult for women to use the law to protect themselves. The criminal justice system is controlled by men, many of whom perceive family violence as a private matter or believe that women could avoid violence if they learned to please their husbands. A wife who asks for protection against her husband's abuse is often divorced by him under Muslim divorce law (talaq).

Several NGOs have conducted sociological surveys on the problem of violence against women. The surveys point to an increase in domestic vi-olence when there is pressure of economic hardships. Then, a woman is subjected more often to violence by her husband, in-laws and sons. The most common form of violence is beating. Generally, these cases go un-reported because women consider it shameful, even though they risk suffering physically and psychologically from pain and diminishing self-esteem. Psychological violence has a high probability of a tragic outcome, such as murder or suicide. Cases of suicide have begun to increase, and "the reasons for suicide and its attempts are socially and personally moti-vated: financial difficulties of the family, interpersonal terms, a family break-up, family squabbling, loneliness and nervous stress".[49]

Although still at an extremely high level, family violence has decreased since 1997. Women attribute this to their greater earning power in the informal sector, a new-found authority within the family and the greater vulnerability of men who are unemployed.

Several female-operated NGOs, including Women Scientists of Tajikistan, Simo, Gender and Development, Tradition and Modernity, Women and Family and others, run rehabilitation centres for women. In these centres, women who have been victims of violence are assisted in regaining social status through psychological training and legal and medi-cal advice.

A sociological study conducted by the Women Scientists of Tajikistan association[50] observed an increased tension within families, mainly due, as mentioned earlier, to economic hardships. Analysis showed that the reason for violence against women is often a lack of will or ability by the parties to resolve the conflict in a rational manner. Often women find themselves in a protracted psychological struggle from which they are unable to extricate themselves.

One of the training sessions conducted for women by the association's crisis centre incorporated lessons that were learned in Tajikistan to settle internal civil conflict. These lessons led to a new two-stage approach for reaching reconciliation within the family: first, a process of dialogue aimed at determining the dynamics of the relationships between the conflicting parties; and second, the development of consecutive steps to change these relationships for the better. The study's conclusions regarding conflict resolution reflect that many women use compromise or negotiations, some use mediation and a smaller number of women use force. Women also choose different patterns of behaviour in conflict situations, where many prefer cooperation, some keep silent and do not interfere in the conflict and a lesser number simply try to avoid conflict. The association believes that conducting training sessions helps in decreasing violence in society.[51]

Violence against women is an obstacle to equality and represents, in part, the powerlessness of women that is embedded in a culture of unequal institutional relations.[52] The legal system does not provide female survivors of violence with adequate and long-term protection. This feeds a social and political environment in which men are able to exert power and dominance over women with virtual impunity.

Currently there are formal and informal institutional barriers that prevent women from improving their well-being, both individually and collectively, and limit their choices to shape their lives, the lives of overall society and the stability of post-conflict peacebuilding environments.[53]

Poverty's effect on children

While women and men perceived poverty differently, the Voices of the Poor study also revealed that children experience poverty differently from adults. Both boys and girls felt that poverty meant lack of food, clothes, footwear and education.

Most of the children who participated in the focus groups were inadequately and poorly dressed. Furthermore, most appeared to be undernourished and physically less mature than their biological ages. Many said they worked at several jobs, which varied according to the area in which they lived. In rural areas children herded cattle, collected firewood, worked in grain-fed agriculture, bought and sold trade goods in the bazaars, dragged cargo on trolleys or carried buckets of drinking water sometimes two or three kilometres.

This section describes the specific effects of poverty on children, including the impact on education and the issue of street children.

Poverty's effect on the education of children

The impact of the war and poverty on the education of Tajik children has been dramatic. Most children reported that their school buildings were largely destroyed during the civil war and those remaining were very poorly maintained, with broken or missing windows, no tables or usable chairs and no water or toilets. Many mentioned a vast shortage of school-books and other supplies. Just as critical, teachers were paid very poorly, and could make more money from cultivating vegetables in their home gardens than by teaching. Because of these stumbling blocks, children reported that their teachers were abandoning their positions. Indeed, there has been an exodus of teachers from school systems.

Almost all children said that, due to their family's poverty, parents asked them to drop out from school to work in order to help support the family. Girls generally stopped going to school because their parents needed them at home either to work or to care for younger siblings. Children stated that they did not go to school in the spring or autumn because they were needed to weed fields and help pick and process the cotton crop during these seasons. In winter they skipped school because they either had no warm clothes or shoes or had to take turns with siblings in wearing them, consequently attending school on alternate days.

There are other concerns about growing gender segregation in primary education and vocational training. Among urban children, there is no difference in school enrolment numbers between girls and boys. However, in rural areas the number of girls attending school is significantly lower. These disparities can be attributed to the civil war and subsequent economic recession, which resulted in a significant reduction of resources for education in rural areas, including the departure of teachers due to low wages. In addition, the requirement for compulsory secondary education is not strongly enforced. In some parts of the country, where there are few traditional and religious barriers, the main obstacle to some girls in obtaining an education is their ability to afford it. Elsewhere, many girls are involved in arranged marriage at an early age, even polygamous marriages, so that the family will have fewer mouths to feed.

In the more religious areas – such as the Karategin Valley, rural areas in Khatlon *oblast* and some communities of Dushanbe city – girls and women are barred from higher levels of education. Such barriers existed even during Soviet rule. To address this problem, the president of Tajikistan issued a decree in 1999[54] establishing a quota system to promote education for girls from rural religious areas. These girls are admitted to institutions of higher education based on region and school performance and receive assistance in the form of stipends, free meals, hostel accommodation and medical care or payments. Between 1997 and 2002 more than 1,900 girls received such assistance.

Empowering women and children after the war – A successful peacebuilding effort in Buston

The areas severely affected by the war became a priority for peacebuilding efforts for the national government, civil society groups and international actors. Included in the peacebuilding programme was Buston, a community on the outskirts of the capital of Dushanbe, where the government, a World Bank social development team (task-managed by the authors) and international and local NGOs joined together to begin work with women from Buston to build a women's organization called Bonuvoni Navovar (BN) or Women Innovators. Based on the results of the gender analyses, poverty studies and social and gender needs assessments referred to earlier in this chapter, the authors designed a "women's empowerment project". Employing a project development concept in which the relationship between agency and structure is emphasized, the project design was guided by the definition that empowerment is "a group's or individual's capacity to make effective choices, that is, to make choices and then to transform those choices into desired actions and outcomes".[55]

Arising from the widespread disharmony, disappointment and disillusionment resulting from Tajikistan's civil war of the 1990s, Bonuvoni Navovar represents something of a rebirth and reaffirmation of the belief that by working together, women and men can make a difference in their own lives and those of others. BN was established in 2002 with the mission of economically and socially empowering women, and is based and provides services in Buston. Using a participatory community-driven development approach and active networking by project staff and community members, the empowerment project has reached a critical mass of over 11,000 beneficiaries and leveraged US$750,000 in cash, in-kind and infrastructure donations, in addition to a World Bank post-conflict grant of US$692,283.

Post-conflict challenges

Buston is an inwardly oriented community, distrustful of outsiders. Conflict was not inherent within the community but was caused by the civil war. Buston can be viewed as a transitional post-conflict community that was severely underdeveloped even before the war. It became an integral part of the armed opposition and was one of the last holdouts against the central government.

Nevertheless, after the opposition by the warlords ended, the central government reached out to Buston with partial compensation for destroyed homes, and requested World Bank gender and social development expertise. In close cooperation with the World Bank team, the government selected Buston to be the site for a women's socio-economic empowerment project.

Economic and social challenges

Women were one of the most marginalized groups in this area. In Buston, widows and wives whose husbands have left the home to be labour migrants generally live with the extended paternal family, where they are often emotionally and economically disempowered. High unemployment caused by the transition and the civil war affected the community as a whole, but women in particular were vulnerable and adversely hit by unemployment. While during Soviet times women often worked together with men in factories, in post-conflict Buston women faced a lack of job opportunities, physical security, education and training.

Objectives of the women's empowerment project

The women's socio-economic empowerment project pursued the following objectives:
- Mobilization of community and external resources to support and empower women heads of households.
- Establishment and enabling of a central community mechanism, a pilot women's membership organization (Bonuvoni Navovar) capable of addressing post-conflict social and economic needs of women heads of households.
- Increase of the employability and access to employment of women living in the project community.
- Documentation of the components of the economic empowerment model for women that can be effectively replicated in other communities in Tajikistan or other post-conflict societies.

Lessons learned

A number of lessons can be learned from the project.

Lesson 1: Ensure that the goal of the project is accurately understood by the whole community

The team succeeded in mobilizing the community to implement the project using a participatory community development approach. Respect for local knowledge, culture and expertise was an important factor in developing trust in the community. In spite of this, the introduction of the project did not come about easily, because male leaders feared that proselytizing might be the motive behind the activities: in the first phase, men in the community were concerned that the purpose of the project was to convert the women to Christianity. To change these misperceptions, the local project team began a dialogue, met with religious leaders from mosques and scholars from the Islamic Studies Centre and offered courses to women on gender in Islam. Male secular and religious leaders from the community agreed that the studies were beneficial for women and the community as a whole. The chief of party, the implementation manager hired by the World Bank and Counterpart International, participated in the dialogue on a day-to-day basis along with local staff.

Community mobilization involved establishing contacts with the *mahalla* (community) leader and the school principal; conducting a series of community participatory assessments of women's self-identified needs; enhancing capacity through training for women to manage BN activities, including management of the women's centre; starting and managing an NGO; and reaching out and developing synergies with other community projects and NGOs. Training priorities focused on basic computer skills; NGO administration and management; accountability; the NGO electoral process; start-up of a business; maternal infant care; and access to credit. Such training raised awareness of the difference between aid dependency, participation and ownership. Interactive seminars were held on themes such as responsibility of Muslims for their neighbours, women's rights under Islam, principles of citizenship and participatory democracy. As the project evolved, continuous community meetings were held to explain, discuss and suggest ways for it to progress.

The project activities were designed for women's voluntary participation and organic emergence of women leaders. Women willingly organized themselves into four groups. As the training and seminars drew to a close, the groups elected their leaders, who exhibited traits such as risk taking and willingness to change their lives and take responsibility without aspiration for personal gain. These leaders comprised the founders of the women's organization. What became apparent, however, was that women who only joined in the hope of material aid or jobs dropped out within a few months – and only the real innovators remained.

Lesson 2: Engage the broader community early on in a project

The team and BN worked within the structure of societal and religious traditions important to the community. At the beginning the project risked marginalizing the extreme poor and drug addicts. The project team addressed these risks by raising awareness of Muslims' responsibility to the immediate neighbourhoods (*guzars*); furthermore, the district leader, as a government appointee, expressed his full support for the project. This was instrumental in convincing the formal and informal community leaders to include the disadvantaged groups. These groups obtained access to water through the water users' associations. Male leaders gained an opportunity to play a larger leadership role in the community and as a result became supportive of the women's organization. Children, too, could learn how to use a computer. This helped them with their studies. Some young men who were members of Islamic extremist groups initially opposed the idea of the project. Surprisingly, over time they began to engage in the dialogue with the members of the women's organization and supported discussions on women's roles and Islam. Thus engaging the broader community early on in a project contributes to reducing the risk of marginalizing other groups of society.

Lesson 3: Effective communication skills are essential for women leaders

In a post-conflict community, skilled women leaders need to establish effective communication skills for smooth operation and implementation of a project. Communication skills are crucial to create synergies between local leaders, powerful interest groups and community residents, thus ensuring that conflict will not arise between these groups. This is important in societies where local legitimate male leaders represent micro-political structures (for example warlords, clan leaders and religious leaders) that are suspicious and distrustful of innovations and social change. For that reason, a line of diplomatic communication was established within the project. The women elders in the community were some of the first to champion this line of diplomacy with the *mahalla* leader. By communicating the purposes of the project to the local male leaders, the women were able to achieve conflict aversion and male buy-in and support. Initially, communication was pursued house-to-house to talk about the project; later the team distributed flyers. Meetings were organized in each *guzar*, and community meetings were held at the school and the women's centre. Flyers were continuously distributed throughout the community to announce and promote the events staged by the women's centre.

BN is now a registered local NGO that helps to empower formerly mistreated women in Buston. It helps women to improve their own socio-economic conditions, as well as those of Buston generally. BN also builds external community relations with national and international partners, including NGOs. The building where the centre is located has been purchased and refurbished. Importantly, the facility created a space where the community felt that women could meet in a sheltered and secure environment for training.

Lesson 4: Fill in the gap between government services and community demands

Community action led by an organization like BN is an efficient way to gain results when the government is not interested in solving community problems such as water supply and distribution. An unintended result was that BN was able to establish a community water system – a problem the local government had ignored for years. To resolve the issue, BN approached and built a partnership with the World Bank's Dushanbe Water Supply Project. The centre established a water users' association that purchases water from the main Dushanbe water utility and is in charge of its redistribution. The success of the water service delivery has resulted in BN gaining the respect and recognition of the local government. This has contributed to further improvement of public relations between the government and the community as an essential condition for averting conflict.

Key benchmarks and results

Based on two-year benchmarks set by the conditions of the post-conflict grant, the project achieved the following results:
- *Communication and mobilization:* Women from the centre mobilized the community's human and financial resources and doubled the value of the project's approximate worth of US$750,000. These efforts included water system and school rehabilitation, labour for BN centre refurbishment and a health clinic.
- *Establishment of a women's centre:* The centre provides both a secure environment and a space where women can learn to make their own choices and regain self-esteem, and where their specific economic and social needs can be addressed through tailored job and skills training as well as community participation. The centre is equipped with computer resources, which can be used by members of the broader Buston community.
- *Smart economics:* There is a need to set up mechanisms for sustainability. One of the first priorities of BN was to develop a financial foundation to sustain the project after World Bank assistance terminated. BN researched numerous types of business endeavours and settled on a bakery; this was chosen as the ideal economic activity because most women know how to bake and the demand for baked goods in Buston is strong. The bakery, named Sladkoezhka (Sweet Tooth), officially opened in August 2004. It is managed by BN and employs 10 women from Buston and two from Dushanbe.

- *Income generation:* BN identified access to credit as one of the major challenges faced by women in the community. Lack of access kept women from the capital resources necessary for improving their economic conditions. With credit, women members of BN now engage in business activities such as animal breeding, retail and small production/processing. A *group lending* strategy created social, moral and economic incentives. Impact evaluation concluded that at the end of the two-year grant project, activities funded by the loans provided the equivalent of a family's income for two months during each three-month loan cycle. The post-conflict grant included a small loan fund of US$25,000. Staff hired a business trainer from Counterpart International with expertise in micro-finance, who trained a woman from the centre. Later this woman set up the loan programme using tool manuals provided by the trainer. The loan programme was based on a credit needs assessment and each woman had to take business training and agree to the terms of a group lending guarantee as a prerequisite to accessing a loan. The loan repayment was 100 per cent. After two years of successful management of loans and mentoring from staff, the loan fund is now operated by a Tajik micro-finance institution that is owned by BN.
- *Results:* The project resulted in a number of achievements. First, it led to the establishment of a women's centre and building for training, assembly meetings and project management, providing business services to the community and a place where women can voice their needs and concerns. Second, it created active community involvement and support, proceeding from respect for local knowledge and expertise. Women's economic and social empowerment was fostered by regaining self-esteem, employment, access to credit and sustainability. And third, it developed a women's empowerment model that was assessed by the government and external evaluators as a best local fit for replication countrywide and was selected by the World Bank as an example of good gender practice.

Conclusion

Tajikistan has had to grapple with major political upheaval following the break-up of the Soviet Union, as well as a brutal civil war that lasted five years. Given the instability of the country's political situation, major economic problems ensued, which were exacerbated by the imbalance of power distribution due to conflicting regional ethnic groups and geographic divisions. With the deterioration of its economic well-being the country plunged into further poverty. Still challenged by problems inherent in maintaining peace, the process of nation-building and the devastation of the war, the country has yet to address the adverse social impact of its economic transition.

Women's responses to poverty have many facets. Economically, women face diminished prospects for employment, and where employment is found, it is concentrated in the lowest-paid formal sectors. Consequently, the majority of women are now self-employed in the informal sector. The effects of social poverty are probably greater for women than for men. Under the Soviet system, women in Tajikistan were brought into the workforce and treated equally. However, this was the public image. In the domestic sphere women had a heavier burden as they maintained all their responsibilities for the home and added the responsibilities in the workplace.

There are many examples of women's limited social power that directly affect their level of poverty. Tajik women currently face such major issues as unequal social relationships within marriage (e.g. workload, polygamy, early arranged marriages, etc.), unequal opportunities for education, crimes by and against women (specifically the trafficking of women and children) and violence against women (an estimated 87 per cent of women experience family violence). Further, the country's gendered cultural and patriarchal traditions, suppressed during the Soviet era, have enjoyed resurgence and have had negative effects for women and men.

The effects of poverty on women and on children are inextricably woven together as their lives are so heavily intertwined. Hence the economic impact of poverty on women, in terms of household income and health, education and social issues, is felt by children. Children are also directly affected in various areas. For example, the impact of poverty on their education has been dramatic, as there has been insufficient money for school supplies, clothes, books and teachers. Due to lack of money, parents have pulled children from school to work to supplement the household income. Yet efforts made by various international and local organizations to find solutions to the problematic effects of poverty on children appear to be insufficient in terms of coverage and sustainability. The government acknowledges that this is a critical issue. It is obvious that children who have been severely affected by the war and post-conflict development require special attention.

All the aforementioned issues are obstacles to equality for women and represent, in part, the powerlessness of women that is embedded in a culture of unequal institutional relations. Gender equality must have a place in Tajikistan's post-war transition; and women as active agents of change must become part of the nation-building processes. It is clear that the solutions should be based upon women joining together in a "politics of solidarity" and should be combined with research and on-the-ground social development work by, about, for and, most importantly, *with the participation of* women and children who have been commonly affected by the war and post-war trauma. As we have shown in this chapter, by building upon gender-sensitive studies and gender-mainstreaming strategies for designing a specific post-conflict women empowerment project in Tajikistan, women's agency and leadership helped to transform a post-war landscape into a peacebuilding community where women and children have become champions of change. This echoes other calls for female leadership in peacebuilding in other contributions throughout this volume. Along with positive change, women and the entire community began to participate in peacebuilding and ultimately in empowering themselves.

Notes

1. Hobsbawn, Eric and Terence Ranger (1992) *The Invention of Tradition*, Cambridge: Cambridge University Press, pp. 1–15.
2. World Bank (2005) *Tajikistan Gender Review*, Washington, DC: World Bank; Shahriari, Helen, Alexander M. Danzer, Renee Giovarelli and Asyl Underland (2009) *Improving Women's Access to Land and Financial Resources in Tajikistan*, Washington, DC: World Bank.
3. Harris, Collette (2004) *Control and Subversion: Gender Relations in Tajikistan*, London: Pluto Press, p. 23.
4. De Soto, Hermine (2001) "Gender-Sensitive Participation Characterizes Tajikistan's PRSP", *Poverty Reduction Strategy Newsletter*, World Bank, Washington, DC.
5. De Soto, Hermine, Peter Gordon and Firuz Saidov (2001) *Voices of the Poor from Tajikistan: A Qualitative Assessment of Poverty for the Poverty Reduction Strategy Paper*, Washington, DC: World Bank.
6. De Soto, Hermine, Firuz Saidov and Svetlana Sharipova (2006) *Social Dimensions of Resource Flows in Education: Role of Formal and Informal Institutions in Tajikistan*, Washington, DC and Dushanbe: World Bank/UNDP.
7. For more information see Atkin, Muriel (1997) "A Country Study: Tajikistan", in Glenn E. Curtis (ed.) *Kazakstan, Kyrgyzstan, Tajikistan, Turkmenistan, and Uzbekistan: Country Studies*, Washington, DC: Federal Research Division, Library of Congress, available at http://lcweb2.loc.gov/cgi-bin/query/r?frd/cstdy:@field%28DOCID+tj0059%29.
8. Bergne, Paul (2007) *The Birth of Tajikistan: National Identity and the Origins of the Republic*, London: I. B. Tauris, pp. 30–38.
9. Abdoullaev, Kamoloudin (1998) "The Civil War in Tajikistan", *Peace and Policy: Journal of the Toda Institute for Global Peace and Policy Research* 3(1), pp. 17–19, available at http://kamolkhon.com/the-civil-war-in-tajikistan/.
10. Tabyshalieva, Anara (1999) "The Challenge of Regional Cooperation in Central Asia: Preventing Conflict in the Ferghana Valley", *Peaceworks* 28, USIP, Washington, DC, p. 7.
11. More detailed information on the causes and consequences of the civil war in Tajikistan can be found in Akbarzadeh, Shahram (1996) "Why Did Nationalism Fail in Tajikistan?", *Europe-Asia Studies* 48(7), pp. 1105–1129; Akiner, Shirin (2001) *Tajikistan: Disintegra-*

tion or Reconciliation, London: Royal Institute of International Affairs; Djalili, Mohammad-Reza, Frédéric Grare and Shirin Akiner (eds) (1997) *Tajikistan: The Trials of Independence*, New York: St Martin's Press; Nijazi, Aziz (1997) "Tajikistan: Regional Aspects of the Conflict (the 1990s)", in Aleksei Malashenko, Bruno Coppiters and Dmitri Trenin (eds) *Central Asia and Caucasus*, Moscow: Ves Mir Publishing; Nourzhanov, Kirill (1996) *Alternative Social Institutions and the Politics of Neo-Patrimonialism in Tajikistan*, Melbourne: University of Melbourne; Roy, Olivier (2000) *The New Central Asia: The Creation of Nations*, New York: New York University Press; Roy, Olivier (1993) *The Civil War in Tajikistan: Causes and Implications*, Washington, DC: USIP.

12. El Bushra, Judy (2003) "Women Building Peace, Sharing Know-How", Gender and Peace-building Programme, International Alert, June, available at www.womenbuildingpeace.org.

13. International Crisis Group (2003) "Tajikistan: A Roadmap for Development", ICG Asia Report No. 51, 24 April, Brussels, available at www.crisisgroup.org/~/media/Files/asia/central-asia/tajikistan/Tajikistan%20A%20Roadmap%20for%20Development.pdf.

14. Sharipova, Muborak and Shahrbanou Tadjbakhsh (1998) "Babel: Widows of Tajikistan", *Index on Censorship* 27(2), pp. 163–168.

15. Weber, Renate and Nicole Watson (eds) (2000) "Women 2000: An Investigation into the Status of Women's Rights in Central and South-Eastern Europe and the Newly Independent States", International Helsinki Federation for Human Rights, Vienna, p. 440, available at www.onlinewomeninpolitics.org/beijing12/Woman_2000.pdf.

16. Shirin Akiner, quoted in Falkingham, Jane (2000) "Women and Gender Relations in Tajikistan", Country Briefing Paper, ADB, Manila.

17. Falkingham, ibid.

18. De Soto, Hermine (1993) "Equality/inequality: Contesting Female Personhood in the Process of Making Civil Society in Eastern Germany", in Hermine De Soto and David G. Anderson (eds) *The Curtain Rises: Rethinking Culture, Ideology and the State in Eastern Europe*, Atlantic Highlands, NJ: Humanities Press, pp. 289–304.

19. Falkingham, note 16.

20. Government of the Republic of Tajikistan (1999) "Annual Report", State Statistical Agency, Dushanbe.

21. De Soto, Gordon and Saidov, note 5.

22. Ibid.

23. De Soto, note 4, p. 3.

24. De Soto, Gordon and Saidov, note 5, p. 24.

25. Falkingham, note 16, p. 14.

26. Ibid., p. 15.

27. *Dehkan* is a private individual peasant farmer who has a lifelong inheritable lease of land from a collective or state farm.

28. UNDP Tajikistan (1999) "National Status Report on Gender", UNDP Tajikistan, Dushanbe, pp. 18–19.

29. Ibid.

30. Harris, note 3.

31. De Soto, Hermine (2000) "Crossing Western Boundaries", in Hermine De Soto and Nora Dudwick (eds) *Fieldwork Dilemmas: Anthropologists in Postsocialist States*, Madison, WI: University of Wisconsin Press, p. 73.

32. Kuehnast, Kathleen (2000) "Ethnographic Encounters in Post-Soviet Kyrgyzstan", in Hermine De Soto and Nora Dudwick (eds) *Fieldwork Dilemmas: Anthropologists in Postsocialist States*, Madison, WI: University of Wisconsin Press, p. 111.

33. Decree of the President of Tajikistan, "On the Advancement of Women in Society", December 1999; "National Action Plan for the Advancement of Women in Society" (based

on Government of the Republic of Tajikistan Resolution 363, 1998), September 1999; "Program on Basic Directions of State Policy for Equal Rights and Opportunities for Men and Women in the Republic of Tajikistan for 2001–2010", August 2001.

34. UNDP Tajikistan, note 28, p. 22.
35. Materials of the Second Forum of Women NGOs of Tajikistan (2001) "Social Partnerships of the Government, NGOs and International Organizations in Solving Gender Problems in Tajikistan", Gender and Development, Dushanbe, pp. 23–24 (in Russian and Tajik).
36. UNDP Tajikistan, note 28, p. 38.
37. Materials of the Second Forum of Women NGOs of Tajikistan, note 35.
38. Paci, Pierella (2002) Gender in Transition, Washington, DC: World Bank.
39. Government of the Republic of Tajikistan, note 20.
40. UNDP and State Statistics Agency (1999) "Gender Statistics in Tajikistan", UNDP and State Statistics Agency, Dushanbe.
41. Akhmedova, Fatimah (1999) "Women's Place in Tajik Society," Central Asian Monitor 6 (US edition), p. 29.
42. De Soto, Gordon and Saidov, note 5, p. 24.
43. Traditions and Modernity Women's Association (2002) Investigation of Polygamy in Tajikistan, Dushanbe: Swiss Agency for Development and Cooperation, p. 5.
44. Akhmedova, note 41, p. 27.
45. Ibid.
46. US Department of State (2011) "Trafficking in Persons Report: Tajikistan", available at www.state.gov/documents/organization/164458.pdf.
47. Falkingham, note 16, p. 12.
48. Weber and Watson, note 15.
49. UNDP Tajikistan, note 28, p. 92.
50. Materials of the Second Forum of Women NGOs of Tajikistan, note 35, pp. 39–40.
51. Ibid.
52. World Bank (2002) Empowerment and Poverty Reduction, Washington, DC: World Bank, p. 8.
53. Ibid., pp. 18–19.
54. Decree of the President of Tajikistan, note 33.
55. Alsop, Ruth, Mette Frost Bertelsen and Jeremy Holland (2006) Empowerment in Practice: From Analysis to Implementation, Washington, DC: World Bank, pp. 9–10.

8

Young mothers as agents of peacebuilding: Lessons from an early childcare and development project in Macedonia

Deborah Davis

This chapter focuses on the lessons learned from an inter-ethnic peace-building project in the mountains of Macedonia,[1] near the border with Kosovo, carried out in quiet defiance of the ethnic wars in the Balkans. The project, called Lifestart in Emergencies, was created by UNICEF to underpin military and diplomatic peacebuilding efforts in the region with social healing and sustainable community-level conflict resolution processes. Carried out in impoverished, isolated communities where the only sources of income were subsistence farming, timber cutting and smuggling, and where women rarely left the home or spoke to their neighbours, the project attracted little attention during its five years of existence. Further, due to the lack of documentation that characterizes many emergency projects in conflict zones, it now has been largely forgotten, and would not have come to the author's attention had it not been for her association with the World Bank, which provided some of the initial funding. However, the principles on which it was based – that conflict-affected families of all ethnic groups need support and protection, and that the empowerment of women within families and communities helps in bridging ethnic, religious and political barriers – continue to have a profound influence on the character of ongoing reconciliation efforts in the region.

Lifestart in Emergencies was launched in 1996, shortly after the Dayton Accords brought an end to the ethnic violence in Bosnia-Herzegovina and created space for other peace efforts in the region. The project was suspended in 2001, when NATO launched air strikes along the Kosovo-

Defying victimhood: Women and post-conflict peacebuilding, Schnabel and Tabyshalieva (eds), United Nations University Press, 2012, ISBN 978-92-808-1201-5

Macedonia border to prevent the ethnic conflict that had spread to Kosovo from also destabilizing its neighbour to the east, Macedonia – one of the few Balkan countries that had not yet been engulfed in ethnic war. The fact that Macedonia had managed to leave the Yugoslav federation in 1991 without an outbreak of ethnic violence was a testament to the effectiveness of long-standing power-sharing arrangements between the country's two largest ethnic groups, the Macedonians and the Albanians. However, Roma, Turks and other ethnic groups had remained marginalized until the government acceded to UNICEF's demands, during negotiations over the design of Lifestart, to include young mothers and children from ethnic minority families, and to allow educational materials in the Romani and Turkish languages as well as in Macedonian and Albania.[2]

At the time Lifestart was launched, the families living in the Macedonian highlands had been "giving all they had – food, clothes, money"[3] to the tens of thousands of Kosovar Albanian refugees pouring over the border to escape the Serbian invasion of their homeland. As the Kosovo crisis continued, however, and the Albanian population in Macedonia grew larger, the Macedonians began to feel overrun by the refugees and resentful of their increasing demands for political power and bilingual education. To help diffuse these tensions, Lifestart in Emergencies trained a multi-ethnic team of family visitors – young mothers from the mountain villages who would meet with Macedonian, Kosovar Albanian, Turkish and Roma families in their homes and speak to them in their own languages. Early childcare and development (ECCD) served as the entry point for these interactions, which soon expanded to community meetings at which parents and grandparents from the different groups sat together to drink mountain tea and discuss what they could do to give young children a sense of security and hope for the future. Programme facilitators talked about children's psychological and physical needs, and the need for adults to encourage them, treat them with kindness and help them develop a sense of self-worth. They also talked about the Convention on the Rights of the Child[4] and its requirement that parents act in the best interests of their children. The parents were then invited to think about how their children were affected by the behaviour of adults in the family – particularly the impact that violence against children and their mothers would have in creating an angry outlook on life and the perpetuation of violence on a larger scale.

From the beginning, Lifestart in Emergencies embodied the link between peace in the community and peace in the region, and an understanding of how both affect the well-being of families. Against the memory of "mass executions; exploitation as human shields; rape; mass expulsions; burning and looting of homes and villages; destruction of

crops and livestock; suppression of identity, origins and property ownership by confiscation of documents; hunger, starvation and exhaustion; and
many other abuses of human rights and international norms of civilised
behaviour"[5] that the Kosovar refugees had endured before reaching
Macedonia, the project aimed "to initiate and develop in the mother and
the other family members [a] culture of communication that would be
supported with love, respect and tolerance", as a UNICEF evaluation of
Lifestart noted, while "the objective ... was to develop the individual
personality of the mother [so she] would understand responsible parenthood".[6] The idea that women's empowerment was central to community
peacebuilding – the organizing principle of the operation – was not articulated. Instead, facilitators took the approach that "the priority functions
and role of the female" were to protect and advocate for her children,
and therefore young mothers had to be given the "personal responsibility
and mobility" they needed to "devote a significant proportion of their
time to the development of their children". Women were given permission by the male elder in the family to become involved in community-
wide children's learning activities, which soon included literacy classes
and, eventually, conflict resolution exercises across both religious and
ethnic boundaries. In this way, the project was able to build on its advocacy for children to "expand and improve community networks and
strengthen ... the position of the women" within their communities.[7]

The strategic value of community peacebuilding

The family-centred approach to peacebuilding was first developed in the
border regions of Northern Ireland, where communities affected by the
many decades of "the Troubles" were showing alarming levels of violence
against women, depression among young mothers and high rates of
suicide – the leading cause of death – among young men.[8] In the mid-
1980s the women of Northern Ireland – peace activists, advocates of
women's and children's rights, women in religious orders, psychologists
and academics – began to organize support networks, mental health programmes and home visits for conflict-affected families, particularly in
rural and Irish-speaking areas. In 1994, with the creation of the EU Programme for Peace and Reconciliation in Northern Ireland and the
Border Counties of Ireland,[9] these grassroots efforts were recognized as
community-based peacebuilding programmes and given EU funding.

One of these programmes was the original Lifestart of Northern
Ireland, founded by the Sisters of Mercy in the late 1980s. Like other
peacebuilding projects in Ireland's border region, Lifestart provided
home-based services for conflict-affected families. However, it was

Lifestart's core parenting programme, built around early child learning research from the United States, which attracted the interest of UNICEF for use in Southeastern Europe.

As evidence emerged from Northern Ireland's peacebuilding programmes that, as noted in a later EU evaluation, there is a need for funding bodies to understand the "strategic aims" of community peacebuilding,[10] UNICEF insisted that the project be inclusive, as described above. The following section discusses the Macedonia project in more detail.

The Macedonia project and peace in Southeastern Europe

As Britain and Northern Ireland made their difficult way towards a peace agreement,[11] women in Southeastern Europe were also building on the self-help traditions of families and communities to create a subculture of peace, in which peace was understood as inter-ethnic early childcare, cross-border mental health and support for conflict-affected families. Peace was considered not just the absence of war, but a dynamic process of coalition-building, mutual respect and understanding at the community level, as well as responsible behaviour on the part of national and world leaders. These sentiments were expressed in a petition to the United Nations in 1997, signed by nearly 100,000 women from Western and Eastern Europe – as well as Africa, Asia, the Middle East, North America and Latin America – and addressed to the governments of the world:

> We are horrified at the levels of violence witnessed during this century, [and we demand] that war ... be delegitimized as an acceptable form of social behaviour, and that governments and civil society together develop new institutions that do not resort to violence for the settlement of disputes ...[12]

One of the women who signed the petition was Dr Flora Brovina, a Kosovar Albanian paediatrician and co-founder of the Albanian Women's League (AWL), which UNICEF had selected as the implementing agency for Lifestart in Emergencies. Dr Brovina was the granddaughter of a woman who had been a resistance fighter. Half a century later, when the Serbian army invaded Kosovo and decreed that ethnic Albanians could not be admitted to hospitals – not even for childbirth, as they would be "giving birth to terrorists"[13] – Dr Brovina set up a network of underground clinics and trained thousands of women in basic medical care. In 1992, as the Serbian assault on her people escalated, she and 50 other Kosovar Albanian women in the fields of medicine, law and academia formed the AWL in an effort to bring the peace work of thousands of grassroots women in the region into public awareness.

UNICEF's selection of the AWL as the implementing agency for Lifestart in Emergencies brought it to the attention of the international community. In 1999 – the year that Dr Brovina was captured by the Serbian army and put on trial for terrorism for treating wounded Kosovo Liberation Army combatants[14] – the AWL became a founding member of the Gender Task Force of the Stability Pact for South-Eastern Europe. One of its early achievements was to have rape recognized as a war crime, leading to the first rape trials by the International Criminal Tribunal on the Former Yugoslavia. The task force was also instrumental in the work leading to the passage of Security Council Resolution 1325 on women, peace and security.[15]

In the midst of ethnic violence, young mothers challenge family violence[16]

When Lifestart in Emergencies was launched in the Albanian-Macedonian border region in 1996, it was introduced as a means to help young children whose lives had been disrupted by ethnic violence. What the children had lived through was described in a poverty assessment carried out in Albania shortly after the war had ended:

> [There] are pockets of severe poverty in the North mountainous ... areas [and] ... the health of young children and their mothers is poor, with maternal mortality nine times higher than the national average and infant mortality three times higher than the national average for 2002. [Nutrition] is often poor because of poverty and misinformation. Living conditions of children and families are not only marked by traditional family structure and various forms of insecurity and isolation, but also by blood feuding and intercommunity tensions and conflicts.[17]

These kinds of conditions had led to a decline in the under-five population in every country in Southeastern Europe. Between 1990 and 1996, the year Lifestart was introduced, Albania lost nearly 9 per cent of its under-five population and Macedonia lost nearly 8 per cent. By 2002, when most of the violence had ended, Albania had lost nearly 30 per cent of its under-five population and Macedonia had lost nearly 25 per cent compared to 1990.[18]

It is remarkable that, under such conditions, Lifestart was able to reach a total of 5,000 Kosovar Albanian, Macedonian, Roma and Turkish families, including 9,000 children, during its five years of existence. The family visitors and educators who implemented the project were trained in family dynamics, the psychological dimensions of the crisis, the physical, emotional and cognitive development of children, mental hygiene and parents' communication skills. As tensions in the region increased, the project also introduced conflict resolution and community cohesion components.

For their initial contact, family visitors spoke first with the grandfather or other male in the household about the goals of the programme. They would then ask his permission to allow mothers of young children to attend community meetings. For Roma women, who generally were not allowed to attend, an educator would work with mothers and children in their homes. At these meetings, small groups of mothers – and often the male elders who accompanied them – would hear discussions about how children learn, the effects of abuse and neglect (beatings when they do something wrong, tying them to trees when the parents are working) and ways to help them feel safer and have hope for the future. This supportive, non-critical approach helped both mothers and their husbands and fathers to see how the effects of political violence can be compounded by family violence. "Every child has the right to grow up in a caring family", a brochure for parents explained, and

> there is support for families who have difficulty providing care. Psycho-social support and home care can help children and their families to cope with mental, physical, emotional and social needs … There are many reasons why some children cannot grow, sometimes due to illness or death of parents, but often due to serious neglect and abuse. [If that happens], there are temporary alternatives that [can] provide such care until the situation in the biological family is better.[19]

Aside from such parenting materials, Lifestart in Emergencies produced little documentation, as is often the case with crisis projects, except for an evaluation by UNICEF, which included a Likert-type survey of 1,400 participating mothers from the different ethnic groups. The mothers were asked about the changes they had noticed as a result of the project – in themselves and their relationship with their child, in their families and in their communities. The possible answers were "little", "much", "very much" or "not at all". As there had been no baseline survey, the results must be viewed as anecdotal. Nevertheless, it is significant that 70–90 per cent of respondents reported experiencing "much" or "very much" change, as opposed to "little" or "none at all", for every one of the 49 indicators.

Additional evidence of Lifestart's impact can be drawn from other projects that were also based on the model of involving parents from different ethnic groups in the education of their children. One such project was Mozaik, funded by the Swiss Agency for Development and Cooperation and implemented by the NGO Search for Common Ground, which focused explicitly on teaching conflict resolution skills to pre-schoolers. While "At the beginning parents were very skeptical and faced a great deal of pressure from their communities to withdraw their children from the Mozaik kindergartens ... Parents are now very enthusiastic about Mozaik's unique approach ... [and] consider bilingual kindergartens as a crucial element in their children's development and extremely important for the 'healthy' future of Macedonia's ethnically diverse society."[20]

Another project, the Children's Theatre Centre, trained parents and older children in tolerance and conflict resolution through the performing arts. The centre was funded by the Stability Pact for South-Eastern Europe and implemented by the Open Society Institute. One activity was Street Stories, in which about 90 children from different ethnic backgrounds (Macedonian, Albanian, Turkish, Roma and Bosnian) turned ethnic conflicts they had witnessed in the streets into skits. Then they acted out the different roles in front of other children, parents and teachers. "Parents had to be convinced that the project [did] not aim to take sides in the conflict", an evaluation noted.[21] Once they understood that the project aimed at creating a better life for their children, most parents cautiously allowed their children to participate.

Both the Mozaik and Lifestart evaluations give a sense of the scepticism and lack of trust that characterized the population when Lifestart was launched. They also provide a broader context for assessing the significance of the changes reported in the project's micro-level evaluation survey.

Lifestart evaluation findings

The Lifestart evaluators looked at a number of indicators of change in the participating mothers, their children, their family relatives and their communities.

Mothers' changes in relation to the children

Between 70 and 80 per cent of participating mothers reported that the project helped them to communicate more effectively with their children, be more patient, create the conditions for them to investigate and play more often, express love and praise, understand their stages of development and teach them personal hygiene. Notably, more than 55 per cent said they no longer physically punished their children, and almost 25 per cent said that as a result of what they learned in the project, they now physically punished their children "very little". However, about 20 per cent said they still punished their children "much" or "very much".

The mothers also had an opportunity to answer an open-ended question on the most important lesson they had learned about their relationship with their children. Their answers included:

- To create various toys and show my child how to use them
- To be less nervous with the child; to soothe my child when he/she is nervous
- To educate myself about my child's needs at his/her age
- To change my behaviour towards my child
- To accept each developmental change of the child as natural
- To spend more time with the child than the grandmother does
- To meet and learn from other mothers

Changes in the mother

Participation in Lifestart helped mothers to understand the critical role they play in their children's development. They also became more aware of their need for socialization and how to seek support when they had problems. More than 80 per cent agreed "very much" with the statement that "parents are responsible for providing conditions for the proper development of their child". In the mothers' own words, Lifestart contributed to their personal change in the following ways:

- I am now more relaxed, more tolerant, more satisfied and more sociable.
- My expectations of the child are now more reasonable; I am now sure that a kind word is worth more than any threat.
- I persuaded my husband to take part in the project.
- I am now more persistent in solving problems.
- Now I can solve problems easily and without frustration.
- I am now sure that the parents are crucial for a healthy family.
- I acquired new knowledge.
- I became more communicative; I made new friends.
- I now have an open attitude towards the children and we try to find a common language.
- My self-confidence increased.
- I now know that there are times when the father can take care of the child as well as the mother.
- I learned that one has to create appropriate conditions first before planning to start a family.

Changes in the family

The survey also found that other members of the family recognized the importance of the mother's work and deferred to her on matters of child raising. Close to 89 per cent reported being treated with "more" or "very much more" respect in the family after having participated in the programme; and 92 per cent reported that relationships in the family were "better" or "very much better". In addition, more than 87 per cent of the women reported that their husbands were "more" or "very much more" interested in learning about the development of children and in creating a better environment for the child's development; and 92 per cent of the mothers said they were the ones in the family who decided what is best for the child. In the mothers' own words:

- The family is thankful for the programme and warmly welcomes it.
- The family members grew closer.
- We solve problems together.
- The father got closer to his child.
- My husband notices improvements in me.
- I consult my husband more often.
- There is greater understanding of family members for each other.
- I communicate better with the other family members.
- Now my husband helps me with the education of the children.

Changes in the community

Relationships in the community also improved as a result of Lifestart. More than 80 per cent of the mothers said they now exchange opinions with neighbours and other people "more" or "very much more" often. Many conversations are about how to improve the conditions for children to play, and the important role of mothers in the family and community. Ninety per cent reported undertaking "more" or "very much more" joint activities with other adults for the sake of the children; 94 per cent said that interest in "schooling for parenthood" had increased "much" or "very much"; and 81 per cent said that both mothers and fathers had become active in creating better conditions for their children's development. In the mothers' own words:

- The residents of the refugee settlements talk about the programme.
- Now there is a need for a kindergarten in our village.
- We talk more with others about the future of our children.
- People's self-confidence and desire to create better conditions for the children have increased.
- We would like to have a place where children can spend some time together in groups.
- Besides the mothers who participate in the project, the meetings were also visited by mothers who were not part of the programme.
- We ourselves organized a meeting of the women from the city and the villages who took part in the programme.

The community-based educators trained by the project also reported that they themselves had gained greater self-confidence through their training and implementation of the project (51 per cent); greater authority in their own family (30 per cent); greater authority in the community (34 per cent); greater knowledge of how to raise their own children (42 per cent); better cooperation with others in their environment (34 per cent); and awareness of how to change their community for the better (42 per cent).

Finally, educators asked the mothers what they would do to stimulate their children's development in the days to come. The mothers said they would show their children more love and respect, help them with their problems, praise them, build their self-confidence, play with them and help them to learn so they can become useful citizens in society.

Discussion

Through Lifestart in Emergencies, women in isolated, ethnically divided regions of Macedonia became aware of their own *value* and *values*, and learned to overcome mistrust and work together across ethnic lines for the sake of their children. Their initiative and self-confidence also had a positive effect on their husbands, who gained more respect for their wives and began to develop relationships with their children and with men from other groups. These activities, in turn, increased social cohesion. Women who met during the project began to organize inter-ethnic festivals and religious celebrations, and to establish local early childhood development centres in ethnically mixed villages. Many of these centres are now supported by local governments, and the dual focus on child development and parental education has been largely mainstreamed into the Macedonian education strategy and school system.

The programme's success was due largely to the fact that it was non-confrontational and was thus able to foster trust. Focusing on children's well-being proved to be an effective, non-threatening entry point for efforts to address socially and culturally sensitive issues such as domestic and inter-community violence.

After the war: Women continue to drive the agenda in Macedonia

The principles of Lifestart have been incorporated into ECCD and community-based development activities in hundreds of vulnerable communities, reaching tens of thousands of children throughout Macedonia. The project was resumed and scaled up after the NATO bombing ended.

The expanded project, supported by a US$600,000 grant from the World Bank's Post-Conflict Fund, covered some 30,000 children in about 700 predominantly Albanian, Macedonian and Roma communities all over the country. It was implemented by the Forum of Albanian Women in Albanian communities and the Lifestart Foundation of Bitola in Macedonian and Roma communities. The second phase of the project was also supported by the Faculty of Philosophy at the University of Skopje, which provided training and continuous supervision of educators; by psychologists who addressed issues of women's voice; and by the Center for Human Rights at the Institute for Social, Political and Juridical Research, which provided technical assistance in conflict resolution, in collaboration with the Ethnic Conflict Resolution Project. The project included technical assistance to central and local authorities related to the institutional, technical and financial sustainability of the ECCD activities.

The scaling up also resulted in the creation of a national network of local NGOs and 150 community educators specializing in ECCD, as well as a system of 11 regional coordinators for monitoring and supervision. These community-based educators and coordinators, many of them women who were trained through their involvement in Lifestart, are now a permanent presence on the national scene. They were instrumental in the enactment by the Macedonian parliament of the Law on Child Protection, which states in part that:

> Care and upbringing of pre-school education children is a form of child protection that includes housing, care, nutrition, upbringing, education, sports and recreational and cultural-entertainment activities, measures and activities for health promotion and health protection and improvement of the intellectual, emotional, physical, mental and social development of the child ... Any psychological or physical maltreatment, punishment or other inhumane treatment or abuse of children is probibited ...[22]

Many of these women were also involved in the drafting of the government's education strategy, gender-mainstreaming strategy and the new constitution, which guarantees equal rights to citizens of every ethnicity. Further, the Ministry of Labour and Social Welfare has endorsed community initiatives in early childhood education as a complement to the formal kindergarten system; and ECCD programmes and projects have been written into a number of municipal budgets.

These programmes have benefited from the participation and guidance of women who were committed to the belief that inclusion, respect for differences and inter-ethnic dialogue for the sake of young children can prevent conflict at the community level, where most ethnic conflicts begin.

Notes

1. While the full and official name of Macedonia is the former Yugoslav Republic of Macedonia (FYROM), throughout this chapter the country will be referred to as Macedonia.
2. Data from Macedonia's 2002 census, the first conducted since the end of the conflict, show the following official population shares: Macedonians 64.18 per cent (down from 65.3 per cent in the 1991 census), Albanians 25.17 per cent (up from 21.7 per cent in 1990), Turks 3.85 per cent (no change), Roma 2.66 per cent (no change), Serbs 1.78 per cent (down from 2.1 per cent), Bosniaks 0.84 per cent (down from 1.5 per cent) and other 1.5 per cent (down from 2.2 in 1990). See *Statistical Yearbook of the Republic of Macedonia 2004*, Skopje: State Statistical Office. These numbers should be viewed with caution, however, as minority ethnic groups, particularly Roma, are perpetually under-counted, as "there are significant disparities between official data and estimates by non-governmental sources, which put the number of Roma living in Macedonia at 80,000–135,000. This would place Roma at between 3.95% and 6.67% of the total population." See "Written Comments of the European Rights Centre and the National Roma Centrum Concerning the Former Yugoslav Republic of Macedonia", submitted to UN Committee on Economic, Social and Cultural Rights, 37th Session, European Roma Rights Centre and National Roma Centrum, Budapest and Kumanovo, 19 September 2006, p. 2, available at http://www2.ohchr.org/english/bodies/cescr/docs/Comments _ERRC_NRC_Macedonia.pdf. The Roma Education Fund estimates that Roma comprise 5–6 per cent of the population in Macedonia. See Roma Education Fund (2007) "Advancing Education of Roma in Macedonia: Country Assessment and the Roma Education Fund's Strategic Directions", Roma Education Fund, Budapest, p. 9, available at http://demo.itent.hu/roma/portal/downloads/Education%20Resources/Macedonia _report.pdf.
3. Solidarités International (2001) "Our Action in Macedonia: Notes from the Field", available at www.solidarites.org/ourprog/maced.htm.
4. UN Convention on the Rights of the Child, adopted by the UN General Assembly on 20 November 1989.
5. NATO (1999) "NATO's Role in Relation to the Conflict in Kosovo", 15 July, available at www.nato.int/kosovo/history.htm.
6. Adamchevska, Snezana and Zoran Velkovski (2000) "Evaluation of the Lifestart in Emergencies ECCD Project", March, UNICEF, New York.
7. Ibid.
8. Reynolds, Colette, Mary Byrne and Margaret Barry (2004) "Final Evaluation Report of the Rural Mental Health Project (Phase 2)", Centre for Health Promotion Studies, NUI, Galway.
9. The EU Programme for Peace and Reconciliation in Northern Ireland and the Border Counties of Ireland, Operational Programme, 2000–2004 can be found at http://ec. europa.eu. This concept for the second phase of the programme, Peace II, summarizes the purpose and results of Peace I:

> In the autumn of 1994, shortly after the cease-fires were announced by the main paramilitary groups in Northern Ireland, the European Commission looked into practical ways for the European Union to support the region's transition to a more peaceful and stable society. The Task Force set up at that time came to the conclusion that the European Union had a clear interest and vital role to play in maintaining the momentum for peace and reconciliation, not only for the benefit of the region most affected, but also for the wider benefit of the European Union as a whole. On this basis,

the European Commission proposed to create a Special Support Programme for Peace and Reconciliation in Northern Ireland and the Border Counties of Ireland (also known as the Programme for Peace and Reconciliation, or SSPPR), to be implemented in the form of a Community Initiative under the Structural Funds for the period 1995 to 1999. The principle of such a special Programme and its initial allocation of financial resources were endorsed by the European Council of Heads of States and Governments at the Essen Summit in December 1994. After a wide consultation of interested parties both in the eligible region and among European institutions and organs, the European Commission adopted Guidelines for the Initiative in May 1995, and formally created the Programme in July 1995, in agreement with the United Kingdom and Ireland. In recognition of the EU's continuing support for the peace process in Northern Ireland, the European Council in Berlin in March 1999 decided to continue the PEACE Programme for a further 5 years (2000–2004). The implementation of the PEACE II Programme will take place in a new political and institutional context created by the implementation of the Belfast/Good Friday Agreement and by the new round of structural funds.

10. Ibid.
11. The Agreement Between the Government of the United Kingdom of Great Britain and Northern Ireland and the Government of Ireland, also known as the Belfast Accord or the Good Friday Agreement, was signed on 10 April 1998.
12. Petition from the Women of the World to the Governments of the World, presented on opening day of 52nd session of UN General Assembly, 10 November 1997.
13. Interview with Dr Flora Brovina, *The Guardian*, 15 November 2001.
14. After establishing Lifestart in Emergencies, Dr Brovina went back to Kosovo and set up field hospitals to treat wounded members of the Kosovo Liberation Army. She was arrested by the Serbian army in 1999, put on trial for terrorism and sentenced to 12 years in prison. She was released two years later after intense pressure from UNICEF and other international organizations. She then set up a centre to care for women and children traumatized by the war, and returned to practising paediatrics.
15. UN Security Council Resolution 1325, adopted on 31 October 2000. The resolution:

> reaffirms the important role of women in the prevention and resolution of conflicts, peace negotiations, peace-building, peacekeeping, humanitarian response and in post-conflict reconstruction and stresses the importance of their equal participation and full involvement in all efforts for the maintenance and promotion of peace and security. Resolution 1325 urges all actors to increase the participation of women and incorporate gender perspectives in all United Nations peace and security efforts. It also calls on all parties to conflict to take special measures to protect women and girls from gender-based violence, particularly rape and other forms of sexual abuse, in situations of armed conflict. The resolution provides a number of important operational mandates, with implications for Member States and the entities of the United Nations system.

See Office of the Special Adviser on Gender Issues and Advancement of Women, available at www.un.org/womenwatch/osagi/wps.
16. This section is based on Adamchevska and Velkovski, note 6.
17. World Bank (2003) "Albania Poverty Assessment", World Bank, Washington, DC; Zafeirakou, Aigli (2004) "Early Childhood Development in Albania: The Transition Effects", paper prepared for Human Development, Europe and Central Asia, World Bank, Washington, DC.

18. TransMONEE database, UNICEF and International Rescue Committee, Florence. TransMONEE is the database associated with the UNICEF Innocenti project on the living conditions of children and adolescents in Central and Eastern Europe and the Commonwealth of Independent States. The database is available at www.unicef-irc.org/databases/transmonee. According to the TransMONEE database for 2003, the wars in Southeastern Europe caused the following declines in the under-five population between 1990 and 2002: Bulgaria 43.5 per cent; Romania 37.4 per cent; Albania 29.4 per cent; Croatia 28.6 per cent; Bosnia-Herzegovina 39.7 per cent; FYR Macedonia 23.6 per cent; and Serbia and Montenegro 29.8 per cent.
19. UNICEF project materials, translated from Macedonian.
20. Swiss Agency for Development and Cooperation (2004) "Mozaik Bilingual Kindergartens: Together We Grow and Learn", Swiss Agency for Development and Cooperation, Bern, available at www.swiss-cooperation.admin.ch/macedonia/en/Home/Facilitating _Decentralisation/Mozaik_bilingual_kindergartens.
21. Task Force Education and Youth, Enhanced Graz Process (2001) "Progress Report: Quick Start Projects", December, Working Table 1, Stability Pact for South-Eastern Europe, Vienna, available at www.stabilitypact.org/education/qsp.pdf.
22. Government of the Republic of Macedonia (2000) "Law on Child Protection", *Official Gazette of the Republic of Macedonia* 98.

Part III

Putting good intentions into practice: National and global efforts to right past wrongs

9

Gender and transitional justice: Experiences from South Africa, Rwanda and Sierra Leone

Lyn S. Graybill

Africa saw in the 1990s both a model for restorative justice in South Africa's Truth and Reconciliation Commission and a mechanism for retributive justice in the International Criminal Tribunal for Rwanda. They preceded Sierra Leone's attempt in 2002 to set up concurrent post-conflict systems – both a truth commission and a special court – to deal with crimes committed during its brutal decade-long civil war. To what extent did Sierra Leone improve on the earlier examples in addressing the issue of gender violations? This chapter discusses how violations of women's human rights committed during conflict were handled by these earlier forums, and how Sierra Leone learned from and adapted the models to suit its unique situation. It suggests in conclusion that the limited successes of all three countries in dealing with gender violations may set the stage for continuing violence against women in Africa.

South Africa

Three hundred years of minority rule in South Africa, culminating in a decades-long low-intensity civil war between resistance movements and the government, ended with the nation's first all-race elections in April 1994. The new government quickly passed legislation creating the Truth and Reconciliation Commission (TRC) to investigate gross human rights abuses (defined as "killing, abduction, torture, or severe ill treatment").[1] Victims were invited to tell their personal stories at hearings conducted

Defying victimhood: Women and post-conflict peacebuilding, Schnabel and Tabyshalieva (eds), *United Nations University Press, 2012, ISBN 978-92-808-1201-5*

by the Human Rights Violations Committee, and perpetrators were encouraged to make full disclosure to the Amnesty Committee for abuses
committed between 1960 and 1994.[2]

Gender crimes during apartheid

In the early hearings, women's testimony before the TRC was largely
about abuses to male relatives, not to themselves. According to Ross's
coverage of the first five weeks of hearings, 60 per cent of deponents
were women but over three-quarters of their testimonies were about
abuses to men.[3] Under pressure from women's organizations and following a submission on "Gender and the Truth and Reconciliation Commission" by Goldblatt and Meintjes, the TRC attempted to refocus its
efforts on women.[4] For instance, the commissioners amended the form
used for statements, cautioning women: "Important: Don't forget to tell
us what happened to you yourself if you were the victim of a gross
human rights abuse."[5] The TRC accepted recommendations that women
be allowed to tell stories on behalf of other women; that groups of
women be permitted to come together and tell their stories as a collective; that hearings be held in camera when requested; and that women,
supported by social workers and psychologists, be permitted to tell their
stories before a panel of female commissioners in a meeting hall where
only women were allowed to attend.[6] Three women-only hearings were
held in Cape Town, Durban and Johannesburg to address abuses of
women.

The TRC gave many women their first opportunity to tell anyone
about their abuse during the apartheid years. Two women at the Johannesburg hearing testified that this was the first time either had told of her
rape. Thandi Shezi, who was gang-raped by the police, testified, "I thought
I'd done something that I deserved to be treated like that."[7] Kedeboni
Dube, who was raped by Inkatha Freedom Party supporters, had only
told her family she had been kidnapped.[8] A woman testifying anonymously at the Durban hearing also said she had told no one of being
gang-raped by Inkatha members as her husband watched. She explained:
"Sometimes I feel like I invited the trouble myself."[9]

In addition to rape, other violations women suffered centred on their
sex and age. Many women testified that they were degraded during their
menstrual periods, forced to stand without benefit of sanitary pads with
blood running down their legs.[10] Women were sometimes made to dis-
robe in front of male wardens, fondled by doctors and police officers and
genitally shocked.[11]

Not all women availed themselves of the opportunity to testify.[12]
Given the assumption of many South Africans about a sexually abused

woman – that she had brought it upon herself – many women chose not to speak out. Many high-ranking women in government who were rape victims during the apartheid years may have worried how they would be perceived if they came forward with their stories.[13] Some women in government were former MK (Umkhonto we Sizwe) soldiers who had been molested by their own comrades in training camps in Zambia, Angola and Tanzania but may have not wanted to discredit fellow members in the African National Congress (ANC).

The TRC's final report identified 140 rapes, although the actual number is certainly much higher,[14] and confirmed the initial impression that women had been reticent to speak about their own violations. Although more than half of all deponents (54.8 per cent) were women, only 43.9 per cent of women identified themselves as victims of abduction, torture or severe ill treatment.[15] Still, this represented an increase in the percentage of self-proclaimed victims over the first five weeks of hearings that Ross's study analyses, and can be attributed in part to the decision by the TRC to hold special women's hearings.

A final curiosity is that while rape victims could identify themselves as victims of "severe ill treatment", this is one type of violation for which no individual amnesty applicants acknowledged responsibility. No member of the security forces or liberation movement applied for amnesty for rape or other sexual violations. This is probably because they assumed that rape would not fall within the guidelines, as an act had to not only have a "political" motive but also be performed "without malice". Can one rape without malice? One view of why rape was not acknowledged by perpetrators is its common occurrence in South Africa – so common that it is not considered a gross human rights violation.

Post-TRC gender violence

One wonders whether the focus on gender violence at the TRC had any impact in directing attention to gender violence in the post-apartheid era. Despite the passage of the Domestic Violence Act in 1998, domestic abuse is rampant in South Africa, affecting 25–30 per cent of women.[16] A study conducted by the Medical Research Council found that 27 per cent of women in the Eastern Cape, 28 per cent of women in Mpumalanga and 19 per cent of women in the Northern Province had been physically abused by a current or former partner. In another study of 1,394 men working for three Cape Town area municipalities, 44 per cent admitted to having abused their female partners. In a third study of 1,800 working men in the Western Cape, 22 per cent reported having forced their wives or girlfriends to have sex.[17] What happens in the home traditionally has been seen as a private sphere out of bounds for government interference, leaving wives who are economically dependent on their abusive spouses with few options.

South Africa also has the highest number of reported rapes in the world.[18] In one study, one in four men interviewed claimed to have had sex without a woman's consent.[19] Interpol predicts that one in two South African women will be raped in her lifetime.[20] To compound this, rape is the most underreported crime in South Africa, according to Human Rights Watch.[21] Even the official South African Police Services (SAPS) statistics – widely perceived as being too low – documented 71,500 rapes in 2008–2009,[22] while the South African Law Commission estimates there may be as many as 1.69 million rapes a year.[23] Most disturbing is that incidents of rape are rising: from an average of 16,000 official cases per year in the 1980s – at the height of the conflict – to 55,000 official cases in 2006. The high-profile acquittal of Jacob Zuma, ANC deputy president, for the alleged rape of his god-daughter highlighted the pervasiveness of the problem throughout all levels of society, as well as the low conviction rates.[24]

Conviction rates hover at just 8 per cent of reported cases.[25] SAPS, whose reforms have centred on race bias, have paid little attention to the fair treatment of women rape victims.[26] Even young girls find themselves objects of sexual assaults. SAPS statistics reveal that 41 per cent of rape victims are girls under the age of 12.[27] Schoolgirls are raped, sexually assaulted and harassed by their male classmates and teachers, causing many to drop out of school.[28]

In addition, circumstances force women to trade sex for goods. The incidence of the "sugar daddy" phenomenon – where women have "transactional sex" with usually older partners in return for food, clothing, transportation, school fees or gifts – is high.[29] Cross-generational relationships associated with low condom use and gender-based violence are linked to high HIV/AIDS infection rates.[30]

In South Africa, where more people are living with AIDS than in any other country, women are affected disproportionately,[31] prompting Stephen Lewis, the UN special envoy on HIV/AIDS in Africa, to describe the pandemic in Africa as a "war against women".[32]

Sexual harassment is yet another area of concern. It is estimated that 76 per cent of women have experienced some form of sexual harassment, 40 per cent of whom left their jobs as a result.[33] Although perpetrators can be indicted under a number of laws, including the Employment Equity Act, there have been few prosecutions.

One theory to explain the high levels of sexual violence is that it is a natural outgrowth of past political violence. Human Rights Watch maintains that there is "at least circumstantial evidence that those areas worst affected by the uprising against the state and by intra-community political conflict are also those areas where reported rapes are highest".[34] Goldblatt and Meintjes hypothesize that men's exposure to torture and violence during the apartheid era has contributed to the current climate of violence against women in South Africa.[35] Conversely, Zwane links rape in the townships to the *end* of armed struggle and the demobilization of youth who are trying to find meaning in their lives when there is no longer a clear enemy.[36] While Skully stresses the historical context for gender violence, harking back to colonialism,[37] Britton suggests contemporary events. She surmises that increased gender-based violence may be a backlash against the constitutionally enforced gender equality of South African women.[38] Whatever the reasons, it has been suggested that currently women are experiencing "as much, if not more, gender-based violence in their communities than was the case under apartheid".[39]

Rwanda

As South Africans were holding their first democratic elections in April 1994, 3,000 kilometres to the north Rwandans were massacring each other in the fastest recorded genocide in history. After the airplane death of Hutu President Juvenal Habyarimana on 6 April 1994, the Hutu went on a killing spree, exterminating an estimated 800,000 Tutsi (and moderate Hutu as well) over the course of 100 days in an effort to thwart the power-sharing arrangement with Tutsi to which the president had agreed under the Arusha Peace Accords of 1993. The genocide ended when the mainly Tutsi Rwandan Patriotic Front (RPF) defeated the remnants of the interim government and stopped the carnage.

Sexual attacks during the genocide

Although the main casualties were men, women were particularly vulnerable to sexual violence. Human Rights Watch described how women were individually raped, gang-raped, raped with objects such as sticks or gun barrels, held in sexual slavery and sexually mutilated.[40] Regarded as prizes to be distributed to subordinates who performed well in killing Tutsi, women were kept in sexual servitude either collectively or through forced "marriages".[41]

Although both Tutsi and Hutu women were raped (for instance a Hutu wife of a Tutsi man, or a Hutu woman who aided Tutsi) – and especially elite educated women of both ethnicities[42] – Tutsi women suffered the most rapes and other forms of sexual violence. Human Rights Watch established that virtually every Tutsi woman and adolescent girl who survived the genocide had been raped. The UN special rapporteur in

Rwanda, extrapolating from the number of unwanted pregnancies after the genocide (with 100 cases of rape resulting in one pregnancy), estimates that the total number of women raped was between 250,000 and 500,000.[43]

Women who managed to avoid murder were nevertheless under a death sentence, since the perpetrators often carried the AIDS virus.[44] According to President Paul Kagame, "We knew that the government was bringing AIDS patients out of the hospitals specifically to form battalions of rapists."[45] According to Lisa Sharlach, statistics from over a decade ago indicated that half of all rape survivors were HIV positive.[46] But more recent figures from the World Health Organization in 2008 estimate that 150,000 Rwandans are living with HIV/AIDS, including 78,000 women, down from its estimates in 2002 of 500,000 with HIV/AIDS, including 250,000 women.[47] One can surmise that the downward trend is due to AIDS-related deaths.

Justice and the ICTR

Contemporaneous with South Africa's "pardon" experiment embodied in the TRC, the government of Rwanda demanded "punishment" through the International Criminal Tribunal for Rwanda (ICTR) for acts of genocide committed by the former regime. Mamdani explains the difference between a truth commission and a tribunal in this way: "if South Africa exemplifies the dilemma involved in the pursuit of reconciliation without justice, Rwanda exemplifies the opposite: the pursuit of justice without reconciliation".[48]

While the ANC was hamstrung by promises to the National Party to grant amnesty as a condition of relinquishing power, the Rwandan Patriotic Front, having ended the genocide and routed the remnants of the Hutu government, was under no such constraint and heartily supported (at least initially) the establishment of a Nuremberg-style tribunal to try those who had fled into exile, and local courts for those detained in jails inside the country.[49] The Tanzania-based ICTR, which is set to complete its work in 2014, has prosecuted the planners of genocide, crimes against humanity and violations of the Geneva Conventions committed in 1994, while the Rwandan state courts have prosecuted those who followed orders. Under the state's Genocide Law, the more serious Category 1 crimes originally carried a mandatory death penalty, with varying sentences for the lesser Categories 2, 3 and 4 crimes.[50] In the years since the genocide, approximately 7,000 people have been tried in the state genocide courts.

Although Category 1 defendants in state courts may include those who commit acts of rape and sexual torture, few if any of the dossiers have included these charges. One reason is that the law does not expressly define the legal elements of either crime, such as force or coercion. Hence court verdicts are inconsistent, law enforcement is confused and sexual violence against women tends to be ignored.[51] According to then deputy minister of justice Gerald Gahima, within the Justice Department's investigation teams "rape has not been receiving the attention it deserves. The main focus has been on the killings and not as many women were killed."[52] It is unfortunate that so few rape cases have been tried in the state courts, since verdicts in local courts would likely be perceived as more legitimate than those in an international tribunal outside the country, and thus have a greater chance of influencing community attitudes towards sexual crimes.

In an effort to deal with the large number of suspects – 130,000 at its height – the government in 2002 resurrected a traditional form of jurisprudence, *gacaca*, literally "justice on the grass", to expedite justice quickly and efficiently. *Gacaca* officially concluded in 2010.[53] It was often portrayed as reconciliatory, rather than merely punitive, because it aimed to restore relationships by reintegrating perpetrators back into their communities once they admitted their wrongdoing. *Gacaca* rewards confession with reduced sentences, and both mandatory apology and compensation to victims are written into the *gacaca* law.[54]

The *gacaca* panels, which heard testimony of Categories 2–4 crimes and reached verdicts through community consensus, were not originally authorized to hear crimes involving rape or sexual torture. Women's rights activists had successfully lobbied the government to categorize rape and sexual torture as Category 1 crimes which deserved the harshest penalties. They argued that sexual torture has lifetime effects on its victims – a slow death more painful than murder – and therefore should be elevated above murder, unintentional homicide and other serious assaults in the hierarchy of crimes. In a sense, this acknowledges that rape is so heinous that it must be prosecuted at the state level, although, as mentioned, few rape cases have actually been prosecuted at that level. Even if the dossiers were to include rape, criminal courts are geographically, procedurally and financially inaccessible to the majority of women.[55]

Although rape could not be prosecuted in *gacaca*, the 2004 Genocide Law nevertheless permitted a Category 1 suspect to confess at a *gacaca* panel. If the suspect's confession (along with an apology) was accepted, he could get a reduced sentence (and avoid the death penalty). In that way, rapists could be motivated to acknowledge their crimes.[56] In 2008 the law was further changed to permit Category 1 cases, including rape, to come under the *gacaca* jurisdiction. The change was opposed by most women's groups, which felt it minimized the seriousness of rape and believed the sentences would be too lenient. Only one out of 20 rape victims interviewed by Human Rights Watch said they preferred *gacaca* over the state courts.[57]

Few rape cases have been prosecuted in the ICTR either. In the tribunal's first year it looked as though it would fail to mount even one rape prosecution. One explanation was the lack of political will among those leading the investigations. The perception of tribunal investigators was that rape is a "lesser" crime not worthy of investigating.[58] However, in July 1996, under pressure from international women's groups, a sexual assault committee was created within the tribunal to address problems related to the investigation of gender crimes. When former mayor of Taba Jean-Paul Akayesu was arrested for genocide, the prosecutor of the ICTR was asked by women's and human rights organizations in an amicus brief to charge him specifically with rape and other crimes of sexual violence. As a direct result of their brief, the prosecutor amended the indictment to include charges of rape and inhumane treatment. In addition, the amendment recognized rape as a crime against humanity and a war crime.[59]

Akayesu was convicted in September 1998 of inciting others to commit genocide (marking the first conviction of genocide by an international court) and of crimes against humanity (including extermination, assassination, torture, rape and other inhumane acts). He was sentenced to life in prison. This case set the precedent that rape can be one means of committing a crime of genocide if it targets a particular ethnic or religious group. It marked the first time that an international court had punished sexual violence in an internal conflict.

Few rape prosecutions

Although the Akayesu case was ground-breaking, after that verdict prosecutors at the ICTR have been reluctant to bring indictments for crimes of sexual violence.[60] At the tenth anniversary of the genocide, only 30 per cent of cases tried included rape charges, and only 10 per cent of those defendants were found guilty for their role in widespread sexual violence. Binaifer Nowrojee writes: "In real numbers, that means that, at the tenth anniversary of the genocide, only two defendants had specifically been held responsible for their role in sexual violence crimes ... despite the tens of thousands of rapes committed during the genocide."[61]

The deputy prosecutor of the tribunal explains: "African women don't want to talk about rape. We haven't received any real complaints. It's rare in investigations that women refer to rape."[62] Although rampant, rape has been underreported by victims. Because of the stigma, most women do not talk of their experiences. Linda Fairstein, a veteran prosecutor of sexual offences, argues that women's reticence to testify at a trial is based on the desire "to avoid what they anticipate will be the rigors of seeing their assailant and being cross-examined; reliving the terror of their victimization, especially in a public courtroom; the humiliations or embarrassment of describing the intimate acts forced upon them so violently; being questioned about their personal lives".[63]

One woman revealed her discomfort about testifying before the tribunal:

> They asked me what I meant by "raping", I didn't know what to do. I looked around me for help. It is not something you do in Rwandan culture. They asked me if it was for a man to put his penis in a woman's vagina. I nodded. They said I had to repeat it. So I repeated it. But then I started to cry because of the shame. For a Rwandan girl to use such words in her life, you don't know: it is awful.[64]

The tribunal has gone some way in attempting to alleviate victims' discomfort. It has eliminated a corroboration requirement, rejected the admissibility of the victim's sexual history and defined the crime in terms of force or threat of force applied, rather than the resistance offered.[65] Rule 34 of the ICTR Rules of Procedure and Evidence addresses the need for witness protection, and Rule 69 relates to non-disclosure of the identity of a witness who may be in danger.[66] Even with these reforms, women have still hesitated to testify. One victim said, "There were no women asking the question. If it was a woman, I would have told her."[67] Some women complained that they had to speak to "returnee" translators – Tutsi who had been in exile often for decades and returned after the genocide. Given the tensions between this group and surviving genocide victims, women only felt comfortable speaking with others who had gone through the same experience.[68]

Many also feared reprisals if they pointed the finger, since witnesses could be protected in Arusha, but their safety could not be guaranteed on their return home. One woman was killed in 1997 after she testified against former Rwandan mayor Jean-Paul Akayesu – a chilling warning to other potential witnesses.[69] Another explanation for women's resistance to testifying is "survivor's guilt". Women often feel shame since they are regarded as collaborators with the enemy for having survived.[70] Still another reason for their unwillingness to testify is poor health due to the AIDS virus, which keeps them from travelling to Arusha. Two-thirds of the members of AVEGA-AGAHOZO (Association of Genocide Widows) are HIV positive.[71]

Post-genocide status

Victims have suffered serious medical conditions from sexual violence, including gynaecological and urinary infections, in a country that has only five practising gynaecologists.[72] Women who became pregnant had the difficult decision of whether or not to have the child. Since abortion is illegal in Rwanda, many women turned to self-induced or clandestine abortions, which resulted in serious medical complications.[73] Others chose to bear these children, whom society refers to as "children of hate", "children of bad memories" or "devil children".[74] Some of the 2,000–5,000 war progeny have subsequently been abandoned or killed by their mothers.[75]

The social consequences are enormous. Because of the genocide, 54 per cent of the Rwandan population are now female and 34 per cent of Rwandan households are headed by women (60 per cent of whom are widows), giving women new opportunities but new burdens as well.[76] Given the number of men who were killed or are in prison, marriage may be problematic even for women who were not sexually "defiled". The shortage of men contributes to increased polygamy and the practice of sharing men, known as *kwinjara*, which has become so common that health officials say it represents the greatest challenge in their efforts to combat the spread of AIDS.[77]

AIDS is also being spread by the growing rate of prostitution. According to Newbury and Baldwin, so-called "defiled" women have been pressured into sexual liaisons with local officials since their experiences have already made them "social outcasts".[78] There is increased prostitution not only for young women but older women and teenage girls as well. Newbury and Baldwin write: "Although fully aware of the risks of HIV infection, these prostitutes could envisage no other way of earning enough to stay alive."[79]

Sexual violence continued after the genocide. Tutsi women who had survived were attacked by Zaire-based *interahamwe* (Hutu militias) to eliminate witnesses.[80] In some cases, Tutsi women survivors were pressured into relationships with RPF soldiers as a reward for ending the genocide. Some Hutu women were raped by RPF soldiers in retaliation for rapes against Tutsi women, but since the ICTR, state genocide courts and *gacaca* are trying just the Hutu who committed genocide and not the Tutsi for revenge killings and affiliated acts, women raped by Tutsi men will not receive justice.[81] Since the genocide, domestic violence has become common, affecting one-fifth of Rwandan women, yet these cases are rarely brought before the courts.[82] However, in 2008 the government of Rwanda passed the Domestic Relations Bill and the Domestic Violence Act.[83]

The TRC and ICTR: Serving women?

How successful were South Africa's and Rwanda's attempts at meeting women's needs for reconciliation and justice? As noted earlier, the TRC privileged reconciliation over justice,[84] and the ICTR justice over reconciliation, but in looking at how the two forums handled gender crimes, this distinction breaks down. It is not clear that women in South Africa experienced the reconciliation between victim and perpetrator that was supposed to be forged from the experience of telling their stories in a safe space, hearing perpetrators acknowledge their acts and forgiving perpetrators. Nor is it true that women in Rwanda feel justice has been done by the tribunal's punishment of Hutu who killed, mutilated or raped female Tutsi. In both cases, the handling of crimes against women was an afterthought. The TRC and ICTR took only halting steps towards recognizing the distinctive ways in which women suffered human rights abuses, and both dealt with gender crimes as an "add-on" that was not central to their work.

Both processes have let down women. For those few women who were even aware of the work of the ICTR,[85] anecdotal evidence suggests they were not pleased with the court's judgments, especially pertaining to women.[86] No doubt few Rwandan women survivors feel they have received the justice that was promised them in the ICTR format. The prison term meted out to Akayesu for rape was just 15 years (concurrent with a life sentence for extermination) – the typical sentence handed down at the ICTR for rape – which to many women whose lives have been ruined seems insufficient.[87] Sentencing defendants to concurrent sentences sends the message that rape is not as important as other crimes, since the punishment for rape is subsumed in the punishment for other crimes.[88] Furthermore, the ICTR is prosecuting those who gave orders to rape but not the actual rapists. Many women presumably live in neighbourhoods with former rapists whom they must see daily, reliving the trauma over and over again.

Although the ICTR represents an unprecedented example of prosecuting rape as a crime against humanity and a means of genocide, it was prosecuted as an adjunct to other war crimes, for instance conspiracy to commit genocide, and not by itself. In effect, this trivializes rape, confirming the view that it is the "least condemned" war crime.[89]

Copelon also criticizes the focus on mass rape and ethnic cleansing, because it represents a transfer of concern from individual women to the nation or group. When rape is attributed to ethnic hatred, she argues, women are given no specificity, which amounts to an added assault on women. To view mass rape as a weapon of ethnic cleansing focuses on the ethnic hatred and makes the gender hatred, and the individual tragedy, invisible.[90]

While victims were allowed to testify anonymously, there were examples where they were in full view of the accused. Several women also spoke of their humiliation when defence lawyers and judges joined in the crowd's laughter during their difficult testimony.[91] Witnesses were subject to hostile cross-examinations from defence attorneys. According to Mertus, "Law does not permit a single witness to tell ... her own coherent narrative; it chops the stories into digestible parts, selects a handful of these parts, and sorts and refines them to create a new narrative – the legal anti-narrative."[92] These procedures are supposedly to protect women and ensure that their suffering is not put on trial, but witnesses long to "finish their story" for themselves. Often the process of telling and observing one's story being heard allows survivors to become subjects again.[93]

In a fashion, this occurred at the South African TRC hearings, although there remained procedural and cultural constraints to women's voices being heard. At the TRC women could testify as injured parties without hostile cross-examinations. Some women testified to the therapeutic value of speaking out. However, after an initial sense of relief at having unburdened themselves, there was a return and intensification of symptoms associated with the original violations as well as the onset of new symptoms that may be related to further traumatization caused by retelling the story.[94] A serious blow to female victims was the fact that no amnesty applicants confessed to rape, creating the situation of victims but no perpetrators. It is difficult to see how women were reconciled in the absence of acknowledgement by their assailants.

Sierra Leone

What did Sierra Leone learn from the earlier experiences in transitional justice? Sierra Leone embarked on a two-pronged process to further both justice and reconciliation: a special court to try those "who bear the greatest responsibility"[95] and a truth commission to hear from lesser perpetrators and victims. In fact, it was the first country where the international community set up simultaneously both a truth commission and a court in a post-conflict setting.

Women during the civil war

The decade-long civil war in Sierra Leone was marked by barbarous attacks on civilians, including killings, amputations and sexual violence.[96] Human Rights Watch estimates that between 215,000 and 257,000 women were victims of sexual assault during the conflict.[97] Physicians for Human Rights concludes that one out of eight households had been subjected to sexual violence.[98]

Women of all ages, from young girls to grandmothers, were both individually raped and gang-raped, often in front of their families. Some women were not only forced to have sex in front of family members, but also with family members. Many pregnant women had their wombs ripped open and their foetuses speared by assailants who took bets on the sex of the unborn child.[99]

Rebels took women as their "wives" – perhaps 60 per cent of girls involved with fighting forces were taken as spouses[100] – and branded the name of their group on their breasts. If pro-government forces found these marked women, they would kill them, accusing them of aiding the enemy.

Virgins, or those perceived to be virgins, were preferred,[101] which explains the young ages of many of the victims. The high value placed on virginity in Sierra Leone culture means that these women were subsequently undesirable as marriage partners; hence the impact on women, families and communities was enormous.

Every side of the conflict perpetrated human rights violations against women – not just the Revolutionary United Front (RUF), the Armed Forces Revolutionary Council (AFRC), the Sierra Leone Army and the Civil Defense Forces (CDF), but also UNAMSIL (UN Mission in Sierra Leone) and ECOMOG (Economic Community of West African States Monitoring Group).[102]

Prosecuting gender crimes at the Special Court

Some of the advantages that accrued to the Special Court of Sierra Leone (SCSL) included the mixture of foreign and domestic jurists and its location within the country where the violations took place. International expertise complemented local understandings – an important contribution since Sierra Leone is not advanced in terms of legal protections for women against rape. For instance, in Sierra Leone law, rape is prosecuted under customary law rather than general law, as most serious crimes are. Only the rape of a virgin is considered serious (in Krio "to virginate"),[103] whereas the rape of a married woman or non-virgin is not considered a crime at all.[104] The diffusion of legal knowledge may help the country to internalize international human rights norms, including norms affirming the rights of women.

As a hybrid court, the SCSL was able to utilize national as well as international law. In addition to the state crime of arson, it covered offences under the Prevention of Cruelty to Children Act of 1926, including "abusing a girl under 13 years of age", "abusing a girl between 13 and 14 years of age" and "abduction of a girl for immoral purposes".[105] Also, the advantage of having the court conduct its work in Freetown made it easier for female witnesses to testify and see justice being done. "In this respect," writes Eaton, "the impact of the SCSL's rulings may be felt more widely by the victims than has been the case with the ICTs [international criminal tribunals] decisions."[106]

On the other hand, its location within the country made it harder to protect witnesses, especially the identity of those testifying anonymously. As with the ICTR, the prosecution limited the number of witnesses, with the goal of having a few strong witnesses in order to speed up the trial. As in all court cases, a witness could be subjected to adversarial cross-examination and not allowed free rein to tell her story in her own way.

Despite the adversarial court setting, witnesses were generally treated with respect and dignity. Unlike most courts, psychological counsellors were provided for witnesses to help them get through difficult testimony.[107] Witnesses often felt a sense of release and closure by giving testimony, and judges intervened to stop defence lawyers' overly hostile questioning of witnesses. Most witnesses were sheltered at a safe house in Freetown once their identity was revealed to the defence, with victims of gender-based crimes separated in their own safe house from other witnesses.[108]

Unlike the ICTR, the SCSL indicted suspects for gender crimes not as an afterthought or an add-on to its central work. The reason for this proactive approach, according to King, is that before the hearings even commenced, women's groups and other civil society organizations formed the Women's Task Force on the Role of Women in the TRC and Special Court to ensure that gender crimes were adequately identified and addressed.[109]

The SCSL statute lists the crimes against humanity that can be prosecuted: "rape, sexual slavery, enforced prostitution, forced pregnancy and any other form of sexual violence" when conducted as part of a widespread attack against civilians.[110] When former prosecutor David Crane handed down his first indictments on 7 March 2003, in four of the five the indicted were charged specifically with crimes of sexual violence, categorized as crimes against humanity. This marked the first time that an international tribunal had addressed the prosecution of rape as a major war crime in and of itself in a situation not marked by genocide.[111] This was an important step in treating the crime of rape seriously.

The seriousness with which the court viewed sexual crimes was indicated by the number of investigators assigned to sexual assault violations (two women, or 20 per cent of the investigation team, compared to less than 2 per cent of the ICTR's investigators who dealt with these crimes).[112] One attorney was specifically dedicated to prosecuting cases of sexual violence. Three out of 11 judges (two in the trial chambers and one in the appeal chambers) were women.[113] Perhaps learning from the poor record of the ICTR when it began its work,[114] the SCSL statute specified that due consideration be given to the appointment of prosecutors and investigators in gender-related crimes.[115] The Women's Task

Force on the Role of Women in the TRC and Special Court also advocated for gender balance among the staff.[116]

The SCSL indicted leaders on all sides. This even-handedness was undoubtedly an advantage over its predecessor, the ICTR (as well as the Rwandan genocide courts and *gacaca*), which just tried Hutu accused of crimes against Tutsi and not Tutsi who were involved in revenge killings (and rapes) in the aftermath of the genocide. However, like the ICTR, the SCSL only went after leaders with overall command responsibility, not the foot soldiers or the actual rapists.

In addition to rape, it was expected that other forms of gender violence would be prosecuted. Crane added the charge "forced marriage" under "other inhumane acts" in the legal category of crimes against humanity, arguing that this was more than just rape as these women were held for long periods of time and forced to clean, cook and porter for their "husbands". This charge was added to the six indictments against the RUF and AFRC defendants. However, in June 2007 the court found the AFRC defendants guilty of rape but not guilty of sexual slavery or forced marriage.[117] It was only in February 2009 with the rulings against the RUF defendants that the crime of forced marriage (in addition to rape) was successfully prosecuted.[118]

The court also refused to allow the prosecutor to amend the indictment of the three CDF defendants[119] to include any acts of sexual violence (rape, sexual slavery, enforced prostitution and forced marriage), which the prosecutor sought to do four months before the start of trial, on the grounds that the prosecution waited too long to amend the indictment.[120] Kelsall and Stepakoff argue that the court failed to appreciate fully the difficulties encountered in investigating gender-based crimes (including reticence of victims to come forward, stigma in acknowledging rape, fear of reprisals and the fact that many CDF combatants are considered national heroes by Sierra Leoneans for helping to defeat the rebels, making it difficult for their victims to come forward). Witnesses who had eagerly come to the court to testify about sexual violence committed against them by the CDF were silenced. Six of the seven who testified (to other acts but not sexual acts) later expressed their profound disappointment at being stopped when they tried to speak of their experiences of being raped. Kelsall and Stepakoff argue that the SCSL "missed an opportunity to include as part of its evidence testimony about a significant aspect of the Sierra Leonean conflict".[121]

Acknowledging violations against women at the SLTRC

Working alongside the Special Court was the Sierra Leone Truth and Reconciliation Commission (SLTRC), which was authorized by the Lomé

Peace Accord of 1999 to placate those who were angry about the amnesty deal given to the rebels to get them to lay down their arms.[122] The amnesty deal was later withdrawn when the RUF broke the terms of the agreement and went back to fighting, and the government asked for assistance from the United Nations in prosecuting the leaders of the rebellion in a special court. Nevertheless, it was agreed that the SLTRC would proceed. Its aim was "to work to help restore the human dignity of victims and promote reconciliation by providing an opportunity for victims to give an account of the violations ... suffered and for perpetrators to relate their experiences, and by creating a climate which fosters constructive interchange between victims and perpetrators".[123]

Including the voices of both perpetrators and victims, it was hoped, would create understanding through respectful listening as conflicting parties heard each other's grievances. Mark Freeman and Priscilla Hayner suggest that this aspect of truth commissions may help build empathy.[124] However, just as there are critiques of the benefits of truth telling/hearing in the South African TRC, there are sceptics of this process in Sierra Leone.[125]

Since the Special Court was mandated to prosecute "those most responsible" – and limited funding has limited the number of indicted to just 13 individuals (four of whom are dead)[126] – the vast majority of perpetrators were exempt from prosecution and instead were invited to participate in a South African-styled TRC. Operating from mid-2002 to 2004, the SLTRC's focus was not punishment but reconciliation of perpetrators and victims. Many more victims were able to testify in what was conceived as a more cathartic, healing environment than had been possible in the SCSL.

With no mechanism to compel testimony and no incentive (amnesty) to testify, it was wondered whether perpetrators would come forward to confess. Despite Crane's insistence that he would not use testimony given at the SLTRC to indict someone in the Special Court, many perpetrators remained suspicious and chose not to testify.[127] The far-from-ideal situation of having two concurrent transitional justice institutions, confusion about their mandates and lack of an amnesty agreement undoubtedly contributed to the low number of narratives from perpetrators – just 1 per cent of all statements collected.[128]

Even fewer numbers of perpetrators actually apologized or asked for forgiveness from their victims, as had been expected by the commissioners. Commissioner William Schabas notes, "in some cases [they asked] pardon or forgiveness of their victims".[129] But Shaw observes: "No commander in ... any of the hearings I attended acknowledged any personal responsibility for child abductions, rape, amputations and other violations, leading to considerable probing and heated exchanges when the

Commissioners questioned them."[130] She also notes that rank-and-file ex-combatants felt it was not their place to speak, leaving that role to their commanders. In particular, few soldiers from the CDF testified, believing they were not blameworthy as they were defending the country against the RUF/AFRC forces. Those who did testify denied committing any crimes.[131]

It is unfortunate that the SCSL would not allow CDF leader Samuel Hinga Norman to testify before the SLTRC, as he had wanted to do. His testimony would have added to the historical record about the war, and he may have apologized for the human rights violations committed by his forces, setting an example for his followers to confess as well. While the SLTRC's final report found that the majority of abuses (60.5 per cent) were committed by the RUF/AFRC, the CDF was also guilty of violations (including rape), especially late in the war.[132] The court's refusal to let Norman testify publicly before the SLTRC, arguing that he had a legal right not to incriminate himself, is especially unfortunate since the SCSL would not allow the prosecutor to add rape to the CDF defendants' indictments, saying their due process rights would be harmed since the original indictment did not include this. Thus, for victims of sexual violence at the hands of the CDF, there was no acknowledgement. Nor was there acknowledgement from UN peacekeepers with UNAMSIL or West African forces with ECOMOG who had raped women, but who did not participate in the SLTRC hearings and were not indicted by the Special Court.

Like the Special Court, the SLTRC paid attention to the sexual abuses committed against women during the war. The Lomé Peace Accord (1999) had urged that since women had been particularly victimized during the war, special attention should be accorded to their needs. The Sierra Leone Truth and Reconciliation Act followed up on this notion of targeting women by ordering the commission to "implement special procedures to address the needs of ... those who have suffered sexual abuses".[133] Duggan and Abusharaf attribute the attention to women's needs by the SLTRC to the pressure from national and international women's groups.[134] Thus, unlike the TRC in South Africa and the ICTR, investigating the special ways that women were targeted was no mere afterthought, but was central to the working of the SLTRC from the outset, as it was to the SCSL. Even before the SLTRC was established, the Women's Task Force lobbied the government, demanding gender balance among the commission's staff. Three of the seven commissioners selected were women, no doubt in deference to the task force's recommendations. Two of the female international commissioners,[135] Ajaaratou Jow of Gambia and Yasmin Sooka from South Africa, had extensive experience of dealing with gender crimes.[136]

Taking a page from the South African book, women were encouraged to testify at special women's hearings held over three days in May 2003. These hearings were dedicated to looking at the specific ways in which women were targeted. Women walked to the YMCA building where the meetings were held, carrying signs that said "Justice for Women" and "No Violence Against Women".[137] They were permitted to testify behind a screen with their identities hidden, or to testify in camera or publicly if they so chose. The sessions were opened by the Ministry of Social Welfare, Gender, and Children's Affairs, and women from family support units were sent by the National Police to observe. Only female commissioners questioned these witnesses. In addition to individual women, a number of women's groups provided submissions and oral testimony. Nowrojee reports that women's groups spoke positively about the special hearings, and that rape victims who testified "appeared to have few complaints about their experience testifying".[138]

Indicative of women's voices being heard, and the crime of sexual violence being taken seriously, is the fact that hearings on gender violence had the largest attendance of any of the hearings.[139] Audiences heard testimony about torture, rape, sexual abuse, sexual slavery, trafficking, enslavement, abductions, amputations, forced pregnancies, forced labour and detention, which were later highlighted in the final report.

The SLTRC's final report established that 33.5 per cent of all victims who gave statements were women, and identified war widows, aged women, girl mothers, victims of displacement and female ex-combatants as particularly vulnerable groups.[140] Many "war brides" – girls captured to serve as wives to rebel forces – have stayed with their "husbands" because of intimidation, lack of viable options and fear of rejection by their communities.[141] In particular, those whose unions produced children are not likely to receive a welcome, given that family lines are patrilineal. It was hoped that the attention paid to these crimes by the SLTRC would provide their communities with the understanding and compassion to accept these women and their children.

But not all women's voices were heard. Women who had fought for the rebel RUF – even if they had been abducted and fought under duress – did not testify before either the SLTRC or the Special Court, fearing they might be prosecuted.[142] Likewise, the shame associated with being a "wife" of a rebel soldier, and the stigma associated with rape, kept some women from testifying.

Still others, according to Shaw, either decided not to give public statements or gave statements that withheld information they thought would be damaging to their families in order to protect them.[143] This probably had more to do with their uncertainty as to whether testimony would be turned over to the Special Court, their fear of retaliation from former combatants or the government and their shame over being defiled, rather than with any cultural aversion to verbal discourse of memories in favour of social forgetting, as Shaw maintains.[144]

Jamesina King believes that the reason female victims hesitated to testify was "because they did not fully understand the SLTRC's objectives, and second, they did not think the commission would meet their immediate needs of medical assistance, micro credit schemes, and shelter programs". Yet once the commission explained the SLTRC's objectives and the possibility of reparations, "women were more willing to talk about the violations perpetrated against them and their families".[145]

Post-SLTRC/post-SCSL legacy?

The two institutions' focus on gender-based violence may help to raise consciousness about such violence as a human rights issue. Nevertheless, the impact of the Special Court will be limited. The force of law alone will not end violence against women; at most, it may provide "symbolic value in condemning the acts, demonstrating intolerance or moral repugnance for acts committed".[146] That a handful of wartime leaders have been charged with rape (one-third of whom – the CDF defendants – had all charges of sexual crimes thrown out) for the acts of their followers will not resonate among those followers unless steps are taken to make rape a serious crime domestically during peacetime.

Likewise, the SLTRC's offer of a forum for women to tell their stories of sexual violations may begin a psychological healing process in which they are reconciled with their memories, and engender sympathy and understanding in their communities. Still, the process had its limitations. While women who testified may be "reconciled" with their memories, it is hard to believe they were reconciled with their assailants, as few perpetrators acknowledged responsibility for wartime violence against women. If contrition is necessary for reconciliation, little was forthcoming.

Whatever consciousness has been raised about the reality of gender violence must be implemented in practical ways, since sexual assault remains a problem even in peacetime. Amie Tejan-Kellah, programme officer for the International Rescue Committee's Rainbow Center, says "Rape has been on the increase since the end of the civil war."[147] But few rape cases make it to trial due to the inefficiencies in the judicial system.[148] In addition, it is believed that HIV rates as a result of the war may be much higher than the official figure of 1.6 per cent. According to UNAIDS, of the 46,000 adult cases in 2009, 28,000 (60 per cent) are female.[149] And the fact that 90 per cent of women have undergone circumcision means HIV infection is much more likely than in uncut women.[150]

In its final report the SLTRC recommended a number of reforms that address women's needs. It called on communities to accept survivors of sexual violence,[151] and recommended that the government provide free psychological support and reproductive health services to these women. It urged the government to give a monthly pension not only to amputees and other war wounded, but to victims of sexual abuse as well. By making victims of sexual violence a prioritized category eligible for reparations, the SLTRC's report elevated rape as a serious human rights violation.

The SLTRC also advocated for reforms in the legal, judicial and police systems to make it easier for women to report cases of sexual and domestic violence. In particular, it mandated that laws which link the prosecution of sexual offences to the moral character of the complainant be repealed – an imperative recommendation.[152] It advised the government to campaign against the customary practice whereby a victim of rape is obliged to marry the rapist.[153] It urged the government to enact specific legislation to address domestic violence, help facilitate the prosecution of offenders and empower women to access protective orders.[154] Pointing to the structural inequality of women, the SLTRC in its report called for the repeal of all statutory and customary laws that discriminate against women, including marriage, inheritance, divorce and property ownership laws.[155]

In response to the SLTRC's recommendations, parliament unanimously passed three gender bills (on customary marriage and divorce, inheritance and domestic violence) in June 2007, which was remarkable since the government has failed abysmally to implement any of the SLTRC's other recommendations.[156] The bills were widely applauded as a positive step towards gender equity, as they banned marriage before the age of 18, required that marriage be consensual and registered with the government, allowed women to acquire property in their own names (and not be required to pay back dowries if the marriage ended), provided for inheritances to pass to the wife and children rather than revert to the parents and brothers (bringing an end to the practice whereby women are forced to marry their husband's brother) and introduced the new offence of domestic violence.[157] The domestic violence bill defines such violence to include sexual abuse and provides mechanisms to address punishment of domestic violence through criminal law and protection of women through civil law. Until the passage of this bill, the law had not specifically prohibited domestic violence; wife beating and forced intercourse were common.[158]

While the passage of the gender bills is a laudable step, there are real barriers to implementation. First, access to justice is nearly non-existent in rural areas in the provinces where customary law judges have no legal training and may be unaware of the formal laws.[159] Secondly, even women themselves believe that domestic violence is justified. Reportedly, "85 per cent of women agreed that beating by their partners was justified for going out without telling a husband, neglecting the children, arguing with a spouse, refusing sex or burning food".[160] Not surprisingly, in 2006 (before the passage of the gender bills) only one successful prosecution was brought for an offence of domestic abuse.[161] Having the laws on the books is a promising first step, but knowing the laws and having access to the formal justice system remain a challenge.

Conclusion

During apartheid in South Africa, genocide in Rwanda and civil war in Sierra Leone women experienced serious human rights violations that centred on their sexuality. Acts of gender violence had occurred before the eras of conflict, but the conflicts exacerbated the situation. Women in post-conflict societies continue to feel the effects of violence as they confront a myriad of problems, including stigmatization, poverty, poor health, AIDS infection and lack of physical security.

It is probably no coincidence that incidents of rape and domestic violence have skyrocketed in post-conflict societies. A US Agency for International Development report on six post-conflict countries asserts: "Domestic violence against women increased as a result of the stress, trauma, and social disorder that emerged during and following the conflict."[162] According to Amnesty International, increased rape and domestic violence have been reported in the Democratic Republic of the Congo, Northern Ireland and former Yugoslavia. These studies suggest that violence against women intensifies after conflicts have ended.[163] Women in South Africa, Rwanda and Sierra Leone, where beliefs in male supremacy, dominance and aggression are widespread, continue to suffer gender-based human rights violations.

These three societies have attempted to deal with past violations (including those against women) through truth commissions, tribunals or a combination of both. All three governments passed gender bills – undoubtedly in response to the publicity about the extent of gender crimes committed during the conflicts. Arguably, Sierra Leone has been the most successful of the three countries in stressing from the outset gender violations as an important component of its transitional work. In particular, Sierra Leone activists were able to take the recommendations from the SLTRC report and lobby effectively for the passage of the gender bills, although as noted in the case of South Africa, having laws on the books that outlaw violence against women is just the first start in entrenching women's rights.

Attitudinal changes are paramount. Recognizing that rape in times of conflict is wrong has not transferred into recognition that violence against women in peacetime is equally prohibited. The systematic subordination of women and entrenched social attitudes that preceded those periods of conflict made the notion of women's *bodies as battlefields* acceptable. Women's bodies continue to be sites of struggle. In the absence of gender equality, violence against women pervades peacetime and will likely erupt on a massive scale should intra-state conflicts reignite.[164]

Notes

1. See Promotion of National Unity and Reconciliation Act 1995, available at www. justice.gov.za/trc.
2. The amnesty agreement was a compromise demanded by the National Party to ensure that its followers would be indemnified from prosecution. Although the National Party favoured a blanket amnesty, the ANC-dominated government insisted on a conditional amnesty – amnesty offered to perpetrators on an individual basis in exchange for full disclosure. In this fashion, at least the truth would come out.
3. Ross, Fiona (1996) "Existing in Secret Places: Women's Testimony in the First Five Weeks of Public Hearings of the Truth and Reconciliation Commission", paper presented at Fault Lines Conference, Cape Town, 4–5 July, pp. 6–7.
4. Goldblatt, Beth and Sheila Meintjes (1996) "Gender and the Truth and Reconciliation Commission", submission to Truth and Reconciliation Commission, May, available at www.justice.gov.za/trc/hrvtrans/submit/gender.htm.
5. Truth and Reconciliation Commission (1998) *Truth and Reconciliation Commission of South Africa Report*, Vols 1–5, Cape Town: Juta. See Vol. 4, Chapter 10, "Special Hearing: Women", p. 283.
6. Seven out of 17 commissioners were women.
7. Human Rights Violation Committee transcript, 28 July 1997, available at www.justice. gov.za/trc/special/women/shezi.htm.
8. Human Rights Violation Committee transcript, 28 July 1997, available at www.justice. gov.za/trc/special/women/dube.htm.
9. Human Rights Violation Committee transcript, 25 October 1996, available at www. justice.gov.za/trc/hrvtrans/HRVDURB3/day2.htm.
10. Human Rights Violation Committee transcript, 29 July 1997, available at www.justice. gov.za/trc/special/women/mokonyan.htm.
11. Human Rights Violation Committee transcript, 8 July 1996, available at www.justice. gov.za/trc/hrvtrans/Mmabatho/thunyisw.htm.
12. Ross asserts that some women activists chose not to give statements, refusing to see themselves as "victims" or preferring to see themselves not as individuals but as part of a collective who resisted. See Ross, Fiona (2003) *Bearing Witness: Women and the Truth and Reconciliation Commission in South Africa*, London: Pluto Press, pp. 17, 158.
13. Krog, Antjie (1998) *Country of My Skull*, Johannesburg: Random House, p. 182.
14. Truth and Reconciliation Commission, note 5, Vol. 4, p. 296.
15. Ibid., p. 285.
16. US Department of State (2008) "Country Reports on Human Rights Practices: South Africa, 2007", 11 March, available at www.state.gov.g/drl/rls/hrrpt/2007/100505.htm.

17. All three studies are cited in US Department of State (2003) "Country Reports on Human Rights Practices: South Africa, 2002", 31 March, available at www.state.gov/g/drl/rls/hrrpt//2002/18227.htm.

18. See Baden, Sally, Shireen Hassim and Sheila Meintjes (1999) "Country Gender Profile: South Africa", Swedish International Development Cooperation Agency, Pretoria, available at www.bridge.ids.ac.uk/reports/re45c.pdf.

19. UNIFEM (2002) "What Do We Want to Teach Our Teachers About VAW?", End Violence list, UNIFEM, 3 May, available at www.mail-archive.com/end-violence@phoenix.edc.org/msg00238.html.

20. POWA (2010) "Shadow Report on Beijing +15", March 2010, p. 7, available at www.powa.co.za/files/SouthAfricaShadowReportMarch2010.pdf.

21. Human Rights Watch (1995) *Violence against Women in South Africa: State Response to Domestic Violence and Rape*, New York: Human Rights Watch, p. 51.

22. POWA, note 20, p. 7.

23. Cited by Britton, Hannah (2006) "Organising against Gender Violence in South Africa", *Journal of Southern African Studies* 32(1), p. 146.

24. See Terreblanche, Christelle (2006) "Women the Losers in Zuma Rape Case", *Mail & Guardian*, 13 August.

25. Human Rights Watch (1997) "Violence against Women and the Medico-Legal System in South Africa", August, available at www.hrw.org/reports/1997/safrica.

26. Human Rights Watch, note 21, p. 115.

27. Cited by Britton, note 23, p. 146.

28. Human Rights Watch (2001) "Scandal at School: Sexual Violence against Girls in South African Schools", March, available at www.hrw.org/reports/2001/safrica.

29. *IRIN* (2003) "Focus on the 'Sugar Daddy' Phenomenon", *IRIN*, 24 July.

30. For a well-documented link between gender violence and HIV infection see Dunkle, K. L. (2004) "Gender-based Violence, Relationship Power, and Risk of HIV Infection in Women Attending Antenatal Clinics in South Africa", *The Lancet* 363(9419), pp. 415–421.

31. In 2008 21.1 per cent of women aged 20–24 were HIV positive, compared to just 5.1 per cent of their male peers. See South African National HIV Survey, available at www.avert.org/safricastats.htm.

32. Quoted in Brown, David (2002) "Study: AIDS Shortening Life in 51 Nations", *Washington Post*, 8 July.

33. US Department of State, note 17.

34. Human Rights Watch, note 21, p. 22.

35. Goldblatt, Beth and Sheila Meintjes (1998) "Dealing with the Aftermath: Sexual Violence and the Truth and Reconciliation Commission", *Agenda* 36, p. 15.

36. Zwane, Pule (1996) "The Young Lions and the Sexual Face of Violence in Black Townships: The Inheritance of the Future Government", Center for the Study of Violence and Reconciliation, Johannesburg.

37. Skully, Pamela (1995) "Rape, Race, and Colonial Culture: The Sexual Politics of Identity in the Nineteenth-Century Cape Colony, South Africa", *American Historical Review* 100(2), pp. 335–359.

38. Britton, note 23, p. 145. See also Moffett, Helen (2006) "'These Women, They Force Us to Rape Them': Rape as Narrative of Social Control in Post-Apartheid South Africa", *Journal of Southern African Studies* 32(1), pp. 129–144.

39. Bennett, Jane (1999) "A Preliminary Assessment of Current South African Research Being Undertaken (or Completed) on Connections Between Gender-based Violence, Peace-building and Development Initiatives in South Africa", paper prepared for Oxfam by African Gender Institute, December, unpublished.

40. Human Rights Watch (1996) *Shattered Lives: Sexual Violence During the Rwanda Genocide and Its Aftermath*, New York: Human Rights Watch.
41. des Forges, Alison (1999) *Leave None to Tell the Story: Genocide in Rwanda*, New York: Human Rights Watch, p. 215.
42. Newbury, Catherine and Hannah Baldwin (2000) "Aftermath: Women in Postgenocide Rwanda", Working Paper No. 303, Center for Development Information and Evaluation, USAID, Washington, DC, July, p. 3.
43. Cited by Human Rights Watch, note 40, p. 24.
44. Turshen, Meredith and Clotilde Twagiramariya (1998) "'Favours' to Give and 'Consenting' Victims: The Sexual Politics of Survival in Rwanda", in Meredith Turshen and Clotilde Twagiramariya (eds) *What Women Do in Wartime: Gender and Conflict in Africa*, New York: Zed Books, p. 110.
45. As quoted by Landesman, Peter (2002) "A Woman's Work", *New York Times Magazine*, 15 September.
46. Sharlach, Lisa (1999) "Gender and Genocide in Rwanda: Women as Agents and Objects of Genocide", *Journal of Genocide Research* 1(3), p. 393.
47. World Health Organization (2008) "Epidemiological Fact Sheet on HIV/AIDS and Sexually Transmitted Infections", available at www.who.int/globalatlas/predefinedReports/EFS2008/full/EFS2008_RW.pdf.
48. Mamdani, Mahmood (1996) "Reconciliation without Justice", *South African Review of Books* 46, p. 4.
49. The UN Security Council authorized the ICTR through Security Council Resolution 955 in 1994.
50. Category 1 includes planners, organizers and leaders of the genocide and crimes against humanity, those who killed with particular zeal or excessive malice and those who committed sexual torture. Category 2 includes perpetrators, conspirators and accomplices of intentional homicides. Category 3 includes those who committed serious but non-fatal attacks. Category 4 covers property offences. The revised *gacaca* law of 2004 collapsed Categories 2 and 3 into one category. The law was changed in 2008 to facilitate the ICTR's transfer to Rwandan courts of those cases it will not be able to hear before its term expires in 2014, and removing the death penalty in order to be compatible with international human rights standards.
51. Human Rights Watch (2004) *Struggling to Survive: Barriers to Justice for Rape Victims*, New York: Human Rights Watch.
52. Cited by Human Rights Watch, note 40, p. 89.
53. Human Rights Watch (2011) "Justice Compromised: The Legacy of Rwanda's Community-Based *Gacaca* Courts", Human Rights Watch, New York, May, p. 3.
54. See Graybill, Lyn S. (2004) "Ten Years After, Rwanda Tries Reconciliation", *Current History*, May, pp. 202–205.
55. Wells, Sarah (2005) "Gender, Sexual Violence and Prospect for Justice at the *Gacaca* Courts in Rwanda", *Southern California Review of Law and Women's Studies* 14(2), pp. 167–196.
56. Ibid., pp. 186–187.
57. Human Rights Watch, note 53, p. 113.
58. Human Rights Watch, note 40, p. 94.
59. Benninger-Budel, Carin and Anne-Laurence Lacroix (1999) *Violence Against Women: A Report*, Geneva: World Organization Against Torture, p. 245.
60. Eaton, Shana (2004) "Sierra Leone: The Proving Ground for Prosecuting Rape as a War Crime", *Georgetown Journal of International Law* 35(4), pp. 873–920.
61. Nowrojee, Binaifer (2005) "'Your Justice Is Too Slow': Will the ICTR Fail Rwanda's Rape Victims?", Occasional Paper 10, UN Research Institute for Social Development, Geneva, November, p. 3.

62. Cited in Human Rights Watch, note 40, p. 95.
63. Fairstein, Linda (1993) *Sexual Violence: Our War Against Rape*, New York: William Morrow and Company, pp. 104–105.
64. Power, Samantha (2003) "Rwanda: The Two Faces of Justice", *New York Review of Books*, 16 January.
65. Niarchos, Catherine (1995) "Women, War, and Rape: Challenge Facing the International Tribunal for the Former Yugoslavia", *Human Rights Quarterly* 17(4), pp. 649–690.
66. Human Rights Watch, note 40, pp. 96–97.
67. Ibid., p. 90.
68. Nowrojee, Binaifer and Regan Ralph (2000) "Justice for Women Victims of Violence: Rwanda after the 1994 Genocide", in Ifi Amadiume and Abdullahi An-Na'im (eds) *The Politics of Memory: Truth, Healing, and Social Justice*, New York: Zed Books, p. 173.
69. Walsh, Connie (1997) "Witness Protection, Gender and the ICTR", Coalition for Women's Human Rights in Conflict Situations, Montreal, p. 1, available at www.womensrightscoalition.org/site/advocacyDossiers/rwanda/witnessProtection/report_en.php.
70. Human Rights Watch, note 40, p. 74.
71. McGreal, Chris (2002) "A Pearl in Rwanda's Genocide Horror", *Guardian Unlimited*, 5 December.
72. Schlein, Lisa (1998) "Rwandan Women", *Voice of America*, No. 2-229521, 11 April.
73. Human Rights Watch, note 40, p. 94.
74. Ibid., p. 3. See also Turshen and Twagiramariya, note 44, p. 104.
75. Nowrojee and Ralph, note 68, p. 169.
76. Newbury and Baldwin, note 42, believe that the figure of female-headed households may be significantly larger but respondents are reluctant to claim that status; see p. 6.
77. Byrne, Bridget (1996) "Rwanda", in Bridget Byrne, Rachel Marcus and Tanya Power-Stevens (eds) *Gender, Conflict and Development, Vol. 2: Case Studies – Cambodia, Rwanda, Kosovo, Somalia, Algeria, Guatemala, and Eritrea*, BRIDGE Report No. 35, Brighton: Institute of Development Studies, p. 38. See also Jones, Adam (2002) "Gender and Genocide in Rwanda", *Journal of Genocide Research* 4(1), p. 86.
78. Newbury and Baldwin, note 42, p. 5.
79. Ibid., p. 9.
80. See Turshen and Twagiramariya, note 44, pp. 101–117.
81. The temporal jurisdiction of *gacaca* is 1 October 1990 to 31 December 1994, and so excludes post-1994 offences of the RPF.
82. Human Rights Watch, note 40, p. 20.
83. Kagire, Edmund (2008) "Country Commended on Domestic Laws", *The New Times*, 7 August.
84. Despite the rhetoric of the government that *gacaca* is reconciliatory, many observers view it as just another tool of an extremely authoritarian government to demonize, marginalize and disenfranchise the majority Hutu population. See Tiemessen, Alana Erin (2004) "After Arusha: *Gacaca* Justice in Post-Genocide Rwanda", *African Studies Quarterly* 8(1), pp. 57–76.
85. In one study, 87.2 per cent of respondents claimed they were not well informed, or not informed at all, about the ICTR. See des Forges, Alison and Timothy Longman (2004) "Legal Responses to Genocide in Rwanda", in Eric Stover and Harvey M. Weinstein (eds) *My Neighbour, My Enemy: Justice and Community in the Aftermath of Mass Atrocity*, Cambridge: Cambridge University Press, p. 56.
86. See Nowrojee, note 61, pp. 4–6.

87. Kamatali, Jean Marie (2003) "The Challenge of Linking International Criminal Justice and National Reconciliation: The Case of the ICTR", *Leiden Journal of Law* 16, p. 129.

88. Eaton, note 60, p. 902.

89. See Wood, Stephanie K. (2004) "A Woman Scorned for the 'Least Condemned' War Crime: Precedent and Problems with Prosecuting Rape as a Serious War Crime in the International Criminal Tribunal for Rwanda", *Columbia Journal of Gender and Law* 13(2), pp. 274–321.

90. Copelon, Rhonda (1994) "Surfacing Gender: Reconceptualizing Crimes against Women in Time of War", in Alexandra Stiglmayer (ed.) *Mass Rape: The War against Women in Bosnia-Herzegovina*, trans. Marion Faber, Lincoln, NE: University of Nebraska, pp. 197–218.

91. Owens, Margaret (2002) "Abuse of Women Witnesses by the International War Crimes Tribunal of Rwanda", 20 August, available at www.fruithome.com/teams/modelun/ai03rwai.html.

92. Mertus, Julie (1997) "The War Crimes Tribunal: Triumph of the 'International Community', Pain of the Survivors", *Mind & Human Interaction* 8, p. 51.

93. Scarry, Elaine (1985) *The Body in Pain: The Making and Unmaking of the World*, New York: Oxford University Press.

94. See de Ridder, Trudy (1997) "The Trauma of Testifying: Deponents' Difficult Healing Process", *Track Two* 6(3/4), p. 32. Hayner notes that 50–60 per cent of testifiers suffered difficulty after testifying: Hayner, Priscilla (2001) *Unspeakable Truths: Confronting State Terror and Atrocity*, New York: Routledge, p. 144. The most recent longitudinal study challenges the conventional wisdom that testifying was therapeutic for victims. See Chapman, Audrey R. and Hugo van der Merwe (eds) (2008) *Truth and Reconciliation in South Africa: Did the TRC Deliver?*, Philadelphia, PA: University of Pennsylvania Press. To date there have been no post-TRC studies that evaluate female victims of sexual assault and their perceptions of the TRC process.

95. UN Resolution 1315, 14 August 2000.

96. The civil war began with the Revolutionary United Front invasion from Liberia in 1991 and officially ended in 2002.

97. Human Rights Watch (2003) "We'll Kill You if You Cry: Sexual Violence in the Sierra Leone Conflict", Human Rights Watch Report 15, 1(A), New York, pp. 25–26, available at www.hrw.org/sites/default/files/reports/sierleon0103.pdf.

98. Physicians for Human Rights (2002) "War-Related Sexual Violence in Sierra Leone: A Population-Based Assessment", Physicians for Human Rights, Cambridge, MA, p. 2, available at www.peacewomen.org/assets/file/Resources/NGO/Disp-Health-VAW_WarSexSierraLeone_PHR_2002.pdf.

99. Human Rights Watch, note 97, p. 35.

100. McKay, Susan and Dyan Mazurana (2004) *Where Are the Girls? Girls in Fighting Forces in Northern Uganda, Sierra Leone and Mozambique: Their Lives During and After War*, Montreal, QC: International Center for Human Rights and Democratic Developments, p. 92.

101. One explanation is the younger the girl, the less likely she would be HIV infected.

102. Ironically, the only armed group not to be implicated in human rights abuses was the mercenary Executive Outcomes, a South African-based company that was hired by the Sierra Leonean government to repel the rebel forces.

103. Human Rights Watch, note 97, p. 24.

104. Nowrojee, Binaifer (2005) "Making the Invisible War Crimes Visible: Post-conflict Justice for Sierra Leone's Rape Victims", *Harvard Human Rights Journal* 18, p. 88.

105. Statute of the Special Court of Sierra Leone, 16 June 2002.

106. Eaton, note 60, p. 913.

107. Human Rights Watch (2005) "Justice in Motion: The Trial Phase of the Special Court for Sierra Leone", Human Rights Watch Report 17, 14(A), New York, p. 8, available at www.hrw.org/sites/default/files/reports/sierraleone1105wcover.pdf.

108. Ibid., p. 35.

109. King, Jamesina (2006) "Gender and Reparations in Sierra Leone: The Wounds of War Remain Open", in Ruth Rubio-Marin (ed.) *What Happened to the Women? Gender and Reparations for Human Rights Violations*, New York: Social Sciences Research Council, p. 254.

110. Statute of the Special Court of Sierra Leone, 16 January 2002.

111. Eaton, note 60, p. 909.

112. Nowrojee, note 104, p. 100.

113. King, note 109, p. 256.

114. See Nowrojee, note 61.

115. Statute of the Special Court of Sierra Leone, Article 15(14), 16 January 2002.

116. King, note 109, p. 256.

117. *The Prosecutor v. Alex Tamba Brima, Brima Bazzy and Santigie Borbor Kanu*, SCSL1-04-16-T Judgment, 20 June 2007.

118. *All Africa.com* (2009) "Sierra Leone: 'Forced Marriage' Conviction a First", *All Africa. com*, 26 February.

119. The CDF, led by Samuel Hinga Norman, was a pro-military militia composed of traditional hunters, known as *kamajors*.

120. The judges found that the prosecutor waited until February 2004 to amend the indictment, although he had evidence of sexual violence as early as June 2003. To amend the indictment would be an infringement of the defendants' rights. See Kelsall, Michelle Staggs and Shanee Stepakoff (2007) "'When We Wanted to Talk About Rape': Silencing Sexual Violence at the Special Court for Sierra Leone", *International Journal of Transitional Justice* 1(3), pp. 355–374.

121. Ibid., p. 362.

122. Lomé Peace Accord, Article XXVI, 7 July 1999.

123. Truth and Reconciliation Act 2000.

124. Freeman, Mark and Priscilla B. Hayner (2003) "Truth-Telling", in *Reconciliation After Violent Conflict*, Stockholm: IDEA, p. 126.

125. See Kelsall, Tim (2005) "Truth, Lies, Ritual: Preliminary Reflections on the Truth and Reconciliation Commission in Sierra Leone", *Human Rights Quarterly* 27, pp. 361–391.

126. CDF leader Samuel Hinga Norman died in custody on 22 February 2007. The other three indicted who are dead, or presumed dead, are RUF leader Foday Sankoh, his military commander Sam Bockarie and Johnny Paul Koroma, the former AFRC junta leader whose bloody coup in 1997 led to the Nigerian-led ECOMOG intervention.

127. Rumours circulated that there was a secret underground passageway between the SLTRC and Special Court and that the two bodies were sharing information. Some personnel who worked for the SLTRC were later seen in the employ of the Special Court, which fuelled suspicion that they were colluding. See Truth & Reconciliation Commission (2004) *Witness to Truth, Report of the Sierra Leone Truth & Reconciliation Commission*, Accra: GPL Press, Vol. 3B, Chapter 6, p. 377.

128. Ibid., Appendix I.

129. Schabas, William A. (2003) "The Relationship Between Truth Commissions and International Courts: The Case of Sierra Leone", *Human Rights Quarterly* 25, p. 1051.

130. Shaw, Rosalind (2004) *Transnational Subjectivities: Reconciling Ex-Combatants in Northern Sierra Leone*, Cambridge, MA: Carr Center for Human Rights Policy, p. 17.

131. Ibid.
132. The CDF's rules forbade sexual intercourse before battle, but once the CDF moved from its native areas the internal discipline was weakened.
133. Truth and Reconciliation Act 2000.
134. Duggan, Colleen and Adila Abusharaf (2006) "Reparation of Sexual Violence in Democratic Transitions: The Search for Gender Justice", in Pablo de Greiff (ed.) *The Handbook of Reparations*, Oxford: Oxford University Press, p. 636.
135. Like the Special Court, there were both local and international representatives.
136. Nowrojee, note 104, p. 93.
137. Ibid., p. 86.
138. Ibid., p. 95.
139. Ibid.
140. Truth & Reconciliation Commission, note 127, p. 47.
141. US Department of State (2006) "Country Reports on Human Rights Practices: Sierra Leone, 2005", 8 March, available at www.state.gov/g/drl/rls/hrrpt/2005/61591.htm.
142. Denov, Myriam S. (2006) "Wartime Sexual Violations: Assessing a Human Security Response to War-Affected Girls in Sierra Leone", *Security Dialogue* 37(3), pp. 335–336.
143. Shaw, note 130. See also Shaw, Rosalind (2005) "Rethinking Truth and Reconciliation Commissions: Lessons From Sierra Leone", USIP Special Report 130, February, Washington, DC.
144. Shaw, note 130, p. 26.
145. Cited by Park, Augustine S. J. (2006) "'Other Inhumane Acts': Forced Marriage, Girl Soldiers and the Special Court for Sierra Leone", *Social & Legal Studies* 15(3), p. 330.
146. Ibid.
147. *TerraViva News* (2004) "Sierra Leone: No End to Rape", *TerraViva News*, 15 December.
148. US Department of State, note 141.
149. UNAIDS (2008) "Country Statistics: Sierra Leone: 2008", available at www.unaids.org/en/regionscountries/countries/sierraleone.
150. There is no law that prohibits female circumcision.
151. It has been easier for perpetrators to return to their communities than for victims of sexual violence to be received home. Coulter attributes this to the fact that they usually return with no material means of support, often with wartime children in hand, and become a burden on their families and communities, rather than because they had been sexually defiled. See Coulter, Chris (2006) *Being a Bush Wife: Women's Lives Through War and Peace in Northern Sierra Leone*, Uppsala: Uppsala University.
152. Truth & Reconciliation Commission, note 127, Vol. 2, Chapter 3, p. 333. The SLTRC had four categories of recommendations: "imperative", "work towards", "seriously consider" and "call on". "Imperative" recommendations are those that are urgent and ought to be implemented immediately. "Work towards" recommendations should be done within a reasonable time period. "Seriously consider" recommendations are those which the government should evaluate but is under no obligation to implement. "Calls on" recommendations are for non-governmental bodies.
153. Ibid., p. 337.
154. Ibid., p. 328.
155. Ibid., pp. 320–321.
156. See Graybill, Lyn S. (2007) "Debt Relief – A Panacea for Sierra Leone?", *CSIS Africa Policy Forum*, 9 February, available at http://csis.org/blog/debt-relief-panacea-sierraleone.
157. See Teale, Lotta (2007) "Sierra Leone Passes the Gender Bills into Law", *The Monitor* 24, June, pp. 11–12.

158. US Department of State, note 141.
159. Amnesty International (2007) "Amnesty International Report 2007: The State of the World's Human Rights", Amnesty International, London, available at www.scribd.com/doc/16274231/Amnesty-International-Report-2007.
160. These figures are based on a UNICEF study, cited by Bureau of Democracy, Human Rights, and Labor, US Department of State (2008) "Country Reports on Human Rights Practices: Sierra Leone, 2007", 11 March, available at www.state.gov/g/drl/rls/hrrpt/2007/100503.htm.
161. Sierra Leone Court Monitoring Programme (2009) "SLCMP Appeals to the Government to Enact the Gender Bills before the Election", 14 October, Freetown, available at www.carl-sl.org/home/reports/270-slcmp-appeals-to-the-government-to-enact-the-gender-bills-before-the-election. The text refers to a press release issued by the Sierra Leone Court Monitoring Programme on 14 February 2007, "calling on the Government to fulfill its obligation to enact the gender bills before the elections scheduled for July 2007".
162. USAID Women in Development (2000) "Intrastate Conflict and Gender", *Gender Matters Information Bulletin* 9, December, p. 2, available at http://pdf.usaid.gov/pdf_docs/PNACP514.pdf.
163. Cited in *IRIN* (2008) "Sierra Leone: Sex Crimes Continue in Peacetime", *IRIN*, 20 June.
164. For a discussion on the link between gender equity and conflict see Dworkin, Terry M. and Cindy A. Schipani (2007) "Linking Gender Equity to Peaceful Societies", *American Business Law Journal* 44(2), pp. 391–415.

10

Empowering women to promote peace and security: From the global to the local – Securing and implementing UN Security Council Resolution 1325

Ancil Adrian-Paul

In a world of continuing instability and violence, the implementation of cooperative approaches to peace and security is urgently needed. The equal access and full participation of women in power structures and their full involvement in all efforts for the prevention and resolution of conflicts are essential for the maintenance and promotion of peace and security.[1]

Despite this clear statement from the world's governments in 1995 and a number of internationally agreed instruments, women's perspectives on peace and security have until recently remained a marginal concern on the global security agenda. Their experiences in armed conflict often go unacknowledged, their roles in peacebuilding efforts are frequently dismissed and they are often excluded from seeking political office.[2]

Over the last few years there has been increasingly strong recognition by the international community of the importance of gender equality and the empowerment of women in the continuing struggle for equality, poverty reduction, peace, security, democracy, human rights and development. In nearly every country and region of the world, progress in different areas has been made towards achieving gender equality and women's empowerment. Yet this progress has been uneven and the gains remain fragile; almost nowhere are women's rights given the priority they deserve.

Despite increased global awareness, in many countries the rights of women are still under threat.[3] Women's peace and security are inextricably linked to development, which suffers greatly during conflict and the aftermath of conflict. In 2000 UN Security Council Resolution (SCR)

Defying victimhood: Women and post-conflict peacebuilding, Schnabel and Tabyshalieva (eds), United Nations University Press, 2012, ISBN 978-92-808-1201-5

1325 on women, peace and security was adopted following concerted advocacy and other initiatives by civil society, UN agencies and member states.[4] It represents ground-breaking international law that recognizes the negative experiences women face in conflict situations. At the same time, SCR 1325 signifies a landmark in the recognition of women's contribution to the maintenance of peace and security and acknowledges their specific needs and concerns in armed conflict and its aftermath.[5] The resolution acknowledges that women are not merely victims but also have agency and are involved in active peacebuilding, mainly through informal grassroots diplomacy in conflict zones.

Resolution 1325 also recognizes that women have generally been excluded from the formal reconciliation, reconstruction and peacebuilding processes in post-war transformations. SCR 1325 is now more than a decade old, and while there has undoubtedly been progress, with a number of initiatives being taken by the United Nations, member states, regional and subregional institutions and civil society organizations, its implementation has been slow and sporadic. Among the initiatives that have been developed are four further Security Council resolutions[6] on sexual violence in conflict, and there has been a concerted effort to develop action plans at national, regional and subregional levels to accelerate the implementation of SCR 1325.

This chapter provides summarized information on the worldwide campaign Women Building Peace: From the Village Council to the Negotiating Table, which was developed and launched by International Alert (IA)[7] in 1999 with support from over 200 organizations around the globe. It describes follow-up activities in the immediate aftermath of the adoption of SCR 1325, and highlights strategies and tactics used and the increasing concerted development of national action plans, focusing on the Liberia National Action Plan as an example. It concludes with lessons learned and some policy and research recommendations.[8]

The context

The Women Building Peace campaign from May 1999 to December 2000 was launched by the IA Policy and Advocacy Department based on the recognition that during armed conflicts women suffer tremendously. As peace support operations generally fail to include women, their perspectives are often marginalized, especially at the decision-making level. It is now a commonly recognized fact that during armed conflicts women become targets of systematic gendered and sexual aggression by different warring factions, with perpetrators ranging from regular armed forces to peacekeepers.[9] Sexual torture, rape, sexual slavery, forced pregnancy, forced abortion, forced prostitution, forced eviction and other such measures are often used to attack women individually and their culture as a whole. As a result, women have been exploring legal strategies in national and international courts to demand accountability, justice and reparation.[10]

The economic impact of conflict on women is also extremely injurious. It includes a marked increase in poverty, a drastic reduction in nutrients and cultural, political and social disadvantages.[11] Furthermore, due in large part to insufficient understanding of the impact of armed conflict on women, a clear gap exists in their protection, specifically in the delivery of humanitarian assistance.[12]

Women are frequently put at risk by a lack of appropriate facilities for refugees and the internally displaced. Often the camps constructed for these groups of people, the majority of whom are women, are ill designed and insecure, thus increasing the risk to women and girls of sexual and other types of harassment.[13]

Although normally less visible than men, women have long been integrally involved in seeking solutions to issues intrinsic to peacebuilding, including ecological balance, demobilization and the reintegration of former child soldiers, along with demilitarization and disarmament. They are highly visible in building street-level peace accords, peace villages and bi-cameral citizen committees and promoting a culture of tolerance at the local community level. Women are also often resource managers, advocates for others in emergency and crisis situations and leaders in community organizations.[14] Yet despite their ability to offer innovative peacebuilding initiatives, women are rarely found at formal negotiating tables, and particularly infrequently at national and international levels.[15] This exclusion from high-level decision-making has confined women's political participation to marginal civil society groups, with a corresponding lack of recognition for their generally innovative and dedicated peacebuilding initiatives.

The history of traditional peacekeeping operations reveals that conflict situations have been further exacerbated because peace support operations have often failed to include women and their perspectives.[16] Peacekeeping, a traditionally male-dominated field, has changed dramatically over the last decade, and UN peacekeeping operations are no longer a one-dimensional matter of deploying military forces to maintain the peace between countries. They now include such varied tasks as civilian policing, elections, human rights monitoring, repatriation of refugees, demobilizing soldiers, demining and humanitarian relief. Importantly, many peacekeeping missions, such as the UN Mission in Liberia (UNMIL), now incorporate senior gender advisers and address sexual abuse and exploitation, promoting zero tolerance through conduct and discipline departments.[17] In addition, it is widely accepted that women peacekeeping personnel, both in the military and in the civilian component, can help to improve the behaviour of male peacekeepers towards local women and assist in minimizing friction between the United Nations and the host-country population. Furthermore, females in peacekeeping missions can be important role models for local women: an example is the all-female formed police unit deployed by India in Liberia.[18]

The campaign – Women Building Peace: From the Village Council to the Negotiating Table

Preparatory steps to launching the worldwide campaign included systematic consultation with and mobilization of women from different conflict areas brought together in an international conference on Women, Violent Conflict and Peace Building: Global Perspectives.[19] The conference was funded by the UK Department for International Development and the National Lottery Board, and organized by IA, the Centre for Defence Studies (King's College London) and the Council for the Advancement of Arab/British Understanding. Women peacemakers, leaders and activists from conflict areas (Palestine, Israel, Rwanda, Burundi, Mexico, Afghanistan and Lebanon) came together to share their experiences of armed conflict, their agency and their positive role in peacebuilding. Participants acknowledged that a number of international instruments and norms to empower and advance women had been developed, but these had remained mainly rhetorical and not become reality.[20] Following discussion, assessment and reflection on existing international mechanisms to promote women's advancement and empowerment, and the degree to which these mechanisms have been interpreted and entrenched into national laws, the participants explored peace and security strategies and the mechanisms by which their concerns could be highlighted internationally.

As a result of the discussions, the participants unanimously agreed on the need for a campaign that would be a rallying point to highlight women's peace and security issues globally. Based upon pre-existing commitments made by the international community regarding women and peacebuilding, they devised five concise demands and decided to run a global campaign to advocate for their inclusion in peace processes and the recognition of their role in peacebuilding. The "Women's Five Demands to the International Community" were that policy-makers, planners and programmers:

- Include women in peace negotiations as decision-makers.
- Put women at the heart of reconstruction and reconciliation.

- Strengthen the protection and participation of refugee, internally displaced and other war-affected women.
- End impunity and ensure redress for crimes committed against women.
- Provide women's peacebuilding organizations with sufficient and sustainable resources – both financial and technical.

The global campaign Women Building Peace: From the Village Council to the Negotiating Table was launched in May 1999 to provide a coherent platform for women's demands and encourage the international community to adhere to the commitments they made at the Fourth World Conference on Women.[21] The "Five Demands" formed the cornerstone of the campaign's aims to achieve policy impact, increased participation and partnership, highlight women's peacebuilding agency and promote the release of funds for women's peace and security activities.

Strategic activities to secure the adoption of SCR 1325

It was expected that a high-level political policy instrument would be adopted by the UN Security Council and incorporate the "Five Demands". Women believed that a resolution, which requires members of the Security Council, member states and the international community to implement it, would carry more weight than a presidential statement, which, while it would raise awareness, would not be binding. A resolution would oblige all relevant stakeholders to examine and incorporate the needs of women into their own national policies, programming and practice.

The UN Security Council was identified as the key policy target for the campaign because of its global focus on the maintenance of peace and security and because its resolutions are generally binding on member states.[22] At the beginning of the campaign the Security Council was gradually expanding its mandate, as evidenced by its thematic debates on such issues as the protection of civilians, children and the HIV/AIDS epidemic. A number of high-level initiatives relating to peacekeeping had been started. In 1999 the UN system was also preparing for the review of the Beijing Platform for Action.[23] This period was therefore an opportune time to highlight the issue of women, peace and security further and engage Security Council members.

The Security Council meeting was to be held in October 2000, thus the challenge to lobby and motivate for an agreed resolution by that date was substantial.[24] Campaign staff were acutely aware that momentous policy initiatives such as the adoption of a Security Council resolution are not achievable by any one organization working unilaterally. Rather, successful global advocacy requires tight multilevel collaboration among a number of actors and demonstrable legitimacy. In order to shape and impact policy at the global level, the campaign had to develop close linkages with a number of key stakeholders in the United States, Europe and around the world to ensure widespread support. As a result, a 19-member international advisory committee comprising representatives from countries in pre-conflict, conflict and post-conflict situations and women's organizations working in non-conflict countries was created to guide the campaign and engage with crucial stakeholders, such as local and international women's groups, non-governmental organizations (NGOs), UN member states, the European Union and UN agencies.[25] Engagement with local and international women's groups was critical to the development of a widespread, supportive and legitimate base. This was accomplished through a series of systematic consultations with women's organizations around the world, including in the United Kingdom, the United States, the European Union, the South Caucasus, West and South Africa and South and Southeast Asia, which helped to define further the aims, objectives and focus of the campaign. These consultations provided a regional, national and local issue focus, while the US and European meetings contributed to the refinement of the cross-cutting themes, adding a global perspective that would appeal to the international community. On the broader front, the campaign mobilized grassroots NGOs with an issue focus on women and peacebuilding as focal points to advocate at local, regional and national levels.[26] Approximately 350 of these organizations wrote to the international secretariat of the campaign requesting that their names be included on the list of supporters.

To manage communication with these different structures, campaign staff created tools including e-mail list-serves and a quarterly newsletter to update the groups regularly on the campaign's progress. A website was set up, a series of posters depicting women's positive involvement in peacebuilding was commissioned and policy research papers were published. The communication materials and information on the first-ever Millennium Peace Prize and opportunities to become involved in the campaign were publicized through women's networks, IA partners, UNIFEM field offices and the partners of the members of the advisory committee and the focal points.[27]

Support for engagement with the Security Council was achieved through policy dialogues on the key campaign issues with a number of UN agencies, funds and departments.[28] These consisted of formal and informal meetings to cultivate personal relationships and understanding. Discussions focused on the critical cross-cutting issues to be put on the agenda of the international community and the target agencies that were most likely to offer support and exercise leverage. UNIFEM's leverage in particular was vital due to its invaluable experience in supporting women in armed-conflict situations and its collaboration with NGOs with different constituencies. This relationship-building with policy officials strengthened the relevance of the campaign and made it realistic to the concerns and issues of the policy-makers.

Research activities included the mapping of the women, conflict and peace policies of 15 EU member states. The information was recorded in an active database that formed the basis for a targeted distribution and dissemination list for research papers, newsletters and documents produced by the campaign. Recipients included women's organizations, policy-makers, UK and EU officials and civil society groups. In addition, bilateral meetings or telephone conferences to foster policy dialogue and keep abreast of the discussions and negotiations were initiated with policy advisers and heads of departments in the United Nations, European Union and country capitals of targeted member states in order to gain essential support for the resolution.

Tactics

The campaign employed a variety of tactics to achieve its goals. These included policy dialogues, local and global campaigning, policy research and recommendations, awareness raising and resource sharing as well as the strategic use of leverage.

Policy research, recommendations and dialogues

A methodology of research and dissemination of policy recommendations conducted in-house by the campaign's policy team or commissioned externally from issue experts allowed campaign staff to engage in persistent, vigilant and informed policy dialogue. Following the dissemination of policy products such as research documents with specific recommendations, campaign personnel engaged in bilateral dialogue with policy-makers, eliciting their response and, where appropriate, engaged in roundtables and workshops to discuss the issues. For example, following the production and dissemination of a policy briefing on gender and peace support operations, staff contacted the relevant UN agencies to arrange follow-up discussions.[29] The campaign staff found this strategy of proactive engagement and constructive discussion to be a particularly effective device, especially as women activists and experts from the local, national and regional levels were involved.[30]

Local to global campaigning

Extensive grassroots support and the participation and inclusion of women's groups at the local level generated much of the momentum for the campaign, especially by translating the "Five Demands" into local languages such as French, Nepali, Spanish, Bahasa Indonesian and Portuguese. The women's groups produced postcards and leaflets encouraging the international community to adhere to the commitments made regarding women, peace and security.

To highlight this grassroots support, the campaign organized a global petition, addressed to the UN Secretary-General, calling for the implementation of the "Five Demands"; and 30,000 leaflets and postcards incorporating the petition were distributed in 10 different languages to more than 8,000 individuals and over 350 organizations around the world. The petition was posted electronically on the campaign website, providing a link for those interested to download and sign. It was also circulated among the campaign's extensive networks. The petition proved an enormous success, with over 100,000 signatures collected. Helen Hakena, head of the Leitana Nehan Women's Development Agency in Papua New Guinea, one of the winning organizations of the Millennium Peace Prize, formally presented the petition to Angela King, then special adviser to the United Nations on gender issues and advancement of women, on International Women's Day 2001.

The work of Portuguese NGOs in the campaign provides an example of local to global engagement. Women's groups in Portugal worked with the local government authorities in Lisbon to produce billboards and extra-large posters publicizing the campaign. They also coordinated with partner organizations in lusophone (Portuguese-speaking) countries to collect signatures for the petition. Regional and global NGO focal points followed a similar format in the production of their campaign leaflets, an initiative that was self-funded by the local, regional and national organizations, generating increased visibility and support for the campaign and enhancing its legitimacy and credibility in policy-making circles.

Awareness raising and resource sharing

The production and dissemination of an electronic and print quarterly newsletter in English and Portuguese enabled the geographically diverse focal points to share information about their involvement in the campaign with others. The production of an interactive CD-ROM on women and conflict, along with a campaign pack and leaflets, contributed to raising the profile of women's organizations and their peacebuilding activities. The dissemination of information increased women's credibility within the international community and strengthened the process of informed constructive dialogue and collective action.

Use of leverage

The importance of leverage with key targets cannot be overstated. The location of the campaign secretariat in the United Kingdom resulted in a cordial relationship and a degree of leverage with the UK Department for International Development and the Foreign and Commonwealth Office. This relationship was invaluable in the strategic and targeted engagement with key member states of both the United Nations and the European Union. Thus during the preparations for Beijing+5, and the subsequent period of lobbying for the UN resolution, the NGO Working Group on Women, Peace and Security, formed in May 2000, targeted member states based on knowledge of a particular country or group of countries and their policy position. Additional leverage resulted from existing relations between a particular NGO within the NGO working group and a targeted state.

UN Security Council Resolution 1325 on women, peace and security

Adoption of UN SCR 1325

The adoption of UN SCR 1325 on women, peace and security in October 2000 was a major success of the campaign. SCR 1325 is a testimony to the strength and fortitude of women the world over who had been campaigning, lobbying and advocating on these issues for over 20 years. Its swift, unanimous endorsement by the Security Council and its incorporation of the sentiments expressed in the "Five Demands" surpassed the expectations of even those advocating and lobbying for its passage.

Resolution 1325 – Gains and gaps

SCR 1325 highlights the need for action in several interrelated thematic areas:[31]
- Participation of women at all levels of decision-making relating to the prevention, management and resolution of conflicts.
- Gender perspectives in conflict and training of military and civilian personnel in peacekeeping missions, including on the protection, rights and needs of women affected by conflict.

- Protection of women's rights during conflict, including addressing the needs of female ex-combatants, preventing and ending impunity for gender-based violence and respecting the civilian nature of settlements for those displaced by conflict.
- Gender mainstreaming in UN implementation and reporting mechanisms, including reporting by the UN Secretary-General on progress towards implementation of SCR 1325.

Following the formal adoption of the resolution, the immediate challenge for the campaign was to bring it back home to women, linking the policy to practice on the ground. Campaign staff facilitated a number of national and regional consultations with women's organizations to inform them of the resolution and provide a platform to discuss their perspectives on its relevance and utility to advance women's peace and security in specific conflict and post-conflict contexts. Regional consultations were organized in the Caucasus (March 2002), East Africa (March 2002) and South Asia (February 2003).[32] National consultations took place in Nepal (January 2002) and Nigeria (August/September 2002). During these consultations women agreed the following:

- Resolution 1325 is a political framework that provides a number of operational mandates with implications for policy-makers, decision-takers, programmers and funders. Stakeholders include the UN system, the Security Council and the Secretary-General, individual member states, civil society, the military, humanitarian agencies and researchers.
- Resolution 1325 could be used as a tool for demanding political accountability and the protection of rights, advocacy and lobbying, negotiation, leverage and securing inclusion and representation in peace processes.

Despite its potential usefulness, however, the resolution contains a number of gaps identified by women and civil society organizations, which impact on women's peace and security. For example, there are no mechanisms for dealing with the needs of women living in unrecognized territories and no benchmarks or mechanisms for civil society groups to monitor implementation or assess impact. There is a lack of early warning and early response mechanisms and no mention of peace education or of internally displaced persons and mechanisms for their protection. The resolution also does not address issues of justice – a prerequisite for sustainable peace.[33]

Lessons learned from the global campaign

The experience with the campaign points to some crucial steps and "must do" actions that could assist organizations interested in initiating similar campaigns:

- *Coherent strategy.* Develop a coherent strategy, including elements of research, dialogue and dissemination of key and follow-up messages. Define clear roles and responsibilities and identify the lead person or organization from the group for each activity or block of activities. Include a list of stakeholders to target, divided into those that are sympathetic, those that are neutral and those that are hostile.
- *Secure sufficient resources.* It is imperative to secure sufficient financial and human resources before launching campaign initiatives. Without such resources, opportunities will be missed and the campaign will suffer.
- *Know your stakeholders.* Always identify stakeholders to a process or an initiative. The Women Building Peace campaign identified key stakeholders as women, UN agencies, key governments and member states of the Security Council and the European Union. Know the name and function of the correct individual responsible for the subject of your concern, especially within the UN system and member states. A well-constructed and continuously updated database is essential for the management of contacts. Its creation enhances the process of effective and timely communication.
- *Engage in systematic and widespread consultations with multiple stakeholders.* This should include regular communication in a two-way channel that disseminates the results of consultations, developments at the policy level and news of unfolding events to the stakeholders. The systematic consultations undertaken with the different constituencies in South Asia, Europe, the Caucasus, West and South Africa and the United States facilitated the refinement of aims and themes and helped to frame women's demands.
- *Network and build alliances.* Coalitions and networks are stronger than individuals or individual organizations, and a collective voice expressing a common concern, informed from experience on the ground, is a powerful tool for promoting change. A single organization is unlikely to make as much impact as a tightly constructed, accountable coalition of NGOs with a well-developed, coherent strategy, adequate resources, consensus on objectives, key messages and well-defined goals and aims. Mutual benefit from networks is derived through exchanging information, building coalitions, developing common strategies, expanding the network, linking various groups with one another and managing cross-constituency relationships with tact and diplomacy.
- *Make use of the media.* The media can be a powerful ally if targeted in the right way. Conduct research to identify journalists sympathetic to the issue. Pool knowledge of media contacts and create a database. Ensure that journalists are informed through regular, targeted and concise briefings that communicate the issues clearly. Press releases

should be short, sharp and to the point. Appoint one or two people within the group to be spokespersons and ensure they are available as necessary. There are now different types of media and more and more groups are making use of e-mails and electronic networks. Consider developing an electronic list of media targets concerned and interested in the issue. Ensure that journalists have information in a timely manner. Where possible, introduce the human-interest angle by offering interviews with women engaged in conflict and peace issues on the ground.

- *Be persistent, vigilant and informed.* NGOs and other organizations employ different methods for advocacy and lobbying. IA and the global campaign did not believe in aggressive campaigning, but rather utilized persistent, informed and vigilant engagement through dialogue. The experience of the campaign to secure the adoption of SCR 1325 demonstrated the value of such dialogue. Constant attention and vigilance through systematic consultations will enable coalitions, alliances and groups to recognize and capitalize on windows of opportunity as they arise.

From the global to the local – Developing action plans for the implementation of UN SCR 1325

In the 10 years since the adoption of SCR 1325 implementation has been uneven, and concrete advancements in the equal inclusion of women in peace talks, justice processes and peacekeeping still need attention. Yet it is widely acknowledged that some progress has been made at the civil society level, within the UN system and by member states.

Civil society

Many civil society organizations have contributed to raising awareness of the resolution, for instance by translating it into different local languages. Women's advocacy groups around the globe have been strengthened and new ones created to focus on its implementation. One such organization is the NGO Working Group on Women, Peace and Security, formed in May 2000 and based in New York, which has systematically monitored the progress of implementation and offered strategic recommendations to help the process. For example, in preparation for the Security Council open debate on women, peace and security on 29 October 2008, the working group argued that concrete advancements in the equal inclusion of women in peace talks, justice processes and peacekeeping are still woefully inadequate and urged a critical assessment of efforts to improve women's participation in all aspects of peacemaking, peacekeeping and peacebuilding, particularly in the work of the Security Council.[34]

The Women's International League for Peace and Freedom in Australia has set up a website dedicated to tracking initiatives on the implementation of the resolution at civil society level. In Germany, the Women's Security Council has set up a postcard campaign and plan of action for accelerating the implementation of SCR 1325.[35] In Sri Lanka, the International Centre for Ethnic Studies has collaborated with women in the eastern zones to produce the film *Educating Civil Society* to advocate women's participation in the peace process. Women affected by armed conflict have successfully used SCR 1325 to lobby for their voices to be heard in peacebuilding processes, in post-conflict elections and in the rebuilding of their societies around the world. For example, the Kosovar Women's Network used the resolution to lobby for the opportunity to meet with a visiting Security Council delegation to Kosovo, and stated that without this framework their efforts would have been completely ignored.[36] In the UK, the Gender Action on Peace and Security Group has been set up to monitor the UK's implementation of the resolution.

The United Nations and the Security Council

The adoption of SCR 1325 has motivated and strengthened the Inter-Agency Task Force on Women, Peace and Security of the Inter-Agency Network on Women and Gender Equality that has been coordinating efforts to implement the resolution. An action plan with timelines for implementation across the UN system was developed in 2005 following a request from the Security Council to the Secretary-General. This was reviewed in 2007 and an updated system-wide action plan (2008–2009) was put in place.[37]

The Security Council has become more engaged with issues of women, peace and security and has developed many innovative initiatives. It has held seven open debates during which it has supported the broadening of the UN's integrated approach to women, peace and security (promoting gender mainstreaming in peacekeeping operations, increasing the number of women at the highest levels of decision-making and taking steps to address ending impunity for those committing sexual and gender-based violence).[38] A number of resolutions have been adopted, including SCR 1807 (2008) on the Democratic Republic of the Congo where the Security Council highlighted the possibility of using targeted sanctions in response to sexual violence in conflict.[39] Of crucial importance is that eight years after its adoption, the relevance of SCR 1325 – and its largely unmet promise – was reaffirmed in the passage of follow-up UN Security Council resolutions that included SCRs 1820, 1888 and 1889. SCR 1820 culminated the Security Council's June 2008 open thematic debate on "women, peace and security: sexual violence in situations of armed conflict". SCRs 1325 and 1820 strengthen the links between gender-based violence, human rights violations and international peace and security. It is envisaged that together they will form the impetus for the establishment of a mechanism to hold the perpetrators of violence and discrimination to account at the international level.[40]

UN SCR 1820 on sexual violence in conflict

SCR 1820 is the first to recognize sexual violence as a stand-alone issue affecting women's peace and security, and was developed in response to women's experiences of sexual violence in conflict situations. There is, however, an ongoing debate as to whether SCR 1820 eclipses SCR 1325. Issues highlighted during the debate in June 2008 include questions around the limited focus of the resolution, the fact that SCR 1325 needs full implementation, the lack of transparency and full inclusive consultation and the debate's focus on Africa to the exclusion of other regions where women also suffer sexual violence in conflict.[41]

Regional and subregional organizations

In an effort to harmonize approaches, contribute to synergy and collaborate with the United Nations as the awareness that conflict transcends borders grows, more and more regional and subregional organizations are recognizing their essential roles in promoting peace and optimizing resources. The African Union is actively mainstreaming a gender perspective in the implementation of SCR 1325, including the creation of its Women, Gender and Development Directorate and the appointment of an envoy to investigate sexual and gender-based violence in Darfur. The Southern African Development Community has implemented similar measures. The Economic Community of West African States and the Intergovernmental Authority on Development in East Africa have worked on action plans to implement the resolution.

Within the European Union, there is the European Parliament Resolution on Participation of Women in Peaceful Conflict Resolution (INI) 2000/2025,[42] and the European Peacebuilding Liaison Office in Brussels has initiated the EU 1325 Partnership to coordinate implementation efforts regionally. The Commonwealth ministers responsible for women's affairs agreed at their meeting in Uganda in June 2007 to establish a working group on gender, peace and security to address gender issues in peace and post-conflict processes. In the Arab region, the Arab Women's Organization held a conference in November 2008 on "Women in the Concept and Issues of Human Security: Arab and International Perspectives".

Member states and national action plans

Many member states have been motivated by the adoption of Resolution 1325 and have taken many initiatives. For example, Canada has formed a committee on women, peace and security that focuses on the resolution and its implementation in Canada. At the UN level, several member states led by Canada have initiated the Friends of 1325 – a grouping of states concerned about SCR 1325 and its gender-sensitive implementation.[43]

The commitment of member states is increasing, demonstrated by the growing number of states that have developed national action plans (NAPs) for the implementation of SCR 1325 on women, peace and security. The creation of such plans by member states was called for by the UN Secretary-General in 2004 and is being supported by the UN Office of the Special Adviser to the Secretary-General on Gender Issues and Advancement of Women with sponsorship from Norway. While there is ongoing debate over the value of separate action plans for gender equality and the implementation of SCR 1325, NAPs are considered to be one of the most effective ways for governments to move forward in translating the resolution's goals, as they recognize the empowerment of women as critical for achieving peace and security.[44] NAPs set out a country's strategy for developing inclusive and effective peace, security and development policies, instituting changes in the government machinery and developing stronger relationships with civil society through consultative processes that lead to a roadmap for the promotion and empowerment of women.[45] The publication "Securing Equality and Engendering Peace: A Guide to Policy and Planning" highlights the fact that NAPS can aid the process of gender mainstreaming by providing opportunities for enhancement in the following areas:[46]

- *Comprehensiveness* – greater understanding of the full picture of gender, peace and security issues in a country and engagement in a planning process that encompasses each aspect.
- *Coordination* – promoting collaboration among all stakeholders involved in implementing SCR 1325 at the national level, including government, civil society, the security sector and international and bilateral actors.
- *Awareness raising* – on the importance of SCR 1325 and women's full involvement in peacebuilding and state-building processes.
- *Ownership* – generating local recognition and acceptance of the importance of SCR 1325 and ensuring commitment to its implementation.
- *Accountability* – establishing specific responsibilities and reporting mechanisms for the implementation of SCR 1325 that will ensure sustainability and deliver results.

- *Monitoring and evaluation* – a realistic look at the concrete impact of a national action plan for the implementation of SCR 1325 in the country.
- *A designated budget* – a realistic assessment of required financial resources, as without adequate resources the NAP cannot be effectively implemented and will most likely sit on a shelf.[47]

Between 2005 and 2009, for instance, 11 European and three post-conflict countries (Liberia, Côte d'Ivoire and Uganda) are known to have developed NAPs for implementing SCR 1325. These NAPs all differ in terms of the process undertaken, content, mechanisms, timeframe for implementation and monitoring and evaluation processes.[48] For the purpose of this chapter, the NAP developed by Liberia is of particular interest.[49]

The Liberia National Action Plan

The Liberia National Action Plan (LNAP) was developed through a rigorous process of inclusive consultation and participation involving roundtable discussions and bilateral interviews to assess issues affecting women's peace and security, map women's positions and decision-making power in institutions and agencies, identify projects directly or indirectly related to SCR 1325 and, in the process, raise awareness and promote knowledge of the letter and intent of the resolution and its principles regarding women's peace and security issues. A priority of both the president of Liberia and the Ministry of Gender and Development was the inclusion and advancement of rural and market women. Consultation was therefore a bottom-up process which targeted representatives of these groups and has resulted in a document validated at the community, county and national levels.

The resulting LNAP (2009–2013) is a four-year "living document" constructed around four pillars that can be adapted according to changes in the Liberian context: protection, prevention, participation and empowerment and promotion. Each pillar contains a number of strategic issues and priority areas to be addressed, with outputs and indicators. The pillars include actions on policy review and development; capacity-building; advocacy and lobbying; construction of facilities; research and documentation; and monitoring and evaluation. The LNAP was validated by strategic county dialogues, presentations to high-level policy forums and discussions with a number of key stakeholders including the technical oversight mechanism – the 1325 National Steering Committee.[50] A short-list of priority indicators was developed at a workshop organized by the Ministry of Gender and Development with support from UNIFEM.[51]

The LNAP is closely tied to both SCRs 1325 and 1820 and complements initiatives such as the poverty reduction strategy and the four joint government of Liberia-UN programmes already in place.[52] It focuses on additional and specific actions needed to promote and advance the inclusion of women in all processes that affect their peace and security, foster gender equality and gender mainstreaming and, ultimately, promote sustainable development.[53] The NAP strengthens efforts to advance gender equality, including Millennium Development Goal 3, which envisions the elimination of gender disparity in primary and secondary education by 2005, and in all levels of education by 2015. Its implementation is not limited to the actions it highlights, but includes activities and measures that can be initiated as necessary, bearing in mind the need for coherence and taking full account of the coordination role of the Ministry of Gender and Development.

Monitoring and impact evaluation are of priority importance in the LNAP and must be mainstreamed into mechanisms already in place for the monitoring of the poverty reduction strategy. Mechanisms for monitoring and impact evaluation will include an "observatory" composed of women's groups and other NGOs, the existing 1325 National Steering Committee and a technical monitoring and evaluation task force comprising experts from government ministries and agencies, including the Ministry of Planning and Economic Affairs and the Liberian Institute for Statistics and Geo-Information Services. At the county level, monitoring and evaluation will be the responsibility of the Ministry of Gender and Development gender coordinators and support teams. Ultimately, however, responsibility and accountability for the implementation of the LNAP will rest with ministers, who must ensure compliance with the implementation and results timeframe.

Reporting requirements include yearly reports to the president of Liberia on LNAP implementation status, an interim progress report to the country at the end of 18 months and a final report to the president and cabinet at the end of the four-year implementation period. At the international level, LNAP implementation will require reporting along the lines of the Convention on the Elimination of All Forms of Discrimination against Women. Successful implementation could contribute to the broad objectives of women's ownership of peacebuilding in Africa and around the world.[54]

Conclusion

This chapter has provided information on the Women Building Peace: From the Village Council to the Negotiating Table campaign that helped secure the adoption of SCR 1325. Ensuring women's participation in the urgent task of peacebuilding facing many countries today will enhance the legitimacy of the process by making it more democratic and responsive to the priorities of all sectors of the population. The engagement of women's organizations during and after the Women Building Peace campaign reinforced this belief. Sustainable peace is inseparable from gender equality. The global campaign was premised on the fact that peacebuilding is a process requiring the equal contribution of both men and women, and women's inclusion from the planning stages to implementation will improve the impact of local and international interventions and make the development of peace more just and sustainable. To further full and effective implementation of the resolution from the global to the local, it is imperative that sufficient resources are allocated for work on women, peace and security, including support for the development of NAPs as a key strategy to advance all four SCRs on these issues. The "accountability gap" identified in the recent monitoring report entitled "Women Count" must be addressed.[55] In conclusion, a number of recommendations are suggested that may be taken up by international, regional, national and local actors, including civil society organizations, member states and the United Nations.

Recommendations for the United Nations and the Security Council

- Where sexual violence is a major and complex challenge, senior gender-based violence advisers or coordinators should be deployed as part of peacekeeping missions, as has been done in the Mission of the UN Organization in the Democratic Republic of the Congo.
- Where possible and feasible, conduct and discipline units should be included in future peacekeeping missions.
- Develop and enforce strong accountability systems for the monitoring and evaluation of SCRs 1325 and 1820, as called for by the Secretary-General. In 2004 Sweden recommended that the Security Council "could consider designating a focal point – possibly supplemented by a working group – with a particular responsibility to monitor its own work on resolution 1325".[56]
- Planning for peace support operations and other field missions should show a familiarity with SCR 1325 and its interpretation, and this should be demonstrated at all stages, including pre-planning, during the mission and reporting back from the mission. This should also be the norm in cases where the United Nations becomes a transitional authority. Of particular importance is the integration of women's interests and perspectives and the implementation of a fair and equitable gender balance.

- Develop, consult and agree on standards of excellence for future NAPS. Such standards could result from research and analysis into the impact of NAPs, and may generate political will to replicate good practice in context-specific NAPs.

Recommendations for member states

- Gender balance and sensitivity in peacekeeping and peacebuilding activities must be assured. Security sector and defence policies should be revised to strengthen pre-deployment gender training for peacekeepers at the national level (see also Chapter 13 in this volume).
- The 2005 Paris Declaration on Aid Effectiveness highlighted the need for greater coordination in gender equality programming among humanitarian actors.[57] Reforms in this area should include aid provision to ensure the equal participation of women and girls in all aspects of humanitarian response, their access to capacity-building and employment, and more accountability for gender mainstreaming.
- Research should focus on more systematic collection of gender and gender-disaggregated data.
- Donors should ensure that funds are set aside specifically to fund women's and pro-women peacebuilding initiatives. Donors should also ensure that these funds can be disbursed rapidly and are sufficient and sustainable.

Recommendations for the development of NAPs

- Ensure that the process of developing national action plans is right for the country and current situation, and that the content responds to the demands and expectations expressed by society. Include as many key ministries as necessary and possible both to house the NAP and to drive and sustain its implementation. In Liberia the cooperation of the Ministry of Gender and Development was invaluable in this context.
- Create a process that is consultative, inclusive, participatory, sustained and bottom-up as well as top-down; and develop a mechanism such as a working group that includes the most appropriate stakeholders and level of representatives for the institutions involved, which are well suited for guiding and informing the development of a NAP and will remain engaged throughout the entire process.
- Create a NAP that is visionary yet realistic, with firm timeframes, accountability mechanisms, outputs, indicators, budget indications and implementation plans; and define gender equality priorities and validate gender-sensitive indicators before the NAP is completed in order to leave some time for required adjustments.

- Explore opportunities to "twin" with post-conflict countries in the process of developing their NAPs. For example, Ireland, Timor-Leste and Liberia are linking their NAPs in a break-out from the traditional donor-recipient relationship.
- Ensure that the NAP is financed adequately before or during its launch.

Recommendations for civil society organizations

- Civil society organizations should be willing to be involved in consultations on the development and implementation of a NAP, including being prepared to develop alternative reports and assist in monitoring the implementation of their country's NAP.
- Faith-based organizations and religious and secular leaders of local communities can be constructive forces for conflict transformation and peacebuilding within society. They should be consulted on SCR 1325 and provided with training on how the resolution could be used.
- None of the four SCRs (1325, 1820, 1888 and 1889) is gender divisive, but rather they seek to be inclusive, involving stakeholders in solutions and programmes to better women's peace and security and their involvement in sustainable development. As such men, especially gender-sensitive men, and children and youth should be more enthusiastically and effectively involved in consultations and initiatives that affect women's peace and security, and especially issues of sexual violence of all types, as they are both perpetrators and, at times, victims.

Notes

1. DPI (2001) "The Beijing Platform for Action with the Beijing+5 Political Declaration and Outcome Document", United Nations, New York, para. 134, available at www.un. org/womenwatch/daw/beijing/pdf/BDPfA%20E.pdf.
2. Post-conflict peacebuilding must be understood as a process where political, security and development aspects come together. It entails both short- and long-term objectives, and incorporates all initiatives that can help a country move from war to peace. These initiatives include, but are not limited to, reintegrating former combatants into civilian society, security sector reform, strengthening the rule of law, improving respect for human rights, providing technical assistance for democratic development and promoting conflict resolution and reconciliation techniques. See www.unac.org/peacekeeping/en/un-peacekeeping/fact-sheets/from-peacekeeping-to-peacebuilding/.
3. Chowdhury, Anwarul K. (2005) "Foreword", in *From Local to Global: Making Peace Work for Women, Security Council Resolution 1325 on Women, Peace and Security, Five Years On Report*, New York: NGO Working Group on Women, Peace and Security.
4. UN Security Council (2000) "Resolution 1325: Women, Peace and Security", UN Doc. S/RES/1325 (2000), 31 October, available at www.uneca.org/daweca/conventions_and _resolutions/Res%201325.pdf.

5. Annex to letter dated 15 October 2008 from the Permanent Representative of China to the United Nations addressed to the Secretary-General, "Concept Paper for the Open Debate to the Security Council", United Nations, New York.

6. SCR 1820 (June 2008) focuses on sexual violence in armed conflict (http://daccess-dds-ny.un.org/doc/UNDOC/GEN/N08/391/44/PDF/N0839144.pdf?OpenElement); SCR 1888 (September 2009) strengthens SCR 1820 and calls for the inclusion of sexual violence issues in peace processes (http://daccess-dds-ny.un.org/doc/UNDOC/GEN/N09/534/46/PDF/N0953446.pdf?OpenElement); and SCR 1889 (October 2009) extends the focus on women's participation in peacebuilding, emphasizing their essential role in political and economic decision-making (http://daccess-dds-ny.un.org/doc/UNDOC/GEN/N09/542/55/PDF/N0954255.pdf?OpenElement). See DCAF (2010) "Implementing the Women, Peace and Security Resolutions in Security Sector Reform", Practice Note 13, Gender and SSR Toolkit, DCAF, Geneva, available at www.humansecuritygateway.com/documents/DCAF_ImplementingTheWomenPeaceAndSecurityResolutionsInSecurity-SectorReform.pdf.

7. International Alert is an international NGO based in London and dedicated to the peaceful prevention, management and transformation of violent conflict. IA works at national, regional and global levels to enhance the capacity of individuals, peace networks, constituencies and organizations to build sustainable peace. See its website at www.international-alert.org.

8. This chapter draws and expands on previous publications by the author: Adrian-Paul, Ancil (2003) "Legitimising the Role of Women in Peacebuilding in the United Nations: A Campaign Approach", in NGOs at the Table: Strategies for Influencing Policy, Dublin: INCORE; Adrian-Paul, Ancil, Kevin Clements, Eugenia Piza Lopez and Nicola Johnston (2004) "Legitimizing the Role of Women in Peacebuilding at the United Nations: A Campaign Approach", in Mari Fitzduff and Cheyanne Church (eds) NGOs at the Table: Strategies for Influencing Policies in Areas of Conflict, Oxford: Rowman & Littlefield, pp. 95–112.

9. See www.incore.ulst.ac.uk/cds/themes/women.htm. See also Chapter 2 in this volume for a description of the experiences women face in violent conflict situations.

10. The UN designation of rape as a crime against humanity within international law, in the Rome Statute of the International Criminal Court in February 2001, represented a major step forward in achieving recognition for the traumas that women suffer in periods of armed conflict. Many scholars and activists believe that this should also be recognized in women's experiences as refugees and internally displaced people. See, for example, Levine, Corey (2001) "The Gender Dimensions of Peacebuilding", paper presented at NPSIA conference on Human Security: Policy Implications for the 21st Century, Ottawa, 21 January.

11. DPI (1995) The Beijing Platform for Action, New York: United Nations. In September 1995 more than 180 governments signed the Beijing Declaration and Platform for Action in Beijing, China.

12. United Nations (2001) "War Affected Children: The Machel Review, 1996–2000", supported by UNIFEM Norway, UNICEF Canada and UN General Assembly, UN Doc. A/55/749, United Nations, New York, 26 February.

13. Adrian-Paul, Ancil (2002) "East African Consultation on UN SC Resolution 1325 with Women and Men", report produced for International Alert, London, March.

14. Manchanda, Rita (2001) "Redefining and Feminising Security", Perspectives, Economic and Political Weekly, June.

15. See Chapter 5 in this volume for an examination of the Burundian women's struggle for inclusion in the Burundi peace process.

16. Karamé, Kari with the assistance of Gudrun Bertinussen (2001) "Gendering Human Security: From Marginalisation to the Integration of Women in Peace-Building", Fafo Report 352/NUPI Report No. 261, Fafo Institute for Applied Social Science/Norwegian Institute of International Affairs, Oslo, available at www.fafo.no/pub/rapp/352/352.pdf.
17. UNMIL has established a conduct and discipline department.
18. Author's personal experience of UNMIL and interview with individual women from the conduct and discipline department, August 2008–April 2009.
19. The conference was held in May 1999 in the House of Lords, London, and brought together 50 women from 48 conflict areas.
20. These demands were based on the 12 critical areas defined in the Beijing Platform for Action and accompanying strategic objectives.
21. The Fourth World Conference on Women was the largest of the UN conferences on women, bringing together representatives of numerous NGOs, governments, UN agencies and other constituencies.
22. UN SCR 1325 was developed under Chapter VI of the UN Charter.
23. The Platform for Action resulted from the UN Fourth World Conference on Women, Beijing, 1995.
24. Locally, nationally and regionally based organizations were informed and consulted about the campaign and whether they wanted to participate. They had to be already working on issues affecting women's peace and security and could choose how they wanted to support the initiative, e.g. through collecting signatures in support of the "Five Demands", or organizing local campaigns of relevance to them or any other initiative that would fit into the campaign's tenets of "join locally, work globally".
25. Participants included the US headquarters of UNIFEM, the Center for Women's Global Leadership at Rutgers University, New York, and the executive directors of the Geneva-based African women's organization Femmes Africa Solidarite and the London-based African women's think-tank Akina Mama waAfrika, together with other organizations selected for their geographical location and their expertise on one or more themes underpinning the campaign.
26. There were 22 focal points attached to the Women Building Peace global campaign in 20 different countries. These focal points operated at the local, national and regional levels.
27. The Millennium Peace Prize was the first of its kind and was supported by UNIFEM. The prize was given to three individual women and three women's organizations. For further information see IA's website at www.international-alert.org/women.
28. These included UNIFEM, UNICEF, the UN Division for the Advancement of Women, the Office of the Special Adviser to the Secretary-General on Gender Issues and the Advancement of Women, the World Food Programme, the UN Department for Disarmament Affairs and Department of Peacekeeping Operations and other key UN agencies and departments.
29. This policy briefing was written by Dyan Mazurana and edited by Nicola Johnston, senior policy adviser to the Gender and Peacebuilding Programme at IA.
30. For copies of the reports and policy documents that were produced, see the campaign's website at www.international-alert.org.
31. After the adoption of SCR 1325 two studies have been produced, one by the UN Secretary-General and the other an independent experts' assessment commissioned by UNIFEM. These reports contain a number of recommendations for addressing women's peace and security and advancing and empowering women. For further information see www.un.org, www.womenwatch.org or www.peacewomen.org.
32. Successful funding led to further consultations in Colombia and Afghanistan.

33. International Alert (2002) *Women's Perspectives on Resolution 1325*, London: International Alert. See also El Bushra, Judy (2003) *Women Building Peace: Sharing Know-How*, London: International Alert; Johnston, Nicola (2003) *UN SC Resolution 1325: South Asian Women's Perspectives*, London: International Alert.
34. See www.womenpeacesecurity.org/media/pdf-2008_October_21_Open_Letter.pdf.
35. See http://un.org for pdf copies of SCRs 1325 and 1820.
36. Nobel Women's Initiative (2007) "Women Redefining Peace in the Middle East and Beyond, Report of the First International Peace Conference", NWI Canada, Ottawa.
37. Many more initiatives have taken place, with individual agencies such as UNIFEM and the UN Department of Peacekeeping Operations leading specific sectors. Further information can be found on websites such as www.unifem.org, www.undpko.org and www.un.org.
38. United Nations (2008) "Women, Peace and Security", Report of the Secretary-General, UN Doc. S/2008/622, United Nations, New York, 25 September.
39. Resolution 1807 (2008) para. 13(e) builds on Resolution 1794 (2007), where the Security Council stressed the need to ensure accountability for the perpetrators of sexual violence (para. 15) and requested the UN Mission in the Congo to pursue a mission-wide strategy on sexual violence (para. 18).
40. Robinson, Mary (2008) "Foreword", in *Stepping Up Ireland's Response to Women, Peace and Security, United Nations Security Council Resolution 1325*, report by Irish Joint Consortium on Gender Based Violence, available at www.dfa.ie/uploads/documents/CRU/consortium%20gender%20based%20violence%20report.pdf.
41. Further information on the continuing debate on SCR 1820 may be found at www.peacewomen.org, www.unifem.org and www.womenwatch.org.
42. Further information can be found at www.europarl.europa.
43. For more information on such initiatives see www.peacewomen.org.
44. There is ongoing debate over whether separate action plans for specific issues, such as gender equality, are necessary or valuable, or whether these issues should simply be embedded into wider workstreams. The pros and cons of both approaches are outlined in UN-INSTRAW (2006) "Securing Equality and Engendering Peace: A Guide to Policy and Planning on Women, Peace and Security UNSCR 1325", UN-INSTRAW, Santo Domingo. The report recommends that both should be in place, i.e. there should be a specific action plan to advance gender equality combined with the integration of gender considerations into wider workstreams.
45. Personal invitation to a high-level meeting on "Increasing Momentum for UNSCR 1325 National Action Plans", organized by Realizing Rights: The Ethical Globalization Initiative and Institute for Inclusive Security, New York, 24 April 2009.
46. UN-INSTRAW, note 44.
47. Cabrera-Balleza, Mavic and Nicola Popovic (2011) "Costing and Financing 1325: Examining the Resources Needed to Implement UN Security Council Resolution 1325 at the National Level as Well as the Gains, Gaps and Glitches on Financing the Women, Peace and Security Agenda", Cordaid/GNWP, The Hague and New York, May.
48. Irish Joint Consortium on Gender Based Violence (2008) *Stepping Up Ireland's Response to Women, Peace and Security: United Nations Security Council Resolution 1325*, report, available at www.dfa.ie/uploads/documents/CRU/consortium%20gender%20based%20violence%20report.pdf.
49. The author was one of two consultants who co-authored the Liberian National Action Plan.
50. Participants in the consultative processes included representatives of 12 government ministries; government agencies; the Women's Legislative Caucus; local authority structures; rehabilitation institutions; national security agencies; the Truth and Reconciliation

Commission Women's Committee; the Liberian Institute for Statistics and Geo-Information Services; local, community-based and international NGOs; media institutions; interfaith institutions; the private sector (finance and micro-credit institutions); UN agencies; various UNMIL departments; and members of the donor community.

51. Workshop on Indicators of Peace Consolidation from a Gender Perspective: The Case of Liberia – Including SCR 1325 and SCR 1820, organized by the Liberian Ministry of Gender and Development and supported by UN-INSTRAW, OSAGI, UNMIL-OGA and UNIFEM, Monrovia, 19–20 February 2009.

52. In this current post-conflict recovery phase, Liberia epitomizes the principles and the letter and intent of SCR 1325, with the UN system playing a critical and central role. UN agencies are supporting the government of Liberia to implement four joint programmes that complement the LNAP: the UN Joint Programme to Prevent and Respond to Sexual and Gender Based Violence, signed in June 2008; the UN Joint Programme on Food Security and Nutrition, also signed in June 2008; the UN Joint Programme on Gender Equality and Women's Economic Empowerment, which brings together various UN agencies to support policy development and programme implementation to achieve gender equality in Liberia; and the UN Joint Programme for Employment and the Empowerment of Young Women and Men, which promotes the employability of young women and men, both as a means to economic growth and as a vehicle for sustained peace and security in Liberia.

53. Liberia's NAP will support the operationalization of policy documents already in existence in the country, including the poverty reduction strategy, the Millennium Development Goals, the UN Development Assistance Framework, the National Gender-based Violence Plan of Action and the Women's National Action Plan. Additional policies that support the LNAP include the gender policy of the UN Department of Peacekeeping Operations, the African Charter on Human and Peoples' Rights, the Convention on the Rights of the Child, the Convention on the Elimination of All Forms of Discrimination against Women, the Universal Declaration of Human Rights, the recently adopted UN Resolution 1820 on sexual and gender-based violence and the Beijing Declaration and Platform for Action, as well as those contained in the outcome document of the Twenty-third Special Session of the UN General Assembly: UNGA (2000) "Women 2000: Gender Equality, Development and Peace for the Twenty-first Century", UN Doc. A/S-23/10Rev.1, United Nations, New York.

54. Liberia National Action Plan for the Implementation of UN SC Resolution 1325, Monrovia, March 2009.

55. Moser, Annalise (2010) "Women Count – Security Council Resolution 1325: Civil Society Monitoring Report", October, Global Network of Women Peacebuilders, New York, available at www.gnwp.org/wp-content/uploads/2010/02/UNSCR-Monitoring-GLOBAL-Report.pdf.

56. NGO Working Group on Women, Peace and Security (2005) *From Local to Global: Making Peace Work for Women, Security Council Resolution 1325 on Women, Peace and Security, Five Years On Report*, New York: NGO Working Group on Women, Peace and Security.

57. The 2005 Paris Declaration on Aid Effectiveness presents a framework for the management of overseas development assistance. Advocates have used this as a key entry point for strengthening accountability for financing gender equality. See UNIFEM (2009) *Progress of the World's Women 2008/2009, Who Answers to Women? Gender and Accountability*, New York: UNIFEM.

Part IV

Deconstructing victimhood: Women in political and security institutions

11

State-building or survival in conflict and post-conflict situations? A peacebuilding perspective on Palestinian women's contributions to ending the Israeli occupation

Vanessa Farr

On 4 May 2011 a historic reconciliation deal was signed in Cairo between the two main Palestinian political parties, Hamas and Fatah. A week later 11 other political groups added their signatures. This agreement attempted to end a four-year split that has severely compromised the Palestinian political landscape, caused internal dissension and given rise to a complex governance system in which parallel institutions are run by Hamas in the Gaza Strip and Fatah in the West Bank. The significant regional changes that are marking the "Arab Spring" have also affected political developments in the occupied Palestinian territory (oPt). The "Palestine 194" appeal of President Abbas at the General Assembly in 2011 has so far met with inadequate Security Council support. However, the Palestinian leader has vowed to continue with his statehood bid. His determination and the unprecedented and escalating regional changes have put the question of an independent Palestinian state firmly back on the international agenda – the culmination of a lengthy process of readying Palestinian institutions for statehood which has been supported by the international community but remains an indigenous project born of a long and desperate struggle to achieve independence and national unity in the face of the Israeli occupation.

The goal of declaring a state was first announced in Palestinian Authority (PA) Prime Minister Fayyad's 2009 "Homestretch to Freedom" government plan. It is reinforced in the National Development Plan 2011–2013, which declares that the "basic institutional building blocks of a modern state ... are now in place" and only impeded from full functioning

Defying victimhood: Women and post-conflict peacebuilding, Schnabel and Tabyshalieva (eds), United Nations University Press, 2012, ISBN 978-92-808-1201-5

by the continued Israeli occupation and denial of sovereignty.[1] When progress towards the goal of Palestinian statehood was reviewed at the April 2011 Ad Hoc Liaison Committee meeting for assistance to the Palestinians, the United Nations, the World Bank, the International Monetary Fund and the Office of the Quartet, based on reports and recommendations from the parties, agreed with this view. The committee concluded that the PA "is above the threshold for a functioning state in the key sectors they studied and that Palestinian institutions compare favourably with those in established states".[2]

This optimistic discourse, however, must be tempered by constant reference to the realities on the ground: Israeli Prime Minister Binyamin Netanyahu immediately renounced the declaration of national unity and the US government fairly swiftly followed suit, including threats to withdraw its foreign aid to the PA.[3] Most significantly, the occupation continues to deepen its grip on Palestinian land and lives through untrammelled illegal settlement activity in East Jerusalem and the West Bank and a full military siege on the Gaza Strip. With such high political and ideological stakes, the outcomes of the increased rhetoric about Palestinian state independence very much remain to be seen.

It is important to understand whose discourses are being given public space in this discussion. As Eileen Kuttab expresses it, "the Palestinian local elite represents the interests of small groups of nationals who have employed political space to develop personal agendas and portfolios that do not in any way include or reflect people's aspirations, or work towards the achievements of people's democratic and national rights".[4]

While the Palestinian leadership continues its highly publicized talks about statehood and expresses its ambitions for the post-conflict moment with little reference to what Palestinians themselves are saying, this chapter reflects on the little-heard voices of women.[5] It examines some questions that are rarely asked in state-building rhetoric but have been eloquently formulated in a recent study on the near-complete absence of gender analysis in state-building processes: "who is represented within each group [seeking statehood], who participates in state-society negotiations, and whose expectations and demands are expressed within these negotiations?"[6] These questions are significant for Palestine. Despite their important contribution to the liberation struggle over many generations, women are strikingly absent from the current state-building discourse and occupy very little of the public political space that produces it. At the same time the male political elites, whether Palestinian or international, do not consider or reference women's organizing or engage with international instruments intended to advance women's participation, such as Security Council Resolution (SCR) 1325 (2000) on women, peace and security and SCR 1889 (2009) on women's involvement in post-conflict reconstruction.[7] In the oPt, as in other emerging-state processes, exclusionary patterns of power are proving hard to shift. However, the small and very recent body of work that is beginning to look at women within state-building processes suggests that it is timely to amplify women's attempts to position themselves within this state-building paradigm, in the hopes that the current exclusionary power relations can be concretely challenged and reshaped and that women can become more effective rights claimants in a post-conflict, sovereign Palestinian state.

This chapter offers a focused analysis of Palestinian women's organizing in Israeli-annexed East Jerusalem as an entry point to a consideration of larger Palestinian statehood questions.[8] The study draws on field research carried out with 12 diverse women's organizations in occupied East Jerusalem by the UN Development Programme – Programme of Assistance to the Palestinian People and the Kvinna till Kvinna Foundation. The research was designed to update both Palestinian and non-Palestinian understanding of what a diverse range of Palestinian women currently focus on in Jerusalem, how they view and contribute to the politics they encounter in their everyday lives and how they prioritize their activities in an increasingly difficult operating environment.

The fieldwork has been embedded in a historical analysis of women's political organizing in the oPt in order to explain better where women find themselves today after decades of resistance. Occasional comparisons have been drawn to another long liberation struggle and state-building process with high levels of women's participation, namely that which ended apartheid in South Africa, as useful lessons can be gleaned from this approach.

The research reveals that the work of Jerusalem-based Palestinian women has become increasingly diffuse and yet simultaneously professionalized as the forced displacement of Palestinians from occupied East Jerusalem worsens. The most important findings are that Palestinian women's organizing in Jerusalem has changed as politically informed activism becomes increasingly constricted in this donor-driven and militarized context, and that the women's liberation struggle, like the national one, is being forced to confront ever-changing obstacles, risks and challenges, yet with limited success. A key apprehension, derived from a comparative understanding of what South African women did to ensure their concerns would be addressed in the post-apartheid state, is that the limited but steady contributions made by women's peacebuilding strategies might not be translatable into real political gains in the post-conflict moment if they remain at their current marginal levels of organization.[9]

A brief overview of Palestinian women's political organizing

Palestinian women, in both grassroots networks and more formal organizations (including trade unions and, more recently, the Ministry of Women's Affairs), have played a consistent, if under-acknowledged, role in non-violent resistance since *al-Nakbah* of 1948, within the oPt since 1967 and in peacemaking with international and Israeli counterparts.[10] The particular liberation struggle in which they are engaged is not, however, one that has intended to advance women's equality as a core goal, and there is little recognition of women's particular organizing strategies and political contributions in mainstream histories of Palestine.[11] Despite their record of contributions to resistance, patriarchal norms on appropriate behaviour for women have proven remarkably resilient in the oPt, and deep structural inequalities between women and men echo and enlarge the deep inequalities between Jews and Arabs. Even while the political reality of the occupation has allowed some women to access public spaces in a way that was until recently unimaginable in other Arab countries, the majority of Palestinian women remain tightly confined.[12]

Nonetheless, as is discussed in more detail later, as in other countries engaged in complex processes of political and social change, there are important ways in which engagement in the struggle has helped Palestinian women oppose existing systems of power and control, both those within Palestinian traditional society and those imposed militarily by Israel to maintain the prolonged occupation. Their efforts have contributed to women's participation in public life and shaped men's reactions to this development. While written histories of women's organizing and its institutional impacts may be difficult to find, in conversation male and female Palestinians alike acknowledge that the depredations of the occupation have been in some measure kept in check by civil society (including women's) organizations and women's other activities at familial and local level. Palestinian women have been and are directly involved in a spectrum of activities, such as provision of basic services, caregiving (including in emergency situations arising from violent conflict) and early childhood education. Organized women have also played an important role in civic education, especially on such taboo issues as violence in the family. They have become quite skilful at helping Palestinians understand the interconnections between public, militarized violence and violence in the home.[13]

Women's organizations throughout the oPt are making proactive contributions to legal reform and implementation, and supporting women's political education (and their right to education in general) and participation in public political life. They are working to ensure that the goal of women's liberation remains well positioned within the broader ongoing national liberation struggle and the protracted political, economic and social crisis produced by the occupation. As Eileen Kuttab explains, "Palestinian women's activism has been influenced by its relation to and identification with the national resistance struggle."[14] The challenges they face are, however, identical to those which confront all women interested in reformatory state-building processes: how to insist that their views are respected and taken seriously, how to position their efforts as essential contributions to state-building and how to enshrine them in public institution-building in a more systematic way. As Shireen Hassim observes in her analysis of women's political organizing in South Africa, "it is self-limiting for the women's movement to pursue inclusion in the state in a piecemeal and depoliticized fashion, seeking to include women into existing policy frameworks without questioning whether the overall policy directions are appropriate for poor women, or how to put new areas of policy or law making on the agenda".[15] As in other protracted liberation struggles, efforts need to be made during the resistance period to ensure that post-conflict institutions will recognize the contributions of women to ending the crisis and enshrine their equality in political, social and economic institutions that are informed by and responsive to women's needs.[16]

Security Council Resolution 1325 and Palestinian women's organizing

At the time of writing, political realities within the oPt continue to be quite divergent as a result of the continued internal political divisions between Fatah and Hamas, which are exacerbated by the Israeli military blockade of the Gaza Strip, lack of access to Jerusalem from the rest of the West Bank and movement restrictions within the West Bank itself. This fragmentation has particular impacts on women's organizing. The tenth anniversary of the passage of SCR 1325 in 2010 was seen as an opportunity to understand better how women are coping with the challenges of geographical and political division, and to assist women in different parts of the territory to know more about each other's plight and strategies for survival.

Three goals of the research were strongly informed by SCR 1325. Firstly, as the "quiet deportation" of Palestinians from East Jerusalem becomes increasingly noisy and violent, it is important to focus on how women in Jerusalem are reacting.[17] Secondly, referencing also SCR 1889, there is a need to offer a gendered analysis of how women are being alienated from their own immediate struggle because of the tendency of the international community and national governments to set limitations on local strategic priorities in line with decisions made in capital cities. Thirdly, highlighting women's struggles is a necessary corrective to the tendency to focus on the big issues of the day as defined by officially recognized leaders in the oPt, Israel and the international community, which neglect the interests of ordinary people and particularly of women. It brings to light the ways in which women in this military occupation may be able to exploit "small, temporary, invisible forms of resistance" by using "tactics that exploit the gaping cracks within urban spaces and the systems of power".[18]

SCR 1325 is a useful lens to use in this discussion, as it was devised to challenge the elitism of peacebuilding and state-building processes and their almost complete exclusion of women at a global level. It establishes a political framework through which considerations of women, peace and security can be integrated into the international peace and security agenda.[19] From this perspective, SCR 1325 provides a framework within which to examine the obstacles faced by Palestinian women organizing in Jerusalem when they try to have their interests represented among national and international strategic priorities for Palestinians: the field research conducted for this study suggests that their most overwhelming challenge is the silencing of their political voice – a problem that is taken up in the more recent SCR 1889.

A traditional understanding of the realm of politics may exclude much of what takes place in the private sphere, in the "politics of small things", the means by which people "address the pressing concerns of [their] time".[20] In Jerusalem, however, every aspect of the political is also personal, and the political decisions made by the state of Israel have explicitly gendered impacts. Women experience two forms of oppression: that stemming from political issues such as the construction of the separation barrier, the occupation and encroachment of illegal Jewish settlements into historically Palestinian parts of the city, restrictions on movement, the emphasis on military instead of human security and frustration with the political elite and failed political processes; and that caused by patriarchal control of their social, economic and political space. This double burden affects every aspect of Palestinian women's life and work in the city. One example is the Israeli residential policies designed to speed up a process of "bureaucratic eviction by cancellation of the residency rights of Jerusalem's indigenous population" that was started with the Law of Entry into Israel in 1952. Under this law and subsequent amendments, Palestinians in Jerusalem have to establish that their "centre of life" is in the city. Unlike Israeli Jews, they may not hold dual nationality. As of 1982 children whose fathers are not Jerusalem residents have not been registered at birth, and from 1994 Jerusalemite women have been unable to apply for resident status for their spouses.[21] The impacts of these laws, especially in cases of separation or divorce, are devastating for the well-being of individuals and families.

Jerusalemite women are also affected by the larger political sphere in which the Israel-Palestine conflict is played out, and again they bear a double burden of exclusion and control. Contrary to the clear directives given in SCR 1325 to include women in all aspects of decision-making in a conflict zone, Palestinian women are routinely excluded from high-level negotiations on the Israel-Palestine question – by Palestinian males, the state of Israel and the international community. The field research shows that this exclusion from both local and international political arenas is extremely negative, as previous gains in women's empowerment are being undermined and the interests of Palestinian women are being neglected, not advanced, despite a significant amount of rhetoric about the need to promote gender equality as a part of establishing an independent Palestinian state.[22]

In these circumstances, the field research shows that an overwhelming depoliticization of the women's movement has taken place in the decade since SCR 1325 was passed, confirming findings already published.[23] Nonetheless, there are important differences between women's organizations. Living and working in the urban centre of Jerusalem, as Hanna Herzog argues in her analysis of women's lives in "mixed cities" where both Palestinians and Israeli Jews live together (albeit divided along ethnic-national lines), may in fact offer women some forms of liberation, especially in terms of access to education and inter-class mobility.[24]

A 2010 study showed interesting differences between Jerusalem women's organizations: community-based organizations (CBOs) and charities are most significantly depoliticized; non-governmental organizations (NGOs) tend to project an image of depoliticization despite engaging in highly political work; and feminist and specialized NGOs and service providers are most likely to discuss openly their political role.[25] Overall, however, Palestinian women's organizations have moved far away from the politically informed and proactive work that characterized their interventions from the 1960s onwards. This finding is extremely troubling in Jerusalem, which represents the heart of Palestinian identity and has always been a home of the Palestinian women's movement.

A history of women's organizing in the occupied Palestinian territory

After the 1948 creation of the state of Israel, the earliest Palestinian women's movements in the 1950s concerned themselves more with economic and social affairs than with political work. This began to change in

1964, after the establishment of the Palestinian Liberation Movement, when the General Union of Palestinian Women was formed and women began to participate actively in political meetings, including the Palestinian National Council, which held its first congress in Jerusalem in 1965. After the Jordanian closure of Palestine Liberation Organization associations in 1965, the General Union continued its work in secret. Women's associations proliferated, growing from a variety of interest bases.[26]

Although they had started from a conservative perspective that did not prioritize women's liberation, after the Israeli occupation of 1967 women's organizations became increasingly involved in the social movements conceived by the Palestinian national leadership from the mid-1970s onwards. This was seen as the best means:

> to mobilize and organize people of different social categories including the youth, women, workers and peasants ... [in] decentralized, mass-based structures that enabled the national movement to challenge the series of economic and political measures implemented by the Israeli occupation that sought to destroy the cultural and socioeconomic infrastructure of the Palestinian society.[27]

Strengthened by their own activism, the idea grew that women could organize as women and should prioritize both social and national liberation. Women began to form networks and associations in rural as well as urban areas, which were more explicitly focused on how the occupation affected women as a distinct group. By the late 1970s grassroots initiatives had begun to proliferate. Women voted for the first time, alongside men, in the municipal elections that were initiated by Israeli Prime Minister Yitzhak Rabin in an attempt to defuse the tensions arising from extensive rioting across the West Bank in 1976.[28]

When the first intifada broke out in 1987, it derived its energy from the mass-based structures set up in the 1970s with a broad base of ordinary people – male and female youth, workers and peasants. Women's participation in various acts of resistance, including the first boycotts of Israeli-manufactured goods and the provision of services as political conditions worsened,[29] was seen as a key part of a genuine, decentralized democratic movement "to respond to the needs of the national struggle and to promote women's consciousness around national and women's issues".[30] Highly localized neighbourhood or popular committees became part of a particularly successful organizing strategy, allowing women to engage with every aspect of political life and lead in the boycott of Israeli-made goods. According to Islah Jad, however, their "role in the popular committees became an extension of what it traditionally had been in society: teaching and rendering services", a factor which may help explain why "the women question" remained subsumed in the "nationalist question" in the sexually segregated mosques, cafés and prisons where political strategizing was done.[31]

Yet despite their political invisibility to Palestinian men, women's popular committees did not escape the attention of the Israeli military authorities, which banned them in August 1988.[32] In December of that year, in trying to mitigate the growing impacts of the uprising, the Higher Women's Committee was established. Comprising the Palestinian Union of Women's Work Committees, the Palestinian Federation of Women's Action Committees, the Working Women's Committee and the Union of Palestinian Women's Committees, it articulated as an explicit goal the need to address women's liberation alongside national liberation.[33] This ideal would not be challenged until the signing of the Oslo Agreement in 1993, one effect of which was to create the local elite described by Kuttab, along with a strong sense of introspection in Palestinian organizing as the full devastation of the agreement began to be felt. By destroying Palestinian unity and heightening Israeli military control over the territory it occupies, the agreement also produced a diffuse sense that women's issues, with those of other marginalized groups, could be a focus of concern removed from the project of national liberation.[34]

The challenges of the contemporary struggle

Civil society in Palestine has undergone dramatic changes since the pre-Oslo period,[35] and women have become less engaged with discussions on how their own liberation struggle fits within the national one.[36] Indeed, after the last elections for the Palestinian Legislative Council in 2006, Hadeel Rizq-Qazzaz observed that women may have participated only as stand-ins for male family members, or because "they are deployed by political factions without any real political participation".[37] She also observes that NGOs purporting to support women's political participation were in fact concerned only with "well-known women activists who had both the ambition and the experience to run for elections ... target[ing] only their own members or members of established political parties" while ignoring women who organized at the grassroots level.[38]

Academic analyses of the contemporary struggle in Palestine note that today many women's organizations are scattered in their objectives and operate much more from within donor-driven global frameworks than they did in the past.[39] The result is that their agenda has become both less indigenous and less politically focused on a national liberation struggle that has the broad-based inclusion of women as a core goal.[40] They argue that among other challenges, such as the geographical divides in the occupied territory, the alienation of young women from organized resistance and the "displacement, confinement and domestication of protest",[41] Palestinian women's organizing has been subject to what they derisively label a "professionalization" or "NGOization" process, through which "a small group of nationals [employ] political space to develop their personal agendas and portfolios that [do] not in any way include or reflect people's aspirations, or achieve people's democratic and national rights".[42]

In Eileen Kuttab's view, this is not accidental. She makes a strong argument that many NGOs were deliberately created to limit the challenges expressed by democratic movements, to replace an analysis of class politics with a community development approach and to undermine and coopt leadership through the creation of technocrats. In her analysis, Palestinian women's NGOs are designed as purveyors of "programs that provide limited services to a narrow group of communities, programs that have become accountable to overseas donors instead of their own people". Their purpose, she argues, is to "transform internal solidarity into collaboration and subordination into the macro-economy of neo-liberalism through exploitation of the local human and material resources".[43]

While their decision to work much more with formal, officially registered organizations than with grassroots constituents could indeed be seen to imply a professionalization of women's activities, the challenge is that such NGOs have largely replaced less-structured or *ad hoc* civil society organizing, drawn in the capacities of the elites and become dependent on (ever-changing) international funding parameters to such an extent that they are no longer able to set independent or longitudinal goals for their activities. All these changes, taking place as they are in an ever-less-free environment, have led to a decline in women's collective action to resist the impacts of the occupation. As the second half of this chapter shows, the different levels of Palestinian women's organizing in Jerusalem reflect an extremely diverse group of women with a broad view of their work and its purposes. Is this diversity the most helpful means to move women's activities forward into reformed institutions in the post-conflict moment? Can more effective organizing methods and donor strategies be put in place today that will facilitate a growth in women's leadership and an expansion in the activities of women's organizations beyond mere survival?

Findings of the field research

While they are all working with issues of poverty in the extremely limited economic and social spaces for women in occupied East Jerusalem, in interviews the humblest groupings, CBOs and charitable organizations, appear restricted by either a fear of being considered political or a limited capacity to articulate their political work. They do not openly engage in discussions of the occupation, party politics or patriarchy as root causes of poverty and women's exclusion. In fact, while the women who represent CBOs and charities may have a thorough understanding of the political situation in their day-to-day life, they do not articulate a political role and are unlikely to identify a connection between their work and the ways in which political issues such as the construction of the separation barrier, restrictions on movement and patriarchal control of economic and political space affect every aspect of work in occupied East Jerusalem. CBOs and charities are among the most depoliticized organizations in occupied East Jerusalem, are completely unable to identify their political partners and prove to be the most vulnerable of all the organizations surveyed.[44]

NGOs, by contrast, may outline missions and objectives which are highly political, discuss the political causes of many of the difficulties facing women and be better able to articulate and analyse (using donor vocabulary) the ways in which the occupation and patriarchy contribute to risks and obstacles for women's organizing in occupied East Jerusalem. Nonetheless, they too tend not to recognize or discuss in explicit terms their political role. Unlike CBOs, which appear to lack the capacity to analyse the political situation in such a way that they can develop campaigns, programmes and policies effectively, NGOs have the ability but hesitate to use it. The implications of this observation will be discussed in more detail below.

Feminist NGOs and specialized NGOs and service providers are the most likely of those surveyed to demonstrate an understanding of the ways in which life in occupied East Jerusalem is politicized. They tend to be more likely to recognize their political role, and simultaneously demonstrate a much more thorough knowledge of the vocabulary and mechanics of the donor system which enables them to negotiate it fairly effectively. Their specialization, rather than detracting from their comprehensive understanding of the situation of women in occupied East Jerusalem, seems to be accompanied by an enhanced understanding of what it means for their organizations to undertake political activities. They are clear about the ways in which political issues permeate almost every aspect of their work. They are able to outline how the occupation, internal Palestinian political divisions and patriarchy affect women, and the ways in which the absence of political outlets and counterparts has made their work (which in many cases would normally be carried out by governmental institutions) necessary. They prove to be among the most politicized organizations working with women in occupied East Jerusalem.

Interestingly, and in confirmation of Eileen Kuttab's perspective that the Palestinian women's movement is becoming increasingly alienated from its "historical political culture", some respondents were confused about what "political" could mean in light of what they see as pressure to be non-partisan and avoid political factionalism.[45] Some considered the political to be confined to the sphere of politicians, political parties, governments, nationalism or, perhaps, mass demonstrations – but not to be something that affected women privately. The extent to which many of the organizations interviewed sought to disassociate themselves from anything political was palpable, and the fear associated with any political organizing in occupied East Jerusalem was very real. This confirmed Kuttab's observation that there is now a deep "structural imbalance" between "women's rights vis-a-vis women's practical and strategic needs, versus requirements for the national liberation struggle".[46] It was also clear from discussions that Palestinian women (including those currently active in women's organizations) have not heard about or benefited sufficiently from feminist and post-colonial forays into political science, which have produced invigorating new perspectives on how everyday, quotidian experience is also worthy of analysis as political activism.[47]

Ultimately, the research demonstrates that, despite international tools such as SCRs 1325 and 1889 and their call to include women's interests in peace processes, there are a number of factors causing women organizing in Jerusalem to disassociate themselves from formal politics, with the result that the historically strong women's movement is disintegrating along with the remnants of a coherent national struggle for liberation. First, women's organizations have come to associate "politics" with political parties and a political elite that is deemed untrustworthy and non-representative. Second, they are convinced that expressing a political opinion will undermine their relationships with their beneficiaries, their partners and the donor community. As Shireen Hassim accurately puts it, they are enduring "the reduction of the women's movement to a 'development' partner".[48] Third, the traditionally patriarchal nature of society and men's domination of public politics means that only elite women in well-connected families feel entitled (and are economically able) to take an active political role. Fourth, political involvement when living under occupation and annexation in East Jerusalem can and does lead to reprisals and violence against those who insist on exercising their rights to political voice. Fifth, the broader impacts of the Oslo Agreement and the continued unwillingness of the international community to curtail Israel's escalating territorial expansionism (which relies explicitly on a divided and fragmented Palestinian population) take their toll on a daily basis.

Contemporary Palestinian society, Kuttab observes, "suffer[s] not only from a colonial occupation but also from a fragmented political system, erosion of civil life, profound disintegration of social networks and class polarization".[49] Indeed, the field research shows that CBOs, charities, NGOs, feminist NGOs and specialized NGOs and service providers are choosing not to work together on a joint platform, operate with different vocabularies, have different areas of expertise and are unlikely to engage in conversations about the political role they might play together. Today, CBOs and charities are not given the opportunity to develop their analytical capacities or engage politically. NGOs underreport their political work and deny the extent of their political engagement, while the political work of most feminist and specialized NGOs and service providers is isolated from that of other organizations working to realize Palestinian liberation.

The isolation between each stratum of women's organizations is compounded by divisions between organizations which are forced to focus on survival-level interventions and those that work, perhaps with less urgency, on longer-term political agendas. Those working on a survival level must make more formal political work a secondary issue, despite the fact that their interventions are only temporary solutions to a problem which is growing precisely because of a lack of durable political solutions. Yet organizations with the funding and mandate to engage in long-term political work are unable to take on a political role because of their dependence on the whims of donors. These observations support the feminist analysis of Kuttab, Jab and Shalhoub-Kevorkian, which shows that the domestication and diversion of women's activities through donor funding are yet another manifestation of external efforts to derail and control Palestinian aspirations for democratic, inclusive and sovereign statehood – a response most recently seen again since May 2011 with the announcement of political unification.

Increasing religious conservatism is also playing a part in undermining women's activism. CBOs and charities do not always wish to be seen as channelling women's leadership, and have become isolated from other organizations that still try to cling to visions of empowering women. Ironically, they remain the most deeply embedded in their communities and focus on a client base which represents the poorest and most marginalized women in Jerusalem. By contrast, while general, feminist and specialized NGOs and service providers offer sophisticated insights into women's vulnerability, they are unable to engage with their immediate communities with the same effectiveness as CBOs.

Impacts of absent governmental and political counterparts

The ongoing colonization and Judaization of Jerusalem mean that Palestinians living there have little direct contact with their leadership. As a result, CBOs, charities, NGOs and specialized NGOs and service providers were largely unable to name governmental and political counterparts and could not identify the authorities to which political issues, as well as concerns regarding risks and obstacles, can be brought. They also expressed the view that their political and governmental representatives are partisan, non-representative and corrupt. They feared that working with acknowledged political structures could lead to alienation from the donor community and local actors.

The unwillingness of CBOs and charities to engage with political issues meant that the majority did not identify anyone to whom they could bring political questions. The highly charged nature of the Palestinian political system means that anyone working with political parties, governments or organizations can be perceived as partisan, which may alienate members of the community, local NGO partners and donors. The implications of this impasse are clear and troubling: women's organizations in Jerusalem do not easily find support from those who are formally meant to represent their interests. This is why there is currently "a desperate paucity of independent-minded and outspoken leaders at both local and national levels and a sense of directionless in how people see and use political processes and structures", a problem which is even more exaggerated among the poorest and most marginalized women.[50]

Women's and feminist NGOs expressed similar difficulties with or fears of identifying political or governmental counterparts. While it would appear logical that NGOs would bring their political issues to political leaders, the research showed that internal divisions between the two main parties, Fatah and Hamas, make it risky to approach any political leader or use any government institution. Furthermore, the Israeli annexation of Jerusalem and the military regime in place to suppress unified Palestinian resistance create innumerable obstacles to political action in Jerusalem for Palestinians who are also active in the West Bank and Gaza, as many larger NGOs are. Women's organizations face a terrible double bind: political and governmental counterparts are not easily accessible to Jerusalemites who live under the administrative control of Israel, but even if it were possible to make better use of their political representatives, women's organizations would not do so, fearing that involvement with these actors might pose a significant risk to donor, partner and beneficiary support. A core intention of SCRs 1325 and 1889 – to help women make visible their peacemaking strategies and actions – would therefore seem unavailable to Palestinian women in Jerusalem. They really do not have anyone effective to whom they can report what they do or from whom they could elicit support to enlarge these interventions and make them more strategic and useful.

For those organizations that do identify their work as being political, another challenge was visible: they identified as important a plethora of political and governmental counterparts in a number of different environments. Indeed, they had such a broad understanding of who their political counterparts might be that they seemed to lack clarity about who to work with. The instability in Jerusalem and the large international observer community the conflict attracts mean that there are countless people to lobby. Organizations listed government representatives (from EU governments, Turkey, Libya, Morocco, Jordan, Saudi Arabia), foreign diplomats, Palestinian Legislative Council members (although problems with this body were emphasized), Knesset members, ministers and Palestinian negotiators among their potential counterparts. Some respondents insisted that they would not deal with Knesset members or Israeli government bodies as a means to avoid normalization.

Many organizations were able to recognize the strategic shortcomings of working with multiple counterparts, and spoke instead of a need for stronger political representation and institutionalized mechanisms of support. These organizations were acutely aware of the absence of government institutions that would be capable of acting as counterparts. Indeed, many only exist as specialized organizations because they provide services that cannot be delivered by the absent Palestinian government and are denied by the Israeli government to Palestinians living in Jerusalem.

It becomes clear that, when faced with political issues, risks and obstacles, Palestinian organizations working with women in Jerusalem are at a loss as to who can or will provide them with the support they need. Nor do they know whose support they can rightfully demand. They are profoundly shaped by what Jad and Kuttab have described as a depoliticization process through which their energy and attention are directed into "dealing with aspects of women's lives such as health, education, legal literacy, income generation, advocacy of rights and research" that cannot be properly addressed in the absence of a state.[51] Trying to provide services that women need but do not officially get, however, means that the most capable and dynamic women are fully occupied and have little time left for political work, whether this takes the form of analysis or lobbying. They know and care little about their potential political support base, while those who should be offering them political support know and care even less about them.

Language and knowledge of international standards

An ongoing challenge is that SCR 1325 is not, "in itself, something that ordinary women can wield effectively as a means to describe their peace and security-building work. Nor does it enhance their existing capacities to apprehend and use the sophisticated language and political procedures that form the currency of high-level negotiations ..."[52] The research showed, starkly, that CBOs do not have the capacity to use the language of the donor community. They tend not to know or engage with international protocols such as SCRs 1325 and 1889 and the Convention on the Elimination of All Forms of Discrimination against Women (CEDAW). While none of the CBOs interviewed had knowledge of these international protocols, when the content of each was explained, the reaction of CBOs was generally to eschew the political protocols. Instead of wishing to become more competent to engage with the language of international standards, CBOs expressed an intention to continue to work with the familiar: the protections for women provided by religion and culture.

Adopting the language of international standards was, perhaps rightfully, frowned upon by CBOs, as they all know of instances in which CBOs have made the jump from CBO to NGO, adopted the language of the international system and ended up removed from their greatest strength – their ability to engage directly with the community. On the other hand, the inability of CBOs to communicate in the same language that dominates the discourse among women's and feminist NGOs, some charitable organizations and specialized NGOs and service providers may be undermining their ability to contribute to a united and comprehensive women's movement. It certainly does cut them off from sources of funding offered by donors who expect a certain type of approach and level of engagement with those they support.

Unlike CBOs, more than half of the women's NGOs surveyed were aware of SCR 1325 and CEDAW. Such organizations used these international standards widely in programming, advocacy, training, media campaigns and work supporting equality and women's rights. Specialized NGOs and service providers are also aware of SCR 1325 and CEDAW. Despite being aware of these international standards, not all of the organizations used them; but those which did had incorporated them into projects, programming and training. However, a challenge they all seemed to face was that adopting donor and NGO vocabulary meant diminishing their ability to communicate with and represent ordinary women rather than the elite and the technocrats. Being able to navigate between the two levels of localized community support and sophisticated international discourse is clearly an obstacle that women's organizations are unable to surmount without considerable effort; and given how difficult it is to do even their essential supportive work, they prefer to focus their time and energies in that direction.

Conclusions

Security Council Resolutions 1325 and 1889 call for an amplification of women's voices in matters concerning peace and security, urging the inclusion of women's interests in national and international strategic priorities. However, this chapter shows that far from benefiting from the intentions of these ground-breaking resolutions or being able to build on their own considerable history of organizing, Palestinian women's groups in Jerusalem are facing intense depoliticization and silencing at a crucial moment in the Israeli-Palestinian peace process.

In Jerusalem, women's well-being is negatively affected by challenges such as the deepening occupation of the Palestinian part of the city, displacement and deportation, an ineffectual and non-representative political system and an entrenched patriarchal structure that stifles women's creativity and energy. Organizations working with women in Jerusalem have opportunities denied to besieged women in Gaza and rural women isolated by the impassable illegal settlement network that carves up the West Bank. Nonetheless, they face risks and obstacles that are unique within the oPt, and have limited access to political and governmental counterparts to whom they could bring their issues and grievances. They face constant threats to their continued existence in Jerusalem. Yet they hesitate to engage with the big political questions of the day, even when these are key contributors to the social, political and economic hardships facing women. To the detriment of those they serve, they leave the root causes of many problems affecting women unaddressed and have a hard time thinking about how they can mobilize to challenge the status quo. They have become so consumed with the difficulties of survival and the daily problems that prevent them from doing their work effectively that they no longer even question why non-governmental service providers in Jerusalem have proliferated and whether they should, in fact, all continue to provide services that are the usual duty of the state.

At this critical point in their history, Palestinian women need to move well beyond service provision. Evidence from other protracted liberation struggles, of which South Africa is probably the closest example, teaches that they will need to have clearly articulated opinions on a number of issues, including the restoration of human rights through a just end to the Israeli military occupation, the achievement of Palestinian sovereignty and independence, inclusive state-building, citizenship rights, gender-equitable institutional reform, social transformation, demilitarization and peacebuilding.[53] Yet Jerusalem-based women's organizations, despite their long experience of participating in the struggle for Palestinian liberation, currently lack a national strategy for the emancipation of women within the state-building process and have no effective means to influence the high-level political discussions of the day.

It is precisely because they are so diverse and disengaged from each other that the work of women's organizations in Jerusalem is weakened. Their inability to communicate effectively among themselves is one factor in undermining a united political women's movement for all Palestinians. South Africa shows that when they demand the right to be equal partners representing the views of all women, no matter how diverse they are, women's organizations minimize the risks and obstacles they face and become more effective at lobbying and mounting an organized challenge to their political leaders and to entrenched male dominance more broadly.[54] The donor community also needs to recognize and overcome its tendency to disempower, even if not intentionally, women's organizations and to develop more effective funding responses that value and encourage women's public political participation.

Whereas Jerusalem women's organizations are now increasingly divided, working in isolation of each other and fearful of losing funding or being considered partisan or factional, an inclusive movement recognizing a number of very different women's organizations as one unified interest group could help to bridge the gaps created by NGOization, donor domination and limitations on certain organizations' ability to connect to the grassroots; obviate the need to focus solely on survival-based interventions; and address the isolation that often faces those who do take up the political cudgels in a conflict zone. By working as an inclusive political movement, Palestinian women (both women in the youth movements that seem to be gaining increasing coherence in the oPt and older women with years of activist experience) might find a means to address their fear of partisan politics and elitism within the Palestinian political system. This is an essential first step in rejuvenating a unified Palestinian liberation struggle with women's liberation as one of its key aims.

Beyond the women's movement itself, respondents made it very clear that they are not being heard by the donor community and feel that their organizations should be partners in policy dialogue. Local and international donor discourses contribute to a feeling among women's organizations that the political is an almost taboo subject to be discussed in hushed tones. SCRs 1325 and 1889 could be useful in overcoming this state of affairs if they were taken up by the donor community and other international actors as a means to recognize, fund and promote a united and inclusive movement for women's empowerment as an important strategic priority;[55] again, there is good experience of cooperation between donors and local women in the South African women's movement from which to learn.[56] Palestinian women are also watching contemporary developments in the Arab world, in Egypt particularly, with great interest, to see whether any precedents will be set upon which they can capitalize in their own activism.[57]

No one escapes the power of politics in Jerusalem, with daily events affirming how vital it is to understand, document and report on everything that happens to Palestinians as a means to counter the ever-enlarging force of the occupying power. Politics, here, has never been confined to the halls of government, but permeates every aspect of every Palestinian's everyday life. To say that they need a politically nuanced approach to their work currently seems burdensome to women's organizations, and is certainly a harsh reminder of a long history of failed resistance, failed peace, a corrupt political elite, factional violence and partisan politics. In such constraining circumstances, developing a women-centred politics and political participation should be seen as an urgent necessity and a previously untried means to challenge the impasse in the elite and male-dominated political processes currently claiming world headlines. As Shireen Hassim observes of the South African process:

> Political transition shows that the degree of inclusion – who gets a place at the table – shapes both the nature and the scope of institutions ... as well as their long-term legitimacy. Formal processes of negotiation tend to favour political and social groupings that are already organised at national level, or have access to national actors. Poorly organised and resourced groupings, such as women and the rural poor, tend to be absent from institutional decision-making processes.[58]

The diversity of women's organizations in Jerusalem may be their greatest strength, but channelling that strength effectively will require a commitment to unified action whose scope is unprecedented in Palestinian history. If they succeed in this goal, given the desperate straits in which Palestinians find themselves today and with particular resonance given contemporary political changes in the Middle East, Palestinian women will stand as a beacon of hope for all women facing the challenge of political, social and economic exclusion in conflict and post-conflict zones around the globe. Other experiences offer insights and warnings that, if they are taken seriously, could substantially change the outcome of the hoped-for post-conflict period for Palestinian women. The most important of these is that the transition period can offer unprecedented opportunities to advance women's citizenship claims, but only if resistance from entrenched male elites is intentionally countered, including through careful donor policies.

Gendered state-building cannot result from technocratic fixes: it is an explicitly political process and requires the broad-based engagement of all who will stake a claim to citizenship in the post-conflict state.[59] In Palestine, women's sophisticated analysis and long-term activism have more than readied them for full partnership in building an independent state whose institutions are trusted and capable of delivering to all its citizens.

Notes

1. The state of Israel was created in 1948 through the expulsion of Palestinians from their land, an event known to Palestinians as *al-Nakbah* (the catastrophe). Israel first began to occupy more parts of the Palestinian territory in 1967, and has expanded its grip on Palestinian land ever since through an organized process of territorial expansion defined by illegal "settlement" activity and the declaration of closed military zones: around half a million Israelis now live in heavily secured enclaves in the West Bank, including East Jerusalem. The Gaza Strip remains under full military blockade. The PA's thirteenth government plan envisions the establishment of a sovereign Palestinian state along the 1967 borders by 2011; this goal is reinforced in the "National Development Plan 2011–2013: Establishing the State, Building Our Future", which is cited here. This chapter, finalized in January 2012, draws inferences for Palestinian women from the political upheavals taking place in the Middle East and North Africa where these are relevant and able to be analysed, for example in the decision by Hamas and Fatah to proceed with unification talks after four years of bitter rivalry and separation.

2. The committee meeting was held in Brussels on 13 April 2011. The citation is from the chair's summary, available at www.ldf.ps/documentsShow.aspx?ATT_ID=3878.

3. For media accounts see "Palestine Rivals Fatah and Hamas on Verge of Historic Deal", *The Guardian*, 27 April 2011, available at www.guardian.co.uk/world/2011/apr/27/palestine-rivals-fatah-hamas-deal; "Questions About 'Hamas-Fatah Reconciliation'", *Electronic Intifada*, 27 April 2011, available at http://electronicintifada.net/node/9879; "US Affirms Aid to Palestinians – For Now", *Reuters*, 28 April 2011, available at http://news.yahoo.com/s/nm/20110428/pl_nm/us_palestinians_israel_usa.

4. Kuttab, Eileen (2008) "Palestinian Women's Organizations: Global Cooption and Local Contradiction", *Cultural Dynamics* 20(2), pp. 99–117.

5. Partly, perhaps, as a result of space opened up in the region through the Arab Spring, Palestinians are again speaking out loudly about what they want – "elections for the Palestinian National Council that include ALL Palestinians, including the majority which does *not* live in the 1967 occupied territories", as Ali Abunimah puts it in his Electronic Intifada blog.

6. Castillejo, Clare (2010) *Militarization and Violence Against Women in Conflict Zones in the Middle East: Integrating Gender into Post-conflict State Building*, Madrid: FRIDE, p. 2.

7. All Security Council resolutions on women, peace and security can be found at www.peacewomen.org.

8. The decision to focus on Jerusalem alone was partly decided by the research team's relative ease of access to the city. It was also because Palestinians revere Jerusalem as the future capital of an independent Palestinian state; and in the face of the current internal political divide, engage more willingly with findings from there than they might do with Gaza-based research or studies conducted in the rest of the West Bank.

9. I thank Emily Scott for conducting the primary field interviews for the research on which this chapter is based (June–August 2010) and Linda Ohmann of Kvinna till Kvinna for supporting the research design intellectually and financially. However, the interpretation of the data presented in this chapter is my own and is not to be ascribed to the UN Development Programme or any other organization or individual. A briefer, less academic version of the research has been published in English and Arabic: UNDP-PAPP (2010) "Palestinian Women Organizing in Jerusalem", UNDP, October, available at www.undp.ps/en/newsroom/publications/pdf/other/womenorg.pdf.

10. Not all Palestinian women have chosen non-violent resistance. From 2002 to 2006, 10 women decided on suicide bombing as their contribution to the liberation struggle. For

more analysis see Berko, Anat and Edna Erez (2007) "Gender, Palestinian Women, and Terrorism: Women's Liberation or Oppression?", *Studies in Conflict & Terrorism* 30, pp. 493–519.

11. For a highly detailed account of Palestinian history see Farsoun, Samih K. and Naseer H. Aruri (2006) *Palestine and the Palestinians: A Social and Political History*, 2nd edn, Cambridge, MA: Westview Press. While Farsoun and Aruri offer a fairly detailed discussion of women as victims of violence and as workers, no mention is made of how women organize politically.

12. The "Arab Spring" has, however, been characterized by a high level of public visibility of women, especially young women, although this is not much commented on by Arab male leaders. Whether or not women's activism will translate into long-term gains, especially through their entry to public office, still remains to be seen. For a useful commentary see "An Arab Spring for Women", *CBS News*, 26 April 2011, available at www.cbsnews.com/stories/2011/04/26/opinion/main20057432_page2.shtml?tag=contentMain; contentBody. On the specific subject of Palestinian women's experiences, it is important to remember that they are not, of course, homogeneous. For an interesting account of Palestinian women living in Israel see Herzog, Hanna (2009) "Choice as Everyday Politics: Female Palestinian Citizens of Israel in Mixed Cities", *International Journal of Politics, Culture and Society* 22, pp. 5–21.

13. This statement is based on interviews and informal conversations the author has conducted in Jerusalem, Gaza and the West Bank from 2008 to 2010. Herzog attributes some of the power of the Palestinian women's movement to the fact that it has emerged in urban settings, which has a "liberating" impact, she argues, on Palestinian women. See Herzog, ibid., pp. 10–11.

14. Kuttab, note 4. For an account of women's struggle for education in a state of siege see Shalhoub-Kevorkian, Nadera (2008) "The Gendered Nature of Education under Siege: A Palestinian Feminist Perspective", *International Journal of Lifelong Education* 27(2), pp. 179–200.

15. Hassim, Shireen (2006) *Women's Organizations and Democracy in South Africa: Contesting Authority*, Scottsville: University of KwaZulu-Natal Press, p. 263.

16. Castillejo explores this issue in comparative case studies of Burundi, Guatemala, Kosovo, Sierra Leone and Sudan. Castillejo, Clare (2011) "Building a State that Works for Women: Integrating Gender into Post-Conflict State Building", FRIDE Working Paper No. 107, March, Madrid, available at www.gsdrc.org/go/display&type=Document&id =4112&source=rss.

17. Farsoun and Aruri, note 11, p. 227.

18. Herzog, note 12, p. 7.

19. Anderlini, Sanam (2007) *Women Building Peace: What They Do, Why It Matters*, Boulder, CO: Lynne Rienner; Cockburn, Cynthia (2007) *From Where We Stand: War, Women's Activism, and Feminist Analysis*, London: Zed Books; Farr, Vanessa (2011) "UNSCR 1325 and Women's Peace Activism in the Occupied Palestinian Territory", *International Feminist Journal of Politics* 13(4), pp. 539–556.

20. This term was coined by Goldfarb, Jeffrey C. (2006) *The Politics of Small Things: The Power of the Powerless in Dark Times*, Chicago, IL: University of Chicago Press, p. 2.

21. Farsoun and Aruri, note 11, pp. 339–341. These authors do not, however, comment on the gendered impacts of such policies, including their erasure of the agency, identity and familial power of women who are spouses and mothers.

22. In my experience, such rhetoric is generally expressed by donors in funding decisions: in project proposals much is made of the need to include a "gender analysis" and sometimes even explicit activities for women. Many donors are meant to be directed in their

funding decisions by SCR 1325 action plans decided at headquarters. However, as this chapter elucidates, there is great wariness about funding what women actually want to do, especially when such activities are seen as politically sensitive.

23. Johnson, Penny and Eileen Kuttab (2001) "Where Have All the Women (and Men) Gone? Reflections on Gender and the Second Palestinian Intifada", *Feminist Review* 69, pp. 21–43; Kuttab, note 4; Jad, Islah (2004) "The NGOization of the Arab Women's Movements", *Review of Women's Studies* 2, pp. 42–56; Shalhoub-Kevorkian, Nadera (2009) *Militarization and Violence Against Women in Conflict Zones in the Middle East: A Palestinian Case-Study*, Cambridge: Cambridge University Press; Shalhoub-Kevorkian, Nadera (2010) *Military Occupation, Trauma and the Violence of Exclusion: Trapped Bodies and Lives*, Jerusalem: YWCA.

24. Herzog, note 12, pp. 9–10. However, Shalhoub-Kevorkian (2009), ibid., paints a somewhat different picture of Palestinian women's educational opportunities.

25. See UNDP-PAPP, note 9, for an in-depth discussion of the organizations.

26. It is difficult to find published sources of information about the early women's movement in Palestine. For one recent account see Tarazi, Rima (2012) "The General Union of Palestinian Women", *This Week in Palestine* 167, March, available at www.thisweekinpalestine.com/details.php?id=1627&ed=112.

27. Kuttab, note 4. Kuttab has been writing on this issue for several years: Kuttab, Eileen (1996) "Women's Movement in Palestine", in *Arab Women Facing a New Era*, Cairo: Arab Women's Publishing House (in Arabic).

28. Farsoun and Aruri, note 11, p. 214. The Palestine Liberation Organization won widespread support.

29. Shalhoub-Kevorkian (2009), note 23, p. 11.

30. Kuttab, Eileen (2009) "Palestinian Women's Organizations: Global Cooption and Local Contradiction", *Review of Women's Studies* 5, p. 67, available at http://home.birzeit.edu/wsi/images/stories/5th__issue/Palestinian_womens_organizations_Eileen_Kuttab.pdf.

31. Cited in Farsoun and Aruri, note 11, pp. 226–227.

32. The sex-specific control of men was far more violent: the Israeli army set up impromptu detention centres in schools in camps and villages and imprisoned all males between the ages of 14 and 60. See Farsoun and Aruri, note 11, p. 227.

33. Torres, Marianne (1989) "Women in the Intifada", Palestine Papers, available at www.sonomacountyfreepress.com/palestine/women2.html.

34. Kuttab, notes 4 and 30.

35. Ibid.

36. The Oslo Accords were signed in 1993 between the state of Israel and the Palestinian Liberation Organization. Intended as a means to define a peace process and establish a timeline for it, the accords did not challenge the military occupation or settlement expansion, house demolitions and other military activities in the West Bank, and in fact left Palestinians worse off than before. The accords eventually broke down and the second intifada erupted in September 2000. The Oslo Accords were negotiated and signed in the presence of a few elite men; women were neither consulted nor present in the process.

37. Rizq-Qazzaz, Hadeel (2007) "The Role of Non-Governmental Organizations in Supporting Palestinian Women in Elections", *Review of Women's Studies* 4, pp. 79–81.

38. Ibid., p. 83.

39. See Kuttab, note 30, p. 70. This may indicate that policies such as SCR 1325 national action plans, which are set in capital cities, may not in fact be responsive enough to women's localized needs, especially in politically sensitive settings such as the oPt. More research is needed on this subject.

40. Jad, note 23.

41. Johnson, Penny (2010) "Displacing Palestine: Palestinian Householding in an Era of Asymmetrical War", *Politics and Gender* 6, p. 298.
42. Kuttab, note 30, pp. 65–66.
43. Ibid., pp. 66–67. Kuttab's views are perhaps more strongly expressed than those of other analysts (but see also Jab, Shalhoub-Kevorkian and other Palestinian feminists cited in this chapter), but they capture the strength of the anger felt by politically engaged Palestinians as their attempts to make autonomous decisions or organize independently are continually thwarted, usually by the Israeli-US alliance and an ambivalent European Union. The responses to the latest announcement of internal Palestinian political unity are just the latest iteration of this habit.
44. The majority of Palestinians in East Jerusalem have residence but not citizenship rights; the PA has no jurisdiction over Palestinians in East Jerusalem, who are therefore not represented by any political entity. Furthermore, the Israeli Knesset is increasingly restricting the rights of Palestinians inside Israel. As recently as 29 March 2011, a citizenship revocation law was passed, among several sets of laws targeting Palestinians in just one week. See http://uprootedpalestinians.blogspot.com/2011/03/knesset-passes-racist-citizenship.html.
45. Kuttab, note 30, p. 71.
46. Ibid.
47. Herzog, note 12.
48. Hassim, note 15, p. 263.
49. Kuttab, note 30, p. 73.
50. Farr, note 19, p. 543; see also Johnson and Kuttab, note 23.
51. Jad, note 23; see also Johnson and Kuttab, note 23.
52. Farr, note 19, p. 542.
53. See Hassim, note 15; Gouws, Amanda (ed.) (2005) *(Un)thinking Citizenship: Feminist Debates in Contemporary South Africa*, Landsdowne: University of Cape Town Press.
54. See Hassim, note 15, particularly Chapter 5.
55. Castillejo's comparative study of gender in post-conflict state-building makes precisely this argument. Castillejo, note 6.
56. Hassim, note 15.
57. I am grateful to the academic staff of Birzeit University's Institute for Women's Studies, as well as to non-academic women activists in the oPt and the region, for ongoing discussions on this subject as events unfold.
58. See Hassim, Shireen (2002) "Negotiating Spaces: Women in South Africa's Transition to Democracy", available at http://wiserweb.wits.ac.za/PDF%20Files/wirs%20-%20hassim.PDF, p. 15.
59. Castillejo, note 6, particularly pp. 18–19.

12

Women's participation in political decision-making and recovery processes in post-conflict Lebanon

Kari H. Karamé

The empowerment of women is seen as a crucial element of all social and economic development during post-conflict transitions, and the success of this process is further seen as a basic requirement for all sustainable peacebuilding. Still, while women are active in most functions during armed conflicts, both civilian and military, and also form the majority of the militants in peace movements, they are usually marginalized from decision-making levels in post-conflict peacebuilding processes.[1]

The post-conflict phase is rarely peaceful, and one of the priorities is therefore to establish security and protection of civilians. In this period women often experience a backlash, which puts them back into their traditional roles in society.[2] If women are not present at the peace negotiation table, neither the experiences they had during the war nor the capacities they developed will be taken into consideration in the planning and construction of the future. The war(s) in Lebanon during the years 1975–1990 did not lead to a comprehensive peace agreement, as the Taëf Agreement signed in October 1989 focused on a modified pattern of power sharing and the disarming of the militias. No women were invited to the negotiation table, and Lebanese women thus had no agreement to lean upon to claim their place in the post-conflict reconstruction process.

It is generally assumed that women and men may have different priorities in post-conflict politics. Many authors argue that women's entrance into the political arena after a war has changed the nature of the political agenda itself. Reproductive health and choice, nutrition, equality in education and work, family-friendly policies and environmental considera-

Defying victimhood: Women and post-conflict peacebuilding, Schnabel and Tabyshalieva (eds), United Nations University Press, 2012, ISBN 978-92-808-1201-5

tions are only some of the topics that women have either brought to or highlighted at both national and international levels.[3] These should not be framed as "women issues" only, as they are of great importance for the well-being of the whole society. It may therefore also be asked whether limited participation of women in political decision-making will have an impact on a state's priorities in the post-conflict rebuilding process.

This chapter uses the war and post-conflict situation in Lebanon as the background for a reflection on women's engagement in peace and recovery processes. It first explores the main obstacles to women's participation in public decision-making, and argues that these are found in the patriarchal culture and the political and electoral system of the country. It then discusses the effect of an almost total absence of women from public decision-making on the priorities of the reconstruction process and on women's peacebuilding activities, which have subsequently not been recognized and supported by international and national actors.

Lebanon – An old country, but a young state

History and population

Lebanon is situated at the threshold between the Mediterranean and the Arab world, bordering on Israel to the south, and Syria to east and north. The population is composed of 17 different religious communities and is today divided into approximately 35 per cent Christians and 65 per cent Muslims. Each of these two main groups is again subdivided into sects, with one dominating Christian community – the Maronites – and two Muslim communities of almost equal size – the Sunnites and the Shiites. The country gives refuge to some 350,000 Palestinians, mainly Sunni Muslims. The size of the population and the balance between its various religious sects have always been subjects of discussion and political discord.

The origin of the modern republic of Lebanon was the creation of the autonomous province of Mount Lebanon in 1861, while it was still under the rule of the Ottoman Empire. In 1919 the country became a French mandate, and in 1920 the Lebanese Republic was proclaimed within its actual borders. In 1943 the country finally gained its independence. The majority of Christians and Muslims had divergent views on the orientation and identity of the new state, in favour of either Lebanese nationalism or Arab nationalism. This resulted in a fault-line between the two communities on both political and social levels. A uniting factor was the use of Arabic as the official language of the state.

The Lebanese political system

Traditionally, political power was in the hands of a few notable families within each religious community. The late Oxford-based Lebanese historian Albert Hourani called this "a Lebanese feudal system, a hierarchy of families having formal relations with each other".[4] The purpose was to balance the interests of these so-called "big families", their clients, their communities and their districts.

In each constituency a certain number of seats in parliament are distributed among the different sects, according to their relative share of the population. An electoral list should therefore contain candidates from several sects, and a strong list in this context means a list with candidates enjoying large popular support in all the sects and sponsored by a sure winner. People usually vote for the whole list, and newcomers thus have the best chances of success when they run on a "strong list".

This form for power sharing became the pattern of the constitution of 1926, and later for the National Pact of 1943. The latter was supposed to guarantee the rights of the respective religious communities, and to assert Lebanese independence and sovereignty. The result was a weak state whose inhabitants' primordial identity is with family and sect.

According to the National Pact, all political offices should be distributed on a sectarian basis, and seats in parliament allocated between the different religious communities and regions. Within this framework emerged "a highly exclusive political circle that was composed of elected and appointed representatives of the various sects who had a common interest in maintaining the status quo".[5] In addition the family ties within the political elite were close: in the 1968–1972 parliament, 43 per cent of the deputies were sons, grandsons or cousins of either former or present deputies.[6]

During the 1950s and 1960s important changes took place within the Lebanese population. The Shiite community outnumbered both the Maronites and the Sunnites, leading to pressure to adjust the mode of political representation to reflect this new reality. The cities – in particular Beirut – grew rapidly, from 50 per cent of the population living in urban areas in 1970 to 85 per cent in 2002. Among the urbanites, the politically active section of the population had expanded and the newcomers turned to ideologies more than to sectional interests. However, due to the continuous lack of security and the problems related to rapid urbanization, people turned for protection and services to parties or organizations that "expressed their own identity" and thereby strengthened them.[7] Hence parties and organizations also took on a confessional character, even those which did not have this in their original political programme.

They were to become the main political and armed bodies during the war from 1975 to 1990, with Hezbollah from 1982 onward.

The wars

Even the nature of the wars in Lebanon has been a subject of disagreement, and they have been given many names: civil war, the wars of others, rounds or events. The conflicts had both a national and a regional aspect, but were played out within a national context of competing identities, diverging views on national orientation and power struggles. These dissensions turned into confrontations after the Palestinian Liberation Organization moved its headquarters from Jordan to Lebanon in the early 1970s, and made the country a base for its fight against Israel. In reaction, the Jewish state invaded Lebanese territory twice, in 1978 and 1982, and occupied a zone along the border until the end of May 2000. Despite the regional aspect, the war has usually been presented – in an oversimplified way – as a conflict between Christians and Muslims, even though almost everybody has been fighting each other, as well as being allies in a continually changing pattern.[8]

When the war broke out in April 1975, the Lebanese Army was confined to barracks to prevent it from breaking up along sectarian lines. The vacuum created led to the appearance of militias that represented the different political trends in the country at the time. In the course of the war the state lost most of its prerogatives, and functions like tax gathering, control over local security, hospitals and food distribution were in many places taken over by the militias, thus increasing their power. Each militia had a hard core of professional combatants, but could also mobilize civilians – mostly men, but also women – during periods of combat.

Lebanon emerged from the war as a devastated country and state: its economy had fallen into shambles, public administration functioned only partly and the physical infrastructure was literally in ruins. One-quarter of the population – mostly male professionals and skilled workers – had left the country. The unemployment rate was assessed at 40 per cent of the active population.[9] More than half the population had been forced to leave their homes due to shelling, snipers or the risk of being kidnapped, and 25 per cent were displaced for longer periods, some of them permanently.[10] The war in 2006 gave another severe blow to the economy, with great destruction of infrastructure, private homes, places of work and property.

The human losses were enormous. From 1975 to 1990, 150,000 people – or 5 per cent of the resident population – lost their lives. More than

300,000 were maimed or injured, and around 100,000 of them were disabled for life.[11] Some 350 civilians were killed in the Israeli-occupied border zone during the years 1990–2000,[12] and more than a thousand during the war in 2006. Landmines and cluster bombs still kill and maim civilians in the south.

Although the war(s) took place in a multi-confessional country and led to the displacement of hundreds of thousands of inhabitants, there are few traces of gender-based violence in either popular narratives or academic publications. The indexes of Shehadeh,[13] the most comprehensive work on women and war in Lebanon, and Collings on peace and reconstruction[14] include no references to rape, mass rape, sexual violence or harassment. It is difficult to imagine that these did not happen at all, but there may have been less than in other conflict areas. This may tell us something about the nature of the conflict, whether or not it aimed at a definitive separation of the different communities. But it may also well be that women who suffered from gender-based violence preferred not to tell, out of fear of the reaction of the traditional and patriarchal society.

The economic and material consequences for Lebanese society were many and heavy. The middle class that constituted the backbone of the society has shrunk; only some of the internally displaced persons have returned to their homes; the traditional pattern of coexistence of people with different religions has faded; and emigration and the death of many young men during the war has led to an imbalance in the numbers of unmarried men and women.

In accordance with the Taëf Agreement (1989), the number of seats in parliament was augmented to 128, equally distributed between Muslims and Christians. At the same time the power of the president (always a Maronite) was reduced and shared equally with the prime minister (always a Sunni Muslim) and the president of the parliament (always a Shiah Muslim). This – and the disarming of the militias – should establish the internal conditions for peace. But many observers feel that the agreement cemented the profound divisions in post-conflict Lebanon, instead of building bridges across the fault-lines, as it did not address the sectarian nature of the political system.[15]

The Taëf Agreement was rejected by large parts of the Lebanese population, mainly among the Christians. One reason was that Syria was given the role as the main supervisor of the terms agreed upon. Syrian troops were deployed in Lebanon in 1976 to separate the belligerent parties and became the main powerbroker in the country. The role of Syria in Lebanon's public affairs and the timing of the withdrawal of the Syrian soldiers had become another question dividing the Lebanese people.[16] The agreement did not address the reconstruction of the country.

Political representation in post-conflict Lebanon

As an immediate consequence of the Taëf Agreement, the old mechanisms of exclusion from or inclusion in politics continued into the post-war period. Many political parties were weakened by inner power struggle, while many traditional elite families made a spectacular return to the political arena. Attitudes towards Syria's role became a new element of exclusion or inclusion in politics. In her study of the 1996 elections in the Mount Lebanon governorate, Harik notes that Christian members of the post-war regime needed to come from the pro-Syrian segment of the community or families whose neutrality was not suspect, while members of other communities were prevented from running for election. The newcomers owed their entrance into parliament to either personal wealth or power bases built up during the war. As Harik notes, "This practice reveals the manner in which list leaders evolve inclusionary and exclusionary mechanisms of their own that have little to do with ideological or programmatic concerns."[17] After 2005, being included in either the 8 March or the 14 March movements has become almost a necessity to run successfully for parliament. Both men and women who do not fit into the pattern were excluded from political participation by these mechanisms. Women in addition have to overcome the barriers posed by the rules of patriarchy, which prefer to see a man at the head of the family, the clan and finally the state.

Women in Lebanese society

When the war erupted in 1975, Lebanese society was – under a modern occidental mantle – still a traditional one, with a neat division into female-private and male-public spheres. Both Christian and Muslim women were socially defined by patriarchal social and cultural norms, as daughters, wives and mothers of men. Each religious community has its own family law, giving different rights to women concerning inheritance, divorce and child custody. Other civil rights, like having your own passport and obtaining it without a male relative's permission, having a personal bank account or opening a business without a male tutor, were granted to women in national civil law, but only as late as the 1990s.[18] Lebanese women still cannot give their nationality to their husband if he is a foreigner, or to their common children.

Girls in Lebanon have had fairly easy access to education, but disparities exist between urban and rural areas, social classes and probably between religious communities. If parents cannot afford to send all their children to school, they prefer to send their sons, who are the future heads of family and should take care of their parents and unmarried sisters.

Education was available to girls of the social elite from the end of the eighteenth century, followed by the opening of Christian missionary schools and colleges in the nineteenth century, and private schools established by local inhabitants. Some 5,000 girls were studying in newly established schools all over Lebanon at around this time.[19] In 1878 the Makassed Philanthropic and Islamic Association founded the first Muslim school for girls, as a response to the many foreign missionary schools.[20]

By the beginning of the twentieth century some privileged women started to seek higher education abroad, and most returned home to work in Lebanon, in professions varying from medicine to nuclear physics and history. They were few, but important role models for the younger female generation who had by then gained better access to education in their own country.

The development of a public educational system took off after the declaration of independence in 1943. Schools were built all over the country, and by 1973 the total number of students in elementary and secondary schools, both private and public, was 665,301, of whom slightly less than half at each level were girls.[21] The Lebanese (State) University was opened in 1951 and, because no tuition fees are charged, gave new groups of the poorer segments of society access to higher education. This was in particular an advantage to girls, because families with limited economic resources usually gave priority to the education of boys.[22] Still, according to the educational statistics report of 1972–1973, there were 14 institutions of higher education visited by 32,230 students, but only 5,600 of them were girls.[23]

Despite the war, educational reform continued in Lebanon. The gender gap in enrolment was narrowed, and female enrolment has become slightly higher than that of males at the preparatory and secondary stages of education. The *Arab Human Development Report 2002* explains the rise in enrolment rates and the curbing of illiteracy during the 25 years when Lebanon was in a state of war as an outcome of an undeclared partnership between the public and private sectors of education and the determination on the part of Lebanese families to get their children educated.[24] A complementary explanation may be found in the nature of the conflict, when periods of tension and combat alternated with calmer periods, allowing schools and universities to function according to the same rhythm.[25] Women's enrolment in higher education today is close to 50 per cent on average; but despite an increasing number of women studying medicine, engineering, journalism and business, most women study literature, education and social sciences, preparing them "for gender-segregated, and hence socially acceptable, employment in the service sector".[26]

Unfortunately, the illiteracy rate has also risen, from 9.6 per cent in the early 1970s to 13.6 per cent in 1996, of whom around two-thirds are women.[27] These apparently incompatible figures reflect the growing socio-economic disparities in post-conflict Lebanon.

Lebanese women's way into the labour force has been hard for both educated and non-educated, due to the traditional pattern of gender roles, where the husband is the breadwinner of the family and the wife takes care of domestic affairs. Between 1970 and 2011 the share of women in the workforce increased from 19 per cent[28] to 27 per cent.[29] Women have slowly made their way into most professions, but rarely into senior posts. It was not until the middle of the 1990s that a woman was appointed as *mudir 'amm* (general manager) of the Ministry of Social Affairs. The rest of the public administration is marked by a dearth of women in senior decision-making positions, except in professions where women are in a majority, like nursing and health. In some areas, like the media, women generally constitute 35–50 per cent of the workforce.[30] More education, demographic changes resulting in a surplus of women between the ages of 25 and 45, and the current socio-economic situation are among the factors that have led more women into the job market. Still, these figures show that women in Lebanon represent an underutilized and underestimated source of labour capacities.[31]

Lebanese women's agency during the war

The war led to fundamental changes in women's lives and roles in society. Women from all religious communities became involved in the war in many ways, varying from combat positions (the few) to supportive functions in different militias, activities within civil society and family and engagement in pacifist movements. These activities brought them into the public sphere to a much higher extent than before.

Engagement in the militias was facilitated by the fact that active involvement in warfare seems to have been to a large extent a "family affair", where brothers and sisters, cousins, uncles and parents fought on the same side. Thus when young girls and women left the private sphere, they were usually close to a male relative who could guarantee their moral conduct in this traditional society.[32]

A number of young girls received military training and took part in combat, some of them for up to 11 years. All the militias had women in their ranks; but taking an active part in combat seems to have been most developed on the so-called Christian side. As the war went on and the militias turned into paramilitary hierarchic organizations, women became more and more marginalized as soldiers, and moved to women's traditional supportive functions behind the lines, such as logistics, messing and medical service.[33]

The vast majority of Lebanese women saw it as their main responsibility to bring their family safely through the turmoil of war. Half the Lebanese population had to leave their homes for safer areas for shorter or longer periods, many of them several times, adding to the sense of insecurity and instability. The pre-war pattern of religious coexistence was rapidly replaced by Christian and Muslim areas, and the capital Beirut was cut by a demarcation "Green Line" into the west part, mainly Muslim, and the east part, mainly Christian.

The economic situation deteriorated dramatically for many families due to the loss of income, death or disappearance of the main breadwinner. The number of women-headed families grew, reaching 25 per cent of households in some regions.[34] During these years of ordeal, the most stable assistance the Lebanese civilian population could count on came from their relatives, religious communities and the socio-medical apparatus of the nearest militia, whereas the state apparatus was quasi-absent.

Women were very active in assistance networks and non-governmental organizations (NGOs), both local and international. More than 130 Lebanese NGOs were created to take care of the numerous victims of war, orphans, handicapped and internally displaced persons.[35] Women also engaged in pacifist movements that worked across the dividing lines. Dressed in white, they met on several occasions from both sides of the demarcation line in Beirut as a way to express their rejection of the division of the capital and its people, triggering the anger of the militias on both sides. Their peacemaking role had a limited impact on the conflict, however, and often took place just within their respective communities, "since it requires power to make peace".[36] Some women completely changed their engagement as the war developed, from the use of arms to pacifist work. This was the case for a group of young women who had been fighting with the mainly Christian militia, the Lebanese Forces. In 1985 they laid down their arms because they disagreed with the policy of the leadership, and after a two-year period of reflection they started a pacifist movement called the Lebanese Woman. The means changed, but the aim was the same: the preservation of a free, multi-confessional Lebanon.[37]

Women's organizations rarely confronted the societal order, because this could be interpreted as going against the interests of their own families and communities. As a result, as Makdisi puts it, "the women's movements become, over the decades, more and more part of the establishment, less and less rebel and adversary".[38] They thus seem to face the same problem as many other NGOs in the country, namely the difficulty in working for a common goal across the many dividing lines of Lebanese society. The struggles for women's rights were put on hold during the war, as many women considered the survival of the nation as the most important cause.[39]

Women and political decision-making in Lebanon

Lebanese women earned their legal political rights in 1952, but until 1992 no women had ever been seated in the parliament, with the exception of Myrna Bustani, who was appointed in 1963 to finish her father's term after he died in an accident.[40]

Over the years women have entered many spheres of public life in the country, but they are still virtually absent from official political decision-making positions. Women have been members of various political parties, although in smaller numbers than men. They have been active during election campaigns, fundraising and the like, but never held positions of a decisive level in a party, except for within women's committees, if they existed.[41] In 1990 40 people were nominated to fill seats left vacant in the first post-war National Assembly. Among them, Nayla Moawad was appointed to replace her late husband, René Moawad, who was assassinated just after he became president of the republic in 1989. She was re-elected in every election until 2009, when she stepped down in favour of her son's candidacy, and has been an advocate for more women in political decision-making.

In the first post-war election in 1992, three women gained seats in parliament, two Maronite Christians and one Sunni Muslim. They all came from one of the elite families, or were related to a former, now deceased, male member of parliament. In the 2005 election six women won seats in parliament, all of them Maronites or Sunnis.[42] These elections took place in the midst of a troubled political situation following the assassination of the prime minister, Rafic Hariri. Although the number of women candidates had dropped from 34 in the 2000 elections to only 14, the result was still the highest number of women ever in the Lebanese parliament.[43]

In 2006 the National Commission on Parliamentary Electoral Law – also known as the Boutros Commission – was established. Among other questions, this commission focused on how to rectify the gender imbalance among representatives. It suggested that each party list should include at least 30 per cent female candidates. Despite intensive work of both international and national organizations with the active support of the Ministry of Interior, the female quota was shelved when a new electoral law was adopted in August 2008.[44] The elections in June 2009 saw a setback in the number of candidates and electoral victories, as only four women were elected. Three former women parliamentarians stepped down, one in favour of a male candidate and two to give way to their sons' candidacies.[45]

Women's absence from, or limited participation in, political decision-making is a general problem in Arab countries. A 2009 UN Development Programme (UNDP) report reveals alarming trends concerning the political and economic exclusion and insecurity of women in the Arab countries, where "many women are still bound by patriarchal patterns of kinship, legalised discrimination, social subordination and ingrained male dominance". Also women are routinely "abused and violated while the public looks the other way".[46] Another UNDP report suggests that human development in the Arab region needs to be assessed in a broader context than a purely economic one, encompassing education, freedom and human rights. It demonstrates how the region is hampered by three key deficits: the freedom deficit, the human capabilities/knowledge deficit relative to income and the women's empowerment deficit. Only sub-Saharan Africa has a lower score.[47] The low number of women in political decision-making positions in Lebanon may therefore be seen as a cultural phenomenon rather than a conflict-induced problem.

For many years Lebanon was among those few states that had never had a woman minister, eight of them members of the Arab League. But Lebanon's neighbours Syria and Jordan have had women in ministerial posts several times.[48] Seen against the background of Lebanon's apparently modern way of life, the relatively high level of women's education and their increasing participation in working life, and because ministers are often recruited outside the ranks of members of parliament, one would expect to find women – at least a few – in the government. As both Christian and Muslim women are seated in parliament, religion should be ruled out as an impediment to women in government. Still, it was not until 2000 that two women were appointed minister, one for education and one for social affairs. Again, the main causes are most likely to be found in Lebanese political culture and patriarchy, which accord little or no space for women in official decision-making positions, and which were perpetuated in the Taëf Agreement.

Women in the Lebanese parliament have as a rule been members or presidents of committees dealing with education, culture, social affairs and women's and children's affairs, but have also been appointed to the influential Budget and Finance Committee and the important Foreign Affairs and Emigrants Committee. This proves that once they are in parliament, they are not limited to what are traditionally seen as committees working with women's issues. They have been very engaged in the reconstruction of schools and the amelioration of access to education in every region and for students from all social levels. They have often acted as spokespersons for various organizations working on women's and children's issues. But because they are so few, they depend on their male colleagues to advocate for the cases they are promoting. Still, their presence in the most public of all national arenas, parliament, is important, as it demonstrates that women can be valuable players in the political game.

Mechanisms of exclusion and inclusion of women in political decision-making

There are no legal barriers to Lebanese women's participation in politics.[49] UNDP's 2000 report on women's political participation and good governance states that women's access to political decision-making can never be seen in isolation from their overall socio-economic status.[50] In many countries women do not possess decision-making power in the private sphere that they can transfer into the public realm.[51] This is less the case in Lebanon, where women usually have a lot of influence over the family's budget and education of children, and are the bonds of the extended family.[52] Women of elite families hold power and exercise influence in the larger society in their capacity as mother, wife, etc., of a male politician. People – mostly women – visit them and ask them to intervene in their favour when they have a request to ask of the politician.[53]

Gender mainstreaming and gender quotas are two of the many tools that have been proposed by international donors to ease the way of women into politics, but the use of such means – often assimilated with Western values – has also been the subject of discussion and discord, above all in developing countries. The question posed for women is whether to join the traditional political institutions, or to change them by means of, for instance, quotas for women. Over the last few years a majority of Arab countries have given full political rights to women, and some have introduced quotas for women's participation in politics. In Lebanon there are different opinions. The Lebanese Women's Council argues that "the quota is the best way for women to forge into politics", but other advocates for women's rights disagree because they fear that these women will come from the same ruling parties as the men, and therefore will not necessarily be able to push for women's rights.[54] As noted above, in August 2008 the Lebanese parliament approved a new electoral law, which was met with mixed feelings as two proposed reforms did not pass: lowering the voting age from 21 to 18 years, and introducing a quota for women.[55]

Lack of freedom of association in the Arab region may be another impediment for women to engage in political activities, as they can rarely count on huge women's associations to support their candidature. Women's organizations do in fact encounter particular difficulties in the rising tensions between some governments and the political Islamic groups.[56] Until this day, no woman has represented the Lebanese Shiite Muslim Hezbollah organization and political party in parliament, despite the participation of women within most fields of the organization's activities.[57] The main limitation to the influence of women's associations on broader female representation in Lebanon is the fact that they have remained a part of the very social and political patriarchal culture they are denouncing.[58] They will thus not automatically support and vote for a woman candidate.

According to Jane S. Jaquette, a number of factors determine whether women's organizations and movements can have an impact on national policy and help shape the ideological environment: a patriarchal ideology; the adoption of pluralist forms of social organization and more transparent decision-making; the importance of identity politics; the degree of religious opposition to gender reforms; and, for some post-communist countries, the association of women's equality with the negative legacy of communism.[59] Several of these factors are relevant for a discussion of the hindrances for Lebanese women's participation in political decision-making, and in particular the patriarchal ideology shared by all the country's religious communities.

Errol Miller gives a definition of patriarchy that fits easily to the family-based, patrilinear Lebanese society.[60] In his words it is a "system of reciprocal social obligations in which final authority rests with the older men of the kinship collective, who exercise that authority over its individual male and female members in the overall interest of the collective".[61] Shared identity, group solidarity, common bonds and mutual obligations differentiate patriarchal collectives from one another. Genealogy and generation combined define the younger males as the potential heirs of the older men. This was pointed out bluntly to the author in a conversation with the president of a municipal council in a village in the mountains north of Beirut. Talking about the upcoming municipal elections in 2010, the author asked him about the chances of seeing women in the council of his village. The man responded that he saw no chance of that happening, as none of the eight big families in the village would accept being represented by a woman. His answer stresses two important factors in the Lebanese gendered political culture: first, the central place that is still occupied by the traditional elite, and, second, the limits imposed by the rules of patriarchy.[62]

According to Miller, gender excludes women who become marginalized. But he also demonstrates how women "of the dominant groups" – like families of the traditional political elite in Lebanon – may be "recruited when the supply of older and younger men of the groups is insufficient to meet the demand".[63] Until now, this seems to be the main mechanism of inclusion of women in the Lebanese parliament, as demonstrated in the following example.

In an interview with the author, former member of parliament Nayla Moawad, widow of President René Moawad, told how she was persuaded to present her candidacy "on the third day after the assassination of my husband", when 4,000–5,000 members of his extended family urged her to continue her husband's work. In this way they gave the necessary legitimacy to her candidacy and later to her mandate. All through her married life she had participated in her husband's political life, but in no official capacity. She was therefore well informed about his activities, and people knew it. They also knew her. As she said: "I took over." But without saying it directly, she also pointed to another important aspect of the confidence vested in her: "My son was only 17 years old at that time, so I was the regent."[64] Nobody seemed to question her capacity to replace her husband, because as spouse and companion she had acquired a broad knowledge of how political life functions and she already knew most of the other political leaders. She is a skilled and hardworking politician who could, without any doubt, have reached the same status on her own – but only within another political culture. In 2005 six women entered parliament, among them Solange Gemayel, widow of the president-elect Bashir Gemayel who was assassinated in 1982, and the wife of Samir Geagea, leader of the Lebanese Forces, who was then still in prison. Women are expected to vote according to their husband's choice, and will only reach political positions when "dressed in black" as widows.

Women elected on such a basis will primarily represent the extended family or clan who form the core of their electorate. However, as the list they run on will have candidates from all the sects present in their constituency, they will to some extent work across religious divides when it comes to regional questions, which are usually of a material character. On a national level, however, these divides seem more difficult to overcome, above all when ideological issues like secularization of the political system and modification of the family laws are discussed.

Attitudes – both in society and among women themselves – may represent another impediment to women's access to political life. A report published by the René Moawad Foundation reveals that 74 per cent of the total population and 100 per cent of members of parliament are in favour of broader participation of women. The last figure suggests that there is a gap between what is said and what is done, as there has been no initiative as such from parliament to encourage women to enter the political arena. Fifty-five per cent of the population declared that a woman might well become minister – yet 80 per cent of those who participated in the survey agreed that the domestic chores were exclusively women's responsibility.[65] Political activity is thus not easily compatible with the traditional conception of womanhood. Exceptions to the rule may still be acceptable, as long as the women manage to combine the roles. In addition, many women express negative attitudes towards political activity in general, even calling it dirty. They do not seem to hold much hope of being able to make a change, and therefore often prefer to work within NGOs.[66] Both the society's and the women's own attitudes may therefore represent hindrances to the participation of women in politics.

Many of the mechanisms of exclusion from politics hinder women and men alike – such as the distribution of the seats in parliament among the 17 religious sects and the regional redistribution of these, which may for some sects result in just one seat in each constituency; the dearth of political parties in post-war Lebanon; the renaissance of the traditional elite families; and finally the diverging views on Syria's role in the political life in Lebanon. In addition, women have to overcome the rules of patriarchy and attitudes – both society's and their own – that still place the burden of all domestic chores on the shoulders of women only, and prefer representation by men. Until profound changes take place and independent parties replace the elite families and the religious distribution of political posts, it is unlikely there will be an increase in the number of women in political decision-making positions in Lebanon. A potential future pressure group may come out of the growing number of young, educated, unmarried women, a result of the imbalance between numbers of men and women due to the many young men who died during the war or emigrated.

The reconstruction of Lebanon

Several reconstruction plans were launched by national, regional and international initiatives throughout the years of armed conflict – from 1975 until 1990 for most of the country, and until the end of May 2000 for the southern border area occupied by Israel. Optimism and hope for a prosperous future in the region reigned for some time after peace negotiations were initiated between Israel and its Arab neighbours in Madrid in 1991. The Declaration of Principles agreed upon in Oslo in August 1993 created new hope, even if it was accompanied by an uncertainty about the future of the Palestinian refugees living in Lebanon – whether they should be definitely integrated in the country or not. The reconstruction process therefore started up within a context of regional optimism, and the ambitious projects can easily be seen as a challenge and a bid for a better future. But the priority given to reconstruction of physical infrastructure, like roads, the airport and official buildings, was put into question. When the public were allowed to visit the government's offices, located in a restored Ottoman palace, for the first time, visitors expressed their anger over money spent on luxury when they were facing a declining living standard. Reconstruction of the electricity network has been particularly difficult, as power stations were destroyed by Israeli bombardment on several occasions after 1990. Much less has been invested in social infrastructure, like schools, hospitals, affordable housing, etc., which all affect people's daily life, and therefore women.

Damage and problems – caused by 15 years of combat, lack of maintenance of both physical and social infrastructure, and disorganized urbanization related to the displacement of more than a quarter of the population – were enormous and represented a great challenge, not least in the management of daily life, which is in particular a woman's affair. Displaced families often lived in overcrowded rooms or flats rented at high cost, or sometimes occupied the homes of people who had been displaced to other regions. Many families found a roof with relatives who lived in safe areas. Purpose-designed shelters were almost non-existent, and people from whole neighbourhoods were forced to spend days and nights together in cellars and underground garages, where the hygiene conditions were deplorable. At home, housewives had to cope with scarcity of water and electricity, which were rarely distributed at the same time. Fetching bread and vegetables became a dangerous expedition. On countless mornings mothers faced the terrible dilemma of sending their children to school or not, and many times they had to run to the school to bring them back again safely as shelling became more intense. Children were wounded and killed in their homes, schools and playgrounds. Many women experienced the disappearance of a son, a husband or a brother after he was kidnapped or imprisoned by the enemy, never to be seen again.[67] Assuring physical security and reconstructing social infrastructure were thus critically important to meeting these women's needs. Peace had to some extent brought security, but the social infrastructure remained inadequate.

A substantial part of Lebanon's stock of residential and office buildings was either damaged or destroyed, but there is no comprehensive and definite survey of this. Many families rebuilt and repaired their homes several times during and after the war, because they chose to stay or had no possibility of leaving. The displacement of a large part of the population resulted in an imbalance between the demand for and supply of housing.

Spending on social infrastructure has always been inadequate in Lebanon. Health services, education, housing, sanitation, electricity and water supply all languished, especially in rural areas. This pattern of inadequate development of public spending continued during the war years. Between 1977 and 1987, 89 per cent of all public expenditure was spent on physical infrastructure, compared to only 11 per cent on social infrastructure. Lebanon's educational system, which was once considered the best in the Middle East – although too expensive for many students – suffered from both damages and repeated displacements. Many public schools had simply closed their doors. Despite courageous efforts to keep education on all levels up and running, the sector faced huge problems – and still does.

According to a report of the Lebanese Council for Development and Reconstruction, for the years 1992–1996 the total amount invested in the reconstruction process was about US$3.8 billion. Of this 68 per cent went into infrastructure projects, 13 per cent into social affairs and education, and only 0.8 per cent into industry, agriculture and irrigation.[68]

During the years of war, and increasingly in the post-conflict phase, the socio-economic profile of the population of Lebanon underwent profound changes. The middle class that constituted the backbone of society before the war has been shrinking. This in turn had a negative effect on the lower classes and the poor. This new reality made a growing number of Lebanese dependent on public social infrastructure. The wealth of Lebanon is now in the hands of 4 per cent of the population, whereas one-third live under the poverty line.[69]

Would more women in decision-making positions have made a difference?

In the introduction the question was asked whether the quasi-absence of women from political decision-making in Lebanon has had any impact on the prioritization of select sectors during the reconstruction process. It was also stated that, in general, women's entrance into politics has changed the nature of the political agenda, where questions related to health, environment, nutrition and equal access to education and work are among the topics that have been highlighted.[70] But other authors claim that the correlation between women parliamentarians and women-friendly legislation remains an unexplored area.[71] We may thus end up with pure speculation alone. Still, if we hold the focus of women in the Lebanese parliament up against the areas that have received least attention in the reconstruction process, such as housing, health and education, we find that they match. There are therefore good reasons to believe that more women in parliament would lead to greater focus on these issues.

Women parliamentarians have seen education as key to a better future for both individuals and the country.[72] They are all active on a regional level and take part in international conferences and workshops. In that way they draw attention to the situation and preoccupations of Lebanese women in the post-conflict phase in regional and international arenas. As a response to their and many other women's efforts, the European Union has started training in political awareness and activities for women in Lebanon. On national and local levels, many Lebanese women use women parliamentarians as spokespersons to promote issues concerning the interests and needs of women in the post-conflict environment.

Still, female parliamentarians work mostly within the framework of the public authorities, as none of them can be found among the main critics of the official plans for Lebanese reconstruction. This may be a choice based on pragmatic assessments of how best to promote a cause from within the country's political class through bargaining. But it may also be a consequence of the basis on which they were able to run for parliament as representatives of elite families or on a strong man's list, which have so far been the only ways in which women have had access to this assembly. As they are part of the political establishment, these are the groups they will be accountable to and whose interests they serve. Moawad is convinced that the only way to have more women in decision-making positions is through abolishing the redistribution of political posts on a sectarian basis, and the introduction of political parties.[73] This will free members of parliament – both women and men – from the pressure of seeing first to the interest of the region and the religious and social groups (i.e. their extended family) to which they belong, thus enabling them to promote issues of national interest.

Conclusion

War exposes women to violence and suffering, and loss of both homes and loved ones. But at the same time war also opens up opportunities for new roles and activities in the public sphere, both civilian and military. The many war-induced challenges they meet in the domestic sphere can even lead to the empowerment of women within the family and community. On the other hand, when peace finally comes, women often experience a backlash that puts them back into their traditional, gender-based roles. Whereas men's participation in war may become the basis for future political power, the empowerment of women due to their war-related activities is usually suppressed.

During the war in Lebanon women were present in all fields – a few in combat positions, and others in supportive functions and the administrative apparatus within the militias. Many worked in the numerous local NGOs that were founded to assist the victims of war, the handicapped, orphans and displaced persons. When the country became divided into sectarian zones, Muslim and Christian women started pacifist movements that tried to meet from both sides of the demarcation line in Beirut, triggering angry reactions by the dominating militias. The majority of women saw it as their main duty to bring the family as safe as possible through the conflict.

Some women in post-conflict Lebanon enjoy a high level of education, while the majority of illiterate Lebanese are women. They have entered the labour market in increasing numbers due to the high cost of living and an increasing number of young, educated, single women. Women gained their legal political rights in 1953 and many were active in the political parties that proliferated during the decades before the war. Against this background it is striking that women are nearly absent from public political decision-making forums. It was not until 2000 that the country had its first two female ministers, while only four of 128 seats in parliament went to female candidates in the 2009 elections.

The Taëf Agreement ended the civil war, followed by the disarmament of all but one of the militias and a 50/50 distribution of all political posts between Christians and Muslims. This, in a way, enshrined the traditional political representation, based on religious, regional and family belonging. Because most parties had become weaker, people again turned to old and new political elite families. To be elected to the National Assembly or a municipal office council, women would have to overcome the rules of patriarchy that make people and groups prefer to be represented by a man, unless no suitable male candidate is available. This is reinforced by a political system that may produce only one seat within the constituency for a specific sect. In addition, prevailing attitudes in society and among women themselves have been impediments to women's participation in political decision-making. Profound changes within both the political system and the patriarchal culture will have to take place before the women of Lebanon can fully participate in the public decision-making of their country.

The war in Lebanon ended in 1990, 10 years before women's experiences and roles during war had come to be considered as a valuable resource in the peacebuilding process, as called for by UN Security Council Resolution 1325 (2000). Although the Taëf Agreement was supported by the United Nations as well as countries such as the United States, women were not invited to the negotiation table and given their rightful position in the reconstruction process. Reconstruction plans focused on rebuilding physical infrastructure, whereas social infrastructure was given less attention. As women in politics have generally focused their efforts on issues related to both social and infrastructure development, including health, education, public housing and protection of the environment, greater involvement of women in the Lebanese parliament and a larger number of female government ministers would have likely resulted in a greater focus on these issues in the context of Lebanese reconstruction efforts.

Notes

1. See Dahlerup, Drude (2001) "Women in Political Decisionmaking: From Critical Mass to Critical Acts in Scandinavia", in Inger Skjelsbæk and Dan Smith (eds) *Gender, Peace & Conflict*, Oslo: PRIO, pp. 104–121; Gierycz, Dorota (1999) "Women in Decision-making: Can We Change the Status Quo?", in Ingeborg Breines, Dorota Gierycz and Betty Reardon (eds) *Towards a Women's Agenda for a Culture of Peace*, Paris: UNESCO, pp. 19–32; Karamé, Kari with the assistance of Gudrun Bertinussen (2001) "Gendering Human Security: From Marginalisation to the Integration of Women in Peace-Building", Fafo Report 352/NUPI Report No. 261, Fafo Institute for Applied Social Science/Norwegian Institute of International Affairs, Oslo, available at www.fafo.no/pub/rapp/352/352.pdf; Miller, Errol (2001) "Gender, Power and Politics: An Alternative Perspective", in Inger Skjelsbæk and Dan Smith (eds) *Gender, Peace & Conflict*, Oslo: PRIO, pp. 80–103.
2. Karamé, ibid., p. 23.
3. See Keränen, Marja (ed.) (1992) *Gender and Politics in Finland*, Burlington, VT: Ashgate; Skjeie, Hege (1997) *Research on Women in Political, Social and Economic Decision Making in Norway*, Oslo: Department of Political Science, University of Oslo; UN Development Programme (2000) *Women's Political Participation and Good Governance: 21st Century Challenges*, New York: UNDP.
4. Hourani, Albert (undated) "Political Society in Lebanon: A Historical Introduction", Centre for Lebanese Studies, Papers on Lebanon Series, Oxford, pp. 8–14.
5. Harik, Judith Palmer (1996) "Principles and Mechanisms of Political Inclusion and Exclusion in Postwar Lebanon: Parliamentary Elections in the Governate of Mount Lebanon", paper presented at Conference on Citizenship and the State in the Middle East, Oslo, 22–24 November.
6. Salame, Ghassan (1986) "Lebanon's Injured Identities: Who Represents Who During a Civil War?", Centre for Lebanese Studies, Papers on Lebanon Series No. 2, Oxford, p. 22.
7. Hourani, note 4, p. 16.
8. For a detailed presentation of changing alliances see Hanf, Theodor (1994) *Coexistence in Wartime Lebanon: Decline of a State and Rise of a Nation*, London: I. B. Tauris.
9. Sbaiti, Ahmed (1994) "Reflections on Lebanon's Reconstruction", in Deidre Collings (ed.) *Peace for Lebanon? From War to Reconstruction*, Boulder, CO: Lynne Rienner, pp. 163–178.
10. Ibid.
11. Saidi, Nasser H. (1994) "The Economic Reconstruction of Lebanon: War, Peace, and Modernization", in Deidre Collings (ed.) *Peace for Lebanon? From War to Reconstruction*, Boulder, CO: Lynne Rienner, pp. 195–214.
12. Ibid., p. 199.
13. Shehadeh, Lamia Rustum (ed.) (1999) *Women and War in Lebanon*, Gainesville, FL: University of Florida Press.
14. Collings, Deidre (ed.) (1994) *Peace for Lebanon? From War to Reconstruction*, Boulder, CO: Lynne Rienner.
15. Maila, Joseph (1994) "The Ta'if Accord: An Evaluation", in Deidre Collings (ed.) *Peace for Lebanon? From War to Reconstruction*, Boulder, CO: Lynne Rienner, pp. 31–44.

16. For a comprehensive introduction to the history of Lebanon see Shehadi, Nadim and Dana Haffar Mills (eds) (1988) *Lebanon, a History of Conflict and Consensus*, London: Centre for Lebanese Studies in association with I. B. Tauris.
17. Harik, note 5.
18. For a thorough description of Lebanese women's life and agency before, during and after the war see Shehadeh, note 13.
19. Shehadeh, Lamia Rustum (1999) "Women before the War", in Lamia Rustum Shehadeh (ed.) *Women and War in Lebanon*, Gainesville, FL: University of Florida Press, p. 35.
20. Makdisi, Jean Said (1996) "The Mythology of Modernity: Women and Democracy in Lebanon", in May Yamani (ed.) *Feminism and Islam, Legal and Literary Perspectives*, Reading: Garnet Publishing, p. 243.
21. General Statistics for Education for the Year 1972–73, cited in Shehadeh, note 19, p. 36.
22. UN Development Programme (2002) *Arab Human Development Report 2002: Creating Opportunities for Future Generations*, New York: UNDP, p. 9.
23. General Statistics, note 21.
24. UN Development Programme, note 22, p. 92.
25. Karamé, Kari H. (1989) "L'expérience des jeunes militantes: Etude de cas et conséquences éducationelles", in L.-M. Chidiac, A. Kahi and A. N. Messarra (eds) *La Génération de la Relève: Une pédagogie nouvelle pour la jeunesse libanaise de notre temps*, Beirut: Publications du Bureau Pédagogique des Saints Coeurs, pp. 179–187. See also Karamé, Kari H. (1995) "Girls' Participation in Combat: A Case Study from Lebanon", in E. W. Fernea (ed.) *Children in the Muslim Middle East*, Austin, TX: University of Texas Press, pp. 378–392; Karamé, Kari H. (1999) "Maman Aïda, a Lebanese Godmother of the Combatants: Fighting Without Arms", in Lamia Rustum Shehadeh (ed.) *Women and War in Lebanon*, Gainesville, FL: University of Florida Press, pp. 195–209.
26. Schulze, Kristen (1998) "Communal Violence, Civil War and Foreign Occupation: Women in Lebanon", in Rick Wilford and Robert Miller (eds) *Women, Ethnicity and Nationalism: The Politics of Transition*, London: Routledge, pp. 150–169.
27. See the investigation performed by the Ministry of Social Affairs for the years 1994–1996, available at www.dm.net.lb/orient/htdocs/10-30-10.htm.
28. For information on women's employment see Shehadeh, Lamia Rustum (1999) "Women in the Public Sphere", in Lamia Rustum Shehadeh (ed.) *Women and War in Lebanon*, Gainesville, FL: University of Florida Press, pp. 45–55.
29. World Bank (2011) "Lebanon Country Data, Women, Business and the Law", available at http://wbl.worldbank.org/data/exploreeconomies/lebanon.
30. Makdisi, note 20, p. 232.
31. Al-Atar, Sahar (2008) "Femmes, au travail!!!", *L'Orient-Le Jour*, Beirut, 8 March.
32. Karamé (1989), note 25.
33. Karamé (1995), note 25; Karamé (1999), note 25; Khweiri, Jocelyne (1999) "From Gunpowder to Incense", in Lamia Rustom Shehadeh (ed.) *Women and War in Lebanon*, Gainesville, FL: University of Florida Press, pp. 209–228; Schulze, note 26.
34. Karamé, Kari H. (2001) "Military Women in Peace Operations: Experiences of the Norwegian Battalion in UNIFIL 1978–98", in Louise Olsson and Torunn L. Tryggestad (eds) "Women in International Peacekeeping", *International Peacekeeping* 8(2), special issue, pp. 86–96.
35. Shehadeh, note 13, p. 40.
36. Schulze, note 26, p. 164.
37. Khweiri, note 33. This is her own story.
38. Makdisi, note 20, p. 237.
39. Karamé (1995), note 25, p. 381.

40. There is no substitute to members of parliament in Lebanon. When one dies, he/she is replaced through a special, almost immediate, election – often by a close relative.

41. Karamé (1999), note 25, p. 202.

42. Committee on the Elimination of Discrimination against Women (2006) "Consideration of Reports Submitted by States Parties under Article 18 of the Convention on the Elimination of All Forms of Discrimination against Women, Third Periodic Report of States Parties, Lebanon", UN Doc. CEDAW/C/LBN/3, 7 July, Convention on the Elimination of All Forms of Discrimination against Women, New York, para. 150, available at www.bayefsky.com/reports/lebanon_cedaw_c_lbn_3_2006.pdf.

43. al-Rahbani, Layla Nkoula (2009) "Women in Lebanese Elections: Second-Class Citizens", *Aswat*, 7 October, available at https://www.aswat.com/en/node/1200.

44. See Pellot, Brian D. (2009) "Politics-Lebanon: Family History Counts for Women in Race to Parliament", *IPS*, 28 May, available at http://ipsnews.net.asp?idnews=47010.

45. al-Rahbani, note 43.

46. UN Development Programme (2009) *Arab Human Development Report 2009, Challenges to Human Security in the Arab Countries*, available at www.arab-hdr.org/publications/contents/2009/ch4-e.pdf.

47. UN Development Programme, note 22, p. 27.

48. UN Development Programme, note 3, p. 18.

49. Makdisi, note 20, p. 243.

50. UN Development Programme, note 3, pp. 7–8.

51. Ibid., p. 8.

52. Fondation René Moawad, Union Européenne and Fundacion Promocion Social de la Cultura (1997) *La Participation de la Femme Libanaise à la Vie Politique*, Beirut: Fondation René Moawad, p. 20.

53. Author's personal observations during repeated fieldwork in Lebanon.

54. Rath, Tiare (2002) "If Lebanon Is an Oasis of Freedom, Why Don't Women Succeed in Politics?", *Daily Star*, Beirut, 1 February, available at www.bintjbeil.com.articles/en/020201-rath.html.

55. Khoury, Doreen (2008) "Lebanon's Election Law: A Cup Half Full", *Daily Star*, Beirut, 10 October.

56. Shehadi and Haffar Mills, note 16, p. 19.

57. Shehadeh, Lamia Rustum (1999) "Women in the Lebanese Militias", in Lamia Rustum Shehadeh (ed.) *Women and War in Lebanon*, Gainesville, FL: University of Florida Press, pp. 153–154; Holt, Maria (1999) "Lebanese Shii Women and Islamism: A Response to War", in Lamia Rustum Shehadeh (ed.) *Women and War in Lebanon*, Gainesville, FL: University of Florida Press, pp. 185–186.

58. Makdisi, note 20, p. 237.

59. Jaquette, Jane S. (1997) "Women in Power: From Tokenism to Critical Mass", *Foreign Policy* 108, pp. 23–37.

60. The term "family-based" means that the family is the basic social unit providing identity, security and solidarity on all levels; "patrilinear" means that ascendance and descendance are defined by the male side, from father to son and so on.

61. Miller, note 1.

62. Author's informal interview in Beirut, spring 2010.

63. Miller, note 1.

64. Author's interview with Nayla Moawad, 23 July 2002.

65. Fondation René Moawad, Union Européenne and Fundacion Promocion Social de la Cultura, note 52, pp. 20–26.

66. Karamé (1995), note 25, p. 391.

67. Based on author's own experiences of life in Beirut during the war.

68. Cited by Salamé-Hardy, Katia (1998) "Liban: Quel avenir pour les 'oubliés' de la reconstruction?", *Arabies*, October, p. 33.
69. Ibid.
70. Keränen, note 3; Skjeie, note 3; UN Development Programme, note 3.
71. Reynolds, Andrew (1999) "Women in the Legislatures and Executives of the World: Knocking at the Highest Glass Ceiling", *World Politics* 51, pp. 547–572.
72. Author's interview with Nayla Moawad, 23 July 2002.
73. Ibid.

13

Combating stereotypes: Female security personnel in post-conflict contexts

Kristin Valasek

A woman in uniform with a baby in one arm and an AK-47 in the other continues to provoke shock, outrage, pride and disdain. With the prevalent sociocultural construct of "man = protector" and "women and children = protectees", the very notion of a woman, much less a mother, as a security provider is often beyond the popular imagination. Predictably, reconstruction, peacebuilding and development initiatives in post-conflict environments[1] often fail to take women into account as actors in the realm of security. As a result, men continue to be highly overrepresented in post-conflict security sector institutions: from 81 per cent of Rwandan police officers and 96 per cent of the Republic of Sierra Leone Armed Forces to 98 per cent of Nepali judges.[2]

In international discourse on women in post-conflict contexts, women have gone from being trapped under the label of "victim" to an expanded view of them as "victims" and/or "peacebuilders". While it is occasionally acknowledged that women are capable of supporting and perpetrating violence (see other chapters in this volume, especially Chapter 2), these roles are usually either silenced or sensationalized. This chapter argues that these three categories do not adequately represent the multiplicity of roles that women take on in post-conflict contexts. Moreover, this form of categorization effectively excludes women from the pivotal role of security providers.

Adopting a broad definition of security provision encompassing both state and non-state security and justice actors, such as the armed forces, police, intelligence, border management, courts, prisons, customary/

Defying victimhood: Women and post-conflict peacebuilding, Schnabel and Tabyshalieva (eds),
United Nations University Press, 2012, ISBN 978-92-808-1201-5

traditional security and justice providers and private security companies, reveals the diversity of security positions that women and men take on. Women and men also play a key role in security sector oversight, as members of parliaments, civil society organizations, government ministries, ombudsperson offices and human rights commissions. However, this chapter focuses on women as security providers within formal state security and justice provision institutions. Post-conflict disarmament, demobilization and reintegration (DDR) and security sector reform (SSR) processes offer a window of opportunity to ensure the increased recruitment, retention and advancement of female personnel within these institutions.

This chapter provides a mixture of theory, policy-oriented information and practical advice directed towards a broad audience, ranging from peacebuilding practitioners and security policy-makers to gender-focused academics. Information in this chapter is gathered from academic and practitioner publications as well as personal experience from working on these issues in Liberia and Sierra Leone. As such, it first includes a section linking peacebuilding, DDR, SSR and feminist theories. Then it moves on to provide a rationale for strengthening the participation of women within security and justice institutions and information on how to overcome common challenges to the increased participation of women, including cultural norms and stereotypes, lack of education, discrimination, sexual harassment and sexual violence. The chapter concludes with practical recommendations for how to increase women's recruitment, retention and advancement in post-conflict security sector institutions.

Setting the stage: Peacebuilding, DDR, SSR and feminisms

Linking peacebuilding, DDR and SSR

Post-conflict peacebuilding is a complex and multidimensional process of transformation from a state of violent conflict to stability, security and peace.[3] Reconstruction and development activities can contribute to peacebuilding if they are oriented towards ending the violent conflict and preventing its reoccurrence (see Chapter 1). In this context, the transformation of security sector institutions is one of the key activities necessary in order to provide justice and security and prevent the resurgence of conflict.

Linked DDR and SSR processes are integral to a comprehensive transformation of the provision of security and justice in post-conflict contexts. According to the UN Integrated DDR Standards, DDR is a "process that contributes to security and stability in a post-conflict recovery context by removing weapons from the hands of combatants, taking the combatants out of military structures and helping them to integrate socially and economically into society by finding civilian livelihoods".[4] As part of this process, former combatants are also integrated into "new" security institutions, including the armed forces, police and border and intelligence services.

The United Nations defines SSR as "a process of assessment, review and implementation as well as monitoring and evaluation led by national authorities that has as its goal the enhancement of effective and accountable security for the State and its peoples without discrimination and with full respect for human rights and the rule of law".[5] In post-conflict contexts, SSR generally entails a wide range of activities with the twinned objectives of ensuring democratic and civilian control of the security sector and developing an effective, affordable and accountable security sector.[6] This encompasses everything from security sector oversight training for parliamentarians and civil society organizations to technical support for the drafting of standard operating procedures for border control.

DDR and SSR processes are conceptually interlinked in a number of ways; both falling under the umbrella of goals such as increased provision of security to all people and post-conflict state-building. In concrete terms, DDR shapes the terrain for SSR by influencing the size and nature of statutory security institutions. In turn, DDR should be undertaken with a comprehensive national vision of the security sector in mind. DDR and SSR are directly linked through the integration of former combatants into "new" security institutions and structures. They both form a part of the broader peacebuilding agenda and should be approached together in order to ensure a comprehensive and sustainable reform process.[7]

Coming to terms with women

With regards to the conceptual debates surrounding the role of women within post-conflict security structures, specific schools of feminist thought approach the issues differently. Generically speaking, feminism is an umbrella term for diverse political and social movements and schools of theory dedicated to achieving the full social, political, cultural and economic equality of women and men. In the context of DDR and SSR, three main schools of feminist thought are often invoked: cultural/essentialist feminism, liberal/equal rights feminism and postmodernist/poststructuralist feminism.

As described in Chapter 2, cultural/essentialist feminists subscribe to the understanding that there are core biological differences between men and women which create physical and psychological differences that impact upon women's and men's role in providing security. Theorists within this field claim that women are inherently more peaceful and more apt to create a secure world because of their biological role of bearing and raising children and/or their "feminine" traits of cooperation, caring and nurturing.[8] The predominance of men in positions of decision-making on security issues is seen as promoting insecurity through men's inherent warlike behaviour and their espousal of "masculine" values of individuality, dominance and violence. With regard to female security personnel, these lines of argument have been used both to declare women unfit for combat duty and to promote women as especially fit to be caring, non-violent security providers.

Liberal/equal rights feminists reject essentialist claims as gender stereotypes, and view men and women as equals in terms of underlying beliefs, abilities and capacities.[9] They focus on women's equal rights as a platform to call for women's full and equal participation in decision-making on peace and security issues as well as their equal right to security. They often highlight the importance of women joining security institutions, including combat positions in the armed forces, in order to be seen as full citizens and security providers rather than as "weak" and needing protection.[10]

Postmodernist/poststructuralist feminists argue against essentialist gender stereotyping but also against uncritically advocating for women's participation in security discourses and structures without a gender analysis of the discourses and structures themselves. A common critique of security institutions involves their perpetuation of a culture of violent, militarized masculinities, which negatively impacts female and male security personnel as well as civilians. Postmodernist feminists also challenge the simplistic categories of "women" and "men" and note that, in addition to gender, other factors can influence access to and provision of security, including ethnicity, class, sexual orientation, religion, ability, etc. They provide an in-depth analysis of the gendered characteristics of security personnel, structures, policies and institutional culture and call for comprehensive transformation.[11]

This chapter draws upon the schools of liberal/equal rights and postmodernist/poststructuralist feminist theories to argue that women and men have an equal right to participate in security institutions, while fully acknowledging that equal participation does not automatically make – and stand for – equitable and gender-responsive security institutions. Equal recruitment, retention and advancement of women within security institutions must be accompanied by the integration of gender issues at the levels of policy and procedures, institutional structures, staffing, training, operations, logistics and budgeting. More importantly, there must be a process of fundamental transformation of the security institution to an institution that is focused on meeting the security and justice needs of men, women, girls and boys.[12]

Female security personnel – Realities and rationale

> Searching for weapons was a regular task in Kosovo ... This is almost impossible without women in the team. If you suspect that weapons have been hidden in a village, going into houses is much easier in teams of both women and men. The female soldiers can talk to the women in the house because they often have more trust in other women, and this reduces the risk for escalation.[13]

Currently, statutory security and justice institutions, ranging from the armed forces, police services, customs, immigration and intelligence service to prisons, courts and private security companies, predominantly employ men. The handful of women who are able to take on the role of security providers face the challenges of being relegated to low-status or entry-level positions and suffering discrimination, harassment and violence from their colleagues. This is true for post-conflict, developing and developed contexts. Post-conflict DDR and SSR processes can provide the space needed to implement measures to increase the recruitment, retention and advancement of women within these institutions. There are many strong arguments for why increasing the participation of women within the security sector is viable, necessary and beneficial – including equal representation, operational benefits and normative compliance.

Equal representation

It is imperative for security and justice institutions to be representative of the population they seek to serve. A representative institution is one that reflects the composition of the general population at all levels of the organization, including in terms of ethnicity, geography, sex, religion, sexual orientation and language. As there is often a larger percentage of women than men in post-conflict societies, it follows that a truly representative security institution should employ a comparable number of women and men. Building representative security sector institutions increases local ownership, legitimacy and trust and is a key indicator and requirement of democratic governance, especially in the aftermath of intra-state conflicts.[14]

As democratic citizens, women are the civic equals of men and thus share the same rights and responsibilities. Women not only have the right to be equally represented in decision-making positions within security institutions, but also have the civic obligation to participate fully within all areas of the security sector.[15] At the international, regional and national levels, laws, instruments and doctrines create a normative framework that binds governments and other actors to guarantee these rights and responsibilities (see subsection below on "normative compliance").

Equal representation is further justified by studies showing that men and women are equally capable of serving as security providers. For instance, research on the effectiveness of female versus male law enforcement officers has not found any meaningful difference in their activities or productivity on patrol, their performance evaluations and their participation in training and other professional development activities.[16] Quite the opposite, as a representative security institution may inspire more confidence and trust on the part of service recipients and may be better able to deliver security and justice to a diverse constituency.

Operational benefits

Not only has it been shown that women and men are equally up to the task of providing security and justice, but in certain cases increasing the participation of women can have clear operational benefits. At a basic level, fully opening up all positions in the field of security to women and other underrepresented groups ensures access to a larger pool of potential staff. This both increases the availability of human resources and creates the potential to select better-qualified staff. In addition, due to socialized gender roles, women tend to bring with them a key set of skills and abilities that have direct operational benefits.

For instance, research within the field of policing has documented the benefits of increased participation of women within security institutions. According to a desk review of research on gender and policing:

> Research conducted both in the United States and internationally clearly demonstrates that women officers rely on a style of policing that uses less physical force, are better at defusing and de-escalating potentially violent confrontations with citizens, and are less likely to become involved in problems with use of excessive force. Additionally, women officers often possess better communication skills than their male counterparts and are better able to facilitate the cooperation and trust required to implement a community policing model.[17]

Not only do women often possess a useful skill-set, but in certain contexts their inclusion is not just desirable but "an operational imperative", according to the UN Department of Peacekeeping Operations policy dialogue on enhancing gender balance.[18]

Hiring female security staff is an operational necessity, as they can undertake certain critical tasks that men cannot. This is especially the case in post-conflict contexts where women are needed for the screening of female ex-combatants, widening the net of intelligence gathering, performing the cordon and search of women, assisting in the aftermath of sexual violence and assuring effective security service delivery where the segregation of men and women is culturally required.[19] Anecdotal evidence also points to women peacekeepers as being better able to gain the trust of civilians and ensure the full involvement of local women, having better communication and crowd control skills and serving as role models for increased women's participation in national security institutions.[20] For instance, UN and Liberian officials hope that the 103-strong all-female peacekeeping unit from India helps inspire Liberian women to join the police force, limit sexual exploitation and abuse by peacekeepers and redress the gender imbalance in peacekeeping missions. The unit is performing police functions in Monrovia, including guarding the Ministry of Foreign Affairs, patrolling the streets, controlling crowds and responding to calls for armed back-up from the national police.[21] As a result, the Liberian National Police received three times the usual number of female applicants in the month following the unit's deployment.[22]

As a further benefit, women are more likely to report violence, including sexual violence, to female personnel. This is crucial considering the appallingly high rates of violence against women during and after armed conflict. For instance, sexual violence was used as a strategy of war in Rwanda and Bosnia-Herzegovina, with an estimated 250,000–500,000 women and 13,000–50,000 girls surviving rape.[23] In post-Khmer Rouge Cambodia and post-apartheid South Africa, non-governmental organizations have reported an increase in the scope and intensity of domestic violence.[24] Post-accord escalation of domestic violence, including spousal rape, has also been documented in Mozambique, Serbia and Guatemala.[25] In addition to providing support to civilian victims of violence, increasing the number of female personnel creates an opening to challenge and change the cultures of security institutions in order to reduce internal gender-based discrimination and sexual harassment.[26]

Although it is important to emphasize the benefits of increased female participation, care must be taken not to portray women as inherently better communicators and peacemakers or more respectful of human rights. Men and women have an equal capability to possess these traits. However, due to processes of gender socialization, girls and women are often taught and encouraged to develop these skills to a larger degree than men and boys – who might even be discouraged in this regard. Taking this into account, it would benefit SSR processes to include more women to ensure operational effectiveness within security institutions and improved service delivery to society at large.

Normative compliance

Taking the initiative to increase the participation of women within security sector institutions is not only a matter of operational benefits, it also ensures compliance with international, regional and national norms, instruments and laws. The current 194 UN member states are bound by the instruments they have signed and ratified as well as by UN Security Council resolutions. Regional and national instruments in post-conflict countries also call for the equal participation of men and women in all public sector institutions, including security sector institutions.

The substantial body of international instruments that address gender issues and women's rights provides specific and detailed mandates for security sector actors. This includes the full and equal participation of women in security and justice decision-making and institutions. The Convention on the Elimination of All Forms of Discrimination against Women (1979) is an expansive instrument which legally binds the 187 states that are party to the convention.[27] It specifically calls for measures to eliminate prejudices and stereotyped roles for men and women; the right of women "to participate in the formulation of government policy and the implementation thereof and to hold public office and perform all public functions at all levels of government"; the right to the same employment opportunities, promotion, job security, equal remuneration and work-life balance; and equality before the law.

The Beijing Declaration and Platform for Action, adopted unanimously at the 1995 Fourth World Conference on Women by representatives from 189 countries, includes 12 areas of critical concern and hundreds of actions to be taken, among which are numerous mandates for security sector institutions. More specifically, the Beijing Platform for Action calls for the development of programmes and procedures to eliminate sexual harassment from workplaces, gender training for security sector personnel and gender balance in public administrative entities and the judiciary.

In addition to these expansive instruments on women's rights, there are several instruments that focus specifically on women, peace and security issues. UN Security Council Resolution (SCR) 1325 on women, peace and security (2000) provides mandates for UN member states, parties to armed conflict and all actors involved in peace agreements and DDR. SCR 1325 stresses the importance of women's "equal participation and full involvement in all efforts for the maintenance and promotion of peace and security". It also calls for all those involved in planning for DDR to consider the different needs of female and male ex-combatants and their dependants. In addition, UN SCR 1820 (2008) requests that DDR and SSR processes include the development of effective mechanisms for providing protection from sexual violence, demands that armed and security forces are vetted to take into account past acts of rape and other forms of sexual violence and encourages the deployment of a higher number of female peacekeepers and police. Combined with the impetus of operational benefits and the rationale of equal rights, this body of international instruments and laws clearly makes the case for the increased participation of women in security sector institutions.

Challenges to increasing women's participation

> I am not a victim of sexual harassment. When sexual harassment occurs in the United States Air Force, the Air Force and the citizens of the United States whom we serve are the victims. Because sexual harassment interferes with our military mission. It interferes with the job that I and other professionals have been highly trained to do. That is why it has to stop.[28]

Despite the strong arguments for implementing measures to increase the recruitment, retention and advancement of women within security sector institutions, numerous challenges arise when attempting to put these measures into practice. These challenges range from deep-seated cultural stereotypes and a lack of educational and training requirements to discrimination, harassment and violence on the job. Men also face many of these challenges, but to a lesser extent than women.

Gender-based norms and stereotypes

In many post-conflict contexts, cultural norms and stereotypes associate the provision of security with men. Depending upon the specific context, this can be a significant barrier to women's participation in security sector institutions. If women grow up in families, communities and countries where there are no role models of female security personnel or support from their family and friends to pursue a career in security or justice provision, recruitment of women will remain an uphill battle. The few women who do join are often stereotyped and marginalized by their own communities – as a form of social disciplining for breaking traditional gender roles. For instance, in Sierra Leone women who join the police and armed forces are often stereotyped as not smart enough to do well in school – so they are seen as having joined up in search of an "easy" source of income.

Compounded with cultural stereotypes, security sector institutions themselves are infamous for their reliance on strict gender roles, including the stereotypes of men as security providers and women as vulnerable potential victims. The institutional structure and culture of security institutions often condone and perpetuate a certain form of violent masculinity. It is therefore not surprising that gender stereotypes imbue security institutions and personnel. For instance, research shows that male law enforcement officers are more likely to express traditional views of women's roles in society, including the conviction that women's main duties should be confined to the domestic sphere and women are unsuited for police work.[29]

DDR and SSR processes can emerge from their own specific cultural context without condoning stereotypes that limit women's participation in the sector. Specific action can be taken to challenge these stereotypes, including participatory and gender-sensitive security and justice needs assessments; community and national-level awareness-raising campaigns on the role of female security providers; gender awareness training for all security personnel; supporting women's organizations working with security sector institutions and female security sector staff associations; and working with gender champions to mobilize political will at the senior level.[30]

Lack of education and training

In post-conflict contexts, access to education is severely limited – especially for girls and women, who already face barriers to their attendance. Due to the security risk and cost of sending children to school, compounded by gender discrimination, school attendance by boys is often prioritized. Girls' and women's lack of access to education becomes a clear barrier to their participation in security institutions, where a high-school diploma is often one of the basic requirements. Initiatives to provide accelerated high-school education can help eliminate this barrier.

As part of the post-conflict reconstruction of the police service in Liberia, a strategic target was set for 20 per cent female officers. However, prevailing gender stereotypes and female candidates' lack of education have posed barriers to their recruitment. In response to these challenges, a programme of accelerated learning started in 2007 to provide 125 Liberian female recruits with the necessary high-school certificate. The three-month educational support programme for women police candidates between the ages of 18 and 35 provided them with training materials, daily lunch and a monthly stipend. It was a pilot project designed by the UN Police and the Liberian National Police in cooperation with the Ministries of Gender and Development, Education and Justice, the West African Examinations Council and Stella Maris Polytechnic. The course ended on 19 May 2007 with the award of a high-school certificate for the successful candidates and their immediate enrolment in the nation's police academy.[31] However, lack of continued on-the-job training has meant that many of these female officers still lack the skills necessary to perform their duties effectively – which in turn forms a barrier to advancement. Thus lack of basic education and ongoing training proves to be a pivotal barrier for women's full participation in security and justice institutions.

Discrimination in policy and practice

The UN Convention on the Elimination of All Forms of Discrimination against Women defines discrimination as any distinction, exclusion or restriction made on the basis of sex which has the effect or purpose of impairing or nullifying the recognition, enjoyment or exercise of human rights and fundamental freedoms. In the case of security sector institutions, discrimination can manifest itself in anything from verbal comments to unfair hiring and promotion practices.

It often starts with discriminatory recruitment processes that are targeted towards men. From only including pictures of men in recruitment materials, to employing only male recruitment officers and interviewers, to height regulations that discriminate against women, unfair recruitment policies and practices are a concrete obstacle to increasing the participation of women. In post-conflict contexts, discriminatory DDR processes reduce the possibility to recruit female ex-combatants into newly formed security sector institutions. For instance, in Liberia an initial needs assessment estimated that approximately 2,000 female combatants qualified to undergo DDR. However, after an awareness-raising campaign by women's organizations encouraging women and girls to participate in the DDR process, 22,370 women and 2,440 girls were disarmed and demobilized.[32] In other post-conflict countries, women and girls continue to be excluded from DDR processes.

Once on the job, women are often relegated to feminized and thus lower-status positions, including administration, health, maintenance and other support services. Cultural stereotypes are often enacted on the job, creating a discriminatory workplace where women are not given access to on-the-job training or promotion possibilities. For instance, in the Sierra Leonean police service "despite the hiring of women and gender training for the lower ranks, 'female police officers are sometimes expected to do little more than cook lunch for the male police officers'".[33] Within the armed forces, an additional obstacle exists in the form of a discriminatory policy that does not allow women to hold combat positions – known as the "brass ceiling". Without combat experience, women often find it difficult to obtain higher positions and move up in rank. Once again, this feeds a self-perpetuating cycle where, due to a lack of role models, women are dissuaded from attempting to obtain leadership positions. Institutionalized discrimination is thus one of the major contributors to low rates of female recruitment and advancement.

Sexual harassment

Although legal definitions of and responses to sexual harassment vary greatly from country to country, working in an environment free from sexual harassment can be framed as a human rights issue. Sexual harassment is generally defined as unwanted conduct of a sexual nature, or conduct based on sex affecting the dignity of women and men at work. This can include unwelcome physical, verbal or non-verbal conduct.[34] As such, sexual harassment encompasses a wide range of behaviours, from sexual advances or propositions, offensive questions or comments about physical appearance or sex life and sexual jokes and insults to leering, the display of pornographic material and inappropriate touching.

Although research on sexual harassment in post-conflict security sector institutions is largely non-existent, the high prevalence of sexual harassment in security institutions in developed and developing countries, along with anecdotal evidence, suggests that it is a serious obstacle to the recruitment and advancement of female security sector personnel. For instance, according to the European Women's Lobby, 40–50 per cent of European female employees have experienced some form of sexual harassment. Sexual harassment impacts its victims, the work environment and the institution as a whole. Not only can it have devastating effects upon an individual's health, morale and performance, but it also affects the work environment and can hinder the proper integration of women. In addition, the institution is impacted by loss of productivity, absence from work and higher rates of staff turnover. In the context of the military, a study in the United States has shown a strong correlation between high incidence of sexual harassment, lower combat readiness and a poor leadership climate.[35]

Studies have shown a high prevalence of sexual harassment within security institutions, especially within the armed forces, where harassment is pervasive and firmly entrenched in the organizational culture. In 2006 an independent study commissioned by the UK Ministry of Defence revealed that more than two-thirds of servicewomen had been sexually harassed.[36] A class-action lawsuit filed by female corrections officers in the United States revealed sexual harassment to be pervasive and systematic, including demands for sex from supervisors, groping and verbal abuse.[37] When victims of sexual harassment file a complaint the tendency is to settle the charges quietly and informally, and often to blame the victim.[38]

One key step towards reducing sexual harassment is to have a clear, comprehensive and implemented sexual harassment policy. The Kosovo

Police Service revised its policy on sexual harassment in 2003. It states that "It is the policy of the Kosovo Police Service to provide a professional work place free from all forms of employee discrimination, including incidents of sexual harassment. No employee will be subjected to unsolicited and unwelcome sexual overtures or conduct. Harassment will be treated as misconduct with appropriate disciplinary sanctions." The policy also provides a definition of sexual harassment, including specific examples, and outlines the reporting procedure and the duties of command and supervisory personnel.[39]

Sexual violence

Rape, sexual assault and other forms of gender-based violence are daily threats for many female security personnel. Allegations of sexual exploitation and abuse perpetrated by peacekeepers, military personnel and private security staff in Iraq, Bosnia, Liberia and the Democratic Republic of the Congo have undermined their operations and tarnished their reputation. Such criminal behaviour has a deep physical and psychological impact upon its victims, diminishes operational effectiveness, creates a work environment of insecurity and impunity and lowers civilian trust. Along with sexual harassment, it is a clear barrier to the recruitment of women as well as one of the reasons why female security personnel leave their jobs.

Female, and to a much lesser degree male, members of security institutions face violence at the hands of their colleagues and superiors. In a 2006 student survey of the US military institute The Citadel, 20 per cent of female cadets reported being sexually assaulted.[40] In the US armed forces, active-duty service members and their spouses report 20,000–23,000 spouse abuse incidents every year.[41] This goes to show that many of the obstacles to women's participation in the security sector are not just issues for post-conflict countries, but for developing and developed countries as well.

In response to a 2004 UN report revealing a "shockingly large number" of peacekeepers engaged in sexual exploitation in the Democratic Republic of the Congo, the United Nations embarked upon a range of initiatives to prevent and respond to sexual exploitation and abuse (SEA) among peacekeepers. In addition to establishing a zero-tolerance policy, it has initiated training on SEA for peacekeepers; complaint mechanisms; conduct and discipline units; policy on victim assistance; SEA focal points; measures to strengthen leadership accountability; improvements in living conditions and welfare for peacekeeping personnel; amendments to legal agreements with troop-contributing countries; and contracts with all peacekeeping personnel to include prohibitions on sexual exploitation and abuse.[42] Between January 2004 and November 2006, 319 peacekeeping personnel were investigated, resulting in the summary dismissal of 18 civilians and the repatriation on disciplinary grounds of 17 police and 144 military personnel.[43] A 2006 conference on the topic recommended additional measures such as DNA samples, new international pacts and additional assistance to victims.[44]

It is imperative to take these various challenges into consideration in order to design effective initiatives to increase women's participation. However, as each post-conflict context is different, adequate assessment of the specific institutional challenges will provide a more solid starting ground.

Entry points for increasing female recruitment, retention and advancement

As noted above, creating representative security sector institutions where men and women participate equally at all levels of decision-making is a challenge in institutions where men are currently vastly overrepresented. Although employment within security institutions is traditionally viewed as men's work, women are both qualified for and – sometimes contrary to popular belief – interested in these positions. In many post-conflict countries, work within the security sector can provide financial security, which is just as highly appealing to women as to men. Comprehensive and inclusive DDR and SSR processes can draw upon the potential interest from women and take concrete steps to build an equitable sector with a non-discriminatory work environment. Good practices for increasing the recruitment, retention and advancement of women include the comprehensive integration of gender issues into reform processes; specific measures focusing upon recruitment, retention and advancement; and supporting female staff associations.

Comprehensive gender-responsive approach

Comprehensive assessment, planning, implementation and evaluation of DDR and SSR processes that fully take into account the experiences, needs, priorities and activities of women and men enable the creation of gender-balanced security sector institutions. Currently, when gender issues are taken into account in post-conflict DDR and SSR, the result is often piecemeal and *ad hoc*. Only a holistic and integrated approach will produce sustainable reform of security sector institutions. For instance, a strategic target for female armed forces personnel needs to be accompanied by recruitment initiatives focusing on women. Penal reform that includes a revision of promotion policies and the adoption of a sexual harassment policy also needs to implement staff training on sexual harassment and build the capacity of human resources to support accountable promotion procedures. To create equitable institutions it is necessary not just to focus on female personnel, but to include initiatives targeting male personnel as well as security sector oversight bodies. A comprehensive process of integrating gender issues – including women's participation – is a must.

In order to increase the number of women working within security sector institutions, recruitment initiatives need to be linked with reforms focused on retention and advancement. Simply increasing the recruitment of women, for example, does not ensure that female staff are retained or have equal access to decision-making positions. As described in the previous section, discrimination, harassment and violence, among other obstacles, pose formidable barriers to women's retention and promotion. However, an integrated set of measures that includes attention to policy, recruitment procedures, human resources policies, training and promotion criteria can ensure that women not only join but stay.

A comprehensive approach also highlights the need to involve a broad range of stakeholders. First, it is imperative to include a focus on men within the security sector. In order to create an equitable workplace it is necessary to involve the vast majority of employees – namely male security sector personnel. This includes adequate vetting of candidates that incorporates checking for a past history of gender-based violence. It also means prioritizing gender training for all personnel, including training sessions on prevention of sexual harassment. Ensuring that male and female security personnel are informed and trained on institutional gender policies is crucial. Senior management must also take the responsibility to enforce these policies and create a healthy work environment free of impunity. Enlisting high-ranking male security personnel as gender champions, advocates and trainers is another good practice.

It is also important to involve civil society organizations and other oversight bodies such as parliaments, government ministries, human rights commissions and ombudsperson institutions. These bodies hold the power to demand that security and justice institutions change their policies and practices to encourage equitable representation. For instance, ombudsperson institutions can document and investigate cases of discrimination, harassment and violence against women. Parliamentarians can pass legislation calling for increased participation of women, including strategic targets for female recruitment. Civil society can lobby for gender equality and, in collaboration with the media, serve as a watchdog to ensure that policies are being fully implemented. Building the capacity of oversight bodies to take into consideration issues of female recruitment, retention and advancement is thus another clear entry point. As with security sector institutions, ways to build the capacity of oversight bodies include increasing female representation, gender training, establishing gender focal points and collaboration with women's organizations and gender experts. Finally, in order to implement effectively a comprehensive and gender-responsive reform process that takes into account all the key stakeholders, it is advisable to conduct a thorough gender audit or assessment of the institution in question.

Specific measures to increase female recruitment, retention and advancement

When the overarching goal becomes the integration of gender into security and justice institutions, it is important not to lose sight of the practical initiatives that are necessary to increase the recruitment, retention and advancement of female security sector personnel.

Current recruitment practices often fail to reach out to pools of qualified and interested female candidates, as is demonstrated by strikingly low rates of female participation within the security sector. Through reforms in recruitment policy and practice, larger numbers of women can take the step to join the police, armed forces, border guards, justice system, prisons and other security sector institutions. Substantially increasing the female applicant pool typically leads to hiring more women. One clear entry point is the DDR process. Ensuring that DDR incorporates female ex-combatants and women and girls associated with the fighting forces opens up an avenue to recruit trained women for new security sector positions. It is therefore important that DDR and SSR processes are well coordinated.

At the policy level, a first key step is the establishment of a strategic target of 20–30 per cent female recruitment, along with a gender assessment and the development of an institutional gender policy. In addition, job descriptions and selection criteria and processes should be thoroughly reviewed to ensure they are non-discriminatory and reflect the actual skills and knowledge required for the positions in question. More specifically, basic initiatives such as hiring female and minority recruitment officers, revising recruitment materials to include pictures and text mentioning women and minorities, giving gender training to recruitment officers and distributing information on job opportunities to women at places where women congregate are crucial. Other good practices include raising public awareness on the role of women in the security sector, for instance by training female personnel to speak at schools and with the media. Scholarships and internships for women can also be provided as incentives for initial exposure and involvement in these institutions.

Similarly, to retain women and ensure equal access to decision-making positions, it is helpful to have institutional policies in place on gender mainstreaming, affirmative action and/or equal opportunities. Additional measures are necessary to prevent and adequately respond to the challenges that block retention and equal promotion, such as discrimination, harassment and violence. These measures include sexual harassment policies, gender-sensitive codes of conduct, gender training, independent bodies to report violations to, hotlines, gender focal points and awareness-raising campaigns. Men and women should have equal pay, benefits, pensions and other non-salaried remuneration. In addition, human resources policies and practices should be reviewed and made as woman- and family-friendly as possible, including flexible work hours, part-time and job sharing, daycare and school facilities, transportation, nursing areas, access to psychological support and paid maternity and paternity leave. At a basic level, logistics and equipment need to be available for women, including separate and adequate numbers of housing and bathrooms as well as appropriate uniforms and equipment.

Specific action needs to be taken to avoid the tendency for women to become trapped in entry-level positions due to discrimination, family responsibilities or the lack of access to educational opportunities. At minimum, objective and non-discriminatory promotion criteria, clear and transparent job evaluation standards and performance-based assessments need to be developed and implemented. In some cases, establishing an independent review board is necessary to avoid discrimination and nepotism. Women also need to have access to career advancement training. The decision can even be taken to fast-track female and minority candidates with high potential. Finally, initiating mentoring programmes for female staff and establishing strong female staff associations can provide crucial support to female staff as well as serving as platforms to call for internal reforms.

Female security sector staff associations deserve to be highlighted as a crucial entry point towards creating equitable security sector institutions. In many post-conflict countries such associations already exist. However, they often focus on general social and welfare issues, such as organizing networking events, hosting dances or providing financial support for weddings and funerals. Although useful as a support system for female staff, these associations have the potential to be a strong force for change from within security sector institutions. By supporting capacity-building and mobilizing existing associations to focus on issues of policy reform, recruitment processes and professional advancement, female staff associations can become real drivers of institutional transformation.

Conclusion

Taking action to support women's right and responsibility to serve as security providers in post-conflict contexts not only transcends the conceptual barriers of women-as-victims and women-as-peacebuilders, but is also essential to the practical efforts to support the creation of peaceful, safe societies. Currently, security and justice institutions predominantly employ men despite the many strong arguments supporting the need for them to be representative. Especially for post-conflict security sector institutions, it is vital that diverse individuals and communities can identify with and feel comfortable with security and justice personnel. Not only does this build legitimacy and trust, but it enables access to security and justice. Increasing the number of female security and justice personnel is also supported by international, regional and national norms, instruments and laws, and is shown to have operational benefits.

However, there are many challenges to overcome when attempting to support the development of equitable institutions. Female security personnel continue to face deep-seated cultural stereotypes that deem security provision an exclusively male realm. In addition, security institutions such as the armed forces are often overtly discriminatory in policy and practice, and characterized by an institutional culture of pervasive sexual harassment and violence. Yet another obstacle is that in post-conflict contexts, due to the limited access to education, especially for girls, women often lack the basic education requirements needed to apply to police and defence academies, not to mention law school.

Despite these challenges, there are numerous entry points for increasing female recruitment, retention and advancement as part of post-conflict DDR and SSR processes. These include practical actions such as establishing strategic targets for female recruitment, career advancement training and support to female staff associations. For example, it is frequently the case that significant gender-related reforms, including strategic targets for female recruitment, have been incorporated into police reform processes but remain alarmingly absent from other key security sector institutions, such as the armed forces, prisons, intelligence service, fire service, border management and the justice system. We can look to these cases of gender-responsive police reform, such as in Kosovo, Liberia and Sierra Leone, for good practices and lessons learned that can be applicable to reform processes in other security sector institutions and other post-conflict contexts. Yet the objective is not simply to increase the number of female personnel in security institutions. The end goal is to have a peaceful, safe society complete with a security sector that is representative, accountable and capable of meeting the different security and justice needs of men, women, boys and girls. Therefore, a comprehensive approach to integrating gender issues is imperative. This means effecting change in deep-seated attitudes, behaviours and cultural norms, within both security institutions and society overall. Rather than *ad hoc* isolated initiatives to recruit more women, it is necessary to take fully into account gender and diversity issues in the entire process of assessing, planning, implementing and evaluating post-conflict DDR and SSR processes.

Notes

1. It is extremely difficult to draw a conceptual line between "conflict" and "post-conflict" contexts. For more in-depth discussion on this terminology, see Chapter 1.
2. The three statistics are based, respectively, on the Rwanda National Police website at www.police.gov.rw/spip.php?article528; Pratt, Memunatu and Kristin Valasek (2011) "Sierra Leone", in Miranda Gaanderse and Kristin Valasek (eds) *The Security Sector and Gender in West Africa: A Survey of Police, Defence, Justice and Penal Services in ECOWAS States*, Geneva: DCAF, p. 231; UNDP Nepal (2006) "More Women in Law a Must for Justice in Nepal", 27 October, UNDP, available at www.undp.org.np/newsroom/details.php?n=195.
3. Schnabel, Albrecht and Hans-Georg Ehrhart (2005) "Post-Conflict Societies and the Military: Challenges and Problems of Security Sector Reform", in Albrecht Schnabel and Hans-Georg Ehrhart (eds) *Security Sector Reform and Post-Conflict Peacebuilding*, Tokyo: United Nations University Press, p. 2.
4. United Nations (2006) "Integrated Disarmament, Demobilisation and Reintegration Standards – 1.20 Glossary: Terms and Definitions", United Nations, New York, 1 August, p. 6, available at www.unddr.org/iddrs/01/download/IDDRS_120.pdf.
5. United Nations (2008) "Securing Peace and Development: The Role of the United Nations in Supporting Security Sector Reform", Report of the UN Secretary-General, United Nations, New York, 23 January, p. 6.
6. Hänggi, Heiner (2003) "Making Sense of Security Sector Governance", in Heiner Hänggi and Theodor Winkler (eds) *Challenges of Security Sector Governance*, Geneva: DCAF, pp. 17–18.
7. United Nations (2006) "Integrated Disarmament, Demobilisation and Reintegration Standards – 6.10: DDR and Security Sector Reform", United Nations, New York, 1 August, pp. 1–34, available at www.unddr.org/iddrs/06/download/IDDRS_610.pdf.
8. York, Jodi (1998) "The Truth About Women and Peace", in Lois Ann Lorentzen and Jennifer Turpin (eds) *The Women and War Reader*, New York: New York University Press, p. 19.
9. Sheehan, Michael (2005) *International Security: An Analytical Survey*, Boulder, CO: Lynne Rienner, p. 121. See also Chapter 2 in this volume.
10. Carter, April (1998) "Should Women Be Soldiers or Pacifists?", in Lois Ann Lorentzen and Jennifer Turpin (eds) *The Women and War Reader*, New York: New York University Press, pp. 33–34.
11. See authors such as Cynthia Cockburn, Carol Cohen and Cynthia Enloe. See also Farr, Vanessa, Henri Myrttinen and Albrecht Schnabel (eds) (2009) *Sexed Pistols: The Gendered Impacts of Small Arms and Light Weapons*, Tokyo: United Nations University Press.
12. For more information on how to integrate gender into SSR see Bastick, Megan and Kristin Valasek (eds) (2008) *Gender and Security Sector Reform Toolkit*, Geneva: DCAF, OSCE/ODIHR, UN-INSTRAW.

13. Wetterskog, Lars (2007) "Too Much 'Moralizing' Before Deployment, Good and Bad Examples: Lessons Learned from Working with United Nations Resolution 1325 in International Missions", Genderforce, Uppsala, p. 29.

14. OECD-DAC (2007) *OECD-DAC Handbook on Security System Reform: Supporting Security and Justice*, Paris: OECD, p. 73.

15. Snyder, R. Claire (2003) "The Citizen-Soldier Tradition and Gender Integration of the U.S. Military", *Armed Forces & Society* 29(2), pp. 185–186.

16. Lonsway, Kim, Margaret Moore, Penny Harrington, Eleanor Smeal and Katherine Spillar (2003) "Hiring & Retaining More Women: The Advantages to Law Enforcement Agencies", National Center for Women & Policing, Berkeley, CA, p. 3, available at http://womenandpolicing.com/pdf/NewAdvantagesReport.pdf.

17. Ibid., p. 2.

18. UN Department of Peacekeeping Operations (2006) "Enhancing the Operational Impact of Peacekeeping Operations: Gender Balance in Military and Police Services Deployed to UN Peacekeeping Missions", Final Report, UN DPKO Policy Dialogue, New York, 28–29 March, p. 3.

19. Ibid., p. 23.

20. Ibid.

21. McConnell, Tristan (2007) "All-Female Unit Keeps Peace in Liberia", *Christian Science Monitor*, 21 March.

22. UN Security Council (2007) "Record of 5766th Meeting", UN Doc. S/PV.5766, 23 October, United Nations, New York, p. 5, available at www.securitycouncilreport.org/atf/cf/%7B65BFCF9B-6D27-4E9C-8CD3-CF6E4FF96FF9%7D/WPS%20SPV5766.pdf.

23. Ward, Jeanne (2002) "If Not Now, When? Addressing Gender-based Violence in Refugee, Internally Displaced and Post-conflict Settings: A Global Overview", Reproductive Health for Refugees Consortium, New York, pp. 28, 81, available at www.rhrc.org/resources/ifnotnow.pdf.

24. Pickup, Francine with Suzanne Williams and Caroline Sweetman (2001) *Ending Violence Against Women: A Challenge for Development and Humanitarian Work*, Oxford: Oxfam GB, pp. 145–146.

25. Ibid., p. 142.

26. Lonsway et al., note 16, p. 3.

27. Number of signatory states according to the UN Division for the Advancement of Women, available at www.un.org/womenwatch/daw/cedaw/states.htm.

28. US Armed Forces Sergeant Zenaida Martinez, quoted in Zeigler, Sara L. and Gregory G. Gunderson (2005) *Moving Beyond G.I. Jane: Women and the U.S. Military*, Lanham, MD: University Press of America, p. 125.

29. Gregory, Jeanne and Sue Lees (1999) *Policing Sexual Assault*, New York: Routledge, p. 199.

30. OECD-DAC (2009) "Section 9: Integrating Gender Awareness and Equality", *OECD DAC Handbook on Security System Reform: Supporting Security and Justice*, revised edn, Paris: OECD, p. 15.

31. Global News Network (2007) "Liberia's Education Minister Expresses Optimism for Women Educational Program in the Police", 9 May, available at http://theliberiantimes.com/blogs/index.php?blog=2&m=200705.

32. Bastick, Megan (2008) *Integrating Gender in Post-Conflict Security Sector Reform*, Geneva: DCAF, pp. 17–18.

33. Naraghi, Sanam and Camille Pampell Conaway (2004) "Security Sector Reform", in *Inclusive Security, Sustainable Peace: A Toolkit for Advocacy and Action*, London: International Alert/Women Waging Peace, p. 35.

34. European Commission (1991) "Protecting the Dignity of Women and Men at Work: A Code of Practice on Measures to Combat Sexual Harassment", Commission Recommendation 92/131/EEC, 27 November, Brussels.
35. Zeigler and Gunderson, note 28, p. 125.
36. Maley, Jacqueline (2006) "Sexual Harassment Rife in Armed Forces", *The Guardian*, 26 May.
37. DeSouza, Eros R. and Joseph Solberg (2003) "Incidence and Dimensions of Sexual Harassment across Cultures", in Michele Paludi and Carmen A. Paludi (eds) *Academic and Workplace Sexual Harassment: A Handbook of Cultural, Social Science, Management and Legal Perspectives*, Westport, CT: Praeger, p. 67.
38. Zeigler and Gunderson, note 28, p. 112.
39. Kosovo Police Service (2002) "Sexual Harassment P-1.48", 27 February (revised 19 February 2003), Kosovo Police Service, Prishtina.
40. National Organization for Women (2006) "From The Citadel to Military Recruiting – Sexual Harassment in the Military More Pervasive than Ever", 1 September, NOW, Washington, DC, available at www.now.org/press/09-06/09-01.html.
41. Taylor, Lauren R. (2001) "Pentagon Says Military Domestic Violence Must End", *Women's Enews*, 4 December.
42. UN Department of Public Information (2005) "UN Establishes Peacekeeping Conduct and Discipline Units: Latest Move in Reforms to Tackle Sexual Exploitation, Abuse", Press Release PKO/120, 3 August, New York.
43. United Nations (2007) "UN Will Enforce 'Zero Tolerance' Policy Against Sexual Abuse, Peacekeeping Official Says", 5 January, UN News Service, New York, available at www.un.org/apps/news/story.asp?NewsID=21169&Cr=sex&Cr1=abuse.
44. United Nations (2006) "UN Hosts Meeting Aimed at Tackling Problems of Sexual Abuse by Field Personnel", 4 December, UN News Service, New York, available at www.un.org/apps/news/story.asp?NewsID=20842&Cr=sexual&Cr1=abuse.

Conclusion

14

Defying victimhood: Women as activists and peacebuilders

Anara Tabyshalieva and Albrecht Schnabel

The chapters in this volume cover a wide range of women's post-conflict peacebuilding experiences in different parts of the world. Post-conflict situations are windows of opportunity during which gender relations can and should be rethought and which, if properly utilized, can serve as the right moment to "rewrite" the rules and practices that previously served as obstacles to the participation of women in society. Overall, our book is meant to challenge the popular and often-propagated assumption that women should be supported, empowered and given a voice merely in their roles as victims. Collectively, we provide evidence in support of the growing understanding at international, national and local levels that while – and because – women are disproportionately affected by war, they can be powerful agents of positive and sustainable change if brought on board and given the chance to participate in every aspect of a society's peacebuilding process.

We now return to some of our main analytical conclusions on how best to reconsider and correctly interpret the roles, contributions, rights and responsibilities of women in post-conflict peacebuilding. We first focus on common experiences of victimization and revictimization observed across the different chapters. These include the need to recognize and overcome multilayered post-war challenges; the political and economic exclusion generally experienced by women in post-conflict environments; the failure to address conflict-related traumas as well as continuing or new forms of gender violence in the aftermath of armed conflict; and the resulting (re)victimization of women based on gender discrimination and the

Defying victimhood: Women and post-conflict peacebuilding, Schnabel and Tabyshalieva (eds),
United Nations University Press, 2012, ISBN 978-92-808-1201-5

re-establishment of patriarchal norms, practices and power relationships in both private and public institutions. While international – donor-driven – efforts should be able to address missed opportunities to create space and access for women to participate actively in peacebuilding processes, weak aid effectiveness and accountability as well as incoherent and possibly even contradictory national and international agendas and objectives for post-conflict reconstruction are obstacles that prevent women's access to post-conflict rebuilding activities.

We then draw on the findings from the book chapters and highlight experiences where women have managed to move beyond victimhood to become active, acknowledged contributors to and owners of post-conflict transformation processes. The reflections developed in this section focus on women's leadership roles; women's empowerment, social cohesion and different aspects of social transformation; evidence of successful partnership with both national and international players; experiences with coping and survival strategies of women at the community level; the role of international aid in empowering women; the value of successful awareness raising, advocacy and publicity; and the need for and impact of enhancing gender equality in a society's security and justice sectors.

We conclude with a number of recommendations – drawing on the experiences shared in the chapters – for facilitating and promoting positive responses to women's places and roles in rebuilding post-conflict societies. The general recommendations focus on the need to enhance women's political participation and empowerment. This includes efforts to increase and assure their effective representation at all levels and in all activities; the need to assure and enhance the physical security of women; and efforts to raise awareness among all stakeholders in peacebuilding about the potential for women to serve as agents of peaceful change in post-conflict transitions. Moreover, women need to be assured of access to economic resources. This requires efforts to push ahead with grassroots economic strategies to empower women on their own or in family units; the introduction and support of micro-credit programmes for women; the promotion of labour, land and property rights for women, including through legal reform; and the integration of women into the transformation and management of post-war security institutions. Specific recommendations cover the need to address war and post-war distress, including through faith-based institutions, indigenous healing ceremonies, truth and reconciliation mechanisms and other such locally relevant methods for assisting traumatized populations; to build coalitions and prepare for peaceful transformation and prevention of violent conflict; and the crucial necessity to work with men – both adults who effectively hold power in society and young men who hope for positive generational change in terms of men's attitudes towards women as equal partners, not inferior bystanders – in building and managing post-conflict societies. We close with some recommendations for international state and local actors, including the United Nations, regional organizations and bilateral donors, but also national governments, civil society organizations and national and international research communities.

Common experiences and recommendations for change

The chapters in this volume focus on the experiences, contributions and roles played by women in post-conflict reconstruction. Women are portrayed in their full complexity: not simply as helpless or innocent victims, but as both victims and active agents of change.

Interactions among members of post-war societies are characterized by new doubts and old concerns about prevailing hierarchical relationships between genders and age groups; and, most importantly, by crucial opportunities to reopen debates about marginalized, thus vulnerable, groups' safety and access to political and economic resources in the critical immediate post-conflict phase. The reflections from different parts of the world draw our attention to the differing dynamics of participation as they play out in various local, national and international settings. Most contributors agree that active facilitation and cooperation by all actors, whether local or international, are crucial in engaging and supporting women in the transformation of all aspects of a post-conflict society.

Although the following findings, recommendations and suggestions draw on a limited sample of conflict and post-conflict experiences, many are worth considering in a variety of other post-conflict and violence-afflicted contexts. Thus each case is relevant beyond its own context and its lessons will likely resonate with the challenges faced and opportunities for change offered in other settings.

Women as victims in conflict and post-conflict environments

During the past decade international and national players have made extensive progress in mainstreaming gender in peacebuilding activities, such as through gender analysis programmes, by focusing on gender equity or with attempts at institutionalizing gender inclusion (Chapter 2). However, these remarkable advancements met with many obstacles and difficulties. While there is a committed network of individuals and institutions that are dedicated to moving a pro-women peacebuilding agenda forward, widespread ignorance of women's right to equality, a refusal to address violence against women and obstruction of women's peace efforts are still real constraints (Chapter 2). The chapters in this volume point to a great number of specific challenges that are characteristic of post-conflict environments (see Chapter 1) and resonate strongly throughout the various case studies. They are detrimental to, but also highlight the need for, creative and feasible solutions to give women more just and meaningful roles, even in the most adverse political, economic and cultural environments.

Political exclusion of women

The absence – and purposeful exclusion – of women in peace negotiations is a common phenomenon in the post-conflict world. Post-conflict processes continue to serve the interests of male-dominated parties and tend to overlook the needs and interests of women, as if they were a special interest group or simply one of many vulnerable groups rather than half or more of society. Despite an international discourse proclaiming that their views are important, women continue to be excluded from peace talks and all other stages of the process. Moreover, women and men are often trapped within patriarchal cultural norms that cause people to prefer to be represented by a man. Women might be considered electorally only if there is no suitable male candidate, while those female candidates who argue from a patriarchal perspective are more likely to be accepted than women who represent the views of other women (Chapter 12). Structural efforts at the local and national levels to overcome this challenge remain operationally weak. At present, whether women will be seen as partners or not depends much more on the personal convictions of individual actors than on a systematic implementation of policies of gender inclusion. Yet individuals with the authority, willingness and diplomatic skill to trigger changes in attitudes and behaviours towards the treatment of women as equal peacebuilding partners remain exceptional in all current peacebuilding operations.

While representatives of international organizations should be much more proactive, regrettably they often remain unreliable due to either ignorance, neglect, a misguided sense of respect for local ownership or their own unexamined prejudice. They rarely enforce their posturing on women's inclusion when it comes to negotiations in reality. For instance, in her discussion of the Taëf Agreement (1989) in Lebanon, Kari Karamé (Chapter 12) notes that even though the negotiation of the agreement was supported by the United Nations and the United States, only men were invited to the negotiation table. As Vanessa Farr shows in Chapter 11, more than 20 years later, "Contrary to the clear directives given in SCR 1325 to include women in all aspects of decision-making in a conflict zone, Palestinian women are routinely excluded from all high-level negotiations on the Israel-Palestine question – by Palestinian males, the state of Israel and the international community." The cases of Burundi and Tajikistan indicate that male-dominated political institutions were re-luctant to delegate authority and responsibility to women during negotia-tions, as issues of war and peace were considered to be "men's issues" (see Chapters 5 and 7). In neither case did international actors override these attitudes in favour of honouring their own stated commitments to advance women's inclusion. These experiences show that unless inter-national actors are ready and willing to promote aggressively the norms now enshrined in lofty statements and reports by the UN Security Coun-cil and Secretary-General, for instance, nothing will change.

Economic and security exclusion of women

In post-conflict environments in particular, women tend to face greater economic problems than men because of their disadvantaged status. Women without direct protection of adult men, including widows, second or unofficial wives, unmarried mothers and single women, are particularly often denied legal rights to land and other resources that were previously owned by their deceased husbands, fathers or other close male relatives. Often they are also unable to engage in productive economic activities and, along with their dependent children, elderly or sick under their care, subsequently suffer from abject poverty and deprivation (Chapter 3). Marginalized by their community, some women support polygamy in the often-vain hope that it will offer protection for themselves and their chil-dren (Chapter 7).

Similar dynamics are at play in a nation's security institutions. Recruit-ment practices often fail to reach out to pools of qualified and interested female candidates, as is demonstrated by strikingly low rates of female participation within many of the institutions of the security sector, includ-ing the police services and armed forces. Even when women do gain access, they face considerable difficulties in coping with discrimination, harassment and violence, all of which pose formidable barriers to women's retention and promotion. Creating representative security sec-tor institutions where men and women participate equally at all levels of decision-making is a challenge, particularly in institutions where men tra-ditionally tend to be greatly overrepresented (Chapter 13).

Failure to address trauma, health issues and post-conflict gender violence

Many women are physically disabled and psychologically traumatized by the wounds of war crimes, which continue to haunt them long after the end of armed violence. The international community has supported some modest programmes for reproductive health and dealing with psy-chological trauma, for instance in Bosnia, Cambodia and Rwanda. How-ever, such programmes usually only managed to reach a small fraction of the suffering women and no precise information is available on their effectiveness. As the treatment of traumatized women is labour-intensive, costly and often misunderstood, poor countries lack the resources, institutional infrastructure and cultural and social capacities to provide such services on a large scale and in a sustainable manner (Chapter 3).

In addition, violence and harassment against women continue in the aftermath of armed conflict. The cases from South Africa, Rwanda and Sierra Leone show that there is an explicit acceptance of peacetime gender-based violence. While wartime rape is increasingly seen as a crime and thus usually prohibited, everyday violence against women in peacetime is not (Chapter 9). Equally, even though rape is now recognized in the Statute of the International Criminal Court as a war crime and crime against humanity, domestic violence is not distinctively recognized as prosecutable under international criminal law. Moreover, in many countries the definition of domestic violence in national criminal justice systems remains ambiguous, such as in East Timor and Cambodia (Chapter 4). As domestic and sexual violence and harassment tend to proliferate during the immediate aftermath of armed conflicts, women are further victimized at an already particularly challenging time.

"Revictimization" based on gender

After war, patterns of gender discrimination and segregation that existed prior to the outbreak of armed violence are often reproduced. In some cases the worst aspects of the male-dominated cultural norms can be rebuilt, such as polygamy, early arranged marriages and segregation. According to Sharipova and De Soto (Chapter 7), the Tajikistan case demonstrates that the "gendered cultural and religious patriarchal traditions, suppressed during the Soviet era, have enjoyed a resurgence and had negative effects for women".

Often, women are seen as victims and passive recipients of benign local and international support; but if, during the course of the conflict, they gained access to previously male-owned institutions, they are also seen as a significant threat to male power. It is also clear that the rhetoric may change without much institutional change being felt on the ground. For example, especially in the aftermath of high-profile mass crimes, human rights are likely to be universally emphasized and appropriate legal and regulatory frameworks established. This is a positive development. Yet such rights – and particularly women's rights – are unlikely to be rigorously enforced by law enforcement agencies, as the institutions and personnel that are meant to safeguard human rights are in reality very difficult to change, especially in traditional societies where women have not previously enjoyed social and political equality (Chapter 3).

In countries such as South Africa, Rwanda and Sierra Leone, where male supremacy, dominance and aggression are widespread, women continue to suffer gender-specific human rights violations. As Lyn Graybill argues, "The systematic subordination of women and entrenched social attitudes that preceded those periods of conflict made the notion of women's *bodies as battlefields* acceptable. Women's bodies continue to be sites of struggle" (Chapter 9). Among the reasons for this problem is the pattern of normalization of violent male behaviour during the years of conflict as a legitimate way to reach socio-economic and political goals – little is done to challenge or change this reality in the aftermath. As a result, private, domestic gender-based violence and the use of violent rhetoric or actual political repression by leaders are far too often seen as acceptable male behaviour by both women and men.

In a post-conflict process, some new forms of patriarchy and gender order may develop. As violence against women and children continues to flourish in a post-war environment, sex trafficking, sexual exploitation and prostitution challenge peacebuilding and recovery efforts (Chapters 4 and 7). It is not only in public institutions run by men and in male attitudes, however, that transformation is difficult and slow. In some cases where there are efforts to reform policing and justice delivery in women's favour, women prefer to cling to the past, colluding in their own victimization by sacrificing themselves to protect their male relatives. An example from post-conflict Tajikistan tells of women who willingly took responsibility for crimes of drug trafficking and murder that were committed by their husbands and sons (Chapter 7).

Lack of cohesion between international and national agendas and mandates

There is little cohesion and insufficient collaboration among national and international players, which greatly impedes cooperation on peacebuilding activities and empowerment of women. For instance, in East Timor and Cambodia the situation of women is challenged by, among other things, an incoherent introduction of international human rights standards and the lack of consolidation with national and local judicial structures. Unilateral introduction of international standards without the human and financial resources to implement them creates confusion and tempts local populations to revert back to customary practices, as these promise faster and more predictable responses (Chapter 4).

Although the establishment of gender units in peacekeeping missions or national governments was intended to enhance the promotion of gender equality in international and national decision-making processes, in reality they may have marginalized the agendas of women and children by creating weak agencies without adequate authority, capacity, financing and expertise. At the same time the existence of such units appears to have created the impression that other relevant offices and institutions are freed from responsibility for addressing the needs of women and children within their mandates and activities (Chapter 4).

Achievements in moving beyond victimhood and towards respecting the agency of women as peacebuilders

These continuing challenges aside, over the last two to three decades there have been positive developments that allow women to play more just and meaningful roles as peace agents in official post-conflict peacebuilding activities. These changes are being supported by both national and international actors, and some could be emulated in other contexts. The following observations highlight some of these positive and replicable experiences.

Women's leadership roles

The value of women's leadership in conflict management and peacebuilding is increasingly visible and recognized in public and official debates and publications. One of the main messages in the volume is that the need for women's equal share of leadership positions in post-conflict activities is overlooked at both international and national levels. Yet even in adverse political, economic and cultural environments and despite a lack of government support and/or international assistance, in many postwar areas women's grassroots groups have consolidated their peacebuilding efforts at local and national levels. When governments are unwilling or unable to address issues of importance to the survival of women in post-conflict societies, women's peace activism and reconstruction efforts, focusing on self-help, mutual support and survival, are the only spaces in which the interests and rights of women and other marginalized groups are discussed (Chapter 5).

There are numerous field stories about peace initiatives of women which are bridging ethnic and religious divides in Africa, Europe, the Middle East and Asia. In Burundi, female peace activists initiated a safe space for inter-ethnic dialogue (Chapter 5). A different inter-ethnic dialogue was initiated in Macedonia by a programme called Lifestart in Emergencies, where female victims of violence contributed to conflict prevention activities at the community level (Chapter 8). In Lebanon, which is divided into sectarian zones, Muslim and Christian women initiated pacifist movements to meet from both sides of the demarcation line in Beirut, triggering the anger of the dominating militias (Chapter 12). The Kenya Women's Peace Forum meets regularly to evaluate and discuss how national policies and events affect women in the country. In addition, Kenyan women's groups played important roles in organizing women voters to support female candidates and create a relatively violence-free election in 2002 (Chapter 3). In the occupied Palestinian territory, women are finding ways to achieve reconciliation between the two main political factions as a means to restore national unity (Chapter 11).

In immediate post-war situations, women's networks and organizations are often the only places where women can go for support, education, protection, shelter or to escape violence, forced marriages and other risks, as well as to provide support for other women. For instance, in Afghanistan women's organizations have been providing a multitude of services that would otherwise be unavailable in many rural areas. They have been running independent girls schools, income-generation programmes, healthcare training and legal aid clinics (Chapter 3).

Women's economic empowerment and social cohesion

Micro-credit programmes supported by multilateral donors have proved successful in empowering women at the community level. Such programmes often aim to support the struggle for survival of poor and widowed single heads of households and abused women in hostile post-conflict environments (Chapters 3 and 6). Many micro-credit programmes bring together women from different ethnic and religious groups and afford them access to financial loans to start up small businesses. In addition, the informal interactions within these groups have therapeutic value. In Rwanda, for instance, women's groups included both Tutsi and Hutu women, who helped each other in rebuilding their traumatized lives (Chapter 3).

Joint economic and social activities also have a preventive dynamic. In the Balkans joint economic activities of women effectively bridged post-conflict divides in society. Good practices include Yugoslavian and Macedonian cases. Women teamed up for the Lifestart in Emergencies initiative in isolated, ethnically divided regions of Macedonia and learned to overcome mistrust and bridge ethnic divides for the sake of their children. The programmes had a positive influence on them and their male and female relatives, inspiring them to develop relationships with men and women from other groups. Such economic programmes have positive impacts in many areas because of their non-confrontational character and ability to foster confidence. Aimed at providing a better future for their families and children, the programmes served as effective, non-threatening entry points for women to address socially and culturally sensitive issues, such as domestic and inter-community violence (Chapters 6 and 8).

A sole reliance on male relatives for peace and economic security does not guarantee women's and families' survival; the contributions by women, in family units or alone, are crucially important. In Burundi many of the women's associations were formed by those who decided to focus on reclaiming their own sense of identity, reviving dormant skills and engaging in a number of activities that were conducive to personal healing and economic productivity (Chapter 5).

Successful partnerships of national and international players

The international community and national actors have made praiseworthy progress in mainstreaming gender concerns in post-conflict reconstruction. The ground-breaking UN Security Council Resolution (SCR) 1325 (2000) has generated many hopes for a gender-sensitive approach to post-conflict reconstruction across the world. The resolution was an important landmark in the recognition of women as peace agents. Although a number of states ignore SCR 1325, it has become popular in the last decade (Chapter 10). In addition, SCR 1820 (2008) focuses on the prevention of sexual violence in war. However, it takes a more limited view of sexual violence and the victimhood of women, and narrows the geographic focus and agenda of SCR 1325. In fact it risks diluting existing international law, limits the number of countries on the Security Council's agenda and thus threatens the full implementation of SCR 1325 (Chapters 1 and 10).

Numerous UN agencies, in partnership with other international and national stakeholders, made a difference in empowering women as resourceful agents of peace. Particularly UNIFEM and several non-governmental organizations (NGOs) have advocated for women's inclusion in all aspects of peacebuilding (Chapter 10). Furthermore, on a regional level the Intergovernmental Authority on Development in Eastern Africa, for instance, has adopted a regional gender policy to enhance the role of women in peacebuilding and post-conflict reconstruction.

Coping and survival strategies of women at the community level

In parallel with actions initiated by governments, civil society organizations and international actors, local communities continue to address war and post-war trauma in time-honoured and traditional ways. Particularly in a post-conflict environment, women and men continue to appreciate the value of peaceful religious practices and indigenous traditions of mutual support. The importance and contributions of traditional responses to war and post-war suffering are often overlooked. The chapters in this volume report on a wide variety of faith-based and cultural practices of survival. In Cambodia, for instance, traumatized women visit Buddhist temples for relief through meditation (Chapter 3). In many tribal areas in Africa, local healers provide help to distressed women. In Lebanon, Muslim and Christian women initiated "pacifist movements that tried to meet from both sides of the demarcation line in Beirut" (Chapter 12).

Experience shows that despite the trauma of war and violence, women are less likely to resort to destructive measures, such as violent retaliation, than men. Instead, more often than not they focus on productive approaches to survival – and thus to constructive peacebuilding. For instance, in Burundi women were proactively engaged in peacebuilding at the grassroots level, where they are not considered to be threatening national and state power structures and are thus free to become socially and politically active. Associations, community groups and social movements offer a much-needed space for social and psychological healing (Chapter 5).

Again drawing on the experience in Burundi, the survival strategies employed by women were often so subtle that even well-intentioned practitioners and academics failed to recognize their critical role in peacebuilding. Women's creative, practical and non-violent approaches to peacebuilding focused less on "victimization" and more on survival strategies and reconstruction initiatives, which enhanced their capacity for serving as effective peace players (Chapter 5).

International aid to empower women

Many field studies show a positive relationship between foreign aid and the empowerment of women. The international community has supported women's organizations in post-conflict societies in order to channel humanitarian assistance and empower women. In many countries, such as Bosnia, Cambodia, El Salvador and Rwanda, women's organizations have used such assistance to support the rehabilitation of female victims of mass crimes and the promotion of women's economic and political rights. However, as Vanessa Farr shows in her case study of the occupied Palestinian territory (Chapter 11), if women's organizations are afraid to touch politically sensitive issues for fear of becoming "politicized" (or being perceived as such by political authorities and donors), they lose their ability to function as advocates for women's rights. She thus argues that "The donor community ... needs to recognize and overcome its tendency to disempower, even if not intentionally, women's organizations and develop more effective funding responses that value and encourage women's public political participation."

Successful awareness raising, advocacy and publicity

Post-conflict settings present new prospects for the participation of women in the political arena. Often, post-war democratic constitutions provide formal equality between men and women. As a result of their increased involvement in public life during and after conflict, some women not only acquire leadership skills and experience but also become keenly aware of their political rights and responsibilities (Chapters 3 and 8).

International and national awareness-raising initiatives and advocacy have encouraged general public and government perceptions of women as peace agents. Due to international advocacy and pressure in Afghanistan, for instance, in 2002 female candidates gained 160 seats in the 1,451-strong tribal council, the Emergency Loya Jirga. The UN Mission in Afghanistan included a gender adviser and the interim government established a ministry of women's affairs, similar to the practices in postwar East Timor and Cambodia (Chapter 4).

In many post-conflict contexts, discriminatory DDR (disarmament, demobilization and reintegration) processes reduce the possibility to recruit female ex-combatants into newly formed security sector institutions. In Liberia, for instance, an initial needs assessment estimated that there were approximately 2,000 female combatants who qualified for DDR, but were not given an opportunity to take part. Following an awareness-raising campaign by women's groups that encouraged women and girls to participate in the DDR process, eventually 22,370 women and 2,440 girls were disarmed and demobilized (Chapter 13).

In many cases, growing publicity about the situation of women triggers responses by the national government. In Sierra Leone, for instance, activists were able to take the recommendations from the Truth and Reconciliation Commission report and lobby effectively for the passage of a number of gender-focused bills (Chapter 9).

Enhanced gender equality in security institutions

The Vienna-based UN Commission for Crime Prevention and Criminal Justice drafted a resolution in 1997 to enhance gender equality in the area of criminal justice systems. Taken up by the General Assembly in December of the same year, it provides guidance on a wide range of issues, including criminal procedures, police powers, sentencing and corrections, and victim support and assistance (Chapter 4).

Although employment within security institutions is traditionally viewed as men's work, women are both qualified for and – sometimes contrary to popular belief – very much interested in these positions. Within many post-conflict countries, employment within the security sector can provide financial and job security, both of which are highly appealing to women, just as they are to men (Chapter 13). Moreover, making security institutions and the services they provide more representative of and relevant to all parts of the post-conflict societies they serve necessitates the integration of women.

General recommendations for change

Enhancing political participation and empowerment

Increase political representation of women!

During times of conflict, many women acquire leadership skills and experiences. They become aware of their political rights and the responsibilities they can and should shoulder in post-conflict settings (Chapter 3). Post-war constitutions and laws should thus provide for formal gender equality and the legal underpinning for assuring women's right and duty to participate in the political life of society.

Both international and national actors should encourage women's participation in political affairs. Modest and sometimes symbolic steps taken to increase women's access and participation should translate into more significant and visible decision-making roles. Programmes need to be developed to facilitate greater representation of women in post-conflict elections, to assist female candidates in subsequent elections on a non-partisan basis and to support women's advocacy organizations engaged in promoting women's participation in local and national affairs (Chapter 3). Especially in male-dominated political cultures, some women have a negative attitude towards political activities and prefer not to engage in politics, choosing instead to become actively involved in the work of NGOs (Chapter 12). Consulting with NGOs in general and women's NGOs in particular may thus offer opportunities to reach women who are willing to play more active roles in society. However, as Farr shows, this presupposes that women's NGOs are free to participate in sensitive political debates without fear of suppression and the risk of scaring women away from participation (Chapter 11).

When attempting to raise women's representation in political, economic and social life, it is important to avoid simplistic applications of gender quotas. While quotas might offer short-term solutions, they do not address the underlying reasons for the absence of women from positions of power and influence. However, it is very useful to incorporate a gender dimension at the design, implementation, monitoring and evaluation stages of peacebuilding programmes and projects. The objective of gender-sensitive peacebuilding programme design and implementation is not merely to raise the number of women involved, but to gain an understanding of the similarities and differences between the needs, priorities and contributions of women and men, thus breaking down outdated and discriminatory stereotypes and attitudes (Chapter 3).

For instance, when post-conflict reconstruction focuses almost exclusively on rebuilding physical infrastructure, the "social infrastructure" tends to be overlooked. More often than not it is women who highlight and prioritize the need to rebuild such social infrastructure, including health, education, public housing and protection of the environment. The Lebanese experience tells us that primarily female government ministers lobbied for investments in social infrastructure, thus addressing a crucial peacebuilding challenge that would have otherwise gone unnoticed (Chapter 12).

Include women in peacemaking and peacebuilding processes!

Peacebuilding consultations should take advantage of – and learn from – the survival and coping strategies of women who have managed their own lives and the lives of their families and communities in the midst of tensions, armed violence and their aftermath (Chapter 11). Both international and national actors should pay greater attention to the voices and experiences of women peacemakers and support their initiatives (Chapter 5). Their experiences should inform the planning of peacebuilding programmes. Equal contribution of men and women from the planning to the implementation of peacebuilding programmes is a precondition for enhancing the impact of local and international interventions and making the consolidation of peace increasingly just and sustainable (Chapters 2, 10 and 11). Commitments to gender equality are thus an essential requirement for peacebuilding activities. However, while one or two programmes dedicated to the inclusion of women or women's organizations may show symbolic goodwill, they do not substitute for a truly participatory process that capitalizes on the contributions of women peacemakers and responds to and advances women's specific needs and experiences (Chapters 2 and 11).

Enhance the physical security of women!

National actors, bilateral and multilateral agencies, international organizations and NGOs need to formulate and implement programmes on enhancing the physical security of vulnerable populations, which, in post-conflict societies, include virtually the entire (male and female) population. Individual requirements of specific groups must be analysed, understood and considered, particularly of those groups which are marginalized in peacebuilding processes and thus prevented from fully determining their own fate and making positive contributions to their society's future. Being one of these groups, women have been marginalized and are now in need of proactive inclusion. Including these groups in programme planning and evaluation processes ensures that their requirements are properly considered. Security institutions are the official providers of security, yet often they are not trusted because of their oppressive and violent behaviour during conflict. Security sector reform is thus an essential precondition for post-conflict reconstruction. The inclusion of women in these processes is key for ensuring that the provision of security responds adequately to security threats experienced by women and eventually giving "greater representation of women in police forces and judicial processes, training to security staff on women's rights, establishment of peace committees to prevent the eruption of violence and special interventions for vulnerable youth" (Chapter 3; see also Chapter 13).

During the post-conflict moment, violence against women must be reduced and cannot be tolerated or accepted as customary, culturally legitimate behaviour. Concerns about unacceptable behaviour towards women cannot be limited to wartime only. For example, the recognition that rape in times of conflict is wrong must lead to the recognition that violence against women in peacetime is equally unacceptable (Chapter 9).

In constructing a gender-equitable post-conflict society, health services for women and girls should be prioritized. It is important to mainstream concerns for the epidemic spread of sexually transmitted diseases, including HIV/AIDS, especially in Africa (Chapters 5 and 9). So far, however, experience shows that in the aftermath of conflict the health needs of girls and women receive less priority than those of boys and men (Chapters 3 and 7).

Strengthen respect for women's human rights!

After war, international and national actors need to work hand in hand to promote women's rights – or, better, to prevent the violation of human rights in general, with particular consideration to understanding and alleviating rights violations as they concern specific groups in society, including women. They need to fund and develop awareness-raising programmes via radio, television and print media. To end cultures of impunity, comprehensive reporting systems need to be created to document abuses of women's rights and support female and civilian survivors of the war in seeking justice (Chapter 3). Following on the suggestions made in the previous section, this needs to include special training for law enforcement agencies, which play an important role in enforcing women's rights at the community level (Chapters 3 and 13).

Raise awareness about women as peace agents in post-conflict transition!

Promoting public debates and media literacy about SCRs 1325 and 1820 (and subsequent resolutions) and about national responses to these important programmes in post-conflict societies is an essential step in raising awareness about and advocating for participatory roles of women.

In order to sensitize society and national actors to issues about gender discrimination, particularly in patriarchal societies, women should be given opportunities to voice their concerns about perceived gender injustices and translate those experiences into supporting and leading roles in transforming their society. In post-conflict reconstruction, particularly girls and women should be publicly recognized and encouraged (and, most importantly, not discouraged!) to play more active roles. This recommendation can be advanced by offering women opportunities to debate and analyse the language of SCRs such as 1325 in order to relate them to the specific conflicts in which they are caught (Chapter 11).

The media can be a powerful and influential collaborator in publicizing and advocating the end to discrimination of previously underrepresented groups of society. Some practical and potentially useful steps drawn from the case studies throughout this volume include the identification of journalists who are sympathetic to calls for women's empowerment; the pooling and sharing of media contacts in an easily accessible database; regular, targeted and concise briefings for journalists; and efforts to focus on positive angles in reporting on post-conflict developments and dynamics by offering interviews with women engaged in conflict and peace issues on the ground (Chapter 10). Moreover, strategies need to be encouraged that promote women's engagement and empowerment in utilizing the media. Stakeholders need to develop and support programmes that create awareness about women's needs and rights through radio, television and print media (Chapter 3).

Women-only forums have proven to facilitate women's participation at community and national levels. Initiatives to establish such forums need to be supported by national and international actors (Chapter 5). Particularly state actors must be convinced of the need to value, not sabotage and repress, women's organizations' intentions to participate in public debates on politically sensitive yet existential issues (Chapter 11). Such women-only spaces are important ways to build bridges between women from different identity groups, collect information about the types and effectiveness of current programmes and set priorities and strategies for addressing violence against, and the political marginalization of, women. They are safe spaces for discussion of highly personal forms of violence and the unique perspectives of women that are often not discussed in mixed-sex forums (Chapter 2).

Support training and education!

Education and training activities can prepare women and men for their roles in post-conflict societies, including the responsibility of providing leadership. Because of alarming trends in gender inequalities in education and training, which affect girls and women in a post-conflict society, the problem of unequal access to education needs to be urgently addressed (Chapters 3 and 5).

Women should be trained and educated to participate in peacebuilding activities as experts, community and national leaders, decision-makers, civil society activists and opinion leaders. Building capacity through leadership and communication skills is of strategic importance for current and potential future women leaders (Chapter 7).

Providing access to economic resources

Push ahead with women-focused economic strategies at the grassroots!

Peacebuilding programmes need to take affirmative action to ensure gender-based patterns of discrimination that prevent women's equal access to resources and political and economic opportunities in post-conflict societies will be broken (Chapters 2 and 11).

Relief agencies, NGOs and community groups should empower women to take the necessary first steps towards independent survival. The Yugoslav example of women owners of shops in post-conflict Sarajevo, Belgrade and other communities is an encouraging model. Providing small interest-free loans to qualified women and teaching them basic small-business practices are effective steps in peacebuilding equality (Chapter 6).

To ensure job security for women and avoid discrimination and nepotism in fragile transition societies, it is crucial to establish an independent review board for applicants for public sector positions. Women should not be trapped in entry-level posts as a result of traditional discrimination, everyday family duties or a lack of access to educational resources (Chapter 13).

Promote micro-credit programmes for women!

Micro-credit programmes should be promoted to serve joint humanitarian and developmental goals. In the context of such programmes, international lenders should continue to address needs of disadvantaged groups of women. Micro-credit programmes in peacebuilding environments also have great therapeutic value through the informal interactions they trigger at the community level (Chapter 3).

Support land and property rights for women!

Peacebuilding leaders often fail to consider the difficulties women face in accessing resources, including their property and land rights. These deserve priority treatment, as in most agricultural societies gender equality in access to land, water and other resources holds the key to women's survival. In this context, the international community and national actors should monitor the implementation of constitutional and legislative reforms, encourage initiatives designed to build public support for women's property rights and support actions to resolve bureaucratic inertia and confrontation (Chapter 3).

Integrate women in post-conflict security institutions!

Established good practices for increasing the recruitment, retention and advancement of women in security institutions include the comprehensive integration of gender issues into reform processes. This includes specific measures that focus on recruitment, retention and advancement, as well as support for female staff associations, raising public awareness on the role of women in the security sector and training female personnel to speak at schools and with the media (Chapter 13).

To create equitable institutions it is necessary not merely to focus on female security personnel, but also to include initiatives directed at male security personnel and oversight bodies. Building the capacity of oversight institutions to demand and monitor female recruitment, retention and advancement should be a priority. Ensuring that male security personnel are informed and trained on institutional gender policies is crucial. Senior management must also take the responsibility to enforce these policies and create a healthy work environment free of impunity. Enlisting high-ranking male security personnel as gender champions, advocates and trainers is thus a particularly useful practice (Chapter 13).

Ensuring that DDR processes incorporate female ex-combatants and women and girls associated with the fighting forces opens up an avenue to recruit trained women for new security sector positions. It is therefore important that DDR and security sector reform processes, if not already approached as complementary and highly interlinked activities, are well coordinated – and that they are more gender-sensitive (Chapter 13).

Human resource policies and practices should be reviewed and made as woman- and family-friendly as possible, including through the availability of flexible work hours, part-time and job sharing, daycare and school facilities, transportation, nursing areas, access to psychological support and paid maternity and paternity leave. Logistics and equipment also need to be available for women, including separate and adequate numbers of bathrooms and appropriate uniforms and equipment (Chapter 13).

Addressing war and post-war trauma

Recognize the role of faith-based institutions in helping traumatized populations!

International and national actors need to consider supporting traditional approaches and institutions that deal with psychological traumas experienced by women, men, girls and boys. Traumas can lead to highly destructive behaviour towards oneself, the immediate family and community and society at large. In this context, local religious beliefs and value systems have customarily provided consolation to suffering populations and should be consulted and utilized (Chapters 3 and 12). However, one must be careful not to harm women's positions by strengthening traditional actors who use their post-conflict activities to reinforce discriminatory practices. It is important to ensure that the goals and objectives of post-conflict actions are correctly understood by local communities. Lack of expertise and respect for the local culture may undermine the fragile trust generated within a traumatized society. In some cases local people also fear proselytizing motives behind external activities. As Sharipova and De Soto report in Chapter 7, in Tajikistan, for instance, men were concerned that the purpose of a particular project was to convert women to Christianity.

Especially in male-dominated societies, support groups among women are time-tested institutions that offer invaluable opportunities to share problems and experiences. Such groups provide joint psychological support and need to be permitted to engage with women on issues that concern their existential needs and concerns (Chapters 3, 5 and 11).

Build coalitions to transform and prevent violent conflict!

Post-war activities should pay attention to proactive approaches to conflict prevention in fragile societies. The tremendous challenges of rebuilding post-war societies serve as reminders of the costs incurred in waiting for conflicts to erupt and picking up the pieces afterwards. Efforts and commitments towards conflict prevention are necessary to avoid the escalation of an intractable spiral of violence and destruction. As a logical consequence, all women and men, young and old, in affected societies should unite, build new coalitions and organize within social movements, civil society organizations or political parties to prevent violence, transform conflict and, in the aftermath of war, create conditions for avoiding its repetition.

Support greater participation of adult and young men!

Gender divides and inequalities can be narrowed only if both women and men join in advocacy and awareness-raising activities. In particular, involving more men, especially gender-sensitive men, in consultations and initiatives that promote women's peace and security and address sexual violence is a crucial requirement for converting the challenges of victimhood into opportunities for leadership (Chapter 10).

Recommendations for international, state and local actors

After these more general recommendations, which focus mainly on themes and actions, the following recommendations are directed at actors that can facilitate positive change towards more sensible and just treatment and opportunities for empowerment and participation of women in post-conflict processes.

International community

United Nations and Security Council

The United Nations is often criticized for – and is in fact guilty of – ongoing gender imbalances among UN country-specific special representatives of the Secretary-General (SRSGs). In 2009 women held only two of the 40 posts of SRSG.[1] Moreover, in 2011 only three out of 14 peacekeeping missions were headed by female SRSGs, while only 45 out of a total of 138 UN resident representatives were women.[2] Particularly where sexual violence – direct and structural violence – is a major and complex challenge, advisers on gender-based violence should be deployed as part of peacekeeping missions, as has been done for instance in the Mission of the UN Organization in the Democratic Republic of the Congo (Chapter 10), and should be properly funded to do their work. Where possible and feasible, conduct and discipline departments or units should be included in existing and future peacekeeping missions.

Particularly as time passes and SCR 1325 becomes more of a historic document, with fewer specific advocacy events and activities, its main messages might become forgotten and the presumption that they have been mainstreamed might turn out to be false. It is thus important to develop and enforce strong accountability systems for the monitoring and evaluation of SCRs 1325 and 1820 and all subsequent resolutions on women's peace and security issues, as called for by the Secretary-General. Planning for peace support operations and other field missions should demonstrate a familiarity with SCR 1325 and its interpretation. This should be demonstrated at all stages, including pre-mission planning, during the mission and in post-mission reporting. It should also be the norm in cases where the United Nations acts as a transitional authority. Of particular importance is the integration of women's perspectives and a fair and equitable gender balance in the make-up of missions, setting positive examples for national counterparts.

Special attention should be given to avoiding the pitfalls of many designated "gender units". As mentioned above, in some cases the establishment of weak gender units in peacekeeping missions or national and local governments may in fact lead to the marginalization of issues related to the support and empowerment of women, thus "wasting" the potential that was generated with the designation of such units for advancing women's concerns in peace operations.

Ensuring national-level adherence to gender-equal practices includes development, consultation and agreement of standards of excellence for future national action plans (NAPs). Such standards could result from research and analysis into the impact of NAPs and may generate political will to replicate helpful practice in context-specific NAPs already in operation (Chapter 10).

Systematic conduct and improvement of gender and socio-economic analyses of post-conflict societies, as well as methodological development, collection and analysis of sex-disaggregated data and gender-sensitive indicators, remain important issues. Gender-sensitive peacebuilding strategies depend on the thorough analysis of reliable and systematically collected gender-disaggregated data (Chapter 10).

Bilateral and multilateral actors, including regional organizations

It is particularly important to engage civil society actors in consultative processes during the planning of peacebuilding programmes. This will help support local and national ownership of the implementation of and follow-up to sustainable efforts, without which real change is difficult to achieve. In this context, the contributions by individual women and women's organizations will be crucial. It would also be helpful to integrate issues of violence against – and security for – women in early warning and response mechanisms by multilateral organizations, or ensure that national efforts are ready and willing to respond to escalating levels of violence against women in a preventive fashion.

International actors can serve as models of coalition-building and cooperation with each other and with national and local actors. Humanitarian actors, for instance, are often on the ground before and during a conflict, and are also among the first international actors present, addressing society's most immediate survival needs, once official fighting has halted. They are thus best placed to expand and deepen the collaborative efforts initiated before and during the conflict with civil society actors from the society they serve. Particularly as part of their work with women, they should be among the first to champion and promote women's rights and ensure that women are an inherent component of all short- and long-term assistance strategies.

There are also a number of post-conflict challenges that necessitate regional approaches by national actors, including those directly affecting the situation of women. In Central Asia, for instance, women and children are illegally trafficked to Russia. Tracking, countering and mitigating such crimes require close collaboration among regional, national and international actors (Chapters 4 and 7).

Development donor community

The development donor community is well advised to increase its support to women's organizations and recognize this work as being political, not just immediate service provision. Aid offered to war-torn societies needs to take into consideration women's human rights violations, government accountability and responsiveness and the involvement of civil society groups in promoting, advancing and maintaining increased participation of women in setting and implementing post-conflict peacebuilding agendas. In addition to incentives for post-conflict governments to create space for the activities of such organizations, a coherent policy of conditionality should entice national and local governmental and non-governmental authorities to support vulnerable groups as active agents of peace and draw on their advice and active contribution (Chapter 11). Women's organizations need to be recognized as an integral part of externally driven efforts to rehabilitate and reconstruct post-conflict societies (Chapter 3). Direct funding should be made available to such groups. However, long-term dependence of these organizations and their activities on external sources of aid should be avoided (Chapter 8). Women's organizations also need to be given the government's assurance that they will not be sanctioned for accepting financial support from external sources and for possibly challenging prevailing cultural and social norms that limit women's rights, freedoms and opportunities to play active peacebuilding roles.

Donors should work with national and local governments in developing mechanisms to support grassroots peacebuilding initiatives that help women leave their victimhood behind and take substantial control of their own futures (Chapters 8 and 11).

Funding should reflect women-sensitive budgeting: aid programmes should show that women are intended to be among the major beneficiaries of peacebuilding projects in war-torn societies. Sufficient and sustainable funds must be set aside specifically for women's peace initiatives (Chapter 10).

Organizations that receive funding need to understand that the inclusion of women at every level of their staff and board is required in order to ensure that these women have the support of other women and women's organizations and are not merely considered as token representatives put in place "to look good but keep quiet" (Chapter 2; also Chapter 11).

Once targeted programme support has been implemented, aid effectiveness and outcomes should be monitored and evaluated by international and national actors, with the assistance of beneficiaries. There are high risks that funds for women are misused in post-conflict reconstruction, do not reach their intended audiences or support ineffective programmes designed without the input of women peacebuilders. Particularly large multi-donor programmes should conduct needs assessments of all community-based peace initiatives and identify those that would benefit from more flexible, untied donor support (Chapter 8).

State actors

International peace operations can have a strong imprint on post-conflict societies. Through their programmes and activities they impart values and practices that may be new to their host societies. Strengthening the roles of women in active participation in rebuilding post-war societies may be among the more drastic suggestions made by international actors accompanying initial peacebuilding efforts. It is thus particularly important that international peace missions practise what they preach – including their own treatment and involvement of women in field operations. The gender balance in peacekeeping missions must therefore be strengthened and pre-deployment gender training for all peacekeepers should be provided at the national level before individuals are sent on bilateral, regional or international missions (Chapter 13).

The 2005 Paris Declaration on Aid Effectiveness highlighted the need for greater coordination in gender-equality programming among humanitarian actors.[3] The equal participation of women in all aspects of humanitarian response, their access to capacity-building and employment, and more accountability for gender mainstreaming within humanitarian missions should be ensured. Research on humanitarian and other peace operations should focus on the systematic collection of gender and gender-disaggregated data, then redesign existing programmes and practices and ensure that new activities are gender-sensitive from the start.

National action plans reflect serious attempts to implement new international agreements or practices (such as the principles enshrined in SCR 1325). The process for the development of NAPs must match the needs and capacities of the country and its current situation. Their contents must reflect the specifically solicited and expressed needs of society. NAPs need to be owned and implemented by as many actors in government and civil society as possible in order to drive and sustain their implementation (Chapter 10). Ideally, such processes are consultative, inclusive and participatory, and organized as bottom-up as well as top-down exercises. They should be driven by mechanisms such as a working group with the participation of all relevant stakeholders involved in their implementation. The working group needs to guide and inform the process. Moreover, NAPs need to be visionary yet realistic, with firm timeframes, accountability mechanisms, outputs, performance indicators and a sufficient budget (Chapter 10).

Civil society organizations

In post-war environments, emerging civil society organizations face numerous unique problems and a lack of credibility (and track record) when working with donors and the local population alike. Some local NGOs are phantom organizations without specific directions and goals, serving primarily the private interests of their founders while consuming donor funds that could possibly be invested more effectively in the interest of intended beneficiaries. It is thus not easy for an NGO quickly to establish a reputation as a respectable and credible actor. This also applies to women's groups and other civil society organizations dedicated to equitable and inclusive peacebuilding. NGOs must therefore improve their capacity and legitimacy – towards the society which they serve and the donors on whose support they depend – in part with the assistance of international actors (Chapter 6).

If at all possible, civil society organizations need to involve men, especially gender-sensitive men, in consultations and initiatives that affect women's peace and security. This applies in particular to issues of sexual violence of all types, as men are both perpetrators and, more often than usually recognized, victims of such violence. It is important to note that neither SCR 1325 nor SCR 1820 is a gender-divisive tool. Instead they are intended to be inclusive and involve all relevant stakeholders, both men and women, in solutions and programmes that are designed to improve women's peace and security and their involvement in sustainable development (Chapter 10).

Civil society organizations should be involved – and should be ready to assist – in consultations on the development and implementation of national action plans. Ideally, they will be in a position to develop alternative reports, offer constructive advice on developing locally relevant NAPs and assist in monitoring their implementation (Chapter 10).

With proper support, including of their political analysis and work, civil society organizations can also serve as pools of future political leaders. This is the case particularly during the immediate post-conflict formation of a new political elite that does not merely resemble a new configuration of wartime elites, but consists of educated and committed persons, both women and men, without direct links to (or even in opposition to) the former conflict parties. In addition, the recruitment of political leaders and their more immediate staff from civil society organizations, particularly grassroots groups, will ensure that voices from civil society are carried into positions of social, economic and political power. They will assure that peacebuilding efforts are relevant to the needs of society and will positively impact all parts of the population regardless of their previous ability to exert influence and have their opinions heard and needs considered. It is likely that the wishes and expectations of previously marginalized groups will be heard much more prominently in decision-making circles if represented by civil society organizations that can now place some of their own in positions of power. Such empowerment can lead to greater governmental awareness of what really matters locally and is expected by the population.

There is, however, one important caveat. One has to be careful not to siphon off all gifted, progressive, well-educated and networked individuals from civil society organizations to work for foreign NGOs or serve in government positions, parliament, security and justice institutions, educational facilities, private companies and any other institution where individuals who are ready and willing to embrace new thinking are a sought-after commodity. This would be detrimental to the creation and consolidation of a functioning and influential civil society during the critical post-conflict years. Foreign NGOs and international missions in particular need to be careful to avoid fuelling a domestic brain-drain that attracts capable nationals away from local NGOs and state institutions by offering higher salaries and privileges than the local market can bear. In addition to aligning international organizations' wages to local levels, it may be necessary to offer special funds to public institutions and local civil society organizations to enable them to pay competitive wages (Chapter 5). Such financial support should be accompanied by demands to pay fair and equal wages to both women and men.

Civil society groups may be in a privileged position to initiate and invest in the creation and expansion of South-South networks of other organizations operating in societies which have experienced or are currently undergoing similar post-conflict transitions. This allows for the exchange of experiences; it may also be useful in pursuing cross-border Track II diplomacy and fostering a common approach to understanding and embracing women's peacebuilding roles in post-conflict contexts. Such coalitions and networks can serve as collective voices to express a common concern for promoting change – and a platform to unofficial Track II diplomacy across borders in contexts where official relations prove to be difficult to establish for reasons that may pre-date or were created by the armed conflict. Moreover, individual, often small, local organizations tend to accomplish much less than well-respected and connected coalitions of NGOs with a well-developed and coherent strategy, adequate resources, members' consensus on objectives and clearly articulated and defined goals and aims. There are great advantages in exchanging information, building coalitions, developing common strategies or linking various groups with similar objectives with one another (Chapter 10).

Religious leaders in particular can be either progressive or reactionary forces in transformation and peacebuilding dynamics in post-conflict societies, particularly if conflicts were fought at least in part over religious convictions. Religious leaders may thus be very influential and should be consulted and engaged in discussions on, for instance, SCRs 1325 and 1820. They should be offered training opportunities on how these resolutions could be used to foster peace and justice at the community and national levels (Chapter 10).

Research community

Many of the calls and suggestions for improvements in the way peacebuilding activities should embrace contributions of women and prepare the path for a more representative and inclusive and less discriminatory society that is responsive to the needs of all its members are based on thorough research, analysis and evidence-based argument. Patriarchal argumentation that has withstood the test of years, decades and centuries may be easy to challenge, yet hard to change. Thorough research into gender-related post-conflict challenges will detail the specific needs of women, but may also unearth previously neglected needs of men. It will support efforts to link specific, gender-disaggregated threat analyses with the most relevant and potentially effective responses. It will show that women's experiences during times of peace and times of conflict are as valuable as those of men in generating critical competencies as peacebuilders, and they can serve as active contributors to post-conflict state- and community-building efforts. Moreover, thorough research will show how both women and society overall will benefit from putting an equal share of post-conflict decision-making and leadership responsibility in the hands of women.

Well-conducted gender analysis can lead to more appropriate programme planning and implementation. Furthermore, research informs – and improves – training. For instance, gender analysis training programmes among police in Cambodia led to new police initiatives to address domestic violence and trafficking in women (Chapter 2). Research also allows a fair examination of the contributions and pitfalls of traditional and customary practices – and the advantages and disadvantages of supporting or opposing such practices during the (partial) redefinition of post-conflict values, norms and practices. Particularly during transition periods in which highly fragile state and society structures need to grow into structures that are self-sustainable, it is important to identify and draw on the support of local patterns or cultures of peace and participation that reflect traditions of mutual support and – quite often – the very central role occupied by women. However, again one needs to be cautious: while some traditional cultures, norms and practices offer innovative solutions, others, such as customary law in Burundi that impedes women's access to land and property ownership, further cement discriminatory and counterproductive practices (Chapter 5). Moreover, as Vanessa Farr observes in Chapter 11, growing religious conservatism may play a significant role in undermining women's activism.

In search of post-war or pre-war identities, some groups of women are manipulated by conservative opinion leaders into accepting traditional hierarchical relationships between the sexes and their victimhood status. For example, when traditions of early and plural marriages, restricted access to education and training and everyday victimization of children and women by both men and women are presented as religious or ethnic customs, great care should be taken in confronting such arguments and practices; they should be questioned, critically examined and openly discussed. Ideally, such customs can be successfully challenged – and changed. Further research may reveal a multilayered picture of gender inequalities in the post-war patriarchy and suggest solutions to reduce gender exclusions and inequalities.

Concluding thoughts: Seizing the post-conflict moment

As the first chapter argued, post-conflict situations offer numerous opportunities for rewriting traditional "rules" and behavioural patterns that would likely continue to determine the roles of women in post-war societies if not challenged during the formative days, months and years following the cessation of armed violence and the onset of building (and in a few cases "rebuilding") a society founded on the promotion of positive peace. Social, cultural, economic and political justice changes the way in which communities and population groups relate to each other. This of course includes the relationship between men and women – a relationship that was often neither just nor equal prior to the outbreak of violent conflict. Yet wars change geopolitical and cultural landscapes, and also the way communities and individuals interact with and are positioned relative to one other. They may show that prevailing attitudes, norms and practices are counterproductive to social peace, stability and well-being.

Post-conflict societies need to change much of what has defined them before and during the outbreak of violence if they intend to live a more peaceful and stable future life. This does not merely mean that injustices suffered during the war need to be addressed. Of course, war creates much suffering – increasingly so among civilians, and disproportionately among women. Post-conflict peacebuilding programmes have to address and redress these tragedies, assist victims in overcoming their suffering and prevent the abuses from happening again, in times of conflict and of peace. However, this book challenges the popular assumption that women should be treated – and supported – only as victims. It offers a perspective of women as active and enthusiastic agents of change rather than passive and helpless victims. There is a growing understanding, from international to local levels, that women can turn the tide – and should be assisted in doing so by local, national and international actors – in converting the challenges of victimhood into new leadership opportunities. Recent research, advocacy work and policy statements and guidance are evidence of this positive and long-overdue development. We hope that this volume, and the lessons and recommendations it has produced, will help in maintaining this positive momentum by contributing to and triggering further debates in research, learning and policy design and implementation.

Notes

1. Steinberg, Donald (2009) "UN Resolution on Women, Peace and Security: Anniversary Worth Celebrating?", reprint of Reuter's article, 19 June, available at www.crisisgroup. org/home/index.cfm?id=6166&l=1.
2. See Anstee, Margaret Joan (2011) "One Woman's Experience at the UN", *New World Online*, Summer, available at www.una.org.uk/new_world/summer2011/5-margaret _anstee.html. See also Anstee, Margaret Joan (2004) *Never Learn to Type: A Woman at the United Nations*, London: John Wiley & Sons.
3. See World Bank (2008) "Aid Effectiveness: A Progress Report – On Implementing the Paris Declaration", World Bank, Accra, available at http://siteresources.worldbank.org/ INTCDRC/Resources/Progress_Report_Full_EN.pdf.

Index

A

abductions, 207, 209, 219, 222, 224

abuse
alcohol and drug, 57
child, 52
of children, 53, 104, 201
by government and rebel security forces, 20
at hands of their male partners, 48
physical, sexual and psychological, 53–54
of single mothers, 54
of widows, 54
of women, 81, 90, 92, 104, 155, 341
of women with disabilities, 54
activist mothers, 64–65
ADB. *See* Asian Development Bank (ADB)
Afghanistan
aid agencies fail to appreciate the complexity of the culture and religion, 17, 31
discrimination against women by warring groups, 59
family structure collapse and Taliban policy, 16
men and women turn to opium, 15
opium industry engages women and men in Iran, Tajikistan and Pakistan for trafficking drugs, 15, 177

polygamy in post-conflict Muslim societies, 19
shortage of funds and critical humanitarian needs, 157
social responsibility of women in post-conflict rebuilding, 16
systematic killing and maiming of innocent people by belligerent groups, 80
Tajikistan refugees fled to, 169
UN Mission in Afghanistan included a gender adviser, 111, 344
women's organizations provide a multitude of services, 93, 341
women's participation in reconstruction of, 111
women wear the burqa, 51
AFRC. *See* Armed Forces Revolutionary Council (Sierra Leone) (AFRC)
African National Congress (South Africa) (ANC), 209–10
Albanian Women's League (AWL), 194–95
amputations, 218, 222, 224
ANC. *See* African National Congress (South Africa) (ANC)
anti-personnel landmines, 14. *See also* landmines
Armed Forces Revolutionary Council (Sierra Leone) (AFRC), 219, 221, 223